STONES
OF
DESTINY

A Story of Man's Quest for Earth's Riches

STONES
OF
DESTINY

Keystones of Civilization

By John R. Poss, B.S., E.M.

Published at Michigan Technological University
with assistance from the estate of Scott Turner

HOUGHTON, MICHIGAN 49931

1975

Library of Congress catalog card number: 74-79993
ISBN 0-915072-01-7

First printing: April, 1975

Manufactured in the United States of America by LithoCrafters, Inc., Ann Arbor, Michigan

To my wife MAREE
this book is
lovingly dedicated

FOREWORD

At no time in the history of the United States has it been more important for us to recognize our dependence upon minerals and metals. Oil is just one of the materials we wrest from beneath the earth's surface. The Mideast oil embargo of late 1973 and early 1974 brought forcefully to the attention of everyone that we could not take oil for granted and that we must change our life styles in order to balance the demand with supply.

Our disproportionate use of almost all of the world's minerals and metals is just as great as our disproportionate use of oil. We don't produce what we use, which leads to many unanswered questions. How long are other nations going to tolerate this? Where will we get our mineral raw materials in the year 2000? How will a mineral shortage affect our standing as a world power?

There is no single or simple solution to such questions, but one thing is certain, there will be no solution without an adequate supply of scientific and engineering manpower in the minerals and metals field.

There has been a steady degradation in the image of the minerals profession since World War II. This has been evidenced by declining higher education enrollments in the field, by an increasing antagonism towards anything related to mining, and by the passage of legislation restrictive to the industry.

Idealistic young people, misled by the argot of the anti-technologists, have turned their backs on one of man's most essential endeavors, the winning of minerals and metals from Earth's great storehouse of treasures—materials vitally needed for survival of the human species.

For years professional educators have tried unsuccessfully to stem this tide. Perhaps their efforts have been too defensive or have seemed too closely related to self-interest. With this book they may have at hand a new tool to reinterest young people once more in the field of mining and minerals.

The author, John R. Poss, has shown the way in his magnificent story, "Stones of Destiny." He takes us from man in prehistory to man on the moon in an authoritative, gently written, profusely illustrated history of mining, minerals and metals. The moral is inescapable—world history has been influenced markedly by man's quest for mineral wealth.

"Stones of Destiny" gives powerful testimony to the adventures of the miner-prospector, the consummate skill of the metallurgist, and the never ending romance between man and Earth's mineral wealth. It is a book touching on the rise and fall of empires as they relate to minerals and metals. It is a book of conquerors—Caesar, Charlemagne, Cortes, and Pizarro, spurred on by visions of gold, silver, and base metals.

The author traveled the world prospecting for facts and pictures to tell this epic of man's search for earth's priceless materials. No prospector could have been more successful. Poss has served as geologist, miner, and metallurgist in locating, collecting, and concentrating a vast amount of material into a single, highly readable volume.

"Stones of Destiny" is a book that should stimulate young people to learn more of the minerals and metals field and one that should furnish all of us with a bonanza of information to help counter the downward trend of interest in our profession. It's a story giving ample testimony to the desire of the engineer to serve society in a highly humanistic venture.

Michigan Technological University wishes to make special acknowledgment to Dr. Scott Turner whose bequest made the publication of this book possible. Dr. Turner, a benefactor of the University, was one of its early graduates. His distinguished career as one of the country's leading mining engineers was a credit to the mining profession.

R. L. Smith
President,
Michigan Technological University

ACKNOWLEDGMENTS

I am indebted to, and greatly honored by my alma mater, the Michigan Technological University, for publishing this book. I especially wish to express my sincerest gratitude to the University's president, Dr. Raymond L. Smith, for it was his interest in the subject that made publication of the book possible.

To William G. Lucier of the University who patiently and efficiently handled the details of publication I extend my deepest thanks. In addition I would also like to extend my gratitude to Joseph A. Romig, for his service in reading every word of the text.

Matters concerning archeology, history, mineral resources and technology which form the textual background of this book, of necessity, rest on the works of many authors. Since my text essentially concerns past events, I have had to turn to the writers who have recorded the past. In doing so I have consulted many, endeavoring to choose those who appear to represent a consensus of accurate and dependable viewpoints.

Those sources are named in the list of Selected Readings in the back of the book, some having provided more information than others. Most chronicles of the past must in some ways resort to borrowings from the actual recorders of history. Similarly, the materials appearing in my text are not original, excepting the emphasis which I have placed upon the roles played by known mineral resources. Nevertheless, I am indebted to the historians who made it possible for me to assemble the facts.

I wish to acknowledge my appreciation of the courtesies offered me by such libraries and historical societies as: The Library of Congress, the Public Libraries of Los Angeles, San Francisco, New York City, University of California at Los Angeles, Widener Library of Harvard, and the State Historical Societies of Arizona, California, Colorado, Georgia, Illinois (Chicago), Missouri, Montana, New York, Oklahoma, Oregon and Utah.

For the thousands of color photographs obtained by me over a score of years, many of which appear in this book, I deeply appreciate the cooperation of such museums as: The British Museum, London; The National Museum, Athens; The Treasury, Topaki Palace, Istanbul; The Louvre and the Musee de l'Homme in Paris; the Vatican Museum, the Capitoline Museum and Villa Giulia Museum in Rome; the Berlin State Museum; Department of Antiquities, Cairo Museum; the Residenz and Deutsche Museums in Munich; the Palestine Archeological Museum; and the National Museum of Anthropology in Mexico.

In the United States helpful museums included: The Smithsonian Institution—Museum of Natural History, Museum of History and Technology and the National Portrait Gallery, Washington, D.C. Also, the American Museum of History and the Museum of The American Indian, Heye Foundation in New York City; the New York State Museum, Albany; the University Museum, Harvard; the Field Museum of Natural History, the Museum of Science and Industry and the Oriental Institute, University of Chicago, in Chicago; the Museum of Natural History and Colorado State Museum in Denver; Wells Fargo History Room and the M. H. de Young Memorial Museum in San Francisco; the Natural History Museum and Museum of Science and Industry in Los Angeles; the Pioneer Memorial Museum, Salt Lake City; the Henry Ford Museum, Greenfield Village, Michigan; the Dahlonega Gold Museum, Georgia, and scores of United States National Monuments, State Parks and Historic Sites.

To my beloved daughter, Marian de Lacy, I am indebted for her careful reading of my first, overly voluminous manuscript and her helpful, incisive suggestions which made this a suitable presentation.

To cartographers, I wish to extend my thanks for preparing the maps in this book.

I owe the greatest debt to my wife, Maree. Without her devotion and companionship through thousands of miles of demanding travel, exploring byways and landmarks of history, and her indispensable help photographing artifacts and realia in museums of the world, the materials for this book could not have been assembled.

John R. Poss

March 1975

CONTENTS

xi

PROLOGUE

Stones in the Ages of Man

One clear November day, some years ago, I left Athens and drove along the blue Saronic Gulf 40 miles to historic Cape Sunion, then turned eastward and climbed to the top of a mountain ridge high above the ancient village of Laurium. The Sunion promontory lay far below, crowned by the ruins of the Temple of Poseidon, God of The Sea. Its white marble columns gleamed brightly against the azure Aegean waters. The air around me was filled with the resinous aroma of pine trees. Their fresh, bright greenery contrasted vividly with the mountain's red, rocky soil—an unforgettable vista of green upon crimson under a sky of blue. Only the murmur of a lazy breeze broke the solemn stillness.

Using a crude sketch-map given to me by an official of the American School of Archeology in Athens, I continued along a lonely, stoney road that squirmed atop the ridge. I was searching for the ancient mining town of Maronea and its adjacent mill-site, Soureza, one of the mines of the famed Laurium district. In its heyday Maronea had stepped into the mainstream of history, and with its great wealth had stemmed an onrushing national calamity. Now the town was in utter ruin, but I wanted to find it and relive its former glory. In America, such a mining camp is called a "Ghost Town." I knew this one would not be of weathered clapboard and clanging iron, as were the many I had visited at home. Meager evidence has often aided me in detecting historic sites, but here in Greece 2500 years could have erased nearly every clue.

After a long search, I was almost convinced that I had been following the wrong trail. Then, I saw a carved white marble slab laying on the ground amid a jumble of limestone blocks. It could have been a lintel of some ancient doorway. Obviously, it had been shaped by the hand of man. I looked about, seeking more signs of human habitation.

Ghost Town—480 B.C.

And then, incredibly, the whole Athenian ghost town of 480 B.C. unfolded before my eyes. It was composed entirely of tumbled white and gray marble structures scattered among the pine trees. Because its materials of construction were as imperishable as the Parthenon itself, the ruins had been preserved all these years. The settlement had occupied a large area along the gentle slope of a wooded valley.

First, I came upon the cisterns used in the milling center of Soureza. Some had been hollowed out of solid rock, 12 to 20 feet in diameter. Most were built of accurately shaped and closely fitted marble blocks. Immediately below each cistern were the remains of marble walled buildings where Athenians, 25 centuries ago, had washed Maronea's crushed silver ores across stone slabs, called laveries, to separate the heavier silver-bearing galena particles from the lighter rock waste.

Water had been scarce on the high, sunny hills of Laurium. Every available drop had to be carefully collected and stored in the cisterns, to be used over and over again. Marble steps, worn deep by many feet, led steeply into the cisterns. Shouldering heavy pottery jars, slaves had dipped the vessels here into the water. Then they carried the jars to the wash tables where the water was used, recovered and returned to the cisterns. The remains of terra-cotta jars were everywhere.

The marble ruins extended along the forested hillside as far as I could see. Within view, at least 50 cisterns, with their adjoining laveries and remains of dwellings, lay almost buried by the encroaching forest. Apparently, the site had been untouched by archeologists. Perhaps it was too far from public roads to warrant restoration. The marble walls lay just as they had fallen long before the beginning of our Christian era. The strong Aegean sun spot-lighted the disarray of marble blocks, as I stood engrossed with the role they had played in a decisive moment of history.

Persian Shadows

For centuries the state-owned mines of Laurium had enriched the treasury of Athens, and the citizens had received their share. In 490 B.C. the dark shadow of an invader threatened the land. But Darius and his mighty Persian army had been turned back by a brilliant Greek victory on the plain of Marathon. Uneasy were the years that followed, for the Asiatic horde, bent on conquest, would surely strike again.

Themistocles, the great Athenian statesman, persuaded his countrymen to forego the customary distribution of profits from the Laurium mines and to use the proceeds to build a fleet of 100 triremes, great warships with three banks of oarsmen. In 483 B.C. a new bonanza, richest of all, was discovered deeper within the limestone strata at a place called Maronea. The find was timely, for just three years later a wave of Persians under Xerxes was again sweeping toward Athens. Leonidas and his 300 brave Spartans had already died to the last man, trying to stop the Persians at Thermopylae. Athens was next. Not only Athens, but all Greece, was in turmoil over this new threat.

Xerxes reached Athens, stormed the Acropolis, burned the temples then under construction, and drove the citizens from the city. The outnumbered Athenian fleet, built largely with the wealth of Laurium, lay nearby in the Bay of Salamis awaiting the next blow. In one of history's most crucial naval battles, the Athenians launched a furious assault, ramming head-on into the huge fleet of their enemy. With great audacity and resourceful strategy the Greeks won the battle. Xerxes withdrew his crippled forces and retired to Persia.

The triremes of Athens and the silver of Laurium had formed the bulwark which prevented the swelling tide of Oriental culture from sweeping aside the glorious civilization of Greece. One of Earth's great silver bonanzas had played a vital part in preserving our Occidental heritage.

The Stones of Soureza

For hours I walked among the ruins of Soureza and Maronea. Spellbound, I studied the fallen stones of the historic settlements. Today's world faded away. The realm of classical Greece became a living reality. Despite the widespread disorder of the ruins, they reflected the intense activity that once pervaded the place. One could sense the bustle and almost hear the voices of state officials and the stern, unfeeling commands of their crusty overseers, directing the hordes of

slaves toiling over the wash tables and bringing an unending stream of water from the nearby cisterns.

Centered here, 2500 years ago, was the destiny of Greece. Such men as Peisistratus, Themistocles, Pericles and hosts more had trod among these stones, watching with grave concern the flow of silver across these very same laveries. The rich mines of Laurium had not only saved the Greeks from Persian domination, they also provided Athens with a monopoly of silver in the Mediterranean world. This gift of the earth greatly bolstered Athens' economic power, which led to and supported Greece's glorious Golden Age of commerce and culture.

As I turned and walked away from Soureza, the murmuring pine trees brought me back to the realities of today. Laurium was only one of the noted districts of the world whose mines had turned the course of history. I was to encounter many more revealing experiences while visiting other regions of prodigious mineral wealth on my long trek into man's fascinating past.

A New Look at History

As the author of many educational films dealing with the history of the Americas and the Old World, during my research pursuits I have been perplexed by the casual regard which historians in general have shown toward the influence of man's natural resources upon the evolution of history. That indifference has been singularly noticeable to me, because, as a mining engineer and geologist, I am familiar with the production and economic importance of the world's outstanding mineral deposits.

From the vantage point of both an engineer and historian, therefore, I felt impelled to examine and correlate the relationship between a people's possession of natural resources and the flowering of their civilizations.

Many circumstances have contributed to man's progress. Beneficial rainfall, fertility of soil, economic geology, and waterways useful for commerce and irrigation are items which depend upon geography. Forms of government, religion, and human creativity in thought and technology have also affected the affairs of mankind. One fundamental element that in the past has stimulated man's development, and even today bears forcefully upon international politics, is the presence of commercial mineral deposits within his domain or under his control, coupled with the venturesome urge to seek their discovery, and the ingenuity to utilize them. To the ancients, and some moderns, these minerals have long been known simply as 'stones.'

Convincing proof of the influence which materials and economics exert upon history exists today. Late in 1973 certain oil-rich Arab states decided to end their embargo of oil to European nations whom the Arabs had considered unfriendly. Their stated reason: "To save Europe from economic disaster." Such is oil's power. But oil is only one of man's strategic materials. Because of a threatening shortage of minerals essential to an industrialized world, nations are growing more dependent upon one another, and more competitive in world markets for raw materials. Obviously, minerals and economics are still vital forces, as they have been throughout history.

After 40 years devoted to writing their monumental THE STORY OF CIVILIZATION, Will and Ariel Durant summed up their views in a recent edition, THE LESSONS OF HISTORY, dealing with the various causes that have swayed man's cultures. Among many other conclusions, the Durants cited examples of 'economics in action.' They declared that Agamemnon's siege of Troy was an attempt of the Greeks to satisfy their 'economic ambition' by gaining control of the Dardanelles; that "the money of the Delian Confederacy built the Parthenon"; that "the Crusades were attempts to capture trade routes to the East"; and that "the banking house of the Medici financed the Florentine Renaissance." I should like to state again that the mineral riches of Attica, to which the Durants referred, also sustained the commercial supremacy and social ascendancy of the Athenian Empire and helped save Greek culture from Oriental subjugation at the hands of the Persians.

The Bonanza Hunters

Delving deeper into man's past we find that it was the discovery of metallurgy, after innumerable millennia of Stone Age darkness, that introduced and boomed the use of metals. The resulting search for metallic ores, in turn, stimulated the widespread diffusion of civilization from its birthplace in Sumer and Babylonia. It was Egypt's long, extraordinary production of gold that enabled her to buy the cedarwood ships of

Byblos which carried the commerce and the heritage of the Nile to all mankind throughout the eastern Mediterranean.

Strabo, the Greek traveler and geographer, acknowledged that it was the silver wealth of Tartessus (Andalusia of modern Spain) that supported the armies and navies of Carthage and maintained her control of the Mediterranean Sea. These same resources of Spain, the Eldorado of antiquity, became the bone of contention between Carthage and ambitious Rome. After Rome defeated Carthage in the Punic Wars and became the dominant power, Spain's storehouse of riches furnished the monetary base for the establishment of the Roman Empire, and gave Rome the appetite and the sinews to seize other mineral-rich regions of the ancient world.

A thousand years later, it was the shining wealth of the Orient that lured Christopher Columbus westward, resulting in his discovery of America. The vast natural resources of the New World, first encountered by Spanish conquerors and the adventurers who followed them, became the economic foundation for mankind's most prolific civilization. The fabulous mineral riches of the West, and other regions of America, brought the prosperity and the power of the United States into full bloom. Later, the discovery of valuable mineral deposits opened Australia and Africa to settlement and civilization.

Throughout history bonanza hunters have explored far away lands, seeking metal supplies, or ore deposits, required for their arts and industries. Thus were horizons widened and new lands discovered, and so were spheres of trade, thought, art and technology expanded by finding and utilizing mineral wealth. It is well that there always have been venturesome men who, as if by some arrangement with providence, have undertaken to unearth nature's treasures at the times and in the places their civilizations have required.

Many pages of history have been colored brightly by these ever hopeful bonanza seekers. Known in modern times as 'prospectors', they form a special breed of necessarily indestructible optimists, hardy and dauntless, attuned to the timeless scheme of nature, the big skies and silent hills, seeking reward only from the hands of earth herself. The word "prospect" is defined as an act of looking forward, of anticipation. Hence, the prospector always has been an anticipator, a forerunner of civilization.

The purpose of this book is to bring into better focus the role of man's material and economic evolution, while viewing it in context with his contemporary social and cultural development. We shall witness here the epic parts played by the 'stones' that man has discovered over the face of the earth, and homage will be paid to that indispensable ingredient of man's nature, his inborn spirit of adventure without which there would be no discoverers or inventors.

From Stone to Metals

We shall follow herein many explorers on their historic quests. The earliest set forth during the stone ages when man's progenitors searched for good flint, the first mineral to be used in art and industry. With implements and weapons of flint man procured his food and clothing and defended his habitations. For over 200,000 years flint was man's most cherished material possession.

Gold, occurring in the native state and readily recognized, was the first metal used by man. Fortunately, gold was malleable and could be worked into desired shapes, but it was too soft to be used as a working metal. Copper, first found in the native, metallic form was also fairly malleable and workable. Since copper was a little harder than gold it became man's first industrial metal. Copper chisels carved the stones for the pyramids of Egypt and copper was the first metal employed in warfare.

Copper, mixed with tin, created the so-called Bronze Age and launched mankind's first widespread industrial boom, which quickened the spread of civilization. The Iron Age was born after iron's troublesome metallurgy was fathomed, and, although iron was first used in terrifying weapons of war, it became the fore-runner and mainstay of our modern industrial age. Later came the Nuclear Age, revealing tremendous opportunities in all the sciences, a bittersweet gift of nature bearing both untold blessings and virulent woes. Then, it was the search for a strange new metal, uranium, that became one of feverish and fate-laden necessity.

With the arrival of the Space Age the whole world watched as man crowned his accomplishments in science and technology by reaching and exploring the moon. Again, as in ages past, 'stones' became the important objective of the hunt. This time it was from the lunar surface that a treasure was gathered and returned to the voyagers' homeland, the United States. In an endeavor to probe the secrets of the universe, man has begun a quest that will lead him to undreamed of frontiers.

Milestones of Progress

Seeking these milestones of man's progress through the ages, my earthbound treks began in England, France and Switzerland where Paleolithic or Old Stone Age ruins reveal the slow, relentless advancements in man's use of flint. The trail led on to include Germany and Austria where salt and amber, together with flint, provided the basis for man's earliest routes of trade, then to the Middle East, Egypt, Palestine and southwestern Asia where civilization dawned and the use of metals began.

The galvanizing effect of man's use and search for metallic ores became increasingly evident as the inquiry led to Crete, Greece, Italy and Spain, where appeared the first westward migrations of civilizations. In Mexico, South America and the United States there was spectacular proof that metallic wealth incited the discovery, exploration and development of the New World, as it did also in Africa and Australia.

Back to England went the study, for there in the mid-18th century hand tools had been replaced by power-driven machines, inaugurating England's Industrial Revolution. The machine-age spread to America. Then, an array of American inventors became the precursors of technological developments that made the United States the leading industrial nation on earth. Again, it was native mineral wealth that played a decisive role.

During the following 200 years, as industrialization spread to other nations of the world, the consumption levels of manufactured goods accelerated enormously. Late in the present 20th century our long plundered planet, Earth, began to feel the pangs of exhaustion. More and more deposits of the earth's resources, fossil fuels and minerals, became depleted, or were nearing the end of their days.

Meanwhile, in certain once impoverished lands new resources such as petroleum were developed which began to dictate a revision of international politics. As this is being written, Russia and the Arab states are arrayed in formidable opposition against Europe, Japan and the United States over the status of Israel, the Biblical Land of Armageddon. But quite another situation is seriously disrupting the relationships of the super-powers. It is the prize of the Middle East's enormous wealth in oil, of prime economic necessity to all concerned, for oil turns the wheels of their burgeoning industries. Actions being taken for control of these resources are threatening the peace of the world, the future of mankind.

Frontiers in Space

Now, a new era has dawned. The dilemma of one shortage crisis after another, especially in energy, oil and minerals, is spurring scientists to scan the realms of space. Even certain portions of our solar system are being envisioned as possible new sources of raw materials needed by our hungry industries. Yes, there are still undiscovered frontiers. As man continues his ceaseless quest for the substances and innovations required by his civilization, this book will provide a view of his long march from the stone ages to the launch pads that will send him upon the pathways of his greatest adventure.

The material sources on anthropology, archeology, history, geology, economics, science, technology and mineral resources of the world are innumerable. For the reader who wishes to pursue certain subjects more in detail, the accompanying list of selected publications should provide opportunities for further 'prospecting' and exploration. While so engaged, it should become evident that earth's riches have played many vital roles in the stirring story of mankind.

Chapter 1

STONE AGE TREASURE

The cry "Revolution" has resounded across the face of the earth during many frenzied periods of history, toppling empires and creating social changes in its wake. But man-made revolutions have been infinitesimal in proportion and insignificant in their consequences compared with the gigantic paroxysms of the planet on which we live. These cataclysmic events in earth's history, aptly known to geologists as revolutions, have also been prime movers in setting the stage and the conditions for man's development.

Before witnessing man's arrival upon the scene, we should first peer into earth's dramatic 5 billion year old past in order to understand the circumstances that controlled his earliest activities. About 70 million years ago, recent as geologic time is measured, during the Cenozoic era, earth experienced violent disturbances of its crust. Titanic forces thrust, squeezed, broke apart or faulted, warped or folded, vast areas of earth's outer shell. Great mountain systems, such as the Alps, Himalayas, Carpathians, the Andes, the American Rockies, Cascades, Sierra Nevada, and the volcanoes of East Africa, rose to lofty heights where seas and lowlands once existed. This era of mountain building, the Cenozoic Orogeny, which included the Cascadian Revolution, the Alpine Revolution and others, shaped our landscapes of today.

Great changes in climate were wrought over the world by these high mountain chains which affected air currents, temperatures and rainfall. The greatest change came with the growth of the polar ice cap and widespread glaciers. At the dawn of the Pleistocene, the most recent geologic epoch, about one million years ago, the northern regions saw the approach of the Ice Age, or to be more specific, four glacial and corresponding inter-glacial ages. Alternation of the ice ages, it is thought, was caused by the rising and declining accumulation of ice due to the fluctuation of cold and warm ocean currents circulating in the polar seas. Since the world appears to have reached a period of maximum warmth about 6000 years ago, apparently today we are in an inter-glacial stage.

The Ice Ages

As the early Pleistocene ice cap thickened an immense volume of water was withdrawn by evaporation from the shrinking seas and held captive as snow and ice. Dry land appeared; the English Channel became a plain into which flowed the Thames, the Seine, and the Rhine Rivers. The Mediterranean area became a great valley, with a ridge connecting the mainland of present Spain and Morocco. These necks or bridges of land, now submerged, which also existed between the East Indies and Asia, became

1

important avenues of migration for a rich variety of animal life and the early races of man who naturally pursued the means of their existence. Conditions were being established for an important step in man's evolution, a sequence of events which never before had occurred in earth's history, and never will again.

During the ebb and flow of the ice sheets from the north, in the accompanying inter-glacial stages Western Europe became the world's finest hunting ground. From no less than five geographic regions, parts of Asia, northern Africa, Siberia, northern Europe and the high mountain areas, a bountiful mammalian fauna congregated in Western Europe. First there were hippopotami, rhinoceroses, mammoths, and elephants; then, as temperatures cooled, these forms migrated to the then verdant Sahara region. Adapting themselves to the changing climate, the woolly mammoth, musk-ox, bison, horse, wild cattle, reindeer, bear, and wolverine, 26 species in all, then appeared and occupied the lush tundra, or the meadows and forests that later appeared with declines of the ice sheets in Western Europe.

Forerunners of Man

Into this remarkable assemblage of mammalian life, during a period of several hundred thousand years termed the Paleolithic or Old Stone Age, came eight successive waves of hominid races, the forerunners of modern man. All were basically flesh eaters and dependent upon animals of the hunt as their means of existence. An abundant supply for food and clothing was thus assured, but there was another essential need, a ready source of good material to fashion weapons and implements of the chase.

Fortune had indeed smiled upon Europe and prehistoric man by also supplying a timely and widespread variety of excellent flint. This material would not only become a great blessing to his budding cultures, his artifacts of flint would also leave an unalterable record of the chronology of man.

Although man's earliest stages of evolution preceding and during the Paleolithic period no doubt originated in east-central Africa and western Asia, it was in western Europe, especially France, that the greatest achievements of the Old Stone Age occurred. Barely outside the suburbs of Paris, near the hamlet of Chelles on the Marne River and at Abbeville and St. Acheul on the Somme River, remains of prehistoric cultures have been found dating from 100,000 to 300,000 years old. These and numerous other sites make France the most complete and accessible stone age museum on earth.

Henry Fairfield Osborn, eminent paleontologist in his MEN OF THE OLD STONE AGE wrote, "France, favored beyond all other countries by men of the Old Stone Age, was destined to become the classic center of prehistoric archeology." France's abundance of flint gave measurable impetus to man's first strides toward civilization.

Flint—The Magic Stone

What is flint and why was it so exceptional? Flint is one of several silica minerals composed of silicon and oxygen, a member of a well known group called the "quartz family." Six sided quartz crystals and a related form called amethyst are *crystalline* varieties. The fine grained, china-textured forms are *microcrystalline* (crystals visible only under a microscope), including agate, chert, chalcedony, jasper, flint, and opal. All, except opal, are harder than steel and will scratch a knife blade or ordinary glass.

The advantageous quality possessed by flint and other microcrystalline forms is their tendency to break or fracture into sharp edged, conchoidal (shell-shaped) flakes under percussion or applied pressure. Flint can thus be flaked or chipped into desired shapes, such as cutting and scraping tools, arrowheads, hammers and axes.

Other stones, such as quartzite, granite, diorite and obsidian, which are rocks rather than minerals, have been used by Stone Age men when flint was unavailable. Obsidian is a volcanic rock of glassy texture and it is widely used because of its excellent conchoidal fracture and very sharp edges, but is found only in regions that have seen volcanic activity.

The manner in which Stone Age man worked and used these materials, and the degree of artistry and perfection which he achieved in fashioning his implements of stone, have enabled anthropologists to reconstruct man's progress throughout the numerous millennia of prehistory. Man himself does not easily become a fossil due to the dispersal of his remains by predatory animals, birds, and erosion. But his stone implements have survived to leave a remarkable and imperishable record of his numerous stone age cultures in many parts of the world.

Not all regions of the earth were blessed with such an adaptable mineral resource as flint. Many areas were soil covered, stoneless lands or regions of igneous, volcanic, or sedimentary rocks that were barren of flint and not easily shaped by flaking. But in sections of France, Belgium, Germany, and southern England, limestone and chalk strata containing layers of flint make up much of the landscape.

Paleolithic Ancestors

Of the eight stages of Paleolithic man's appearance in Europe, evidence of the first, although dim, was the discovery of a jaw bone in a sand pit at Mauer near Heidelberg, Germany, in 1907 by Dr. Otto Schoetensack. Among the fossil bones were the straight-tusked elephant, primitive rhinoceros and hippopotamus, indicating that *Heidelberg Man*, named *Homo erectus*, lived during the second inter-glacial stage about 300,000 years ago. This rugged, small-brained creature, tearing and eating raw meat from his kills, had just become aware that sharp edged stone could be used to replace his bare hands for dismembering animals of the hunt. His first tools, picked up at random because they possessed sharp edges and readily fit his hands, were stones now known as eoliths.

Arrival of a new race in western Europe during the long third inter-glacial stage about 250,000 years ago launched an important epoch in prehistory. Apparently the newcomers came across the Mediterranean land bridge from Africa, near present Gibraltar, and established their first crude habitations along the valley of the Somme at Abbeville, St. Acheul and Montieres, and at Chelles on the river Marne near present day Paris. The flint tools which accumulated at these sites provided evidence of the Paleolithic or Old Stone Age's firm establishment in Europe.

The first culture, the *Abbevillian*, produced extremely crude hand axes, or *'coups de poing'* made by roughly chipping cores or chunks of flint. The *Chellean* culture showed improvement in symmetry and removal of the crust covering the flint nodules. In late *Acheulean* times, a notable breakthrough occurred in the art of retouch, or flaking of flint. Workers became aware that freshly excavated flint taken from the limestone and chalk strata of the river banks and low hills contained a certain amount of underground moisture and was easier to chip than the tough, desiccated flint nodules found among the stream gravels. It was then that mankind's first prospectors began to roam the countryside in search of the best flint, and it was then that the first miners started to dig, seeking treasures of the earth.

With more workable flint, daggers and knives could now be made for dismembering game and cutting up pelts; scrapers, borers, and discs began to show increased perfection in flaking and in the evolution of new forms. The masterpiece of late Acheulean industry was the *Levallois* flake, sharp edged and beautifully symmetrical, which first was found at Levallois-Perret, today a suburb of Paris.

If we could stand upon the Pont de Levallois, which now spans the broad Seine in a northwest section of the city, and instantly replace the present scene with a vista of 100,000 years ago, the commercial buildings that now line the river would fade away and in their place we would see a cool, arid, sub-arctic landscape, sparsely forested, stretching unspoiled to the horizon. Browsing here and there might be seen a woolly mammoth or a woolly rhinoceros that had been driven southward by the advancing Scandinavian ice fields.

Within view on the right bank of the river is a tribal community living in the open, scantily clad in skins. Menfolk squat on the ground, chipping razor-sharp flakes from rough cores of flint; womenfolk of the tribe, using the retouched flints as scrapers and knives, are busy dressing hides of the hunt. In their day these people won wide renown for their inventiveness and artistry, reflected in the wares that later became known by their *Levallois* flakes.

The abundance of excellent flint around the great Acheulean communities made them noted hubs of industry. Beginning with the Paleolithic to its close, culture after culture occupied these busy sites over a span of more than 200,000 years. How incredibly long and how infinitely slow was man's progress over such a period of years compared with the spiraling of events in our modern age.

The Neanderthals

The next wave to appear in growing numbers was characterized by *Homo Neanderthalensis*, named after the fossil remains of a man found in the Neander Valley near Dusseldorf, Germany, in 1856. His race arrived in Europe at the beginning of the last inter-glacial stage about 80,000 years ago. As the climate grew severe with the advancement of the polar ice sheet, marking the Fourth and last ice age, the Neanderthals were forced to live in sheltered caves and seek warmer clothing. Thus, a change in nature's cycle of events brought about new and important progress in man's mode of existence.

Although some anthropologists feel that the heavy, bony brow and receding forehead and chin of the Neanderthals separate them from being ancestors of man, they possessed a cranial capacity akin to modern races. The Neanderthals were sufficiently intelligent to forsake the open air and move to the cave entrances, or grottoes. Bears and other denizens of the caves undoubtedly resisted these invasions. In caves at Le Moustier on the Vezere River 50 miles east of Perigueux in Southern France, excellent fossils of early Neanderthals were found which gave the name *Mousterian* to their widespread culture.

The First Technologists

Since the Neanderthals were the first race to endure a glacial age, they were forced to develop new forms of weapons and tools of the hunt in order to increase their supply of clothing. They tracked down the woolly mammoth, giant cave bear, bison and reindeer; used flint tipped spears and darts for the first time, together with throwing stones placed in leather slings; and made earth-dug pitfalls. Such were the primitive, perilous methods that man then employed to overcome his powerful adversaries.

Cave life favored communal and social evolution, tribal lore, and the simple beginnings of religious beliefs and ceremonies. But after 60,000 years of slow, rudimentary development the Neanderthal race disappeared from the scene and apparently became extinct. Degeneration caused possibly by the unbearable hardships of the Fourth glacial age, together with the scarcity of mammalian life, may have contributed to their annihilation. One certain condition that threatened Neanderthal existence was the appearance of a new race, highly superior in physique and intelligence. These were the Cro-Magnons, the first true *Homo sapiens* to arrive in Europe.

Armed with new weapons in warfare, improved stone tipped spears, the Cro-Magnons could have driven the Neanderthals from their grottoes and flint quarries, destroying an inferior race. The time was approximately 35,000 years ago. The Fourth and last glacial age had ended, and the present post-glacial period had begun. Coming somewhere from western Asia, the Cro-Magnons are believed to have spread westward through central Europe perhaps seeking better hunting grounds.

Some of the Neanderthals may have survived the last glacial age but there is no evidence of an admixture of their blood with the Cro-Magnons who apparently disdained the Neanderthal's heavy brows, stocky, slouched figure, features reminiscent of the apes. Cro-Magnon man, on the other hand, was tall and straight, his chin was square and prominent, his forehead high and his brain case was as large as modern man. The Cro-Magnons also had the creative and artistic spirit that made their rise in Europe a giant step forward in the emergence of *Homo sapiens*, the first western man.

The Cro-Magnons, Progenitors of Man

The name *Aurignacian* was given to the first stage of Cro-Magnon culture because his bones were first found in a cave at Aurignac, 40 miles southwest of Toulouse, France. In 1868, Louis Lartet, one of the founders of modern paleontology, discovered similar skeletons in grottoes above the hamlet of Cro-Magnon, 25 miles east of Perigueux. In caves at Les Eyzies and Lascaux in the Dordogne Valley more rich finds were unearthed, all of which were attributed to an advanced race, named the Cro-Magnons.

The newcomers quickly took advantage of their European environment, the cave shelters and hunting grounds, and especially the abundance of splendid flint. Their finds of this material fostered an important discovery: by applying pressure to flint cores with wood or bone points a more precise method of flint flaking resulted, which replaced the old percussion system, a hit and miss practice of striking the core to produce chips.

The peak of Cro-Magnon flint working occurred during the *Solutrean* stage, named after its type locality, a huge open air hunting station at Solutré in southern France, where the bones of 100,000 horses and other animals indicate that Solutré was a great gathering place of the hunt. By then man was showing signs of organization; families joined to form groups or clans in order to cooperate in large scale hunting. The clever, well built Cro-Magnons were proficient hunters, and the development of their flint implements was stimulated accordingly.

With their new system of pressure flaking the Cro-Magnons made notable advances in the art of retouch. They produced very thin, sharp flint blades with perfect symmetry. A famed invention was their narrow new type of javelin head distinguished by its laurel leaf shape. Then came more important innovations; the notching of very slender, artful darts and spearheads for the purpose of holding the weapon in the flesh; then a stem was added to hold the flint to the wooden shaft. Spear points were now beautifully flaked on both sides. Very small implements were also made that found a new and very significant use in fishing, offering a new means for procuring food.

One can imagine how proud the first producers were of these new wares when they were placed on display for the benefit of admiring tribes from neighboring lands. For then, flint alone was the aristocrat and luxury stone which made up man's sole mineral possession, and it would remain cherished for thousands of years to come. The *Aurignacian* and *Solutrean* stages covered approximately 10,000 years of painfully slow progress.

Zenith of Stone Age art

It was the *Magdalenian* culture which marked the final Paleolithic epoch, beginning about 15,000 years ago. Its type station was at La Madeleine, in the Dordogne region of France. Nearby, some 15 stations and industrial sites were found below limestone cliffs along the Vezere River. The art and industry of the Magdalenians are the best known and most fascinating of the Old Stone Age cultures. Branches of art, painting, engraving, and sculpturing, reached their highest points of perfection in this period of the Upper Paleolithic. Well known are the remarkable paintings on the walls and ceilings of the caves at Les Eyzies and Lascaux in France, and in other caves of the same period in Spain and Italy, illustrating the amazing ability of Magdalenian culture 12,000 years ago.

Using chisels and scrapers of flint, bas-reliefs of ice age animals were carved or engraved, then were painted red, ochre, brown and black with pigments of iron and manganese. Magdalenian engravings and sculptures also included beautifully incised decorations on their personal possessions of bone and ivory. Thus, finely wrought flint implements played an important part, not only in fashioning the weapons that secured early man's food and defended his communities, but in attaining his art forms as well.

Magdalenians also used antlers of the ever plentiful reindeer, during the so-called Reindeer Period, and invented delicate bone needles to sew their carefully worked leather clothing. They also developed the bone harpoon, first with barbs on one side, then with barbs on both sides. This was a great new invention, and it spread swiftly, for

large fish were abundant. Using a new means of catching food with greater ease and less danger, the habits of the people changed. The arduous and perilous pursuit of large game grew less popular. The nomadic spirit waned, people grew indolent and less industrious, life had lost some of its challenge.

Inventive progress in flint working slackened, although small tools to bore and fashion bone were developed and used considerably.

After some 7,000 years of preeminence, the Magdalenian culture faded and the talented Cro-Magnon race deteriorated. Perhaps it was because of climatic changes, one of those moods of ecological processes which man seems powerless to understand and anticipate. Deserting Cro-Magnon man, the glaciers and tundra, the reindeer and steppe mammals had retreated northward. Food, clothing, and the bone supply for industry had grown less plentiful. In the face of these obstacles no doubt the former hardy, venturesome way of life became less attractive. The creative spirit of the Magdalenians grew weaker, as clearly shown by subsequent artistic designs. Cro-Magnon's long cycle of superiority, lasting some 25,000 years, came to an end about 8,000 years ago. And with it came the close of the Paleolithic, or Old Stone Age.

After 300,000 Years—

But by then man had at last invented most of the fundamental stone tools that would serve his descendants for many millennia to come. Men of the Old Stone Age had been the first to find and utilize one of earth's primary mineral resources, a revelation of momentous importance. The use of stone, and particularly flint, had opened the door to man's first organized and creative efforts in industry and art.

The final fate of the Cro-Magnon race is unknown. Either they were obliterated after a long period of dormancy, or they were assimilated by newer races who began to invade western Europe, bringing with them cultures which would mark the begining of the Neolithic, or New Stone Age. There are some who believe that traces of the Cro-Magnons still exist in people of the Dordogne area.

One fact, however, is outstandingly clear. Although Paleolithic evolution was also taking place far to the east, placing Europe on the western fringe of development, it was in France that man attained his highest degree of communal life and industry, including the art of flint and bone shaping, relief carving and painting. As it was creative Greece that expressed the classical age of antiquity, so it was Upper Paleolithic man of France who established the classical period of the Old Stone Age.

This land of abundant game and protective grottoes was indeed blessed with the necessities of primitive life, including the providential presence of excellent and plentiful flint. It was this flint that provided early man the means of his livelihood and the instruments and inspiration which nurtured his first great achievements, and made France the cradle of Stone Age maturity.

Following the Paleolithic period dramatic changes in environment took place in western Europe. The Fourth and last ice sheet had retreated northward, followed by the tundra and steppe animals. In the warming soil, forests and meadows appeared, and then came new forms of life, the stag, moose, wild boar, fox, rabbits, beaver and wildfowl. Into this happy hunting ground, about 8,000 years ago, new races of men came into Europe. They came from the Baltic region, from the eastern Mediterranean, and also from northern Africa.

Perhaps because big game had roamed northward, these new races concentrated upon fishing and hunting wildfowl with spears and arrows tipped with small flints, and fishhooks and harpoons of bone. This has been called the Mesolithic or Middle Stone Age. It culminated over 300,000 years marked simply by a few innovations in the shaping of stone, bone, and primitive art, and it raised the curtain on a new period in man's progress, the Neolithic or New Stone Age.

The New Stone Age

The Neolithic has been called the Age of Civilization, for it was during this period of the New Stone Age that the earliest signs of organized society appeared. Arrival of the Neolithic brought several revolutionary changes in man's mode of life. Outstanding features were the polishing of some of his stone tools, the making of pottery, the domestication of animals, and the awakening use of seeds and plants leading to the most important invention of all, farming and agriculture. Man's tempo of progress was now becoming more rapid.

Preparation of the soil and the harvesting of crops encouraged a more settled existence and the establishment of villages. The strictly nomadic way of life became less vital, although the hunt

still provided clothing and food. The need for and use of flint and other durable stone assumed importance as never before. Sharp, heavy stone axes or celts, saws, and adzes were developed to cut trees and clear the land. Sickles made of flint, and some of bone set with flint chips, were used to harvest crops.

The increasing population and widening demand for stone tools made flint a valuable and all important natural resource. No doubt the first industrial boom came to those who were fortunate to possess good, workable deposits of flint. It was natural that certain members of a community, still imbued with the old, restless, hunting spirit would leave the comforts of their grotto hearthstones to venture forth toward the frontier in search of flint.

Such a man was a bonanza hunter as eager as those who would explore other lands in ages to come. In his day, the prehistoric prospector also had grown experienced in noticing indications that pointed to nature's riches. He knew that it was along the river banks, where erosion had exposed the limestone and chalk layers, that fortune might reveal an unusual deposit of his treasured material.

The First Miners

Certain localities became famous for the quality of flint mined, and implements produced. In England, at Cissbury, Sussex, Grimes Graves, Norfolk, and at Spiennes, Belgium, at Grand Pressigny and south Auvergne, France, and in Sweden, shafts have been sunk and galleries driven into chalk and limestone to mine the prized flint.

Crude mining tools consisted of rough picks and hammers of flint and pointed stone hafted to stag horns. Picks of red deer antlers were used to pry loose fragmented chunks. Shovels were made from the shoulder blade of an ox or deer. Fire setting, the building of log fires against a stone face or wall, and subsequent quenching with water, was used to drive drifts or openings through the rock, a slow and tedious process.

The skeletons of Stone Age miners have been found in ancient workings where they were trapped and crushed to death by heavy falls of rock. One was found with his hands still grasping his crude stag horn pick. Imprints of his fingers on the dusty handle were clear and undisturbed all these years. Stone Age man, burrowing into the ground with his crude tools in the dark, cramped, twisting passageways, became the world's first miner seeking riches of the earth.

One of the most renowned and prolific flint industries of all Europe centered around a village now known as Le Grand Pressigny, about 40 miles south of Tours, France. It was one of the great flint deposits worked during the Neolithic period. It must have provided its discoverer with much joy and pride.

The Bonanza of Grand Pressigny

We can see a Stone Age prospector, some 5,000 years ago, walking slowly and gazing intently at the low yellowish limestone wall that borders a river now known as La Claise, near the present village of Grand Pressigny. This man has wandered into a remote wilderness far from the comforts of his native community. A few scattered pieces of unusual honey-colored flint, found among the river pebbles, have caught his eye.

Farther on the pieces increase in number and size. He quickens his pace. Suddenly, all about him are large, butter-colored chunks of flint, more beautiful and plentiful than any he has ever seen. He has indeed discovered a bonanza. He races along the river with overflowing exuberance, enlarging with every step the area of his precious find. Large yellow nodules lay imbedded in the chalk layers of the limestone walls rimming the river, and generously cover the ground on the alluvial fields above. It is a find of major importance. Not only is the flint in great abundance, but it transcends any variety he has ever seen in its rare color and workability.

"Livres de beurre," or pounds of butter, as these chunks of flint would later be called because of their butter-yellow color, size and shape, averaged 12 to 14 inches long. East of the junction of La Creuse and La Claise rivers, prehistoric flint working stations, quarries, and caves now dot the valley for a distance several miles east and west of the present villages of Grand Pressigny and Abilly. In its day, this was a mining district as important as later day Cornwall of England or the Comstock Lode of Nevada.

Neolithic Industry

Here, a great industry of the Neolithic age came into being, as the fame and popularity of its products spread over the land. One can imagine the bustling activity of this Stone Age boom camp as it became more and more noted for its honey-colored wares. Grand Pressigny flint, or whatever name it was then known by, found its way into what is now Brittany, Belgium, Switzerland, and as far east as Italy. Its artisans became increasingly adept in fashioning flint knives, scrapers, axes, sickles, daggers, and picks. Not only these finished products, but raw materials as well, long flint cores and "livres de beurre" found their way into channels of commerce.

The polishing of flint objects was also an important part of their industry. Silex, as flint is called in France, was polished on large grooved slabs of stone, still to be seen in the museum at Grand Pressigny. This rare variety of flint attracted traders from distant lands. Earliest routes of commerce began to criss-cross the land. Ideas were exchanged; art, technology, and religious beliefs spread from one area to another. An awareness of new worlds and other peoples beyond the horizon developed.

The industries of Grand Pressigny flourished during a period that began with the mid-Neolithic about 5,000 years ago and continued through the chalcolithic or copper age and the early part of the bronze age. Even with the later discovery of copper and bronze, stone implements continued to be used widely. Because metals were not in early abundance, only the rich could afford such a luxury. The population as a whole continued to use stone for implements and common tools.

The time eventually came when the increased use of metals sounded the death knell for the flint industries of Grand Pressigny, after it had enjoyed several thousand years of prosperity. But it was not until advent of the Iron Age that Grand Pressigny's long history came fully to an end.

Grand Pressigny Today

A village which the Romans in the 6th century called Prisciniacus now lies sleepily in a green valley between La Creuse and La Claise rivers in southern Touraine, France. Today the little village is known as Grand Pressigny. Residents go about their chores hardly aware that 5,000 years ago the clatter of stone upon stone echoed over the same ground upon which they now live. From the lookout of Le Grand Pressigny's 11th century chateau tower, now surrounded by ruins, one can see a full circle panorama of the farm fields, the river valley, and the chalk cliffs which once provided Stone Age man with the flint that gave this region its first claim to fame.

A museum in a newer 16th century hall of the

chateau contains a remarkable collection of the products of Grand Pressigny's ancient workshops which farmers have gathered from their fields for ages. Several large grooved stones, which were used to polish the silex, or flint, bear testimony to the nature of the industry carried on here. The quaint village, nestled peacefully in the green valley below and surrounded by rare pastoral beauty, offers a place for intriguing reflection and an impressive perspective down the long, long trail of time.

Salt and Amber

As Neolithic man turned to agriculture, his diet came to include more grains and vegetables of the soil and less proteins of animals of the hunt. Just as herbivorous animals seek the salt licks to augment their diet, man now began to value salt as a necessary ingredient of life. Later the use of salt would become intimately connected with religious ceremonies, covenants, enduring compacts and expressions of friendship. Cakes of salt were later used as money in some parts of the world, and allowances of salt were given to men of ancient armies. Salt, as well as prized types of flint, played a big part in establishing ancient highways of trade, as people began to embark upon a new venture—commerce.

The mountainous region in Austria which came to be called the Salzkammergut, meaning "salt exchequer property," of which Salzburg is a well known city, was an important early source of European salt. Later, in the same region, Hallstatt would lend its name to an important phase of the Iron Age. In ancient times, salt and flint, not readily available in all lands, were not the ordinary commodities they are today; they once were items of necessity and luxury.

Another early and highly sought trade item was amber. On the island of Crete, amber beads were found in remains dated about 2500 B.C., and amber articles were later found in Egypt and Mycenae, Greece. These were far flung points of trade, for the amber came from the distant shores of the Baltic Sea.

Amber, a fossil resin, was greatly valued for decorative use. It occurs in irregular, rounded nodules of varying yellow to brown color. It is relatively soft and easily carved to form beautiful ornaments. It possesses an unusual quality. When rubbed on cloth it develops a magnetic charge of electricity. The Greeks, who prized it highly, called it electrum, from which has been derived the word electricity. Drops of water, vegetable matter, and often insects, were trapped and imbedded in clear amber. The shores of Denmark, Sweden, Poland and Germany have been sources of amber for ages. Prussian amber from the coast of Pomerania, now Poland, was most desirable.

The First Trade Routes

Thus began the world's first trade routes. Stone Age merchants loaded amber, salt and flint upon their pack gear and started forth to seek reward and items of exchange in far away places. One of the earliest and greatest routes of commerce extended from east to west along the Danube River, reaching into the eastern Mediterranean. A north and south route came from the Baltic coast and coursed southward over Brenner Pass to the Adriatic. Other routes of trade developed as men ventured beyond the frontiers of their homeland. Aristotle later described these trade routes as sacred to all users, who by general agreement were to receive the protection of the Gods and be free of molestation. Safety was important to both merchants and customers, for trading was a two way enterprise.

Far to the east, in a haze of mythology, were the lands of the Fertile Crescent, encompassing the valleys of the Tigris and Euphrates rivers, and of Asia Minor, of Syria, Palestine, Crete, Mycenae, Egypt and Mesopotamia, where other races were slowly rising. In the rich valleys of the Middle East a warmer climate, longer growing seasons and the existence of wild grains induced the next great step in man's evolution, the invention of farming which would lead to the birth of civilization. But, as we have seen, it was European man who, favored by protective grottoes and flourishing mammalian life, arose from the depths of his Paleolithic beginnings to the greatest heights of the Old Stone Age culture, in which his abundant supply of excellent flint played an inspiring and stimulating role.

Chapter 2

THE CRADLE OF CIVILIZATION

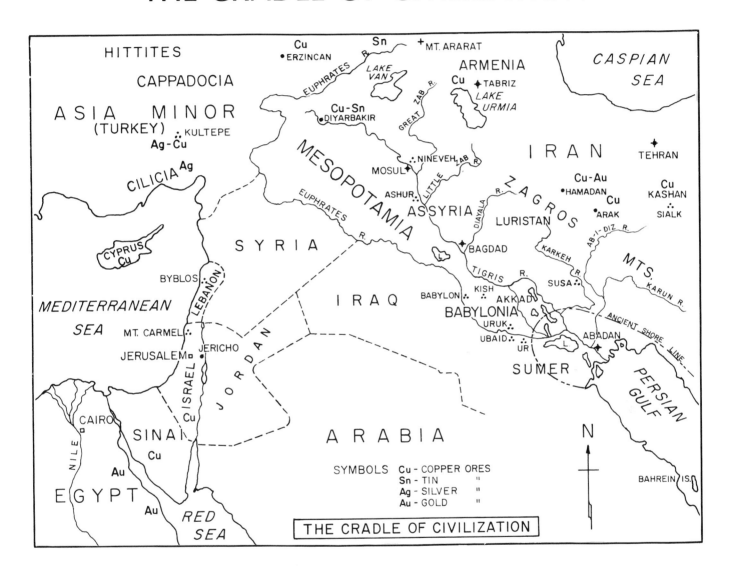

THE CRADLE OF CIVILIZATION

The forces of Nature had smiled upon western Europe, especially France, with those elementary, environmental circumstances which favored and nurtured the emergence of *Homo sapiens* and the greatest development of Paleolithic industry and art. But, it was in the Middle East that the most revolutionary changes took place during the Neolithic or New Stone Age. There, wild barley, wheat and other plants, bolstered by a climate milder than Europe's, and wild prototypes of cattle, swine, sheep and oxen already existed which fostered the invention of farming and the appearance of stabilized communities. There the stage was set for the beginning of civilization.

The Fertile Crescent

The eminent historian, James H. Breasted, coined the term *Fertile Crescent* for that region in western Asia and the Middle East where history began. The term has since become widely used. The eastern portion of the Fertile Crescent begins in the alluvial valleys of the Tigris-Euphrates Rivers. In the southern region near the Persian Gulf, cities such as Ubaid, Uruk (Erech) and Ur, Kish, Nippur and Babylon played dramatic roles in this area. Farther northward, up the Tigris River, were Assur and Nineveh. All of these ancient cities were located in a land once called Mesopotamia, now known as Iraq.

The northernmost arc of the crescent swept to the southern border of present Turkey, an early source of important mineral wealth, and curved westward to the eastern shore of the Mediterranean Sea, taking in Byblos, Mount Carmel and Jericho, in lands that became known as Lebanon and Palestine. The southwest limb of the crescent ended in Egypt, where the rich valley of the Nile nourished a civilization that became remarkable for its duration and culture.

The Caves of Carmel

During the Old Stone Age the eastern Mediterranean area had been experiencing a cultural evolution somewhat older but less advanced than that of western Europe. Many sites of Paleolithic activity, and of the succeeding Neolithic period which saw man's first adventures in farming, may still be seen today. Some have been excavated disclosing with amazing clarity the ruins of prehistoric habitations, while others such as the famed Caves of Carmel have remained untouched

and unchanged by nature or man.

Today one may visit and inspect the Caves of Carmel, alone and undisturbed, by driving a few miles south of Israel's modern city of Haifa. In a high ridge of hard, enduring limestone which overlooks the nearby Mediterranean shore, one will find three large black voids in the rock wall staring starkly across the narrow plain toward the sea. Low dirt terraces form approaches to the cave entrances. Walking cautiously into the larger cave one finds the interior, some thirty feet in diameter, blackened with the soot of thousands of years of prehistoric fires. The cold, dismal walls are shrouded in abyssal silence and haunting mystery. One may peer through the cave opening to the sea beyond, as have many prehistoric men in the long past. It is almost impossible to realize that this unchangeable place, the ultimate in permanency, was once home to humans, and near humans, for over 100,000 years.

On the dirt terrace and in the cave known as Mugaret el-Wad, the prehistorian, Professor Dorothy Garrod, unearthed 60 skeletons of Natufian hunter-fishers of the Mesolithic period. Mortars and pestles of basalt found around the caves suggest that the Natufians were beginning to harvest and grind the wild barley and emmer of the region, about 7500 B.C.

In the Skhul and Tabun caves, Professor Garrod found 10 skeletons of Neanderthal inhabitants and a large quantity of Mousterian flints shown by Carbon 14 tests to be 50,000 years old. In still lower layers were found Paleolithic remains corresponding to the late Acheulean of France, of a period more than 100,000 years ago. This residence, as enduring as the mountain itself, lost its usefulness only when the relatively late comers, the Natufians, moved out into the open to seek an agricultural way of life, 9500 years ago. The Caves of Carmel are noted over the world for the remarkable sequences of habitation which they sheltered. Today the setting is virtually unchanged.

Mounds of The Ages

When Neolithic man abandoned his caves and embarked upon a life of sowing, reaping and stock raising, communities arose centered around certain favored locations. The sites were chosen because of a dependable water supply, nearness to good soil and other resources, and convenience to routes of trade. Since nothing man-made endures forever, eventually a settlement would be destroyed by pestilence, fire, or war. But, as the site was still strategic in location, perhaps a century or more later a new wave of inhabitants would take it over, easily level the old village of sun-dried bricks and rebuild for another generation.

Over thousands of years, this process was often repeated as many as 10 to 25 times. Long use of the site added to prestige and tradition and tended to perpetuate its existence. Such a series of settlements, one upon another, created a mound rising higher and higher until the area at the top became too small to accommodate another community. Then it would be abandoned, to crumble away and be forgotten under centuries of dust and debris when new races came to the land.

Hundreds of these mounds, called "tells," exist in the Middle East. Many are made of the adjoining soils and are barely discernible from the low, natural hills of the countryside. Until recently many sites famous in ancient history have remained obscure and unexplored. Now, one by one, they are giving up their secrets as teams of archeologists from various countries unearth them stone by stone endeavoring to unravel their misty past.

The Walls of Jericho

At the base of Tell es-Sultan 19 levels down, on the site of ancient Jericho, excavated remains of huts made of sun-dried bricks, and sickles of flint revealed that the Natufians here had moved from caves into the open and had begun the harvesting of grain. Carbon 14 tests place Jericho's beginning at about 7800 B.C., making the site with its 10,000 years of continuous occupation the oldest known city in the world. It was also a walled, fortified city, surrounded by a moat-like space. Since it was located in one of the hottest, driest places on earth, and apparently unsuited as an agricultural center, the reason for the famed walls of Jericho presents a mystery.

According to Emmanuel Anati, an Israeli archeologist, Jericho lay astride one of the oldest trade routes of the Middle East in a region possessing certain natural resources. Along the Dead Sea nearby were three precious commodities, salt, bitumen and sulphur. A booming trade in salt had developed to satisfy man's newest dietary requirements in the use of cereals and vegetables. The use of bitumen had increased to fasten flint heads to sickles, axes and

hammers, and for caulking boats. These articles, together with sulphur used in medicinal and ritualistic practices, placed Jericho in the heart of a bonanza land and on a trade route of importance. Even then wealth was tempting envious marauders, forcing Jericho to become mankind's first fortified city. It was then also that the blessings, woes, and complexities of society's economic structure first cast its shadow over the world.

The widespread beginnings of agricultural communities in the Fertile Crescent were disclosed by other excavations of noted Neolithic sites such as Byblos north of Beirut, Lebanon, Hacilar and Catal Huyuk farther northward on the Anatolian plateau of southwestern Turkey, Jarmo in the foothills of northern Iraq, and Hassuna near modern Mosul. Evidence showed that rudimentary farming and the domestication of goats and sheep began as early as 7000 B.C.

The Metalworkers of Susa

A site of great significance is that of Susa, about 15 miles south of Dizful in southwestern Iran, some 125 miles north of the mouth of the Tigris River. In this land that became known as Elam, then Persia, and now Iran, a culture existed about 4500 B.C. which cultivated grain, domesticated animals, and was famed for its beautiful colored pottery with delicate geometric designs. Susa, and Sialk near Kashan farther north, claim our special attention because archeologists have here unearthed some of the oldest tools and weapons of copper and ornaments of gold, indicating that in Iran man had taken another momentous step forward, one of the most consequential in all history. He had discovered the use of metals.

Twilight was falling upon the long, seemingly endless era when man's solitary material resource was stone. A great new age, the Age of Metals, was coming with its myriads of unforseeable benefits; but it was coming very slowly. The early use of copper implements found at Susa and Sialk is important evidence that it was the land of Mesopotamia which saw the dawn of civilization.

Man's First Metals

Unquestionably, gold was the first metal to attract early man's attention. Gold has been found adorning stone knives in many Neolithic remains. Man has long valued its resplendent sun-like luster, always bright and unchanged, and its ability to remain free of tarnish throughout the ages.

Gold must have first caught man's eye when he saw shining flakes and nuggets in stream beds or water holes as placer gold, and as free, native gold in rock outcrops. Gold's charm rested not only in its enduring, brilliant color, but also in its malleability. It could be hammered into all forms and shapes, and pounded into the flimsiest sheets, making it ideal for covering images of wood. Its adaptability to shaping was fortunate, for man was unable as yet to produce heat sufficiently intense to melt any metal. In lovely ornaments gold was man's most cherished possession, but it was much too soft to be used in making tools.

Copper, which also was found first in native nuggets and masses, was far more important than gold as a working metal. But native copper, unlike gold, corrodes quickly in the air to form the green carbonate, malachite, or blue azurite, and in some cases, the red oxide, cuprite. Beneath the carbonate coating, no doubt it was soon discovered that a glancing blow, or stream abrasion, exposed copper's shining red sheen. Man also found that native copper was fairly malleable and could be hammered into desired shapes.

For a long time native copper had been thought of simply as another stone that, like gold, could be hammered, bent, and cut crudely in the shape of man's stone tools. This is known as the *chalcolithic*, copper-stone, period. Then about 5000 B.C., perhaps accidentally someone dropped a lump of copper into the fire and found that heat had made it more malleable, easier to shape, tougher and less brittle.

Thus did heating, annealing or tempering of copper launch man's use of another of his primitive elements, fire, to improve the appearance, durability, and efficiency of his wares. In the use of tools, annealing followed by hammering could now produce sharper edges hard enough to cut stone. Granulated abrasives such as corundum or other hard stones were used to assist the cutting action. But copper tools had to be re-shaped and re-sharpened often. Contrary to popular belief, the ancients did not possess a secret means for hardening copper other than by frequent hammering.

The Discovery of Metallurgy

Animated by the miracle wrought by fire, the next difficult step was an endeavor to melt the copper and pour it into molds in the form of

castings. Man was at last on the road to discovering the science of metallurgy, how to wrest metals from their complex stony ores, as an eminent English archeologist expressed it "one of the most dramatic leaps in history." With the exciting revelation that fire could be used to obtain metallic copper by smelting the blue and green carbonates and the red and black oxide compounds, as well as other copper ores, prospectors were not limited to the search for native copper alone. These new colorful stones of copper then led men to explore the far frontiers.

Where and how the science of metallurgy became known has several schools of thought, the two most favored being the campfire or the pottery kiln. Following one theory, we can visualize some chalcolithic prospector as he climbs the walls of a rugged canyon looking for an exposure of native copper, his only known ore. He has sensed a promising area in the canyon and finally comes upon a rock outcrop brightened by the carbonates of copper, green malachite and blue azurite. Powdered malachite, he already knows, is being used as a greenish eye shadow for rich ladies of the land. The prospector gathers some of the more colorful pieces and prepares to make his camp beside the outcrop on the canyon slope.

Twilight shadows fall across the primeval hills. Perhaps it is in the Zagros Mountains of Iran, or somewhere in Asia Minor. A chilly wind sweeps down the canyon in which he has camped. Stacking a generous supply of wood into his newly dug fire pit, he circles his bright stones around the pit, lights his fire, and sits back to enjoy its warmth.

The wind whistles, and his campfire blazes fiercely in the strong canyon draft. Before long the firewood is a mass of hot, glowing embers of charcoal. And then, before his unbelieving eyes, the prospector sees tiny rivulets of glistening fluid trickling from what had been his green and blue stones. Mystified and weary, he huddles close to the embers and sleeps the night through.

In the morning, as the rising sun chases the shadows from the canyon, he pokes around in the ashes of his fire and cautiously withdraws the gleaming rivulets which are now cold and solid. Incredibly they are formed of metallic copper, the very same metal he has been seeking in its native state. By some miracle he has wrung copper metal from these magical green and blue stones.

The miracle has an explanation. The

prospector's campfire, under the forced draft of the canyon wind, had given the fire a temperature of over 800 degrees centigrade, enough to melt the oxidized ores malachite and azurite with the aid of some lime flux in the limestone which made the material more fluid. His wood fire produced charcoal, a reducing agent which liberated the carbon monoxide that had combined with the oxygen of the carbonates, thus freeing metallic copper from the ore.

Substantiating the campfire theory, such authorities as T. A. Rickard and W. Gowland have referred to the primitive wood fires used even in modern times to obtain metallic copper by the natives of the Belgian Congo, central Africa, the Malay peninsula, and elsewhere. Beads of copper have been found on remnants of copper ore in the ashes left in crudely dug firepits of the inhabitants. Trenches on hillsides or canyon slopes, arranged to catch the prevailing winds, have been used to provide the draft of air necessary to raise temperatures to the melting point of oxidized copper ores.

Other historical and technical authorities, such as R. J. Forbes and H. H. Coghlan believe that it was in the prehistoric pottery kiln that metallurgy was discovered, for only therein was early man able to produce the temperatures required to smelt metallic ores. Several late neolithic cultures were quite adept in producing fine, highly baked and well glazed pottery, using bellows to obtain the necessary forced draft of air and high temperatures. Employing such a process, with the addition of charcoal, copper ores could thus have been reduced to obtain the desired metal. But, one thing is certain; after countless millennia, in which his only material resource was stone, man had now taken one gigantic step into the beckoning Age of Metals.

Stones of Antiquity

Where were the ores of copper to be found and where and who were the people that first realized the potency of this new stone in the remote past? Copper ore bodies, and even minor surface showings of copper minerals of non-commercial value, occur widely scattered over the earth. Considering the numerous sites in Europe and also in western Asia where copper is known to have occurred, it is possible that the secret of smelting copper ores was discovered simultaneously at several places. In England, prehistoric men could have found copper in Cornwall, Devon and Chesire, and also in west central France,

Italy, the Spanish peninsula, and abundantly in Saxony and Bohemia, and on the island of Cyprus.

In western Asia, however, during the late neolithic period, there were not only cultures well advanced in the use of the high temperature pottery kiln, there was also a widespread supply of ores available. Surrounding the Fertile Crescent, in Armenia and such regions of modern Turkey as the Pontus, Anatolia, Taurus, and Kurdistan and in Turkestan east of the Caspian Sea, there were numerous deposits rich in various types of metals. There was also copper in the southern Negev desert of Israel, the Sinai Peninsula, and Egypt.

The particular region that appears to have spawned man's earliest use of copper included Persia, now known as Iran, and the adjoining territories of Afghanistan and Baluchistan. The excavation of copper artifacts in the prehistoric sites of Susa and Sialk in Iran have been already mentioned. It is possible that an alert, discerning prospector could have acquired the secret of melting the colorful oxidized stones of copper from a canyon campfire not far from Susa. But it is just as probable that the pottery kilns of Susa saw the beginning of smelting, for Susa was famed for the attainments of its pottery industry.

Andre Parrot, noted museum curator and archeologist, not long ago wrote "the Louvre's magnificent pottery collection proves that no similar industry of the Ancient East could vie with the pottery of Susa." Parrot called Susa "the Sevres of antiquity." Whichever was the method of discovery, the hoard of copper implements found at Susa and Sialk disclosed that their craftsmen knew the art of annealing and casting metal, the first steps in developing the science of metallurgy. This discovery would lead to the invention of writing, the prelude to history and the birth of civilization.

As primitive populations increased and the need of a greater food supply became evident, inhabitants of the stony highlands began to seek easily cultivated soils and a dependable source of water. Southward from Susa there was such a land midway between the Persian Gulf and modern Baghdad. Today it is known as Iraq.

Pioneers on The Euphrates

A similarity in pottery designs and copper ornaments unearthed in this region indicates that among the first to settle in the fertile valley was a group of enterprising pioneers from Susa. There is a possibility, however, that the early migrants came down the Tigris or the Euphrates from northern Armenia or the Caucasus, an area which was also rich in metallic ores. The exact origin of these first settlers may be somewhat obscure, but an amazingly complete record of the cities they built, following their arrival in the land, has been found by archeologists. The land became known as Sumer. Now fallow and deserted, no place on earth except Egypt is so steeped in the lore of prehistory and the dawn of civilization.

Traditionally this land included the Biblical Garden of Eden. Indeed, during the pluvial period of heavy rainfall which followed the last Ice Age in the north, the Tigris-Euphrates Valley was lush and verdant. It must have seemed a garden paradise to the wandering neolithic highlanders. But today this same valley is a scene of drab desolation. A broad, monotonous expanse of sand dunes now stretch to the horizon. Out of the shimmering heat waves rise the forlorn tumbled mounds or tells which mark the once thriving cities of Sumer.

It is almost beyond belief that here one of the first, if not the very first, notable waves of civilization was set in motion. Yet, this was once a land teeming with energetic, ambitious people astir with creative ideas. From this fountainhead of mankind sprang agriculture, irrigation, metallurgy, commerce, writing, mathematics, religion and the world's first empires.

The Birth of Agriculture

When civilization flowered here, this was a region of low, grassy islands and marshes. The waters of the Persian Gulf, now over 60 miles away, then lapped upon a nearby shore. The silty soil was rich and covered with reeds. It was in this promising land that the first settlers, a short, stocky, non-Semitic race, decided to start life anew, about 4500 B.C.

Utilizing reeds growing abundantly in the marshes, the settlers covered the damp silt with matting and built their homes of mud and thatching. Then they began to cultivate the deep, fertile soil. The great rivers, the Tigris and Euphrates, assured a constant water supply by means of irrigation systems, which the settlers ingeniously learned to develop.

The climate was mild, often hot. Long growing seasons and the rich soil produced bountiful crops. Eventually the pioneers developed a flourishing agricultural economy, adding to the

number and growth of their settlements. In the ruins of Al Ubaid, one of the earliest communities, archeologists later found stone hoes, knives, primitive stone mills for grinding corn, painted pottery and copper ornaments. Inhabitants grew grain and dates, herded sheep, gathered wool and made clothing, while the metalsmiths, the magical craftsmen of the age produced copper wares with increasing diversity. The land was devoid of mineral resources other than bitumen deposits, the surface seepages of oil pools then unknown. But ores of copper were not far away in the highland of Iran. Lacking suitable stone, the settlers resorted to sun-dried brick to erect shrines to their gods and to build other structures.

Epics of The Great Flood

Sometime prior to 3800 B.C. the budding civilization of the Ubaid people was overcome by calamity. Poets and priest-historians of a later age sang epic tales of a great flood that had completely destroyed the early settlements. Archeologists digging in the prehistoric ruins found evidence of a deluge that strikingly resembled the story of the Great Flood recited in the Bible. Since the Great Flood, and the cities that were later built upon the Ubaid ruins, seems to mark the emergence of mankind from the mists of prehistory, the legend deserves examination.

By considering the climatic and physiographic conditions of ancient times, and by inspecting the drainage pattern of the lower Tigris-Euphrates Valley and the topography of the adjacent highland region, it is possible to reconstruct the circumstances that could have triggered a cataclysmic event such as The Deluge described in the Book of Genesis.

During the long periods of the geologic past, the Tigris-Euphrates and tributary river systems had been filling the Mesopotamian depression, including the Persian Gulf which in earlier times reached far north of its present shoreline. When the prehistoric Ubaid people arrived they built their first crude shelters and later their mud-brick cities scarcely above the water line of the marshes. Ubaid, Eridu, and Ur were among the early settlements that arose upon these dangerously low sites.

Stretching a hundred miles southward from the shoreline the upper arm of the Gulf was very shallow. Acting in concert with the efforts of the

Tigris and Euphrates rivers to fill the Gulf and decrease the water's depth, there was a gradual upwarping or uplifting of the land and the sea bottom, as shown by ancient beach lines which can now be seen considerably above the present sea level. This was a condition that eventually could drastically change the physiography of the area.

Unknown to the unsuspecting settlers of early Sumer a third river system was in position to devastate the land. Entering the valley from the northeast and opposing the course of the Tigris-Euphrates outfall, was the river system that included the Karun, the Karkheh, the Jarrahi, and the Ab-i-Diz rivers. Their widespread tentacles reached far upward and eastward into the Zagros Mountains and highlands of Luristan and Khuzestan of western Iran. This large river complex, draining an area of craggy mountains and high detrital valleys, for ages had been dumping huge amounts of silt into the shallow northern arm of the Gulf, slowly building its own submerged alluvial bar, an unseen dam, across the course of the Tigris-Euphrates waters flowing into the Gulf.

The pluvial period, which had produced the savanna-like vegetation of the north African belt, had waned, but occasional periods of heavy rainfall were not entirely of the past, as seen by the silt deposits of the Tigris-Euphrates Valley and those found later covering the Ubaid ruins. Meanwhile, the upper reaches of the Karun-Karkheh watersheds stood ready to disgorge gigantic tonnages of silt down tumbling grades, out and onto the deltaic barrier already grown to considerable height in the shallow, constricted throat of the Persian Gulf. Only a rare and ruinous act of nature was necessary to complete a catastrophic cycle.

Came The Deluge

Then came the terrible deluge. From all the Zagros highlands came a vast flood of alluvial debris, spilling into and filling the shallow neck of the Gulf, adding to the height of the transverse bar that was damming the frustrated waters of the inflowing Tigris and Euphrates rivers. Rapidly a great lake arose in the valley and drowned the low-lying villages. Several hundred miles northward and a hundred miles from east to west extended the inundated area, the whole adopted world of the prehistoric settlers.

As the Tigris and Euphrates rivers entered the newly created inland lake, they dropped their load of sediments just as our rivers do today in man-made reservoirs. Six thousand years later, Sir Leonard Woolley, after making one of the greatest archeological discoveries in history while excavating the fabulous Royal Cemetery of Ur, would feel impelled to probe deeper. Below Ur's ruins, Woolley found no relics or signs of life, only an eight foot layer of clean, barren, water-laid sand and silt. But, beneath this lifeless strata, further digging revealed the remains of a much earlier city. This was physical confirmation of a flood that had buried the towns of the pioneers who had preceded the Sumerians.

The deltaic dam which impeded the Tigris-Euphrates outlets exists today in the form of a neck of land between Basra and Khorramshahr, and the islands of Abadan and Bubiyan. Near the junction of the Tigris and Euphrates rivers, not far from the ruins of Ur and Ubaid, one can see the inland lakes of Hor al Hammar, Hor Sanniya and S'adiya, the shrunken remains of the flood-made sea that gave mankind the immortal legend of the Great Deluge which once covered the ancient world.

Arrival of The Sumerians

Upon the flood debris covering Ubaid and Ur rose the cities of a new people, the Sumerians. Nearby at Uruk, called Erech in the Bible, now known as Warka, they established their capital. The Sumerians were a highly advanced non-Semitic race, skilled in the use of gold, silver and copper. They had begun to record events, including the Great Flood and epic tales of their hero-king Gilgamesh, using pictographic inscriptions on tablets of clay. These chronicles formed the groundwork for the beginning of history, the written record of man's evolution. Dr. S. N. Kramer and other noted Sumerologists recently deciphered the 5000 year old inscriptions revealing that the Biblical story of The Deluge apparently had not originated with the Hebrews. Sumerian legends had been copied by the Babylonians who later ruled the land, and were adopted by the Hebrews, Phoenicians, Greeks, Romans, and finally the Christians.

Evidence as to the possible origin of the Sumerians and the source of their talents in metalworking was contained in other tablets deciphered by Dr. Kramer. They disclosed that King Enmerkar, of Sumer's First Dynasty, sent a herald to Aratta a city-state far to the northeast, perhaps beyond the Caspian Sea, demanding that gold, silver, copper and precious stones be sent together with skilled workers to adorn the temple of the watergods in ancient Eridu, or face destruction. Aratta's ruler replied with equal arrogance by demanding grain, a surplus commodity in Sumer, in exchange. After many threats and counterthreats the people of Arrata finally received the grain and in turn delivered the metals and semi-precious stones to Eridu, heaping them in the courtyard of the temple. This is perhaps history's first recorded instance of economic rivalry resulting in a trade agreement over material resources of the land.

Enmerkar's inclusion of silver in his demands is noteworthy. Silver then was valued even more than gold. Since silver seldom occurs in the metallic state, native silver finds were fairly rare. Silver generally corrodes or oxidizes to form various compounds, although it has occasionally been found even on nuggets of copper. Silver became more plentiful later when the smelting of silver-bearing lead ores proved to be the main source of metallic silver.

The story of Aratta shows that Iran was an early source of Sumer's metals, and that the working of metals was already under way in that region or farther north. But it was the energetic and inventive Sumerians who, bolstered by their prolific agricultural activity, seized the opportunities offered by the use of metals to expand their economy. Under Enmerkar's enterprising leadership and aided by his skillful craftsmen, Uruk and nearby Ur became the enterpreneurs of Sumerian culture.

The Royal Cemetery of Ur

Sir Leonard Woolley's famed excavation of The Royal Cemetery of Ur, in 1927, disclosed fantastic examples of wealth and art of Sumer's Early Dynastic period. Nearly everything had turned to dust; but, an immense treasure of imperishable metal objects had survived to reveal a priceless record of Sumerian prosperity 5000 years ago.

Digging through millennia of debris, excavators found copper spearheads attached to golden shafts, vases of alabaster, shields and daggers of gold and copper, and bowls of silver, surrounding the graves of royalty. The coffin of Prince Mes-kalam-dug revealed a skeleton turned to dust, but the gold, silver and precious stones were found unmoved since the day they were placed upon the body. Attached to a belt of silver,

now altered to a purplish trace, was a dagger of solid gold. Between the hands was a large bowl of gold and a mass of lapis lazuli and gold beads. Against the shoulder was a heavy double axe-head of electrum, a natural alloy of gold and silver. A pile of bracelets, earrings and amulets of gold, a gold headdress, and spiral rings of gold, were behind the body. The most spectacular find of all was a marvelous helmet of solid gold, beaten from a single sheet and beautifully engraved, so perfectly formed that the top was made to fit waves of hair, and the sides formed open circles about the ears. It was a masterful example of the Sumerian goldsmith's art.

Sixteen royal graves were found, but only two had escaped being plundered. The magnificence and perfection of the articles found in the undisturbed tombs have not been surpassed by any modern craftsmen. Among the finds is the famous gold dagger of Ur. Its blade is of solid gold, with a hilt of heavy gold studs and lapis lazuli. Its sheath was exquisitely worked filigree and granulated gold. Wooden harps were frequently found, ornamented with bulls heads of gold with horns and eyes of lapis lazuli.

A common practice, which is still the subject of debate as to its meaning, was the presence in the tombs of the remains of numerous servants, numbering from a few to 80, ornately dressed. Soldiers in full regalia and copper helmets were also interred with the royal remains. Presumably, this was a sacrificial ritual of the times.

A finely worked cylinder seal identified the royal tomb of Queen Shub-ad, which was also a storehouse of treasure. The upper part of the body was entirely hidden by masses of beads of gold, silver, and semi-precious stones. Vessels of gold, silver and copper, and harps with golden bulls heads, and a profusion of golden amulets, pins and pendants, surrounded the coffin.

Two large, intricate headdresses of gold were decorated with gold-shaped flowers and fruits and replicas of golden stags, bulls, and gazelles, all beautifully interwoven with hair ribbons and ringlets of gold. Upon silver tables stood shell-shaped lamps of gold, and shells containing powdered green, red, black and white cosmetics. Twenty-eight ladies of the Queen's court, wearing gold and silver hair ribbons and necklaces of gold, dutifully stood by in the tomb chamber just as they had when presumably they were drugged and put to sleep.

Close by was the tomb of the Queen's husband, King A-bar-gi. The room was filled with men and women servants, soldiers bearing insignia of their rank, and musicians carrying harps. Even chariots were there drawn by oxen and asses, with drivers still in their places, and grooms still holding the heads of the animals. All had taken their allotted positions in the tomb and in the shaft leading down into the tomb. A guard of soldiers, now turned to dust except for their metal trappings, barred the entrance to the passageway.

Another great discovery in the Royal Cemetery was a magnificent mosaic of lapis lazuli and shell inlaid upon two panels measuring 22 inches in length by 9 inches in height, known today as the 'Standard of Ur'. Upon a background of lapis lazuli, delicately engraved shell figures depicted scenes of a Sumerian king reviewing his army, infantrymen holding axes and spears, chariots drawn by asses and driven by spear-carrying warriors, and a 'phalanx' of soldiers crossing a battlefield. The so called 'Standard of Ur' is not only a remarkable example of Sumerian art, it is also a fine historical record. Costumes, equipment, and manner of warfare show how metal armory gave the Sumerians superiority over their adversaries which enabled them to become the first people to dominate the civilized world.

Civilization Begins in Sumer

It was beneath this Royal Cemetery of Ur that Sir Leonard Woolley delved deeper and found the lifeless, sandy strata that provided evidence of a great flood which had submerged the earlier Ubaid cities. Excavations at Ubaid itself disclosed man's oldest known decorations made of copper. Today, one may see in the British Museum, London, nearly life-sized bulls made of copper hammered over a core of wood and bitumen, with eyes and teeth of inlaid shells, which expressed the first artistic use of metals, created by the early pioneers who made the Euphrates valley their home. Thus, upon Ubaid's culture of copper and stone, and the splendid early dynasties of Uruk and Ur, was laid the foundation of civilization in Sumer.

It was during the Uruk period that industry and commerce first bloomed and boomed in Sumer. Lacking deposits of metallic ores in their own land, and increasingly in need of raw materials to supply their growing metal crafts, Sumerians went forth in many directions to trade their agricultural products and finished metal wares in exchange for gold, silver, copper, semi-precious stones and rare woods. Where and how far afield did they go?

Analyses have been made to determine the percentages of impurities contained in Sumerian copper articles, such as iron, antimony, and especially nickel which was commonly present, in order to locate the regions from which the copper ores had been imported. Various minerals which occasionally occur with copper ores are characteristic of certain regions. Many of Sumer's copper objects contained nickel, which suggests that some of the ores came from veins in the Akhdhar range in Oman near Sohar on the Persian Gulf. But there were other places on the Gulf that were well known to the Sumerians.

From a fabulously rich land known as Dilmun, on the northeastern coast of Arabia, probably near Bahrein Island, came boats to Sumer's docks loaded with copper, gold, semi-precious stones, ivory, rare woods, and pearls. The waters of the Gulf then were close to such cities as Eridu, Uruk and Ur. It is even possible that the Sumerians migrated from this southern region by boat when they first came to Sumer.

Copper River

There were also copper ores containing nickel in a region far to the north of Sumer in the rolling hills and rugged mountains of ancient Armenia, reached by traveling the long, winding Euphrates. It is significant that the Sumerian word for copper was 'Urudu' and that the name for the Euphrates was also 'Urudu', meaning 'copper river.' Obviously the Euphrates was a lifeline of commerce into the important metal regions of the far north, reaching even into frontiers of the west.

The Euphrates was also a pioneer trail that took the Sumerians into their "Far West" where traders obtained cakes of copper near Sakcagoz bordering present Turkey. Still farther west in the Taurus region of Cilicia, caravans were loaded with silver as well as copper, then took to the 1200 mile trail homeward to Sumer. Plodding over bare, rolling hills, they reached and crossed the precipitous ravines of the Seyhan River and finally found the welcoming arms of the Euphrates. The great river then carried them on the last 800 miles of their lonely, grueling journey. The Euphrates indeed was a 'copper river' to early mankind.

Traders and Metal Seekers of Sumer

Peoples in all directions on the barbarian fringe provided a lucrative, virgin market for Sumer's civilized wares. Many of these lands were important sources of metallic ores for the resourceful Sumerians. The nearest ore deposits were those of present Iran. Threading the dry, dusty passes of the jagged, upthrust Zagros Mountains, Sumerian traders went into the highlands of Iran beyond Susa. They obtained gold near Hamadan, and copper near Kashan, Arak and Isfahan. Some traders went farther east into Kerman and even so far as the mountains of Afghanistan, a land which supplied them also with lapis lazuli.

Much of the lapis lazuli that was so popular and found in such abundance in Sumerian graves came from the Badakhshan region of Afghanistan which has long been famed for this highly prized gem stone. Not far beyond, an amazing civilization was forming at Harappa, and farther south in the Indus Valley at Mohenjo-daro, about 200 air miles northeast of modern Karachi. Clay seals resembling those of early Sumer have been found on trails of commerce, linking the adventuresome Sumerians with the cultures of India. Thus, from the Indus Valley on the east to Asia Minor on the west, and from the Caspian Sea on the distant north to Arabia on the south, such were the far reaches that lured Sumerian traders and metal seekers. With them went the rudiments of art, science and writing to a world awaiting the birth of civilization over 6500 years ago.

Nature's Golden Hoard

In this dawning age of metals, nature was revealing to man for the first time her hoards of resplendent wealth, countless outcrops of virgin ore deposits that had been basking untouched under the timeless sun during the long geologic past. In the gravels of primeval streambeds, the earliest prospectors came upon glistening flakes and nuggets of gold. Later, they learned to recognize the precious but infrequent patches of this untarnishable metal that were found in veins and prominent ledges of rock.

For millions of years, the abrasive agents of erosion had been attacking these gold bearing outcrops. From both large outcrops and myriads more that were infinitely small, bits and pieces of free (native) gold were liberated and transported below to the ravines and streambeds of the region. Due to gold's high specific gravity (about six times

that of average rock) the washing action of water sorted and concentrated the gleaming metal along streambeds, in depressions, holes and crevices, or upon obstructions such as river sand bars. These alluvial accumulations are known as placer deposits, the principal source of ancient man's gold.

The sorting of gold from sand and gravel by stream water was noticed by early man who imitated this process by using hand held pans filled with gold bearing gravel. Shaking the contents of the pan and removing the lighter rock with a washing action, he was able to obtain free gold in the bottom of the pan. The same gravitational process and results were obtained by using hand rocked "cradles" in which larger amounts of gravel could be washed. Gold bearing sands were also washed across sheep skins, or fleece, which held the finer particles of metal, accounting for the legend of the "Golden Fleece." These were man's earliest and simplest methods used in mining and concentrating metallic ores.

The gold that was so profusely used by the Sumerians came from the various regions with which they traded. Gold was obtained in the mountains of present Iran west of Hamadan, and in the highlands of Armenia south of Lake Van, and beyond to the north as far as the Corun River near Artvin. It was but a short distance farther to Polti (Phasis) on the eastern shore of the Black Sea, doorway to the legendary land of Colchis, home of the Golden Fleece which is described later in these pages. Egypt, as we shall see, was very rich in gold and no doubt supplied Sumer with much of this precious metal.

Copper's Colorful Ores

The discovery and means of using a deposit of copper involved circumstances entirely different from those governing gold. After man had graduated from the use of native copper alone and had invented metallurgy, which enabled him to separate metals from their ores, he began to prospect for the colorful ores of copper. Delighted with nature's silent, peaceful places, and brimming with anticipation, the lone treasure hunter plodded patiently over the untrod hills and mountains of Iran, Armenia and Luristan, inspecting hopefully every slope and gulley for tell-tale signs of ore.

It was a patch of the green and blue colors of malachite and azurite, the carbonates of copper, perhaps mixed with certain oxides, reddish cuprite and black melaconite, that finally caught his eye. If these colored 'stones' were in sufficient strength and proportion in the outcrop and covered an area large enough to warrant mining, he had found the indications of a copper ore body. Further digging would determine the value of his discovery.

These eye-catching minerals that he had found were the weathered and oxidized surface exposures of a deeper and long buried deposit of copper whose original, primary minerals, such as bornite or chalcopyrite, contained sulphur and were known as "sulphides." The absence of sulphur in early Sumerian copper objects indicates that only the carbonates and oxides of copper, and not the sulphides, were first used in Sumerian metallurgical processes.

The Early Smelters

The Sumerians taught their native henchmen in the distant mining regions the rudiments of smelting the carefully selected copper carbonates and oxides. The first smelting furnaces were open hearths, mere holes in the ground, one or two feet in diameter and lined with fire-resistant clay or stone. A layer of charcoal was covered with a layer of ore in the furnace; the charcoal gave the fire a higher temperature aided by a draft of forced air. Gases produced by the charcoal formed the chemical agent which reacted with the oxidized minerals and reduced them to metallic copper. The vitreous slag, or waste, being lighter floated atop the molten mass. After cooling, the brittle slag was easily pounded loose leaving a cake of copper metal.

Perhaps accidentally some molten copper escaped from an early hearth and flowed into a small depression on the ground, then cooled in the form of the natural earth mold. From such an experience sprang the idea that molten, flowing metal could be poured, or cast, into man-made molds of desired shapes. This was another technological step of immense significance and would lead to a tremendous increase in the types of metal objects that could be produced.

Following the simpler open hearth smelting, came the crucible, a pot of fire-resistant clay in which the charge of ore and charcoal was placed, thus providing a cleaner metal cake. By means of a bellows, often made of goat skins, a fiercer heat could be developed in the furnace or kiln which contained the crucible. The resulting ingots were cast into bars, rings and ox-hide shapes which were useful as mediums of exchange and convenient to transport to the metalworkers of Sumerian cities.

Oxidized ores were sought not only because they were more amenable to early smelting processes, but since they were confined to or near the surface, they were also less difficult to mine. Inasmuch as more untouched, unexplored ore deposits were available and open to detection in Sumerian times, only the richest and easiest to mine were worked, which partially accounts for the widely diverse areas of mining and trading activities.

The richer ores could be skimmed or "gophered" from shallow depths, confining production to the oxidized ores and eliminating the need for deeper hard rock mining. It should be remembered that the only way that solid rock could be broken and loosened in mining was by setting fire to a pile of dry wood stacked against a face or wall of rock, followed by dousing and cracking the hot rock with water, a method known as "fire setting." Men armed with copper picks could then pry loose the partially fragmented rock. This slow, tedious process was the only means of making progress through hard, solid ground for over 4000 years. It was not until A.D. 1627, in the mines of Germany, that gunpowder was first used in blasting operations.

Sumerian Technology and Trade

During the ascendancy of Uruk there was a remarkable expansion of the copper industry, stimulated by great improvements in making castings of copper. Both open and closed molds were used, as well as the intricate cire-perdue process. In the latter, a carved model of an object to be cast was covered with a thickness of wax. An impression was then taken creating a reverse mold of the model. Heat was then applied to melt and expel the wax between the model walls, and, into the space thus vacated, metal was poured to form the final casting, a process also known as the lost or waste wax method.

Craftsmen of both Uruk and Ur attained a degree of perfection in metalworking never before known to man. An enticing array of new copper wares were made which won wide acceptance on the trade frontiers. Copper picks, axes, nails, bowls, mirrors, fishhooks, ornaments, religious figures, and especially weapons of war, spears, and helmets, were loaded aboard high-prowed boats together with grain, textiles, leather goods and pottery, to be dispersed to a ready, virgin market, man's first outstanding venture in commerce. With these products also went Sumerian ideas and culture. The first rays of civilization were creeping across a long darkened world, fostered by the everlasting search for and use of metallic resources and motivated by the inborn incentive to trade, man's first example of 'economics in action.'

Making full use of their fertile valley to produce surpluses useful in trade, agriculture continued to play a major role in Sumerian economy. Many first-class citizens became merchants and free land owners. They worked their lands with numerous slaves, for conquest and spoils of war brought about another discovery, that man too could be subjugated and domesticated. Thus did slavery become an inhuman part of man's existence.

Ox drawn plows were used to till the fields. The Sumerians invented the wheel and harnessed Asiatic onagers, or asses, to four wheeled carts and chariots of war. Warfare between rival city-states even then was becoming the mother of invention. Military vehicles were equipped with tires of leather or copper, and carried soldiers wearing copper helmets and armed with copper headed spears. Stimulated by demands for better tools and weaponry, the science of metallurgy was becoming of increasing importance. Unfortunately man became more war-like as his weapons improved, and he continued to seek and devise new aids to conquest.

Temples of Sumer

Uruk's rise to prominence was reflected in the magnificence of its architecture, symbolized by its great ziggurat, a towering temple 'raised to the heavens' in the shape of a stepped pyramid crowned by a shrine to the local god and reached by long flights of stairs. The Ziggurat was an outstanding feature, making its first appearance early in Sumerian history. Accustomed to the eminences of their original homeland, Sumerians found the vast, level Tigris-Euphrates Valley lacking in elevated places, therefore they built their temples on raised platforms of mud brick, faced with burnt brick, since stone was scarce. During a millenium, older shrines were filled in with brick to form the foundation of a new temple, adding to the height of the pyramid or ziggurat. The gleaming White Temple of Uruk, built about 3100 B.C., could be seen for miles around.

Long before the Greek builders of the Parthenon in Athens, the Sumerians achieved the remarkable optical illusion of perfect perspective and proportion by erecting the sides of the ziggurat on carefully calculated curvatures. The Sumerians made use of the arch, painted walls, and mosaic covered columns. Copper was used generously to adorn temples and in architectural details.

Spacious courtyards surrounding the temples were beehives of activity. Huge store rooms were filled with the city's commodities, and clerical quarters hummed with scribes preparing labels and records inscribed on thin clay tablets, while others engraved small stone cylinders used in making impressions upon seals of clay. The cylinder seal was almost a trademark of Sumerian culture. Small cylinders of stone, baked clay, or metal, were engraved with a signature or distinctive design, and then rolled over a soft, unbaked strip or jar of clay, leaving its identification mark. Seals often depicted scenes of worship or of battle, and other important details of community life, an invaluable record of history.

The Invention of Writing

It was this burgeoning economic development and community activity that spurred the invention of writing. A tremendous number of records were now required; labels, price tags, bills, receipts, letters, land surveys, school texts, and epic poems made the old system of crude pictograms, of which there were 2000, obsolete. Abandoning the pictographs, the Sumerians devised a system of marks representing syllabic sounds corresponding to the phonetic value of their language arranged in the order of speech. Since Sumerian words were mainly monosyllabic, some 600 signs were sufficient to meet their needs. The Babylonians would later improve this system; but, along with metallurgy, man had added another invention of momentous significance, a form and method of writing which heralded the arrival of civilization and the beginning of history.

With sharp, wedge-shaped reeds, scribes impressed these signs upon soft clay tablets, for paper was then unknown. Such markings became known as cuneiform, meaning wedge-shaped. Surviving tablets describe a ruler dictating a letter to a secretary, or scribe, seated by his side. After the message had been inscribed upon the soft clay tablet, powdered clay was sprinkled over the tablet to prevent an envelope of clay from sticking to the letter. The name and address was inscribed on a clay strip, wrapped around the letter and sent out to be baked in a furnace. The recipient of the letter broke the clay envelope, read the inscription, and filed it away. Fortunately, tens of thousands of these priceless records have been recovered by archeologists throughout the Middle East, vividly bringing back to life the cultures of ancient times.

The Sumerians also devised a sexagesimal system of mathematics, based upon units of 60, still in use today in computing divisions of time, angles, and the circle. Their texts included multiplication, squares and square roots, and other formulae. The leading unit of Sumerian weight was the mina, divided into 60 shekels. Sixty minas made one talent. The mina was equivalent approximately to our modern pound in weight. There was no real coinage as yet; trade was carried on by barter. Using their system of weights the Sumerians made ingots and rings of gold, silver and copper their standards of value in relation to various commodities. Credit was available with interest rates varying from 15 to 33 percent.

Economic Rivalry

While Uruk was laying the foundation for the first civilization in history, other city-states, such as Lagash and Ur, were thriving in Sumer. But economic competition and wealth were introducing new problems to mankind—a plague of petty, corrupt officials, confiscatory taxation, and greedy tyrants. Sumer's city-states had long been rivals for supremacy of the land. Now they began to quarrel over water rights, boundary lines and fancied wrongs. Perhaps the glitter of gold was exerting its lure, and such a matter as a canal location was only a convenient provocation.

Weakened by centuries of strife, Sumer became easy prey to another race which had risen to power in the Euphrates Valley. As early as 4500 B.C. the Semites had settled about 150 miles northwest of Uruk, establishing a kingdom known as Akkad. Near Kish, their capital, the Tigris and Euphrates were barely 20 miles apart placing the Semitic city astride the main route into the metal-rich mountains to the north and west. By 2350 B.C. Akkad had grown prosperous and strong. For over 200 years leadership of the land swayed between the rulers of Akkad and conquering tribes from Elam.

About 2100 B.C. order was restored in the region by the ascendancy of a new dynasty under the great Sumerian King Ur-Nammu (some authors call him Ur-Engur), who succeeded in uniting Sumer and Akkad. Led by Ur-Nammu and his son Shulgi (Dungi), the first two rulers of the Third Dynasty, Sumer entered a period of brilliant revival, the most active and progressive era of its history. Extending his rule over all western Asia, Ur-Nammu brought unity and peace to the region and proclaimed his Sumerian code of law, the first such code in history.

The Golden Age of Ur

Having grown rich with Sumer's thriving industries and the trade which coursed through Ur from the hinterland, the wise and pacific king launched a lavish building program, determined to make Ur the worthy capital of his great empire. Over an older temple, Ur-Nammu erected his noblest monument, the great Ziggurat of Ur.

At ground level the Ziggurat of Ur measured about 200 feet in length by 150 feet in width. It was built around a core of mud-brick and faced with expertly glazed brick each of which was inscribed with the name of its builder, Ur-Nammu. Rising into the sky in three stepped stages it was an awe-inspiring sight. The lowest stage was black with bitumen, the second stage was gleaming white with gypsum; brilliant red brick made up the third stage. The shrine crowning the top, reached by a stairway of 300 steps, was of glazed, sky-blue brick. The great Ziggurat of Ur, venerated later by rulers of Babylon, became the prototype for the famous Tower of Babel.

The Third Dynasty marked the Golden Age of Ur. The ancient city, then 1500 years old, grew increasingly rich and powerful. Sumerian science, architecture and art flourished as never before. Great libraries of enduring clay tablets were established, recording for posterity the epics of Sumer's past as well as contemporary events. Their agricultural economy boomed. It provided a life of abundance and furnished also the surpluses which the Sumerians used through trade to obtain great stores of metals. Such was the base upon which the Sumerians developed the highest order of community organization mankind had ever attained. In doing so Sumer became the first great commercial nation in history.

The Legacies of Sumer

Sumer's legacies to mankind, transmitted through the many cultures that followed in her wake, indeed were monumental. In Sumer began the evolution of writing, leading to the dawn of history. In Sumer the first literature, poetry, and school texts were written, and the first libraries were formed. Sumerians made the first expertly crafted jewelry and ornamental decorations, and established the first affluent society. They built the first architectural structures including the arch, column, vault and dome, and erected the first lofty temples. The Sumerians devised the first methods in mathematics; were the first to develop irrigation; conceived the first code of law, the first credit system, and the first business transactions. Even today, almost everywhere throughout the western world one may see reflections of these remarkable Sumerian achievements, introduced over 4000 years ago.

In the 'land between two rivers' now known as Mesopotamia, civilization had at last gotten under way. It had begun in Sumer perhaps not far from the Garden of Eden. Its arrival had been signalled perhaps by a Great Flood. For certain, its birth and march forward had been propelled by man's discovery of writing and the science of metallurgy.

Chapter 3

EGYPT

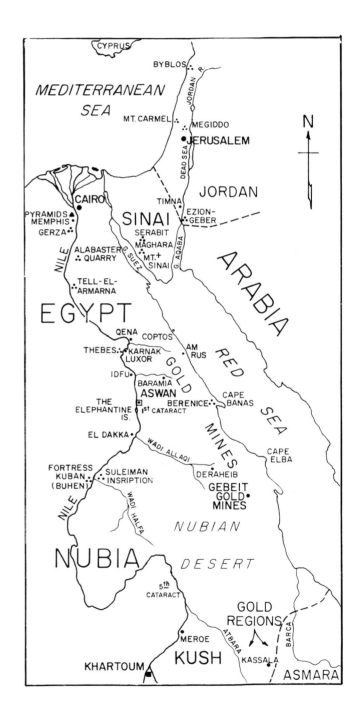

The River Nile

The most phenomenal and by far the most lasting of the ancient civilizations was born in the Valley of the Nile in the land called Egypt. For more than 3,000 years Egyptian art, science and thought influenced most of mankind. During the ages that followed, western civilizations borrowed freely from Egypt and in turn handed down an inestimable heritage to the modern world.

The Nile River was the cradle. Considered to be the longest river on earth, if not the greatest in volume, the Nile rises in Rwanda southwest of Lake Victoria, flows northward through Uganda

23

and the Sudan, joins the Blue Nile of Ethiopia, and ends its 4,000 mile journey at the Mediterranean Sea. North of Khartoum, which lies at the junction of the White Nile and the Blue Nile, the river enters a desert tableland of Nubian sandstone. The landscape with its layers of colored stone, sand dunes, and clumps of thirsty vegetation resembles the Colorado River regions of Arizona and Utah. Here and there, rising above the tableland are rugged, naked hills of granite, schist, and basalt. These resistant rocks have created the six cataracts of the Nile, from number six below Khartoum, to number one downstream and northward at Aswan.

After passing the granite crags of the first cataract near the historic Elephantine, an island in the Nile opposite Aswan, the river is released from its tortuous course and begins a serene, unobstructed flow to the Sea. Thenceforth, the river becomes entrenched between gray and buff limestone walls in a fertile, silt-filled valley varying from 10 to 30 miles in width.

One hundred miles from the sea at the apex of a triangular shaped region, which the Greeks called the "Delta," the Nile becomes divided and forms several lowland channels. In this uniquely shaped country, 750 miles long and less than 30 miles wide and surrounded by desert wastes, we shall witness the beginning and the end of the ancient civilization of Egypt.

Stone Age on The Nile

Man's evolution in Egypt during the Old Stone Age was similar to his progress in western Europe and other regions of the Middle East. Flint relics of the Paleolithic period, including Acheulean hand-axes, have been found on the lower desert plateau and at the heads of the wadis, or dry streambeds, bordering the Nile Valley. In early Paleolithic time the tablelands west of the Nile had received enough rainfall to maintain a verdant, savanna-like landscape. Elephants, hippopotami, gazelles, antelope, wild cattle and asses were among the animals hunted by prehistoric men. As the pluvial or rainy period waned about 13,000 years ago the uplands gradually grew arid. The mammals began to seek the lush lowlands along the Nile where feed and water were abundant. The hunters naturally followed. This singular act of nature eventually ended the nomadic life of these ancestral Egyptians and led them to settle along the Nile Valley.

The slow transition from nomad to settler

came over a period of about 8,000 years. When these early men first looked upon the valley of the Nile it was an endless papyrus marsh, inundated yearly by the river's overflow. The prehistoric hunters of the upper and middle regions of the Nile were members of an African or Hamitic branch of the 'Brown Mediterranean Race.' They came northward from the upper reaches of the river, including Northern Sudan and eastward from the highlands of Libya. By the dawn of the Neolithic, or New Stone Age, many settlements had formed in the Nile Valley. The lower or Delta region of the Nile had become inhabited by mixed races who differed from the hardy hunters of the Upper Nile. The Delta people were more sedentary. They lived on fish and water-fowl and bred sheep, goats, and pigs. They had begun also to cultivate barley and emmer.

From Nomad to Farmer

About 5000 B.C. these Nilotes of the New Stone Age began to show great improvement in the art of flint flaking. Their flint knives were beautifully chipped with small, precise, sharp edges. They made stone tools and vessels which were ground and polished with corundum that probably came from Asia Minor. When these early Egyptians began to develop agriculture they undertook to regulate the flood stages of the Nile. As had the Sumerians and the river peoples of the Tigris-Euphrates valley, the settlers of the Nile region received their first inventive impetus from the need for developing methods of irrigation. The study of engineering requirements for river control and celestial events related to flood cycles sharpened their scientific instincts. The challenge of mastering these problems did much to stimulate national fervor and to advance their civilization.

Between 5000 and 4000 B.C. cultures similar to the Natufians of Palestine, in their use of stone implements and reaping knives, lived in the Middle Nile region at Tasa and Badari, and at Merimdah in the west Delta area. In settlements built of mud and reeds the Badarians cultivated grain, domesticated animals, made fine pottery, and used green malachite for eye shadow. Their decorations of hammered native copper announced the arrival in Egypt of the chalcolithic period, and the appearance of trade relations with the venturesome Sumerians.

The Metalworkers of Gerza

About 3500 B.C. there was a noteworthy influx

of a race from Mesopotamia highly superior to the indigenous Egyptians in the art of metal-working. At Gerza on the Nile River near the Faiyum basin a culture arose to prominence energized by the significant introduction of copper metallurgy. No longer were the coppersmiths confined to simply working native metal. Cylinder seals of the late Uruk Period of Sumer were found in Gerzean graves providing evidence that this revolutionary discovery had now spread to Egypt. And, as it had in Sumer, this most recent of man's inventions would herald the beginning of civilization in Egypt.

These newcomers from the east also introduced new techniques in the carving of lapis lazuli, amethyst, carnelian, malachite and other foreign stones which they brought with them. They especially animated the will to trade. The Gerzeans produced copper axes, daggers, knives, bowls and even sewing needles from ores of copper. Using their knowledge of the high temperature pottery kiln they fused cores of powdered quartz and applied a glaze of colored glass, creating an ornamental material known as "faience," which became a hallmark of Egyptian artistry. As Gerzean industries flourished, trade expanded and their society grew strong and prosperous. With a mixture of Semitic and Nilotic elements, a form of writing developed, the fore-runner of Egyptian hieroglyphics. As in Sumer, writing was developed to aid a booming commerce. Thus, Sumer's legacies in writing and metallurgy led Egypt into the age of history.*

The Gerzean culture was a long, formative period which preceded the brilliant dynastic era of Egypt. Unlike the Tigris-Euphrates valley which was surrounded and open to attack by warlike highlanders, the Nile Valley was insulated from outside depredations by vast deserts bordering the river. Thus protected, the Dynasties of Egypt were free to develop their creative urges undisturbed, except for the power struggles within their own domain.

*Another legacy from Sumer appeared with the introduction of buildings made of mud-brick, a forerunner of Egypt's marvelous monumental structures.

Several historians, such as Elliot Smith and A. Lucas, believe that Egypt was the actual inventor of metallurgy. Since the writer feels that this is not the place to present a compendium of controversial facts, dates, and other pertinent material, here and elsewhere in these pages he has chosen to offer only the prevailing consensus of opinion in such matters. Other viewpoints may be found by consulting the publications and authorities named in the list of Selected Reading.

Egypt's First Dynasty

Egypt embarked upon its enduring civilization about 3300 B.C. when the legendary king named Narmar, better known as Menes, succeeded in uniting the feuding tribes of the Lower and Upper Nile. Menes invaded and subjugated the Delta region and moved his capital from the Upper Nile to a site not far from modern Cairo. It was called the city of 'White Wall,' later named Memphis by the Greeks. Under Menes began the 1st Dynasty of Egypt.

One of the first needs of the Egyptians was to measure the periods of the Nile's overflow. Noticing that the rising of the bright star Sirius, or Sothis, after its invisibility due to conjunction with the sun, corresponded with the rise of the Nile, the Egyptians made the star's first appearance at sunrise the beginning of their calendar year. They divided their year, man's first calendar of 365 days, into three seasons of four lunar months: first the fertilizing inundation season; second the winter or sowing time; and third the summer or harvesting time.

Astronomers and Egyptologists who have investigated the risings of Sirius set the invention of the calendar at either 4241 B.C., or 2781 B.C., depending upon interpretations of 5th and 6th Dynasty inscriptions. 4241 is the generally accepted date. It was a remarkable achievement for that early time. Julius Caesar introduced the Egyptian calendar in 46 B.C., after certain modifications. Later, the Julian calendar was revised slightly by Pope Gregory XIII. Thus, the calendar commonly in use today is basically the same as the one devised by the Egyptians 6000 years ago.

Before the founding of Memphis by Menes, Hierakonpolis in Upper Egypt had been the capital of the Nile's earliest rulers the Thinite kings, so called because of their ancestral home at Thinis near modern Girda. Their royal tombs were nearby at Abydos which was believed to have been the burial place of the mighty god Osiris, worshipped widely over Egypt as the fertilizing power of the Nile, teacher of science, the crafts and architecture, and god of the dead. But Egypt's founding fathers had never been enshrined in huge monuments of stone as were the pharaohs of later generations.

Mud of the Nile, molded and baked to form mud-bricks, was used in Egypt to build the first tombs and structures, in a manner reflecting methods used in Mesopotamia. Sixteen kings would rule before one would inaugurate Egypt's magnificent use of stone. And then it would be an art inherited from the Gerzeans, the use of copper, that would inspire and enable the Egyptians to carry out their grandiose ideas in architecture by using metal to quarry and shape the stone that was found so abundantly bordering the Nile Valley.

The Copper Trail to Sinai

Egypt's desert wastes between the Nile and the Red Sea contained a few unimportant deposits of copper. But even in Gerzean times it was to the Sinai Peninsula that Egyptians went to procure copper. There, they obtained the purest malachite, the copper ore which was easiest to reduce to metal. Closely associated with the malachite was another important mineral, the gem stone turquoise. It was highly prized by ancient craftsmen. It was this dependable supply of oxidized copper ore, amenable to simplest smelting methods, and the abundance of turquoise, that lured Egyptians into foreign lands on one of the earliest conquests and bonanza hunts in history.

As early as the 1st Dynasty the Sinai mines were important sources of copper ore and turquoise. Expeditions which included prospectors, and donkey trains loaded with supplies, went to the Sinai under the protection of military leaders appointed by the king. Troops were necessary, for these fortune hunters were invading the land of unfriendly tribes. Among Egypt's oldest known inscriptions are the pictographs found sculptured on the canyon wall of an ancient mining district. It vividly depicts Semerket, the seventh king of the 1st Dynasty, smiting a chief of the Bedawi or Bedouin tribe during Egypt's conquest of the Sinai region. The land was equally hostile. It was hot and waterless, and laced with tortuous, deep, winding ravines and canyons called wadis. Only in winter months could humans withstand the stifling heat.

An ancient inscription describes the ordeal of an expedition led by a court official named Harrure. The throng threads its way ankle deep in the sands of the bone-dry streambeds, twisting endlessly beneath towering walls of pink and reddish colored sandstone. Overcome with weariness and despair, many of the men prepare to desert the party. The procession halts while its leaders call upon Hathor, goddess of joy and good fortune, to aid them in their search. The column resumes its tiresome march. Suddenly, rounding a curve in the meandering canyon it comes upon a bright green layer of malachite

starkly exposed on the canyon wall. To the jubilant expedition it is a sign that their efforts will be richly rewarded. They have experienced one of those rare moments which nature evokes when she reveals one of her long hidden, untouched treasures.

Goddess of Turquoise

The Egyptian word for malachite, and perhaps for turquoise as well, was *Mafhat* or *Maghara*. Wadi Maghara was the name given to the earliest Egyptian mining district in the Sinai, and Hathor became known as the 'Lady of Turquoise.' For nearly a thousand years of the Old Kingdom and into the 12th Dynasty of the Middle Kingdom, over 40 pictorial inscriptions were incised on the timeless sandstone cliffs of Wadi Maghara. Egypt's conquest of the Sinai and the exploits of her kings and military leaders were extolled in bold relief. On the edge of the waterless wadi beneath the canyon wall, one may still see the crude stone huts that housed the miners and the stone ramparts that protected the settlement from the flash floods that occasionally occurred in desert country.

Later, another important mining district arose at Serabit el-Kadem north of Wadi Maghara. An extensive shrine to Hathor 250 feet long and now in ruins marks the site. There, over 180 inscriptions made from the 12th to the 20th Dynasties bear witness to Egypt's long and continuous exploitation of the Sinai mines, covering a period of over 2000 years in all. So well preserved are the inscriptions, because of the dry climate and their freedom from vandalism on the inaccessible walls, they appear to have been carved recently. After Sir W. F. Petrie deciphered them in 1905 many inscriptions were removed to the National Museum in Cairo.

Measured in terms of modern mining, the Sinai deposits were not large. They occurred in pod-shaped layers 2 to 5 feet thick composed of the carbonates malachite and azurite and the hydrosilicate chrysocolla, closely associated with the nodules of turquoise which owes its blue color to small amounts of copper. Unlike the huge requirements for copper in our industrial age, in ancient times the demand was relatively small. Copper then was used only in making tools, architectural decorations, ornaments for the rich and as a medium of exchange in the form of rings and ox-hide shaped ingots. Stone was the material used by the masses in fashioning their ordinary im-

EGYPT   27

plements. Copper was virtually a precious metal.

Fortunately, copper ores proclaimed their presence to prospectors by the brightly colored outcrops that appeared on the canyon walls of the wadis. Situated thus, the deposits were convenient to mine by means of open caves and adits driven into the soft, friable sandstone walls. Earliest miners used picks and chisels of copper which were sharpened by constant hammering. The pure oxides and carbonates of copper from the Sinai were also the most responsive to smelting methods of those times.

Ancient Mines of Sinai

Heaps of black slag mark the ancient sites of other mining districts in the Sinai such as Wadi Nasb, Wadi Kharg and Wadi Malba. Crucibles found nearby show that the ores were smelted and cast into cakes and ingots for transportation to Egypt. Much of the slag still contains 2.75% copper, indicating that smelting methods were very crude. Charcoal used as fuel and as a reducing agent was a problem in this barren, arid land. Sparsely distributed desert shrubs had to be gathered over wide areas and be converted to charcoal.

According to the Harris Papyrus now in the British Museum, the last Pharaoh to mine actively in the Sinai was Ramses III of the 20th Dynasty about 1150 B.C. Ramses boasted: "I sent my messengers to Atika the land of Mafkat and my mother Hathor to the great mines which abounded in copper. It was loaded by tens of thousands (cakes?) and sent forth in Galleys to Egypt and heaped at the palace with hundreds of thousands (of ingots?) being the color of gold (metallic copper)." After Ramses' reign most of Egypt's copper came from the Island of Cyprus.

However, it was Sinai's copper that propelled Egypt into the Age of Metals, much to the credit of Snefru of the 4th Dynasty who worked the Sinai mines so intensively that he became the patron god of the region. He commemorated his deeds on slabs, or stelae, and enlarged the shrine of Hathor, the 'Lady of Turquoise and Malachite' at Serabit el-Kadem. He built ships to carry an increasing supply of ingots across the Red Sea and thence by pack train over the desert to the Nile.

Copper to Build The Pyramids

Snefru developed navigation and increased trade by sea endowing Egypt with a period of great prosperity. But his most significant contribution to progress was producing the copper metal which enabled Egypt to quarry her abundance of stone. In the tomb of Snefru's queen were found a number of copper relics, the most portentous of which were the copper tools used by stonemasons. Egypt had begun to put copper to work in the creation of her colossal pyramids. Describing this brilliant age, James H. Breasted, eminent historian, wrote: "Such rapid progress in man's control of mechanical power can be found in no other period of world history until the Nineteenth Century of the Christian Era."

An outstanding belief which came to pervade Egyptian life was the divinity of their kings. The king was personified as a visible god with total power over the people. This fundamental concept profoundly united the Egyptians and inspired marvelous attainments in behalf of their rulers. Following the nine kings of the 2nd Dynasty, who by then had disposed of Mene's successors, came the kings of the 3rd Dynasty.

It was during the 3rd Dynasty that Egyptians first looked upon stone as a wondrous material with which to build funerary monuments to immortalize their god-like rulers. Unlike the Sumerians in the stoneless Tigris-Euphrates Valley the Egyptians possessed an abundance of durable white and gray limestone, red and gray granite, black diorite, and even magnificent white and peach colored alabaster. And now at hand was the metal to carve these stones.

Egypt's Marvels in Stone

The first great stone structure was erected for King Zoser (Djoser) founder of the 3rd Dynasty about 2900 B.C. Aided by the engineering genius of his wise and talented minister Imhotep, the Pyramid of Saqqara consisting of five stepped terraces was raised not far from modern Cairo. After 4900 years the pyramid still towers 190 feet above the desert, the world's oldest standing structure. Around it other tombs were built for the royal family.

The Step Pyramid of Saqqara inaugurated Egypt's awesome use of stone in construction, architecture and sculpturing. Imbued with a passion for building heroic and eternal resting places, the 4th Dynasty launched the building of a number of pyramids. Snefru erected two, one in steps at Medum and the Bent Pyramid at Dashur between Memphis and El Faiyum. So fascinated and energized were the Egyptians with their newly found creative power that only 100 years separated Zoser's pyramid from the building of the Great Pyramid at Gizeh for King Khufu (named Cheops by the Greeks), followed by tombs for his son, Khafre (Chephren), and grandson, Menkure. These three mammoth pyramids are the greatest stone tombs built in all history.

Within sight of modern Cairo at Gizeh the pyramids stand undiminished in size except for the white limestone facing which was stripped away by the Arab conquerors of Egypt a thousand years ago. When Herodotus stood in awe before the pyramids in 450 B.C. they were then more than 2000 years old. And then came Alexander the Great, Julius Caesar, Mark Anthony, Napoleon and countless others. There they stood, gazing intently and marveling at Egypt's genius everlastingly preserved in stone. It was fortunate that such durable material was conveniently close to such a splendid highway of transportation as the Nile.

In limestone quarries bordering the Nile Valley, Egyptian workers toiled to fulfill their religious duties. Slaves from subjugated lands labored to cut huge blocks of stone, using copper tubes and chisels hardened by hammering. Mauls of hard, tough diorite helped to dress the rough surfaces. Down from the quarries on long, earth-filled ramps the workers lowered the stone blocks with ropes and rollers onto barges on the Nile River. Then they were floated downstream to Gizeh. There the stones were unloaded and rolled up ramps to the pyramids, growing skyward tier by tier, and fitted into place with joints no larger than one-tenth of an inch.

The Great Pyramid built by King Khufu, or Cheops, is approximately 756 feet square at its base and covers 13 acres. It is over 470 feet high and contains about 2,300,000 blocks of stone averaging 2½ tons in weight. Many blocks weigh as much as 45 tons. Herodotus stated that 100,000 men labored for 20 years in the quarries, on the river and on the site, to build the Great Pyramid at Gizeh, called one of the Seven Wonders of the Ancient World.

During the Old Kingdom alone, which included the first eleven Dynasties, more than 20 pyramids were built to honor Egypt's kings. Grouped about the pyramids were numerous, flat-topped, rectangular shaped tombs of stone called "mastabas" for less important members of the royal families, nobles and well-to-do officials. The cemeteries consisting of mastabas were laid out in regular streets beside the pyramid.

The Pillars of Karnak

The prodigious use of stone was one of the most impressive manifestations of Egyptian culture. Later, during the 18th Dynasty, between 1400 and 1280 B.C., under Amenhotep III and Ramses II, Egyptian love of grandeur was expressed in the columnal halls, carved pillars, obelisks and statues at Luxor and Karnak, near Thebes. There Egyptians erected to their god Amon the largest stone structure of free standing columns ever built—over 3,000 years ago. From one end of the Nile to the other, great edifices and statues stand in silent tribute to Egypt's mastery of stone. Nowhere else in the world has such a wealth of colossal ruins been preserved to bear witness to ancient man's inspiration and use of the natural materials at his command.

Egypt also employed stone in the art of sculpturing, as lasting as the pyramids themselves. Using red and gray granite from Aswan, black diorite, reddish sandstone, quartzite and serpentine, Egyptians carved life-like portraitures of their kings and gods with splendid vigor. These ranged in size from gigantic statues to the smallest perfectly wrought figurines.

Egyptians searched their desert domain far and wide for the hardest and most attractive stone. From diorite quarries, northwest of the rock-cut temple of Abu Simbel on the Nile, blocks were hewn for the magnificent black statues of the temple of Khafre and for the stone floors of the temple of Khufu. From Aswan, and the eastern desert region, came beautiful pink granite porphyry used for the carving of many heroic figures of Egypt's rulers. Some of these are now displayed in prominent museums of the world. Not far from Heliopolis, the ancient holy city of the Lower Nile, east of modern Cairo, a stone quarry in the Mokattam hills produced a dark, yellow quartzite. It was highly prized for sarcophagi and statues. A burial chamber in the Saqqara pyramid, hewn from a single block of this exceptionally hard, tough stone, has been estimated to weigh 150 tons.

Many monumental monoliths, obelisks of carved stone, were erected in Egypt. Two obelisks were set up at Karnak by Queen Hatshepsut; one measured 97 feet high and weighed more than 300 tons. They were cut and formed in the granite quarries near Aswan by the difficult process of using tubular drills, chisels of copper and copper saws set with teeth of flint or corundum. Final shaping was done with hard stone mauls.

Seven months were required to cut and free the stones from the quarry. During a high water stage of the Nile the huge obelisks were floated down the river on barges and hauled on rollers to Karnak. The obelisks were sheathed with a great quantity of electrum, a mixture of gold and silver, shining in such splendor as to be seen for many miles around.

Obelisks were erected by other rulers of Egypt. Some of them now grace public squares in capitals of the world. In Rome an obelisk 132 feet high stands in the Piazza of the Basilica of St. Peter. It was brought from Heliopolis in the first century. Egyptian obelisks stand also in New York, Paris, and London. The greatest of the obelisks lies unfinished in the quarry south of Aswan, partially shaped, but still held by the quarry. It was to have been 137 feet in height and to have weighed over 1,000 tons.

Science and Art in Egypt

Egyptian creativity reached a high point during the Old Kingdom. In addition to the invention of the solar calendar, Egyptians made use of the papyrus plants bordering the Nile to produce mankind's first paper, and they made ink to be used with it. They became remarkably adept also in astronomy, medicine, and mathematics. The Egyptians believed serenely in the hereafter, and acquired material wealth in order that it might be buried with them to be used in the after-life. Fortunately, the recovery of immense treasure through archeological excavations has provided posterity with the means of reconstructing details of Egyptian life with great accuracy, more than any other ancient civilization.

Egypt's marvelous art-work in faience, and in small carvings of lapis lazuli, turquoise, carnelian, obsidian, and amethyst, prevailed for ages. During the 12th Dynasty, scarab making attained the peak of perfection. The scarab, or dung beetle, was sacred to the Egyptians. Noticing the beetle pushing a small ball of dung, in which it lays its eggs, Egyptians developed the idea that the sun, which they worshipped, was a mighty ball of fire that was pushed across the sky by a gigantic beetle, a sun god. Scarabs became symbolic of immortality. They were produced in varied and immense quantities and were widely used as talismans and ornaments. Scarabs in the form of amulets were placed on mummies as symbols of resurrection, and were highly valued trade items in Mesopotamia and in lands of the Mediterranean Sea.

Another outstanding form of Egyptian carving was in alabaster, often called "onyx marble." Again nature had endowed Egypt with deposits of beautiful varieties of this material. From the royal quarries of Hatnub near el Amarna came translucent peach and cream colored alabaster, which was carved into jars, vases, shrines and figurines of enchanting beauty. A 60 ton block of alabaster was hauled on a sled 10 miles to the Nile by 172 men and then carved into a statue 20 feet high and erected in a temple.

Hatnub was worked by Khufu and later furnished the alabaster floor for Khafre's mortuary temple. Now 100 feet deep and 300 feet wide, the Hatnub quarry in ancient times was a royal monopoly worked by convicts and prisoners of war. They lived miserably in tiny stone huts which still can be seen above the quarry. From such a place of wretchedness came the magnificent material long known as Egyptian alabaster. From it, exquisite articles were carved by Egyptian craftsmen thousands of years ago and now excite world wide admiration in many famous museums.

Hardly beyond the dawn of civilization, it was Egypt who gave the world its first and grandest architecture in stone. Egypt's monumental columns, capitals and entablatures with papyrus and lotus designs were copied by later civilizations. Greek sculptors came to study Egyptian statuary and to admire its perfection and vitality and the superbly carved figures of Egypt's rulers. Egypt's splendid works in all types of stone amazed the world. But none of these achievements would have been possible had Egypt not been blessed with a providential abundance of durable stone and her potent tools of copper metal. These were the resources required for the awakening and stimulation of Egypt's dreams of grandeur.

Tutankhamen's Treasure

The use of stone was outstanding, but the Egyptians gained equal renown for their accumulation and profuse use of gold. No other people as yet had such abundant sources of gold in their own and nearby lands. The Egyptians embarked upon history's first great adventure in gold seeking and gold mining. The hoard of gold they acquired was destined to play a vital role in their civilization and the affairs of the ancient world.

The fabulous treasure found buried with King Tutankhamen, who ruled in the 18th Dynasty about 1350 B.C., is a well known example of Egypt's golden opulence. The find represented the only unplundered tomb of a Pharaoh ever found. The tomb was discovered in the Valley of the Kings near Thebes in 1922 by the Englishman, Howard Carter, with the aid of his patron, Lord Carnarvon. Most of the treasure can be seen today in a remarkable exhibit at the Cairo National Museum.

Tutankhamen's tomb, deep within the valley hillside, consisted of several rooms, one of which Carter named the "treasury." The outer rooms were crowded with extraordinary objects, a gold plated chariot, a throne of carved wood plated with gold inlaid with lapis lazuli and carnelian. Life-sized statues of black ebony and gold guarded the tomb amid many alabaster vases and boxes of food and flowers for daily use in the King's after-life.

When Carter first flashed his light into the dark, inner burial chamber it presented a thrilling sight. In the rock-bound room was a large, 10 by 16 foot box of gilded wood, shining in the reflected light. It almost filled the chamber. Within this first outer shrine were three more richly carved, gilded boxes fitting closely within each other. The second box was found to be covered with a yellowed veil sprinkled with daisies of gilded bronze. Ebony latches on the doors of the huge boxes were still tied with bronze rings and sealed with clay, untouched since the day of burial.

After the first and second boxes had been carefully opened, the discoverers came to the third box, which was carved with scenes of the young Pharaoh and his Queen and heavily gilded with gold. Next came the fourth and final box, inside of which there was a magnificent red sandstone sarcophagus. It was inscribed with names and titles of the king and bore a carved relief of a goddess with outstretched, protective wings.

A Pharaoh's Tomb

A subterranean tomb hidden in a rocky hillside with walled and sealed ante-chambers, a burial room, four sealed gilded boxes and a stone sarcophagus, were not enough to protect the sacred mummy of a Pharaoh. For inside the stone sarcophagus were three golden mummiform coffins, one within the other. The first body-shaped coffin was of wood heavily plated with gold. Within it was another coffin fitting so exactly a finger could not be placed between them. It, too, was gold plated, inlaid with lapis lazuli and blue glass paste. A necklace of olive and willow leaves and blue lotus flowers lay across the top of the coffin.

The third and innermost coffin was a glittering, undreamed of treasure, a life-like image, a coffin of solid, beaten gold. The body-like form shaped in gold was elaborately incised with religious patterns, and wings of a goddess enfolded the Pharoah's outstretched image. Upon the king's golden headdress were figures of the vulture and the cobra, symbols of the Upper and the Lower Nile. In the king's hands, folded across the coffin, were the crook and the flail, emblems of royalty and power. The elongated form of the king's beard, symbolic of Osiris, god of the dead, was reproduced in lapis lazuli.

The Solid Gold Coffin

This inner coffin was of solid 22 carat gold, 1/8th to 1/10th of an inch thick. It weighed 2,448 pounds. Within the gold coffin was the mummy of the king, who was about 18 years old when he was buried. Covering the face of the young Pharaoh was the most startling of the treasures, the finest funerary mask ever found. It was of solid gold, inlaid with lapis lazuli and blue glass paste; a remarkable example of the goldsmith's art adapted to portraiture. It was life-sized and presumed to be an exact likeness of the king.

More than 140 ornaments of gold and carved semi-precious stones, rings, necklaces and bracelets were distributed over the swaddled, mummified body. A crown, even sandals of gold, and a great array of beautifully carved alabaster vases, figures, and an alabaster funerary boat were in the tomb. Most of the king's treasure was taken to the Cairo National Museum, but the young Pharaoh's mummy, encased in its coffin of gold and stone sarcophagus, was left to rest in peace in the royal tomb near Thebes, in the ancient and silent Valley of the Kings.

The lavish use of gold, as shown by the treasure of Tutankhamen, reflects the wealth that was available to many of the Dynasties of Egypt. Not only was the gold supply considerable, but it continued to flow with amazing regularity into Egyptian art and commerce for thousands of years. Where did the Egyptians find their bonanzas of gold?

The Gold Fields of Egypt

Some 30 miles down the Nile from Tutankhamen's resting place in the Valley of The Kings

PLATE 1. Flint and obsidian, first minerals used by man, for eons were his prized possessions.

PLATE 2. Stone Age hunters used stone tipped weapons to procure food and clothing.

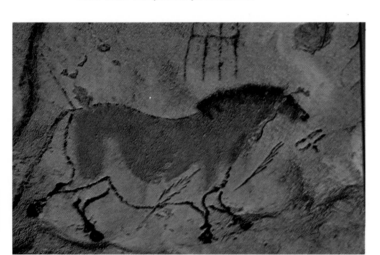

PLATE 3. Magdalenian bas-reliefs carved with flint chisels in caves of Lascaux, France, the peak of Stone Age art.

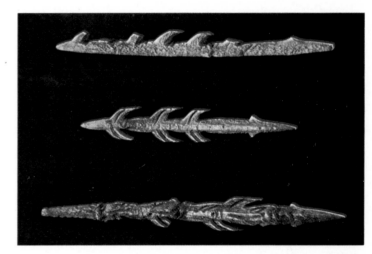

PLATE 4. Bone harpoons made of reindeer antlers climaxed Cro-Magnon culture.

PLATE 5. Amber, a fossil resin, with flint and salt formed the basis of earliest commerce.

PLATE 6. Chateau Grand Pressigny, site of a flourishing flint industry 5000 years ago.

PLATE 7. The Caves of Carmel near Haifa, Israel, ageless home

PLATE 8. Byblos, Lebanon, reveals remains of Neolithic, Amorite, Egyptian and Roman periods.

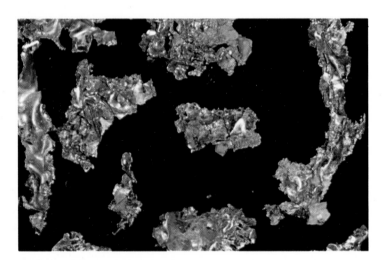

PLATE 9. Native gold was the first metal used by man.

PLATE 10. Native copper, man's first industrial metal, was used to carve the stones for Egypt's pyramids.

PLATE 11. Azurite and malachite, carbonates of copper, aided the discovery of metallurgy.

PLATE 12. Gold daggers from the Royal Cemetery of Ur reflect Sumer's wealth in 2750 B.C.

PLATE 13. The Sinai desert was the goal of Egypt's earliest copper mining expeditions.

PLATE 14. The Saqqara Pyramid, the world's oldest structure, overlooks the fertile Nile.

PLATE 15. The pyramid of Khufu (Cheops) and the Sphinx at Gizeh near Cairo are dated about 2800 B.C.

PLATE 17. One of Tutankhamen's three gold-plated mummiform coffins signifies Egypt's vast wealth in gold.

PLATE 16. King Tutankhamen's funeral mask, found among the treasures in his tomb.

PLATE 18. The king's pendant in gold cloisonné and hands shaped in solid gold.

PLATE 19. Pectoral in gold cloisonné with carved scarab protected by goddesses.

PLATE 20. Alabaster boat adorned with gold leaf and precious stones. Egypt was rich in rare alabaster.

PLATE 21. Papyrus plants of the Nile, made into paper by the Egyptians, aided the spread of writing and civilization.

PLATE 22. From the Cedars of Lebanon Egypt obtained wood for her far-ranging ships of commerce.

PLATE 23. The Nile, flowing past modern Cairo, has given life to 5000 years of civilization.

PLATE 24. Ores of tin, cassiterite crystal (R), nourished the Bronze Age boom.

PLATE 25. Lead, zinc, copper, silver and sulphur minerals. The Sumerians classified over 150 minerals 5500 years ago.

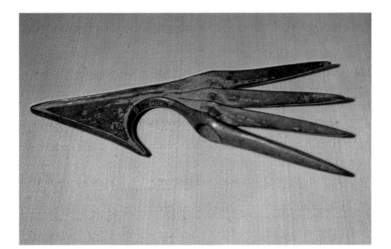

PLATE 26. Luristan bronzes were being made in present Iran as early as 3000 B.C.

PLATE 27. Cuneiform writing on clay tablets left lasting records of widespread Babylonian commerce.

PLATE 28. Akkadian cylinder seals used to mark personal items and trade articles (2100 B.C.)

PLATE 29. Argentiferous galena, silver-lead ore, sought by Hammurabi's prospectors.

PLATE 30. Excavated palace of Minos at Knossos, Crete. It was a great trade emporium in 1600 B.C.

PLATE 31. Typical Cretan architecture. Minos' splendid three story palace covered six acres.

PLATE 32. The Labyrinth, or store rooms, beneath the palace. Trade created Europe's first civilization in Crete.

PLATE 33. The Lion Gate of Mycenae. This acropolis was the birthplace of Greek civilization.

PLATE 34. The Inner Grave Circle and Royal Tombs of Mycenae in which amazing treasures were found.

PLATE 35. This was the face of Agamemnon thought Schliemann, excavator of Mycenae.

PLATE 36. Extensive trade in Mycenae bronze wares took civilization into Europe along the Danube.

PLATE 37. The modern Kupferbergrau mine is in a region that once supplied copper ores to the Danubian Civilization.

PLATE 38. This lovely region has a remarkable history. Here, the Salzach River flows on to Salzburg, heart of a prehistoric salt region, the Salzkammergut. Here also, amber traders passed ages ago. At nearby Bischofshofen and Muhlbach mountains yielded metals during ancient, medieval and even modern times.

PLATE 39. Magnetite and hematite, ores of iron.

PLATE 40. Hittite metalwork was unrivaled. The Hittites are credited with the discovery of ironmaking.

PLATE 41. The Philistines introduced iron to the coast of Palestine (Canaan) about 1175 B.C.

PLATE 42. Grinding wheels at Achzib (Israel) were used to produce purple dyes for Phoenicians.

PLATE 43. King David's tomb on Mount Zion, Jerusalem.

PLATE 44. The site of Solomon's temple in Jerusalem.

is a settlement called Qift, once known as Coptos, perhaps the world's first boom town whose streets of silt became mixed with the dust of gold. East of this river town lies Egypt's forlorn Eastern Desert which rises gradually to meet a range of hills and mountain peaks that overlooks the Red Sea. From this region came gold for the predynastic cultures of Gerza, and for Naqada opposite Coptos, Egypt's earliest source of domestic gold. This golden land came to be known as Coptos, named after its bustling river port on the Nile.

Coptos was the terminus of a very old, historic route which meandered eastward up a dry, sandy wash called Wadi Hammamat. The road crossed a land of multi-hued sandstone mesas and then climbed over desolate granite hills to the Red Sea port of Quseir, which itself has a fascinating past. For ages copper and turquoise had come by ship from Sinai to Quseir to be transported thence by caravan over the Wadi Hammamat trail to Coptos. Not only copper from Sinai but also gold from Coptos for thousands of years coursed their way down the dusty wadi to the Nile.

Egypt's earliest gold field extended from Wadi Dib near present Gemsa on the north to Am Rus 200 miles southward on the Red Sea. The wadi streambeds were first worked for alluvial or placer gold which had been eroded and washed down from the gold-bearing veins found later in the hills of granite and schist. Gold was obtained northward up Wadi Quena at Hadrabia and eastward near the Wadi Hammamat trail at Abu Gerida and Semna. At Fauachir (Foakhir) the ruins of over 1100 stone huts of the miners reveal the size and importance of this early Egyptian gold camp.

Man's Oldest Map

The famed papyrus map of the Ramessides in the Turin museum, perhaps the world's oldest map, shows a route to the Coptos gold mines. It indicates the 'mountains where gold is washed' and the huts of the gold workers and refers to a temple erected to Amon and a memorial stele to Seti I who reigned about 1300 B.C. But Coptos had furnished Egypt with gold several thousand years prior to Seti I. Due to the gold's natural mixture with silver, a metal which was scarce in Egypt, Coptos gold possessed a lighter color and was a highly prized alloy known as electrum.

It was from this blistered desert range of mountains along Egypt's eastern border fringing the Red Sea, and reaching even into northern Sudan and Ethiopia, that the Egyptians reaped their vast harvest of gold. They were attracted by the gleam of gold in the white quartz veins of these highlands and in the sands of the valleys below. Gold was obtained in many districts scattered over a great area. Hundreds of ancient mines have left evidence of their past. The stone huts of the miners, primitive tools, and washing tables, which now lie forgotten under the broiling sun, testify to the exploitation of mankind's first extensive gold field, the treasure vaults of Egypt's opulent Pharaohs.

Farther southward went Egypt's search for gold. Opposite Idfu on the Nile, about 100 miles south of Thebes, another route crossed the desert to the ancient mines of Baramia and Dungasch which produced much gold for the Pharaohs. Seti I vigorously worked this region and built a temple in Wadi Abbad which contained inscriptions describing the operations of his Baramia mine and its golden output which he donated to the shrine of Osiris at Abydos. Feeling compassion for the sufferers who journeyed to his mines over the blazing desert, according to the inscription, Seti had a well dug in 'this bad waterless way ... that they may remember my name all the years to come.'

Across the desert east of Aswan, in hills of black schist and reddish granite near Cape Banas, the gold bearing veins were small. But a plentiful supply of slaves, toiling in sweltering sun, made it possible to work even the tinest showings of gold. As late as the 3rd century B.C., Ptolemy II founded Berenice on the coast of the Red Sea near the ancient mines of Um Eliga, Betan and Rahaba. According to Strabo, Ptolemy established a lucrative trade along the Red Sea reaching out as far as India, and then built a canal joining the Red Sea with the Nile.

Wadi Allaqi's Golden Stream

It was from the Wadi Allaqi region that the Pharaohs of the First and Middle Kingdoms received the greatest abundance of gold mined within their own domain. Sixty miles south of Aswan, near El Dakka, the long, winding Wadi Allaqi leaves the Nile and trends southeastward into a highland area near the Egyptian-Sudan boundary close to the Red Sea. So important was this ribbon of gold to the Pharaohs that forts were built near the entrance of the wadi at Kuban on the east bank of the Nile and on the opposite bank at Semneh and Kummeh.

Leaving the friendly waters of the Nile, the

wadi slowly creeps its sandy way through a desolate but colorful desert of mauve, gray, and pink
sandstones and shales, capped now and then with
a layer of black basaltic lava. Only an occasional
cloud of swirling dust called "dust devils" mar
the prevailing deep blue sky. Thorny, thirsty
shrubs dot the slopes and dry washes. Here and
there rise hills of granite and schist, bare and
sunburned. In veins of white quartz gold can be
found even today. Most of the veins are too small
or too low grade to be worked profitably with
modern labor. Only when slaves provided an inexhaustible supply of cost-free labor was every little
showing of gold made to yield its precious metal.

Some of the veins were richer. Attracted by
accounts of early Greek historians such as Herodotus and Diodorus, engineers of modern times
launched a search for Egypt's more productive
mines. Several yielded substantial amounts of
gold; Seti's Baramia mine gave up over $700,000
in gold; the mines of Wadi Allaqi, including Um
Garaiart, Um Haimur and Seiga, produced gold
valued over one million dollars. At Am Rus
modern miners were amazed to see ancient
workings extending over 1200 feet along the vein
and at depths up to 300 feet.

Above the headwaters of Wadi Allaqi in the
mountainous coastal region southwest of Ras
Hadarba (Cape Elba) on the Red Sea, efforts were
made to revive the ancient mines of Um Narbardi
and Gebeit. But not all the Pharaoh's properties
met with success in modern times, although "Gebeit Gold Mines" is a name that still appears on
maps of this area. At nearby Deraheib the walls of
over 500 tiny, wretched stone huts of the ancient
miners still can be seen, a poignant reminder of a
miner's life under slavery in one of the world's
earliest gold camps. But such was the common
source of manpower used for endless centuries to
wrest metals from the earth.

Slavery in the Mines

In some of the ancient mines crude picks made
of flint have been recovered in the workings, thus
dating gold mining there from a very early beginning. Copper and bronze chisels of subsequent
times, found in the labyrinth of workings by
modern engineers, reveal the various ages and
great spans of time during which slaves labored to
mine gold for the Pharaohs of Egypt. Underground excavations or rooms known as "stopes"
were supported by unmined pillars of rock or
dry-wall masonry. Burning fagots and oil lamps
supplied a dim and malodorous light.

During the many dynasties inscriptions have
described the gold fields and the manner of working them, and historians such as Diodorus have
added their comments. Slaves, prisoners of war,
condemned criminals, exiled political enemies,
and some with their families, were guarded by
soldiers and often fettered. They provided an
endless supply of labor without cost. Thus, even
the poorest veins, as well as the richer bonanzas,
could be gleaned for their gold. Many of the
laborers, as well as their guards, spoke different
languages, adding greatly to misunderstandings
and hardships.

The hardiest adults were selected to work
underground, groveling in small, cramped, winding passages that were dark and badly ventilated.
Many were crushed by rock falls and left to die
where they were buried. An incredible number of
bones have been found in the ancient workings.
Fire setting, the building of wood fires against a
face of rock, was used to crack the rock, after
which it was loosened with stone or copper picks
and chisels. Young children carried the broken
ore in baskets strapped upon their backs to the
surface. There the chunks of ore were spread
among old men, women and children, who further sorted the richer from the poorer portions of
ore and then broke them into pieces small
enough to be placed into small hand mortars.

Gathering Pharaoh's Gold

With stone pestles the ore was laboriously ground
by hand in the mortars to a powder. Then it was
mixed with water and poured over rough stone
slabs which sloped at a gentle angle. The golden
grains being heavier collected in ridges of the
rough slab, while the lighter waste material was
washed away. After being dried the grains and
dust of gold were bagged for shipment, or melted
and cast into rings, ready to be packed and taken
across the desert to the Nile.

Loaded with their heavy golden burden hundreds of doughty donkeys and an army of watchful
soldiers set forth upon the Wadi Allaqi trail. For
seven days the caravan plodded through blinding,
choking dust and searing heat, finally reaching the
welcome embrace of the Nile. Then, donkeys and
men alike would rush to the river's edge to drown
their thirst and cool their tired bodies. Efforts to
establish water wells along this arduous route had
failed for centuries. Memorial tablets erected by
generations of Egyptians testified to the bitter
ordeal suffered by the caravans and the lives that
were lost in bringing gold to the Pahroahs.

Nubia, Egypt's Eldorado

Although Egypt's own domain contained an abundance of gold, it was Nubia, the ancient land of Kush, farther up the winding Nile in present northern Sudan, that became Egypt's gilded Eldorado, her richest storehouse of gold. Nubia is a name derived from the Egyptian word *nub*, meaning gold. Prehistoric migrants traveling northward down the Nile from Nubia into Egypt probably brought information with them concerning their homeland's wealth in gold. Gold found on predynastic flint handles, and the animal cults and shrines of this southern region, are circumstances which suggest that the lords of the Upper Nile, who became the unifiers of Egypt, may have derived some influence through their resources in gold.

Hierakonpolis and its twin city Nekheb, the oldest capital of Upper Egypt, obtained much wealth and power from the gold fields of the Nubian desert. From earliest times Nubia had been the gold seeker's paradise, but the region was hard to reach and dangerous to explore. Many cataracts barred river travel up the Nile. A formidable desert and the hostile, barbarous Wawat, Yam and Mazoi tribes made overland treks painful and perilous. Gold has always seemed to occur in remote and inaccessible places and in lands possessed by peoples who have fiercely defied foreign intruders. So it was in Nubia.

The prize, however, was great and irresistible. Since the time of Stone Age men, there have been adventurers eager to challenge unknown lands regardless of the risks. These were the men appointed by Egypt's rulers to take up their stations on the southern border. They became known as the "Keeper of the Door of the South." Among these hardy barons was Harkhuf the first man to search far up the Nile into inner Africa. In due time such men became Nomarchs and were eventually rewarded with provinces of their own. Following Harkhuf came the opening of a new frontier, the conquest of Nubian tribes and the winning of much treasure.

South of The Elephantine

The first organized expedition seeking the gold of Nubia started from the Elephantine, an island in the Nile River below the first cataract at Aswan. This was the door to the south. The Elephantine was so called because of the ivory of the elephant and other riches which came northward from the Upper Nile to the frontier post at Aswan. The old fort was located around a temple on the southern end of the island. Hundreds of rock inscriptions on the island tell stirring stories of the kings, viceroys and caravan leaders who passed this way, either on campaigns of conquest or journeys to reach the gold fields of Nubia.

Southward from the Elephantine, into a region clouded with mystery and fearful legends, went one of the oldest roads of commerce and exploitation ever blazed by man. The Nubian desert was a scorching, waterless wasteland. Rugged, rocky hills seamed with veins of white quartz, holding forth their promises of gold, rose out of the barren uplands. Opposite the second cataract, on the Hill of Sheikh Suleiman and on the Rock of Abusir eight miles south of Wadi Halfa in the Sudan, there are inscriptions placed there by King Djer of the 1st Dynasty about 3100 B.C. They describe his military campaigns and the capture of Nubian cities.

According to the Palermo Stone, Snefru of the 4th Dynasty, who so vigorously mined copper in the Sinai peninsula, was another conqueror of Nubia. After Snefru came a long succession of punitive raids that kept Nubia in submission from the reign of Pepi I of the 6th Dynasty to King Sesostris of the 12th Dynasty. Amenemhet II, 1200 years after Djer, memorialized his victories over Nubia with a temple up the Nile at Wadi Halfa on Egypt's southern border. A chain of blockhouses, and forts on islands and banks of the Nile, tightened Egypt's stranglehold on the rich trade route that passed through the Elephantine. They guarded the flow of Nubian gold which so lavishly gilded the palaces of the pharaohs and adorned the temples of Egypt's gods.

The first gold won from Nubia had been in the form of plunder, and with it were taken hordes of slaves. Later, gold was sent by Nubian chiefs as tribute to the powerful rulers of Egypt. Finally, hungry for greater riches, the Pharaohs sent their own expeditions to squeeze the fullest measure of gold from the Nubian mines.*

*The Nile was not only Egypt's fountainhead of life-giving water and fertile silt. Its great southern tributaries including the White Nile, the Blue Nile and the Atbara, as well as numerous headwaters as far south as Lake Victoria, led to regions of immense mineral wealth, especially gold. The first tributary southward was the Atbara. Leaving the Nile, just north of modern Ed Damer, the Atbara heads southeasterly across a desert tableland that was often swept by violent sandstorms.

In districts bordering the Anseba, Barca and Mareb

Gold Placers of Sudan

Above the junction of the Blue Nile and the White Nile at Khartoum in northeast-central Sudan, gold placers occurred in the Tira Mandi district in the Nuba Mountains which rise above the vast, barren steppe-lands west of the White Nile. It is not known for certain how far southward into the source lands of the Nile the Egyptians went. But some of the articles included in the cargo that was proudly brought back to King Pepy II of the 6th Dynasty by Harkhuf, Lord of The Elephantine and 'Keeper of The Door of The South,' indicate that his bold expedition had indeed reached the headwater region of the Nile.

In addition to gold, Harkhuf's cargo included ebony wood, panther skins, ostrich feathers, ivory of the elephant and surprisingly, a dwarf or pigmy obviously from central Africa. We know that many gold bearing districts were to be found adjacent to Lake Victoria in present Tanganyika. Along the eastern border of present Belgian Congo, rich and highly productive gold placers were to be found at Kilo and Moto west of Lake Albert, which have yielded considerable gold in modern times.

In Harkhuf's travels through Nubia, of which he later became governor, he found the river banks green with acacias and the hinterland dotted with woods of hashab trees, producers of gum arabic. In the Upper Nile he found forests of ebony and mahogany and grassy savannas containing elephants, lions and brightly plumed birds. The Upper Nile supplied Egypt not only with gold but also with the legends and animal cults which became popular subjects of Egyptian artists. The importance of the Nile as a lifeline of wealth, commerce, and cultural origins is dramatically emphasized by the numerous fortresses, temples and inscriptions that now line the river for hundreds of miles, from Gizeh on the north to the ancient Kushite capital, Meroe, on the south. These testify to the longest parade of national endeavor and accumulation of treasure known to man.

The Fabled Land of Punt

The period between the 13th and 17th dynasties was marked by 350 years of internal strife in Egypt. About 1700 B.C. a Semitic race from Syria, known as the Hyksos, took over the weakened country without a blow. One hundred years later, with the rise of the Thutmose Pharaohs of the 18th dynasty, the Hyksos were expelled from Egypt, leaving a legacy of new equipment in warfare, the horse and chariot.

During the Hyksos occupation Nubia had regained a fair measure of independence. But in 1510 B.C., Thutmose I erected a fortress at the 3rd cataract, penetrated Nubia, and returned down the Nile to Thebes with the body of a conquered chief hanging from the prow of his royal barge. Fired with ambition, Thutmose warred with the Hyksos at Kadesh and expanded his empire to the Euphrates River. The daughter of Thutmose I inherited the empire and became Egypt's first woman ruler. Hatshepsut was a capable queen; she sought peace and prosperity and new sources of wealth to adorn a temple for herself and her father. About 1490 B.C. Hatshepsut revived an ancient tradition by launching a voyage to the fabled land of Punt.

Several dynasties in the past had sent expeditions to Punt. The earliest of record was under Sahure of the 5th Dynasty, about 2700 B.C. Amenemhet II also sent a successful party to Punt about 1900 B.C. Exciting tales of adventure had become legendary concerning voyages to this land of great riches. Two years on the sea were required to make the journey and return, but the lure was tremendous. Punt was not only famous for its gold, but also for the myrrh trees that yielded aromatic gum-resin and incense. The green, living myrrh trees could be transplanted in temple gardens. Incense was almost as precious as gold. It was used in temple rituals all over the ancient world, and journeys were made to far off lands in order to procure it.

Also highly prized was Punt's ivory, ebony

Rivers placer gold was found in the canyon bottoms, while veins of white quartz found streaking reddish tinted hills of granite and schist produced not only gold but also copper and antimony. Near modern Asmara close to the Red Sea, placers and veins were worked for gold. One mine, the Medri Zem, has been worked in the early 20th century. South of Asmara in the Quala district the Dasé mine also became a modern producer. This northern plateau corner of Ethiopia, formerly known as Eritrea, was an important contributor to the rich caravan trade that once flowed through Meroe, ancient capital of Nubian and Ethiopian kings.

Farther southward, the Blue Nile was the next important tributary. Its river gravels and highland regions produced great wealth in Nubian gold. From Sennar southeastward to Er Roseires the sands and gravels of the Blue Nile were worked for gold that no doubt had been brought down from the veins and placers of the mountainous Walaga region of western Ethiopia. In the Beni-Shugul district west of Nejo placers yielded gold for 40 miles along the Dabus River, one of the headwater streams of the Blue Nile.

wood, panther skins, monkeys, and dwarfs or pigmies. Stibnite, an antimony mineral used for eye shadow, was a significant item included in the cargo. Due to small amounts of associated minerals such as silver, antimony and possibly copper, Punt's gold had a distinguishing greenish cast, offering a clue as to the location of this mystic land.

The Mystery of Punt

Due to hazy concepts of global geography that existed in those days, the exact whereabouts of Punt has long puzzled historians. Perhaps in order to maintain secrecy, maps were never made. The long period required for the voyage and particularly the nature of the articles brought back to Egypt provide useful hints as to Punt's location. The records show that Queen Hatshepsut's five galleys, built of timber from the cedars of Lebanon, propelled by sail and 30 oarsmen, left an ancient seaport near Qusier on the Red Sea bound for 'God's Land of Punt' in 1490 B.C.

One of the indisputable sources of incense which no doubt was used by the Egyptians was the Hadhramaut region of southern Arabia, bordering the Gulf of Aden. As early as 2500 B.C. caravans bearing gold, spices, incense and exotic goods from the Far East, India and the Persian Gulf had traveled through the Hadhramaut and then northward from Aden to Egypt. But as a land rich in gold, the Oriental region must have been overshadowed by more exciting rumors emanating from the south, particularly eastern Africa, a land which was also near the source of the Nile.

Although Somaliland, adjoining Ethiopia, has often been mentioned as the land of Punt, it seems obvious that once a venturesome seaman reached Somali shores he could hardly have escaped stories of the gold that lay farther ahead along the coast of what is now Mozambique, in view of what we know today of the gold occurrences of that area.

Watersheds of The Zambesi

Near present Chinde the great Zambesi River disgorges its huge load of water and sediments from one of the great mineralized areas of the world located in Southern and Northern Rhodesia. The Zambesi's southern tributaries reach out to drain gold fields along the northern rim of Southern Rhodesia, including the important districts of Salisbury, Que Que, Gwela and Bulawayo. For

millions of years gold has been available to man in the rocks of this area.

Farther south along the Mozambique coast over the Zambesi divide and draining the eastern watersheds of this golden heartland, rivers combine to form the Sabi and Save rivers, which empty into the Indian Ocean near Nova Mambone. This river system also comes down from a land rich in gold. Quartz veins in schist had been worked in ancient times in the Umtali and Manica gold fields, which straddle the Southern Rhodesia and Mozambique border.

During our modern era, over 3500 mines have been developed in these widely productive areas in which, according to reliable estimates, ancient miners had recovered gold amounting to over $750,000,000. Even a more conservative estimate would not alter the fact that the golden wealth of this region could hardly have hidden its glitter from prospectors of the dim past.

It is true that most of the gold fields have attained commercial production in modern times. Nevertheless, many mines have uncovered ancient placers, open pits, and evidence of primitive firesetting methods of mining. A highly mineralized area such as this, with its numerous gold bearing veins and placers produced by eons of erosion and sorting, must have been known to those who sought gold for the pharaohs. Here too, were the myrrh trees, ivory, ebony, panthers, pigmies and the characteristically greenish gold containing the tell-tale antimony mineral, stibnite, a mineral which is also found today in the ores of the Que Que district, a land which would require two years for a return voyage.

Hatshepsut's Golden Temple

The historic journey of Queen Hatshepsut's ships to the land of Punt is dramatically recorded in colored reliefs and inscriptions on the walls of her magnificent, terraced temple at Dier el-Bahri near Thebes. It is the best available account of a voyage to Punt. But there is nothing resembling a map to help us pinpoint 'God's Land.' Its secret was well kept. Casts of some of the reliefs may be seen in the Egyptian Room of the Metropolitan Museum of Art in New York City.

One of the great reliefs in Hatshepsut's temple depicts a long Byblos-ship, 'very heavily laden with marvels of Punt, fragrant woods, fresh, living myrrh trees, sacks of myrrh resin, ivory, ebony, cinnamon wood, eye-cosmetic, monkeys, dwarfs and the green gold of Emu. Nothing such as this has been brought for any king since the beginning.' The living myrrh trees were planted in the courtyard of the temple and great weights of gold and myrrh resin were presented to the god, Amon. Queen Hatshepsut had successfully completed, as had her ancestors, one of the earliest and longest voyages on the high seas of adventure. But the famed land of Punt still remains a tantalizing mystery.

Reigns of The Pharaohs

Following the death of Queen Hatshepsut her half brother, Thutmose III, also of the 18th Dynasty, became Egypt's ruler. He had jealously and impatiently awaited his succession to the throne. Vengefully, he had statues of the Queen defaced and overthrown, endeavoring to erase completely the memory of her rule. Dreaming of conquest and empire, Thutmose III went on to become one of Egypt's ablest Pharaohs and most skillful military leaders.

With his war chariot richly plated with gold, Thutmose invaded and conquered Syria. He subjugated Palestine, winning the battle of Megiddo in 1479 B.C. After 16 expeditions and 18 years of warfare, the empire of Thutmose spread from Nubia on the south to the Mediterranean on the north and eastward to the Euphrates River. He had taken Egypt to the peak of its power and had established Egypt's first great, organized empire. Then, turning to his own land, Thutmose intensified mining in Nubia and the Coptos country, even though more gold in spoils and tribute continued to come from conquered lands.

The fourth ruler to follow Thutmose III was Amenhotep IV. A dreamer and aesthetic intellectual, he endeavored to revolutionize Egyptian beliefs in many gods to the broad concept of one, the sun-god, Aton. He changed his name to Ikhnaton, abandoned Thebes and with his beautiful Queen, Nefertiti, built a new capital midway between Thebes and Memphis, about 1370 B.C. Here, while he lived in a dream world of harmony, love of nature and joy of living, the empire of his forefathers fell into ruin and disorder.

The second ruler to follow Ikhnaton was the young Pharaoh, Tutankhamen, who re-established Thebes as the capital and restored the worship of the god Amon; otherwise his reign was unimportant, except for the accumulation of wealth placed in his tomb, which we have previously witnessed. About 1340 B.C., a vigorous, able, military leader, Harmhab, became first king of the 19th Dynasty and revived the power and prosperity of the kingdom.

In the ruins of Ikhnaton's palace, now known as Tell el-Amarna, a large number of records and letters in the form of clay tablets were found in 1887. More than 300 "letters," written in Akkadian, from the kings of Assyria, Mitanni, and Babylonia to Egypt's rulers, reflect the glorified reputation Egypt had acquired during its long period of gold accumulation. In their letters the kings begged the Pharaohs to send them gold in exchange for slaves saying, 'My brother, pray send me gold in great quantity, such as cannot be counted. Gold is as common as dust in thy land.'

Egypt, Trade Center of The World

Egypt indeed was rich in gold but poor in many of the raw materials needed for her way of life and commerce. More important than military might, it was this possession of the ancient world's greatest gold filled treasury and gold mining reserves that enabled the Pharaohs to establish Egypt as the dominant power in the Middle East. Gold, which was relatively scarce in most lands, more than her armies, gave Egypt the means to spread her influence, set up and maintain her subject states and trade centers and command the materials required for her civilization. She bought copper from Cyprus and the Mesopotamian Kingdom of Mitanni, silver and lead from Asia Minor, tin from the Seafarers of Phoenicia, and from Lebanon she obtained wood for her temples, ships, and homes.

From earliest times, even in the predynastic Gerzean period, Egyptians had found their way along the eastern Mediterranean shore past Carmel to Gebal, later named Byblos by the Greeks. High in the mountains above the coastal port of Byblos, which had been inhabited even in Neolithic times, were the coniferous so-called "Cedars of Lebanon." The brash, knotty acacia and sycamore trees from the wadis of Egypt were useless for ship building. It was the timber from Lebanon that became the world's mainstay in history's first sea ventures of commerce.

Egypt's first ships were probably built on the spot at Byblos, by means of an ancient method of 'fitting-together.' They could be dismantled, sent anywhere and reassembled perfectly. Immense quantities of Lebanon timber left the busy port of Byblos bound for Egypt. One convoy contained '40 ships of cedar-wood from Lebanon' on its way to Egypt, according to inscriptions on the Palermo Stone. The royal dockyards at Memphis, using the 'meru-wood' of Byblos, constructed the large maritime fleets which sailed to many ports of the Mediterranean and the Red Sea. As were Queen Hatshepsut's ships, the vessels that plied the Nile, Egypt's long lifeline of commerce and communication, were built of lumber from Byblos. For ages, ships of the world made of Lebanon wood were known as 'Byblos ships.'

With the decline of Memphis, following the rise of the Thutmose kings, Thebes became the imperial capital. As the most magnificent city in the world, famed for its temples, statues, obelisks and sphinxes now seen at nearby Karnak and Luxor, and for the tombs in the Valley of Kings, Thebes symbolized Egypt's greatest period of power and achievement. To this busy center came caravans bearing spices, incense and aromatic woods from the East and a variety of metals from provinces of the Empire.

The Artisans of Egypt

As Egypt's imports of raw material expanded so did her production of finished products. Her expert metalsmiths fashioned exquisite jewelry and useful implements for home and agriculture; her artisans created marvelous and popular works in ceramics, faience and glassware, superb textiles, especially linens, and masterful carvings in wood and stone. As commerce grew, a stream of galleys ascended the Nile from as far away as the island of Crete, where an Aegean civilization was taking form. Trade flowed down the Nile to Rhodes, Cyprus, and to Mycenae on the Greek mainland. The spread of Egypt's unequalled cultural attainments through trade to the rest of the world exerted a momentous influence upon mankind, a turning point in history.

Egyptian art, science and architecture inspired and stimulated the budding civilizations of the Aegean Sea. It was Egypt's wealth in gold that sustained her industries, prestige and authority, and the fertilizing benefits of her widespread commerce. Gold flowed copiously from the mines of Nubia and from Egypt's parched deserts despite the heavy toll in human suffering. From the hands of countless humans, living in misery and serfdom, came the gold that gilded Egypt's thrones and temples and built the ships that carried her inestimable heritage to mankind. As tiny ripples emanate from a pebble tossed into a pond, so did gold mined by these humble beings set in motion the waves of a great culture radiating to many distant shores.

The Ramessides

After Seti I failed to find water along the route to the Wadi Allaqi mines, his son Ramses II, anxious to enrich himself and his temples, succeeded in the attempt. Where the route left the Nile at Kuban a stele was erected to commemorate the event. With a treasury full of gold and a mind full of conquests, Ramses launched a program of warfare against the Hittites. After several years of struggle, including the gallant but indecisive battle of Kadesh in 1288 B.C., Ramses agreed to a treaty of peace. Then he married a daughter of the Hittite king and settled down to rule his empire.

In the long reign that followed, Ramses became an insatiable builder of monuments to his own glory. He built the mortuary of the Rameseum containing colossal statues of himself. At Abu-Simbel, which has been moved to avoid flooding by the waters of the new Aswan dam, Ramses built a rock-cut temple guarded by more enormous figures. He added temples at Karnak and Luxor, built temples at Abydos, El Qurna, Memphis and a great palace at Qantir. With Ramses' conquests a large number of slaves and immigrants appeared in Egypt. Much of the labor for his temples was composed of captives. Some historians believe that it was the enforcement of slave labor and oppression of some of the Hebrew tribes during this period that induced the Exodus of the Jews from Egypt. While many slaves were employed in building temples, more than 4,000 slaves were working the royal stone quarries of the Wadi Hammamat.

Ramses II apparently was a handsome, dashing, picturesque, and no doubt a popular king. He ruled for 67 years, from 1304 to 1237 B.C. He sired more than one hundred sons and daughters and lived to be 90 years of age. By means of his own tremendous building activities and usurpation of many monuments of former kings, he spread his name everlastingly across the land. But he had lavished the wealth and the strength of Egypt upon the temples, sending them immense stores of grain, cattle, wine, fruits and great riches in gold, silver and copper. The wealth of the Priesthood of Amon grew to rival that of the king.

Degeneration Sets In

Gold from Egypt's conquered provinces and from her mines was used in almost everything and everywhere, to the point of vulgarity. Gold gilding on an extravagant scale became an obsession. Except for goldsmithing, under Ramses art had begun to degenerate. Much of the sculpturing had become coarse and rough. Egypt had experienced the final burst of her creative glory. But the reign of Ramses II had gained such renown that during the 20th Dynasty which followed, ten rulers covering a 110 year period assumed the exalted title of Ramses. Egypt, however, was growing weak and vulnerable. Libyan bands from the west began invading and plundering the western Delta region.

In 1198 B.C., Ramses III, first of the late Ramesside line, warred with Libya and the Amorites of Syria and finally subdued them. In triumph, more spoils and more captives were brought back to Egypt. Uneasy peace and prosperity prevailed for a period and commerce with the outside world continued. The temple cults of Amon and others, now grown strong and powerful, sent their own fleets to trade across the Mediterranean and the Red Sea. Ramses III sent expeditions to the Peninsula of Sinai where a considerable amount of copper was mined and returned to Egypt, together with a large quantity of turquoise and malachite to be given to the temples. After 31 years, in 1167 B.C., the rule of Ramses III came to an end. Nine weaklings bearing the proud name of Ramses followed. One ruler, Ramses IV, sent 9,000 men into the Wadi Hammamat for stone to perpetuate his name. Nine hundred men perished in the desert heat. Only one small temple survives to his memory.

In the succeeding reigns, disorganization and disorder marked the times. Thebes, which had been abandoned for several hundred years, had become only a burial place of the royal dead. Staggering accumulations of golden wealth, objects of art and ordinary trappings, were piled high in the burial chambers. Eventually, grave robbers, perhaps emboldened with the knowledge and assistance of corrupt officials, readily and systematically despoiled the tombs. Even Ramses II, who had desecrated the pyramid of Sesostris II, in turn had his tomb and that of his father, Seti I, broken into and robbed. Tombs of the whole line of Pharaohs, from the 18th to the 20th Dynasties, were ransacked of their golden splendors and even the bodies were disturbed.

Egypt's Decline and Fall

As the tombs of the mighty Pharaohs were tumbling, so was the Empire which had witnessed their power and glory. The swift decline of the Ramessides and Egypt's growing helplessness was being watched by foreigners and former subjects who were now thirsting for retribution. For generations Egypt's military force had been based upon conscriptions of subjugated peoples. The disenchanted and unwarlike Egyptian masses and their impotent descendants, bereft of any real national feeling, had long since lost interest in military service. Their stomachs and their hearts had been left empty in order to fill the ravenous needs of the temples, the priesthoods, and their rulers.

The temples owned over a hundred thousand slaves, replacing willing workers of the realm, and nearly a million acres of the best land. The temples possessed enormous quantities of gold, silver, and copper, a half million cattle, great stores of grain and fruits; they owned fleets of trading vessels and 169 towns. Everything belonging to the cults was exempt from taxation, adding further burdens upon the people.

Drained of its vitality and its challenge, Egypt soon found her ancient foes and new rivals pressing upon her. An Ethiopian conqueror came from the Upper Nile to found the 25th Dynasty. He too suffered conquest, at the hands of the Assyrians in 670 B.C. Next came the Persian conquerors. In 332 B.C., came Alexander the Great, followed by the Romans, Arabs and Turks. Egypt's ship of state and its long, brilliant civilization became only a fading wake in the sea of history.

Egypt's Gifts to Mankind

Egypt's great wealth had rested mainly in the hands of the Pharaohs, temples, high priests, nobles and their households, landed nomarchs, and an administrative bureaucracy. The masses were benefited the least. The long era of building colossal pyramids, temples, palaces and memorial monuments, useless for creating industry or commerce, sapped prodigious amounts of national labor and substance. With thousands of years of effort squandered and great bonanzas of wealth dissipated, Egypt's forward march became as stilled as the vast piles of stone which once marked the peak of her power.

Gold had been a salient force in elevating Egypt's civilization to commanding heights. Gold from the forlorn deserts of the Nile, spawned by millennia of human anguish and sorrow, played an important role in the spread of Egyptian culture around the ancient world. Although Egypt's supremacy persevered for a very long period it failed ultimately, as would other civilizations to come, because those fundamental freedoms of the individual, which are the seeds of national greatness, in Egypt were ignored and left to wither, fallow and unused.

Nevertheless, Egypt's gifts to mankind are almost incalculable. She bequeathed to posterity the calendar and chronology, the art of stone masonry, architecture, achievements in agriculture, geometry, medicine, jewelry and the perfec-tions of the smith's art, sculpturing, glass making, paper, fine weaving and various principles of orderly government. All these gifts would be hand-ed down to mankind by the Phoenicians, Syrians, Hebrews, the Cretans, Greeks, and Romans, who would follow in Egypt's illustrious path. Its extra-ordinary duration, more than 3,000 years, and its cultural and scientific attainments, entitle the civilization of Egypt to rank in many ways as perhaps the greatest yet known to mankind.

Chapter 4

THE BRONZE AGE BOOM**

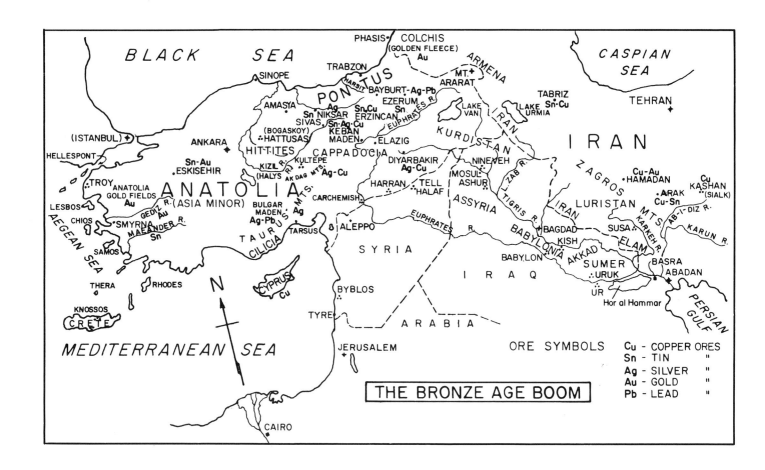

ORE SYMBOLS Cu – COPPER ORES
Sn – TIN   "
Ag – SILVER "
Au – GOLD   "
Pb – LEAD   "

THE BRONZE AGE BOOM

Plate 24 *Ores of tin*, cassiterite crystal (R), nourished the Bronze Age boom. p. 35

Plate 25 *Lead, zinc, copper, silver and sulphur minerals.* The Sumerians classified over 150 minerals 5,500 years ago. p. 35

Plate 26 *Luristan bronzes* were being made in present Iran as early as 3000 B.C. p. 35

Plate 27 *Cuneiform writing on clay tablets* left lasting records of widespread Babylonian commerce. p. 35

Plate 28 *Akkadian cylinder seals* used to mark personal items and trade articles (2100 B.C.). p. 35

Plate 29 *Argentiferous galena, silver-lead ore,* sought by Hammurabi's prospectors. p. 35

**The terms "Bronze Age" and "Iron Age" refer only to the generally accepted order of man's material evolution in most areas of the Old World. In the Pacific region and in parts of Africa the use of metals began with various metals other than bronze.

The Miracle of Tinstone

No event in the history of ancient man had such a momentous impact upon his cultural development and the diffusion of early civilizations as did the discovery and use of a stone today known as cassiterite, a mineral of tin, commonly called tinstone. For ages relatively pure copper had been mankind's sole working metal. But it was soft and had to be hardened and sharpened by constant hammering. By adding a small percentage of tin to their copper, men of antiquity produced a metal much harder than copper and a melt which was more fluid and easier to cast into desired shapes. This "new and better copper" eventually acquired the name 'bronze.'

For over 4000 years following its discovery bronze formed the cornerstone of the world's industry and art. Different types of bronzes were used to fashion a wide assortment of tools, weapons, household utensils and bells, and a vast variety of statuary, vessels, mirrors, ornaments and trinkets. Even today, in this age of widely used metals, bronze is an important material. To the ancients it filled a diverse and potent need and launched a wave of creativity that stimulated peoples of the world everywhere.

Tin is rarely found in the native or metallic state. Although there are several minerals of tin, it is mainly cassiterite, or tinstone, that forms the chief ore of tin. The comparatively few localities in which commercial tin deposits occur in the Old World (no economic deposits at all occur in the United States) have evoked varied opinions among historians and technologists as to where the secret of mixing tin with copper to produce bronze was discovered.

Tin Sources of Antiquity

In considering Europe, one of the great tin producing regions of the world since Grecian and possibly Phoenician times was Cornwall, England. Ancient Iberia, or Spain, and the Erzgebirge Mountains of Saxony and Bohemia also contained important tin deposits. But it has been well established by archeological findings that bronze making reached Western Europe a thousand years following its development in the ancient Middle East.

As for Egypt, despite its early use of copper, the land of the Nile was not the originator of man's newest metal. No traces of tin occurred in the copper producing regions of the Sinai peninsula, nor was tin present in the gold placers that so enriched the Pharaohs, except in the unim-

portant Meuilha district near the Baramia mine. Small deposits of tin occurred near Byblos, with whom Egypt had traded since earliest times, but it was not until the 18th Dynasty that Egypt began fashioning weapons and splendid articles of bronze. Using her abundant resources in gold, Egypt then procured tin from Cretan traders. The art of bronze making was brought to Egypt by the venturesome traders of Mesopotamia.

It is to Asia Minor, Iran and Mesopotamia, even though occurrences of tin in those regions were less prominent, that we must therefore look for the circumstances that favored the discovery of bronze; namely, an available supply of tinstone and the people who were most advanced in the knowledge of metalworking. As we have witnessed, the Sumerians were the first to benefit from the discovery of metallurgy. Since they were keenly alive to improving articles of trade, they would have been among the first to recognize bronze's greater adaptability to precise casting, owing to the molten metal's fluidity. As early as 3000 B.C. the Sumerians were highly skilled in making closed mold castings and in the use of the intricate cire-perdue or lost wax process, as was so clearly revealed by the remarkable metal treasures found in the Royal Cemetery of Ur.

The Highlands of Iran

The inventive metallurgists of Sumer undoubtedly first obtained their copper from the same regions in the highlands of Iran that had furnished the coppersmiths of prehistoric Susa and Sialk, villages of the 5th millennium B.C.; these smiths were among the first users of copper. Less than 60 miles north of Susa copper ores exist today. It is worthy of note that they are associated with tin and tungsten, according to S. H. Lorain, a district director for the Bureau of Mines, who recently made a survey of this area.

Located about 40 miles southwest of the present town of Arak, this region is near the eastern border of Luristan. Significantly, Luristan is famed for its many Bronze Age sites, dated about 3000 B.C., and for the numerous and magnificent Luristan bronzes that now grace nearly every important museum in the world.*

*There are other regions in Iran northeast of Susa, near modern Kashan, that contain copper ores which probably supplied nearby Sialk. The Shari-fabad mine 30 miles northwest of Kashan, and the Temmessi and Meskani copper-nickel mines northwest of Isfahan are deposits which today confirm the existence of (Cont. p. 50)

The supply of tin from these early sources may have been meager and limited but so was the relative demand in that small world. Whether the Sumerians were actually the first to discover the process of making bronze cannot be stated with certainty, but there is little doubt that they were the first to avail themselves of the potentialities of bronze as a trade item. They were also the first to set forth and acquaint far away peoples with the advantages of man's latest and most promising invention.

Tin Veins or Placers?

Where the ancients first obtained their tinstone, whether from stream placers or from veins in rock, has been considerably debated. The sands and gravels of the rivers had long been man's chief source of gold. Due to its relatively high specific gravity tinstone also accumulated occasionally with grains of gold in the streambeds of certain localities. But to ancient prospectors perhaps the blackish, lusterless tinstone went unnoticed. For stream-tin is unimpressive in appearance; it is usually dullish brown, black or earthy gray in color. Before its importance became known, cassiterite in placers more likely would have been separated from the gold and discarded. Even in modern times gold seekers, in order to obtain clean gold, habitually parted and threw aside other unattractive but valuable minerals that clogged and contaminated their gold pans.

Veins in rock, however, first mined for their copper ores which in some instances also contained cassiterite, could have provided the fortunate combination of tin and copper, the ingredients of bronze. Smelting such an ore could have led accidentally to the discovery of the useful new alloy, bronze. Since such copper ores naturally varied in their percentages of tin content, one would expect these first crude "accidental" bronzes to differ in their tin composition. This has proven to be true.

Tin in the first "natural" bronzes varied from 2 to 12 percent. Results later revealed that bronze containing about 10 percent tin made the most useful metal. Earliest bronzes also contained other impurities present in the ores such as lead, zinc and antimony. These minerals are also widely associated with copper ores throughout

metallic ores in these areas. Ancient smelters have also been found at Fahradj near Bam 120 miles southeast of Kerman. There, tin is also found near deposits of copper.

western Iran, notably near Arak, Hamadan, Kashan, and Isfahan.

The First Mineralogists

The Sumerians became adept in recognizing and cataloging the physical properties of over 150 minerals which they met in the course of their trade and travels. Color, and variations of color, hardness, sheen or luster, crystal forms, cleavage or fracture habits, relative heaviness or specific gravity, and the substances which were contained in the mineral, all received a logical classification. Thus were taken the first steps in the science of mineralogy. Although the Sumerians attributed certain magical, religious, and even male and female qualities to various minerals, they nevertheless were alert to their practical usefulness.

The discovery of a new alloy of increased hardness and greater fusibility must have created a sensation among the metalsmiths. Upon investigating the reason for this new metal's behavior, the Sumerians logically isolated the previously unknown impurity, which in the past they had shunned in searching for the purest carbonate ores of copper. Thereafter, this valuable oxide of tin was sought on all the frontiers. Later, the Chaldeans named the mineral *Kasdir*, and the Greeks called it *cassiteros*. In modern terminology it became known as cassiterite.

The gold seekers of antiquity knew that particles of gold were released by decomposition of veins in rock and transported by agents of erosion into streambeds, to form deposits of placer gold. When men realized that the heavy, dark, durable grains of tinstone also accumulated in streambeds by means of the same processes, then placer deposits containing tin also became an early source of supply.

Bronze Spurs Warfare and Trade

It was the demand for weapons of war that provided the greatest stimulus to metallurgy and especially the production of bronze. Not only household articles such as bowls, vases, mirrors and knives, but also swords, battle-axes, spearpoints, daggers, helmets and shields of bronze were fashioned in growing quantities. The rulers of Sumerian city-states built up stores of newly invented weapons for their own use; then, lured by profits and the need of raw materials they traded similar wares to barbarian tribes on the distant frontiers.

Advantages accruing from the development of

man's first durable metal, therefore, made warfare a tempting and profitable pursuit. And from warfare emerged another discovery, slavery. Reaping rich rewards in both trade and human spoils, conquerors returned homeward with hordes of slaves who were used as servants and as workers in the fields and workshops.

As the nearby deposits of tinstone in Iran became more difficult to work and less productive, or were insufficient to meet demands, Sumer's tradesmen searched farther for their metallic ores. Into the upper reaches of the Tigris-Euphrates, which even in chalcolithic times supplied the early coppersmiths, went traders now seeking tin. In northern Turkey near Eskisehir, Kastamanu, and Sivas, and at Tillek near Erzincan in Armenia, tin ores associated with or near copper deposits have been mentioned by ancient and modern writers.

In the Caucasus region near Gori west of Tiflis, and near Alaverdi north of historic Mount Ararat, and also in the foothills of Mount Kuhisahand in northern Iran, tin and copper ores occurred in regions which were well advanced in the earliest use of metal and metallurgy. The riches of these vast regions, and of Asia Minor where ore deposits contained a wide variety of metals, were to exert an important influence in the spread of civilization westward into Europe.

Compared with the spiraling advancements of our modern era the Bronze Age represented a wave of infinitely gradual but inexorable progress. Nevertheless, the Bronze Age in reality was a boom because of its widespread, stimulating effect upon the welfare, enlightenment and inventive impulses of nearly all mankind.

As certain peoples with progressive societies acquired both the knowledge of bronze making and an available mineral supply, they launched their own commercial ventures and increased the scope of their achievements as they entered the dawning Age of Metals. Through a study of their explorations, enterprises and trade systems we are able to trace the rise and fall of one culture after another as they take their places in history while riding the crest of the Bronze Age boom.

Sargon I of Akkad

While the city-states of Sumer were rising to power, a strong Semitic center known as Akkad, located about 150 miles northwest of Uruk, had been forming in the Euphrates Valley. For countless centuries, Semitic nomads had been roaming out of the desert wastes of Arabia, flowing into Syria and Palestine. Some tribes, seeking better pastures for their flocks, settled in lands north of Sumer. Kish became their capital, the first city to arise in the region following the Great Flood. This was about 4500 B.C. Near Kish, the Tigris and Euphrates were barely 20 miles apart, placing the city in position to command the main routes into the metal-rich mountains to the north and west. Strengthened by expanding commerce, the Semites grew prosperous and increasingly aggressive.

About 2350 B.C. a skilled warrior named Sargon I, proud of his humble origin, became king and easily conquered the strife torn city states of Sumer. Sargon succeeded in uniting the kingdoms of Akkad and Sumer, then extended his conquests eastward to the mountains of Elam in Iran, westward to the Mediterranean Sea and southward to the Persian Gulf. Encouraging private enterprise among a growing class of merchants, Sargon sent his armies into Asia Minor to protect the trade in metal coming from the 'silver mountains' of that remote region. Sargon I became the first great leader of the Semites and the first in history to establish an empire.

A Sumerian Heritage

The nomadic tribesmen who had founded Akkad, however, had known nothing of industry or writing. Their Semitic language appeared in written form for the first time after they adapted the wedge-shaped characters of Sumerian cuneiform. The Semites also adopted the Sumerian Pantheon of gods and legends (including the Great Flood), the Sumerian calendar, weights and measures, numerical system and trade methods. From the Sumerians the Semites learned also the use of copper weapons and helmets in warfare, and eventually the expert fashioning of bronze. Although the Semites later replaced the Sumerians as the rulers of Mesopotamia, it was Sumerian writing, language and technology that dominated Semitic life. Sumer's vigorous and ingenious civilization was thus perpetuated and bequeathed to the ancient world.

Sargon's empire was maintained by three sons who succeeded him. The third son, Narim-Sin, was a ruthless warrior and great builder. The famed stele of Naram-Sin depicting his invasion of Elam, armed with metal spears and battle axes, is known for the artistry of its carving, but it illustrates also the purpose of his conquest, to seize the metal riches of Iran. Far north of

Akkad, Naram-Sin erected the largest known building of the Sargonid period, a huge palace, fortress and storehouse. Within the excavated ruins an amazing treasure of metalwork was found. The building had been used as an important depository and to protect the lines of communication into remote, mineral-rich Asia Minor. The need of mineral resources for Mesopotamia's growing metal economy was even then pushing the frontier of civilization westward toward Europe.

The Sargonid dynasty suddenly collapsed in revolt about 2150 B.C. For over 200 years the leadership of Sumer-Akkad wavered between Semitic and non-Semitic rulers. Under Ur-Nammu, as we have seen, Sumer experienced a great revival, its Golden Age. Then, to threaten Sumer anew, appeared another migration of Semites described in the Bible as Amorites, meaning 'out of the west.'

Hammurabi of Babylon

When the unpredictable Euphrates changed its course and deserted Kish, the ancient Akkadian capital, the Amorites settled about a little village known as Babylon on the new course of the river. As time passed the Amorites came under the reigns of several kings with such names as Jacob and Abraham. The sixth and greatest of these rulers was Hammurabi. *About 1900 B.C., as had Sargon I hundreds of years before, Hammurabi again united the kingdoms of Sumer and Akkad. Thenceforth Sumer faded from history as a leading political force, leaving her culture to become the foundation for all subsequent civilizations in Mesopotamia.

Hammurabi extended his conquests and went on to establish the First Babylonian Empire. He drove the Elamites back into the mountains of Iran and held in check the growing threat of the Assyrians on the north. He built great temples, set up a state religion and proclaimed his famous code of 300 laws governing social and economic life. These laws, everlastingly inscribed upon a black diorite shaft 8 feet high, contained over 3,000 lines written in the Semitic speech of the Amorites and Akkadians. They defined codes for the protection of the weak and oppressed and established a state-controlled economy by setting minimum wages and fixed prices for basic com-

*Certain interpretations of the Mari clay tablets, according to some historians, set Hammurabi's reign at about 1750 B.C.

modities. It is one of the most important records in history and may be seen today in the Louvre, in Paris.

Economic Systems of Antiquity

In order to account for the glittering opulence which attended the rise of the city-states of Mesopotamia it is useful to understand the nature of their basic economies. After examining the cuneiform tablets of clay found so abundantly in the archives of Sumer, Babylonia and Assyria, authorities have been able to reconstruct the economic systems of ancient times. These records make it clear that it was primarily man's inborn instinct to trade with his fellowmen that led to the development and spread of civilization.

Mesopotamia suffered a critical lack of suitable stone, timber and metals for structural and ornamental use. In order to obtain these necessary raw materials she was forced to produce export commodities such as grain, textiles, and finished wares. The resultant agricultural, industrial, and trade economy that developed served as a vital stimulus to the ascendancy of the city-states. Commerce in coveted metals was based upon peaceful treaties of reciprocity, but just as often conquests evoked the same results.

Beginning in Hammurabi's time, long distance trading became the source of Babylon's riches and an important energizer to her growth. Forced urbanization developed when colonies were established as trade and supply centers on the far frontiers. There, raw materials were procured and Babylonian wares were distributed by traders appointed by the king, temple priests or their bureaucratic administrators.

These traders were very important, carefully selected, time-tested individuals or families of long standing experience and reputation, governed by stringent rules of conduct and inviolable codes of ethics. As middlemen representing both their city-states, as well as the native princes on the frontier, the traders were entrusted with considerable authority and responsibility.

Unlike modern merchants most traders of antiquity were not buyers and sellers of commodities for a profit. Their compensation consisted of a fixed scale of commissions on goods consigned and delivered. So far as trading operations were concerned, therefore, as a general rule they were economically risk free, but the same could not be said of the lonely trails which were extremely arduous and often fraught with the dangers of marauding tribes. Because trade was the life-blood of ancient civilizations, the severest of penalties were dealt to the murderers of these important emissaries of commerce.

The Venturesome Breed

Occasionally a few favored appointees of the palaces and temples were vested with land grants, special fees and private trading privileges. Certain rulers, such as Sargon I and Hammurabi, encouraged traders to become merchants engaged in private enterprise. Whichever system was employed, whether it was reward through fees and commissions, or private ventures, the trader-merchants of ancient times were a venturesome breed and made up an affluent class.

Metals such as copper, silver, lead, and tin, which were the chief items sought on the trade frontier, were exchanged for fine cloths, useful textiles, leather goods, and finished wares brought from the civilized centers. Metal procurement involved many complex duties for the trader. Natives had to be efficiently trained in mining and smelting methods, and caravans had to be organized for transporting the metal ingots to the storage rooms of the faraway cities.

Palaces of the rulers and temples of the principal gods contained the warehouses where all raw materials and agricultural products of the realm were stored. These sanctuaries were also the manufacturing centers. There, a wide variety of finished articles were made by a complex hierarchy of artisans and laborers attached to and supervised by the state. Redistribution of these wares was left entirely to the discretion of the palace and temple officials.

A Controlled Economy

One of the outstanding features of the system was that all raw materials procured and all finished products dispensed were assigned proportionate values in terms of "equivalencies." Under this system most ancient civilizations engaged in a controlled economy administered by the king, temple priesthood or merchant guilds who were empowered to do so. Thus, unlike the free-dealing, money-based market places of modern days, in ancient times there was no central marketing facility.

Remuneration to natives on the frontiers was guaranteed in advance, payable on delivery of the materials they produced. Thus assured of being rewarded with trade wares valued on a fixed scale of equivalencies, natives were encouraged to increase production. Since the trader himself operated also on a no-profit, no-loss basis, the combined no-risk activity served to balloon the flow of raw materials which were enriching the palaces and temples of the cities.

The accumulations of stored wealth through a controlled economy provided abundant means of enhancing the prestige and power of civilized centers and their rulers. By fostering civic pride, rulers and communities sought to transcend the glory and creative spirit of rival cities, which added to the fame and longevity of their realms. The Babylonians made effective use of this system.

Hammurabi's Empire

Hammurabi's unified, disciplined and peaceful reign marked the Golden Age of the First Babylonian Empire. Great canals were dug to harness the Tigris and Euphrates rivers. Important strides in mathematics and especially astronomy were made. The positions of the sun and moon were first recorded and predictions of eclipses were made. Crafts and trades flourished. Agricultural production and a thriving industry in bronze making made Babylon exceedingly rich and powerful. Donkey caravans ventured into expanding frontiers and returned with supplies for the city's metalsmiths.

Babylon's military strength protected such outposts as Mari and Harran in the north and guarded the lonely trade routes far into Asia Minor. In the bustling courtyards of these outposts stores of grain, wool and metalwares were piled high, marked by clay tablets identifying the merchant owners. These bills of goods were written in Babylonian cuneiform, and in turn were copied by frontier officials who were becoming acquainted with the art of writing. Thousands of these records have been found in ruins across Asia Minor, testifying to Hammurabi's enlightened and prosperous reign. They also reveal with convincing clarity civilization's relentless march from cultured centers of the Middle East to what was then Mesopotamia's Far West.

The booming trade in bronze, supplying an awakening world with a magical new metal for use in the home, for the rich adornment of temples, for tools in the fields, and for implements of war, had created another requisite for progress. Man's urgent need now was a convenient standard medium of exchange. The old fashioned bartering of cattle, grain and other commodities, based upon a system of equivalencies was growing awkward. Ingots, bars and rings of gold were used in exchange, but gold was relatively scarce and the value of copper fluctuated according to supply. A metal which would serve as a reliable standard to support the economic advancement of mankind proved to be silver. Then, prospectors of antiquity began their search for greater supplies of silver, along with gold, copper, and tin.

The Search for Silver

Articles of silver have appeared in many of the finds of early antiquity. Beautiful silver bowls, urns and ornaments of silver found with gold and copper-ware in the Royal Cemetery of Ur indicate its ancient use. Silver was first encountered by early metal seekers in the form of electrum, an alloy of gold containing about one-third silver. Often intimately associated with gold, silver lightens the color of gold as the silver content increases. Egyptians placed added value on the gold which came from the Coptos country, as well as Punt, because of the rarity of color that silver had imparted to the gold. The magnificent headdress of Mes-kalam-dug, prince of the royal house of Ur, actually was of the gold-silver alloy, electrum.

Silver in the form of native metal occurs only in small amounts and rather sparsely over the world, and it quickly corrodes to form a black, oxidized coating. Under arid conditions a soft, greasy, greenish chloride of silver which prospectors call "horn-silver" (cerargyrite) sometimes is found in exposed silver deposits. The early objects of silver, no doubt, were made from native metal, but neither native silver nor cerargyrite were available to the ancients in sufficient quantities to have been the metal's principal source. In the Americas, however, some lucrative deposits of "hornsilver" have been worked by modern miners who were termed "chloriders."

Galena's Affinity—Silver

It was from the argentiferous ores of lead (in which silver was intimately associated with lead) that the ancients obtained their chief supply of refined silver. One of the brightest minerals known to nearly everyone is the sulphide of lead, galena. It has a strong affinity for silver. Not all, but many, lead ores contain silver, and sometimes gold. Although galena oxidizes in surface exposures to cerussite, a nearly clear, colorless, carbonate of lead, remnants of shiny galena often survive at or close to the surface.

Galena's brilliant luster, perfect cube-like cleavage and crystal habit, must have caught the eyes of earliest metal seekers. Even in prehistoric times, galena was gathered, powdered and used as a cosmetic eye paint, as was antimony and malachite. For ages it was unknown that this bright, heavy lead mineral also harbored a valuable white metal, silver. Its discovery perhaps came about accidentally.

Somewhere in the highlands to the east beyond Sumer, or possibly Asia Minor, during the smelting of copper ores an early metallurgist undoubtedly also mixed lead ores unknowingly in the melt, and through the same process of reduction, he obtained not only metallic copper but also metallic lead. If this alert metalsmith left a piece or batch of galena in his hot charcoal fire long enough, he would have noticed a new, grayish sheen to the metallic fluid finally trickling through the embers. It was molten, metallic lead.

Cupellation Discovered

But lead was a dull, soft, heavy metal of little use in implements or weapons of war, and although sheet lead hammered over a few images of wood have been found, together with lead weights and other trinkets, lead was long considered a "cold," unimportant metal. Then, someone either carelessly left the reduced lead metal in the fire, or with scientific intent, applied further heat to the dull, gray metal, leading to another discovery.

As the fire burned fiercely, the ancient metallurgist saw the metallic lead slowly wither and disappear in a faint haze of vapor. As the last vestige of lead vanished, most astonishing of all, a bright globule of shining white metal alone remained. That metal was a bead of silver. A method for producing silver from lead had been found. The discovery of lead's affinity for silver and its volatility under increased heat, leaving a residue of the white metal, marked the beginning of a process known as "cupellation" which would have great importance over the ages to come.*

Shekels of Silver

As silver became more plentiful through its release from ores of lead, Babylonian merchants

*The lead ores now so well known in Iran probably were the early sources of Mesopotamian silver. In the mountains northeast of Sumer, where the early metallurgists obtained their supplies of copper, and some tin, there were many deposits of lead and also zinc. Even today a considerable number of lead deposits can be found around Arak, Yezd, Anarak, Isfahan, Kashan and Kerman.

made it man's first widespread standard of exchange. They used disc-shaped pieces of silver called a shekel about the size of an American quarter, but only as a unit of weight, for the coinage of money was yet to be invented. A shekel was the sixtieth part of a mina. A mina weighed about 18 ounces. Sixty minae equalled one talent, which was about 67 pounds. Commodities were given values compared to weights, or shekels, in silver. During Hammurabi's reign, silver had a relative value of six of silver to one of gold, but decreased as silver became more plentiful. One unit of silver was valued at about 180 units of copper and 40 units of lead. While most payments continued to be made with precisely weighed ingots of gold, copper, and lead, silver was maintained as the actual standard of money.

The ancients called their silver 'the white, bright, shining metal.' It played important roles in religion and mythology of ancient times, because its beauty was reflected in the brilliance of the moon. Egypt's Hathor was the moon-goddess of silver, and the bones of the supreme deity Re, or Ra, the Sun or Creator, were believed to be made of silver. The Mesopotamian deity, Sin, was also god of the moon. Even in modern times, there has been no dearth of composers enraptured with the magic of the "silvery moon."

In Babylonian times, it was Asia Minor that became the most important source of silver, which was widely and abundantly distributed over the vast region. Babylon's enterprising traders sent their caravans westward loaded with articles of bronze in order to procure the raw materials for the city's newest industries, which were humming with activity.

First Industrial Revolution

Indeed, through the discovery of metallurgy and the burgeoning use of the newest metals, mankind was experiencing the first industrial revolution. To the ancients, but a few centuries removed from an age in which stone alone furnished their chief material need, the dawning use of metals was a soul-stirring revelation, far more than when man at last learned to harness steam to do the work of his hands, and invented the telegraph to replace the Pony Express, and the automobile to supplant the horse.

Inured to the wonders of our blasé age, it is difficult to comprehend the human reaction that attended man's emancipation from using articles of stone to fashioning new tools, utensils,

weapons and ornaments made first of copper and then bronze, augmented by marvelous new creations in gold and silver. No wonder civilizations were galvanized into establishing industries dealing in metalware in order to capture the virgin markets beyond their frontiers. Hand in hand with industrial growth went the expansion of agrarian activity. For the first time in history, not only Babylon, but all civilized nations as well, boomed with economic and cultural productivity, induced by the stimulating use of metals, especially bronze.

The Grandeur of Babylon

For a hundred years following Hammurabi's wise and fruitful reign, Babylon enjoyed peace and growing prosperity. The booming city overflowed with indolent luxury. The great Sacred Way bustled with men and women clad in bright, many colored tunics reaching to the ground. Men wore turbans and their ornate girdles contained intricately carved signature seals with which they signed letters and documents of clay. The women were heavily jeweled with golden necklaces and bracelets, and wore their hair in stylish coiffures.

Lush, shady groves of date palms and family gardens lined the great canals. Towering temples shone with gold and bronze ornamentation, for Babylon had become the grandest and richest city mankind had ever known. But the opulence that had made Babylon famed over the world also became its undoing. In pursuit of luxuries, Babylon had left her defenses neglected. She became easy prey to envious raiders.

First came the Hittites from Cappadocia, a region in Anatolia (as Asia Minor was later called). They quickly overcame Babylon, then sacked and burned the city amid scenes of horror and bedlam. That ended the dynasty of Hammurabi and his successors. Ironically, the Hittites had attained civilization and power through the cultural and technological advancements brought to them by the traders of Babylon. After the end of the First Babylonian Empire, fire, death, and confusion stalked the land. Into this vaccuum of helplessness came the Kassites from the northeast to raid and rule. For several hundred years, under Kassite domination, Babylonia lay in a state of stagnation. But far to the north, a new and vigorous empire was slowly taking shape in Assyria.

The Rise of Assyria

Near the modern oil-rich city of Mosul, Iraq, as

early as 6000 B.C. stone age villages had existed at Tepe Gawra (called the "Great Mound") and Hassuna. At Tepe Gawra archeologists have unearthed 26 levels of occupation, 20 of which existed before the dawn of recorded history. This region lies about 300 miles northward, up the Tigris River, from Babylon. Ashur and Nineveh were cities that became famous in Assyrian history.

About 3000 B.C. Sumerian adventurers became the first of an advanced culture to move north and settle in the area around Ashur. Later, the Akkadians took over control of Ashur. The primitive site was then on the border of the rich mineral regions of the Kurdistan Mountains on the north and east, and the Taurus Mountains of Asia Minor on the west. Ashur was an important outpost station on the trade routes to these areas. Perhaps the early Sumerians had been enticed by new opportunities on this frontier, as venturesome pioneers would be in ages to come in other parts of the world.

Pressed by raiding Hittites on the west and Mitannians on the east, Ashur led a precarious existence. In order to protect their strategic position, these hardy settlers and their descendants became adept and toughened in the art of defense and reprisal. They built a standing army, utilized the horse and chariot, developed a strong, united government and became a great military power. In Hammurabi's time, Ashur had been a vassal state of Babylon, although it was relatively independent. Compared with Babylon's culture, however, Ashur was at first crude and inferior, but it was more vigorous and masterful in warfare. After the Hittites had destroyed Babylon's domination of Mesopotamia and returned to their Anatolian homeland, the Assyrians were free to expand their growing kingdom and even take over the old Babylonian routes of trade.

The Metal Seekers of Assyria

Looking westward to the great mineral resources of Asia Minor, Assyrian merchants made agreements with native princes of Anatolia and Cappadocia and prepared to exploit the mineral wealth of the land. As early as 1900 B.C., they had established trading posts, each of which was known as a Karum. One of the most important and centrally located was Kultepe, now known as Kanish, near the modern city of Kayseri in central Turkey. To Kultepe from prospering Assyria came a great variety of linen and wool fabrics, rich and luxurious and highly prized by the native population and princes. The cargoes first had to be inspected by the local rulers who selected the choicest articles, levied taxes, and then permitted distribution of the goods. In return the Assyrian merchants obtained gold, silver, copper, and no doubt some tin from the Sivas region, and occasionally a little iron, which was then a novel luxury worth five times the value of gold.

The Assyrians reaped great rewards in silver, for which the mines of Asia Minor were so famous. A nearby source were the mines of Ak Dagh, between Sivas and Kultepe. But one of the richest areas was the Pontus region south and west of Trabzon. The mineral wealth of the Pontic mines is believed to have been worked in earliest times by the Chalybes and other tribes. Some historians credit this region with the earliest practice of metallurgy. The Cappadocian tablets from the ruins of Kultepe, letters and business agreements dating back to the days of Ur, about 2400 B.C., reveal that the Chalybes of the Pontus had become proficient in the smelting of lead-silver ores, with which they were so abundantly endowed. Some writers suggest that lead-silver smelting had its origin here and spread southward into the ancient Middle East.

Bonanzas of Anatolia

Pontus, so named by the Greeks, was a region which bordered the south shore of the Euxine or Black Sea. It has a long history of rich mineral production. Near Niksar (Neocaesarea), silver mines have been worked since early antiquity. They were still rich enough to furnish Pompey with 6,000 talents of silver, or roughly 6,000,000 ounces. South of Trabzon, at Bayburt rich silver-lead mines were producing when visited by Marco Polo. Farther north, at Gumusane, the lead ores were especially rich in silver, and the deposits still contain considerable amounts of ore. On the Cappadocian border near modern Elazig, was the important district of Keban Maden. A little farther south on the upper reaches of the Tigris River near modern Diyarbekir, there were the rich mines of the famed Arghan Maden district which also contained copper as well as silver.

One of the most productive sources of ancient wealth was the great lead-silver lode of Bulghar Maden, not far from the Cilician Gates north of Tarsus. Prehistoric implements of polished greenstone indicate that the lodes were worked in very early times, and they have continued to produce through many ages. A huge Hittite inscription reveals that the valley entrance to the mines was guarded by a large fortress when the Hittites shipped silver ores to Egypt, where silver was scarce. The silver mines of Bulghar Maden have been used by the Babylonians and the Assyrians, have been extolled by Homer and the Greeks, and have been worked even during modern times.

The tremendous mineral wealth of Asia Minor not only became a mighty stimulant to the westward trend of civilization, but it also served to incubate the development of Anatolian writing, sculpture, and technology. As the caravans from the rich and cultured eastern centers brought their wares and their ideas to Anatolia and Cappadocia, life quickened in all respects on this far western frontier.

The Caravan Trail to Ashur

The activity taking place in one of the many Karums of Cappadocia, let us say Kultepe for example, is typical. The courtyard bulges with exotic goods which have just arrived. Supplies are also being made ready to be sent southward and eastward to the great cities of the ancient world. Silver ingots in the form of rings, plates, wire, but mostly bars weighing about 10 minae, or 11¼ pounds, form an important part of the shipment.

A licensed caravan master stalks about organizing his crew and cargo. He is a stout-hearted frontiersman, brown and leathery from the hot eastern sun. He knows every mountain pass and the slippery dangers that lurk therein, all the precious water holes and the hostile tribes who jealously guard them. He knows where to expect marauding nomads and how to make his stand against them. Caravan travel is hard and grueling, but it is this mode of transportation which civilization has always used to reach faraway lands.

The caravan is ready to move out. Seven hundred miles of primitive trail, barren uplands, mountain passes, and unbridged streams lie between the security of the karum and the civilized comforts of Ashur. The valuable cargoes have been saddled upon the backs of the little black Cappadocian donkeys. The long line of animals at last gets under way. They pass through the gates of the Karum and head eastward from Kultepe across the upland plains. They plod steadily onward, skirt the northern slopes of Asia Minor's highest peak, Mount Argaeus, and cross a pass through the northern end of the Taurus Mountains. They make one camp after another under a great star-lit canopy. Then they turn southeastward climbing mountain spurs and

descending into lonesome valleys until they come to the Ceyland River where Ebistan now stands.

Descending and following the valley of the Ceyland southward, the caravan patiently labors across meanders of the stream until it reaches Marash, where it then turns southeastward. Crossing a long stretch of rugged country it finally reaches the upper Euphrates River at Birecik, not far north of Carchemish. Now traveling in the highlands of northern Mesopotamia, the caravan is past the half-way point when they reach the old Babylonian outpost station of Harran. It is to Harran that the Hebrews, Terah and his son Abraham, and Lot, the son of Harran, will come from Ur of The Chaldees and settle for awhile, before going on to the promised land in Canaan. But we won't pause to probe that story now.

The patient, heavily burdened donkeys and their perspiring escort soldiers cross another barren stretch and come to the very old Tel Halaf. Over 3,000 years before the clattering hoofbeats of the passing donkeys are heard echoing against its ruins, Tel Halaf was just beginning to use copper in place of stone tools. Now, men in 1500 B. C. are freely using a wondrous, modern new metal, bronze, all over the known world.

After crossing the Nahr Khabur River the caravan makes its last weary climb through the rolling, grassy Jabal Sinjar hills and finally emerges upon the Tigris Plain. With shouts of joy the men hail the sight ahead, the rocky headland upon which stands the great walled city of Ashur. High above the ramparts rises the towering temple of their god, Ashur. Eagerly the caravan pushes on. Shouts of welcome greet the men as they pass through the great gate of Tabara, the "gate of the metalworkers." They are home at last!

Assyria's March To Empire

In the same manner that trails blazed by American traders and pathfinders later became highways of national progress, so did this caravan trail of the ancients become a 'Royal Road' across Anatolia for commerce, as well as for conquerors yet unborn. It was the mineral wealth of Asia Minor that furnished the foundation from which Assyria rose to take its place in history. By 1276 B.C., taking advantage of Babylon's weakness under Kassite rule, Shalmaneser I united the city-states of the north, moved the capital from Ashur to Calah (Nimrud) and claimed supremacy over western Asia.

About 1100 B.C., Tiglath-Pileser I, renowned hunter and warrior, led his horsemen and chariots on ruthless campaigns of conquest, seized the Hittite realm and its riches and settled colonists in Cappadocia, defeated the King of Babylonia, and extended his rule to the Mediterranean Sea. Replacing Babylon as the master and the strongest military power of the Middle East, Assyria was now on its march to empire.

Before running its course, it would leave the bloodiest trail yet known to the ancient world, armed with weapons of a newer metal, iron, a metal of a later age which, as we shall see, is to be discovered by the Hittites, another contribution from the Anatolian frontier. Utilizing history's earliest system of nation-wide highways and a terrifying, armor-clad war machine, Assyrian rulers were able to clinch their hold on lands of the ancient Middle East. Meanwhile, their primitive caravan trail, and the 'Royal Road' that followed, became the course which led the civilizations of Mesopotamia, and the Bronze Age boom, westward to the shores of the Aegean Sea, and eventually on to the distant uncivilized lands of Europe.

Civilization Spreads Westward

As early as 3000 B.C., civilization with its arts, religions, and sciences, as recorded on primitive tablets of clay, had begun its spread westward from its place of origin in the valley of the Euphrates, born of man's desire to trade his surplus commodities for materials foreign to his own land. Two main routes carried the traffic: one went by sea from Egypt across the Mediterranean, the other by land through northern Mesopotamia thence across Asia Minor. In earliest antiquity, Egyptian ships had taken to the sea to obtain sorely needed timber at Byblos. Swinging eastward they obtained copper on the island of Cyprus, and even went on farther west to trade with another island in the Aegean known as Crete. We shall witness Crete's outstanding development later; for the present we wish to follow the trail of the caravans which are taking their wares and cultures to western frontiers.

We have already seen the enterprising Sumerians, Babylonians, and Assyrians, pushing the earliest trade routes across Asia Minor. It is quite obvious that the primary motivation behind these expeditions into foreign lands was the search for mineral wealth and trade. Caravanists certainly were not seeking lands more fertile than their

own lush valleys, for their excursions into Asia Minor and Iran were mainly into rugged mountains and barren plateaus.

These hardy merchants were not embarked upon crusades to spread their religions, nor were they seeking superior culture or opulent cities, for they were already leaders in such matters. Only resources which they lacked and needed at home, such as minerals for their busy industries and profitable trade for the disposal of their surpluses and manufactured goods, could have enticed them to endure the extreme toil and hardships of long months on the frontier trails.

The Mound of Hissarlik

Even farther beyond the Assyrian trade station of Kultepe, in central Anatolia, another outpost had developed on the west promontory of what is now the Turkish peninsula. For ages it had been a strategic crossroads of trade. It would become known as the legendary city of Troy. It was Heinrich Schliemann, an American citizen of German birth, who first brought to light the ruins of Troy. Dedicated to the belief that Homeric tales dealt with facts as well as fiction, in 1870 Schliemann led a band of Turkish laborers to a weed covered mound known to the natives only as Hissarlik, which rose about 125 feet above the surrounding plain. The excavators set about digging a deep shaft, but before they had reached the bare, virgin hilltop upon which the first Stone Age village had been built, they had dug through nine successive layers, or city sites including legendary Ilium, each built upon the ruins of its predecessor.

The ancient cities had been fortresses located on a promontory in the Aegean Sea, about three miles from the coast. Commanding the approach to the Hellespont, or Dardanelles, of northwestern Turkey, the site controlled a north-south sea route from the rich Black Sea regions on the north to islands of the Aegean on the south. Hissarlik also straddled an important land route running from the Fertile Crescent in the east to Europe in the west, by way of Asia Minor.

Hissarlik's lowest or first layer contained ruins of a small late Stone Age village built about 3000 B.C. It had been surrounded by massive walls of Cyclopean stones, huge rough-cut, squared stones which the ancient Greeks believed could have been built only by the one-eyed Titans called Cyclopes. In the ruins of the Stone Age village were found tools of flint and obsidian, ivory beads and remnants of black pottery. Even in the late Stone Age, Hissarlik had been a bridge from Asia Minor to Europe, and a meeting place for backward Europeans and venturesome traders from the Middle East. Precious amber from the Baltic region was exchanged here for highly prized glazed blue beads, rare pottery, and ivory.

Troy-Crossroads of Commerce

The Second City, called Troy II, Schliemann mistakenly believed to be Homer's Troy. It was also built of Cyclopean walls, massive stone gates, and houses of brick and timber set upon stone foundations. Numerous implements of copper, bronze, and pottery showing the first rare use of paint, dating the Second City from 2500 to 2000 B.C., reveals the early march of metallurgy toward Europe. A hoard of gold and silver jewelry, ornaments, bracelets, discs and coils of gold led Schliemann to believe that the Second City was the fortress, the "Pergamos" of Homer's Troy, but it was later established that Troy was the Sixth City.

During the period of 2500 to 2000 B.C., Troy II had become a busy commercial center. For centuries preceding the discovery of bronze, Hissarlik had been in touch with Mesopotamia and was familiar with Sumerian techniques in smelting and casting copper. With the dawn of bronze making, and the fortunate occurrence of the nearby metal deposits of Anatolia, Hissarlik's wealth and importance increased, aided by its monopoly of trade routes by land and by sea. Gold, silver, copper, and lead came from nearby lands, lapis lazuli came from Iran, and amber came from the Baltic Sea. Expert craftsmen journeyed from western Asia to settle in the prosperous city of Troy II. The hoard of jewels recovered by Schliemann reveals not only the wealth that resulted from Troy's strategic position, but also the wide range of its commerce. Gold earrings, spiral filagree work, gold discs, beads and pins show the influence of Sumerian and even Egyptian goldsmiths. Other ornaments represent the techniques of Anatolia and the Aegean Islands.

Bronze implements clearly made in Troy II and imitations of such objects have been found westward along the Danube River basin and on into what is now Germany. When backward barbarians of Europe first visited and looked with awe upon the exhibits of Troy's merchants, axe-heads, tools, and ornaments made of a gleaming new metal which was harder and thinner than stone or copper, the commerce of man was ready to continue on its westward way, for the Bronze Age boom had come to Troy.

Spread of The Bronze Age

Supplies of copper and some tin needed for making bronze existed in Anatolia not far from Hissarlik, but it so happened that nature had especially favored the homelands of the western barbarians of Europe with even more useful deposits of the necessary minerals. Then the ancient trade routes, which had first carried flint, beads and amber, now brought copper and tin to Hissarlik. In the Erzgebirge, or "ore mountains" of Saxony and Bohemia, so named because of their many ore deposits, copper and tin minerals still occur together in the same or nearby veins in granite. After the discovery of bronze making, it is noteworthy that the metallurgy of bronze developed in this region on an important scale, as we shall later see. Altenburg and Zinnwald in Saxony and the Muhlbach-Bischofshofen region in Austria would become important production centers in Bronze Age and Medieval times. Although the Bronze Age culture came to Europe a thousand years after its discovery in the Middle East, it spread rapidly westward and northward in Europe when the unimpressive, brown, lusterless stone, cassiterite was found in the rocks of European lands.

As for Hissarlik, wealth and prominence had always attracted covetous marauders and the Second City was no exception; fame and fortune led to its destruction. Nearly a thousand years before Homer's city of Ilium fell, disaster came to the Second City in the form of fire. Solid masses of baked and vitrified brick, charred timbers and masses of calcined rubble unearthed by Schliemann's excavators, revealed the ferocity of the conflagration which destroyed the early bronze city of Hissarlik. And in the many centuries to come, other cities including Homer's Ilium, would be laid low by avaricious conquerors.

The layered mound of Hissarlik has witnessed many stirring events during its long history. Although it won its greatest renown mostly due to Homer's epic tale of the siege of Troy, the ancient and important trade post played a more vital role in transmitting civilization westward to the awakening peoples of Europe. The Bronze Age movement which passed through its portals would not cease until it had covered all the lands of Europe.

Minoan, Mycenaean, Greek, Etruscan, Roman, French, Spanish and English craftsmen would astonish the ancient and modern world with their magnificent works in bronze, as most of mankind reached for its greatest height of ancient culture during the Bronze Age boom. We shall meet again at historic Hissarlik and witness the epic encounter between the Acheans and their legendary Greek heroes under King Agamemnon of Mycenae and the embattled Trojans led by King Priam of Troy, as we watch the rise of a new civilization in the Aegean Sea.

Chapter 5

CIVILIZATION SPREADS TO EUROPE

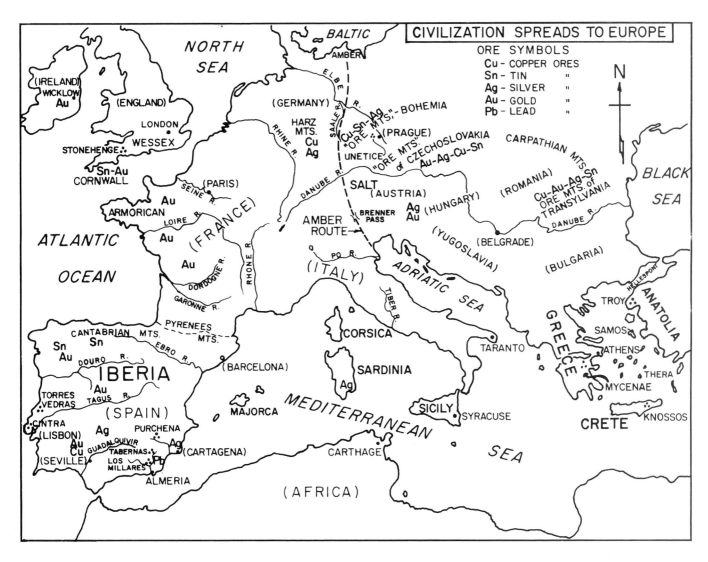

Plate 30 *Excavated palace of Minos at Knossos, Crete.* It was a great trade emporium in 1600 B.C.   p. 36

Plate 31 *Typical Cretan architecture.* Minos' splendid 3-story palace covered six acres.   p. 36

Plate 32 *The Labyrinth, or store rooms, beneath the palace.* Trade created Europe's first civilization in Crete.   p. 36

Plate 33 *The Lion Gate of Mycenae.* This acropolis was the birthplace of Greek civilization.   p. 36

Plate 34 *The Inner Grave Circle and Royal Tombs of Mycenae* in which amazing treasures were found.   p. 36

Plate 35 This was the *face of Agamemnon* thought Schliemann, excavator of Mycenae.   p. 36

Crete The Stepping Stone

While the first rays of civilization were creeping slowly across the valleys of the Tigris-Euphrates in Mesopotamia, and the Nile Valley in Europe, Europe remained in the darkness of the late Stone Age. Gradually, knowledge and technology began advancing westward over two routes, first by the Mediterranean Sea and then by land through Asia Minor.

We have seen the caravans of Mesopotamia plodding across the wastes of Anatolia on the land route carrying their wares and cultures westward through the portals of Hattusas, Kultepe and ancient Troy. The ships of Egypt, however, were the first to spread civilization into Europe, and the island of Crete became the stepping stone. It remained for an English archeologist several millennia later to bring Crete's ancient past to light.

The German archeologist, Heinrich Schliemann, who already had excavated and rediscovered Troy and Mycenae, visited Crete in 1886 planning to seek the legendary palace of Minos at Knossos. When the owner of the land set an exorbitant price on excavation rights, Schliemann withdrew and died a few years later. In 1893, Dr. Arthur Evans, an English archeologist, after seeing a number of engraved stones in an antique shop in Athens, traced them to the site in Crete first designated by Schliemann. In 1900 Dr. Evans and 150 men unearthed one of the most remarkable archeological discoveries ever made. In the ruins of Knossos and other Cretan cities, Dr. Evans found the remains of Europe's first civilization. The record disclosed 10,000 years of the past, including the Stone Age, the Copper and Bronze Ages, and a fabulous era of Cretan wealth and sea power. The story ended with a volcanic explosion and a foreign invasion which brought Crete's brilliant culture to a swift and terrible end.

At Knossos 35 feet of prehistoric rubble was found crowning the top of a low hill that had been occupied first by a Late Stone Age culture. Polished celts, stone axes and some well made pottery were unearthed, representing periods from 10,000 to 3500 B.C. From later levels, a copper axe was discovered on the floor of a prehistoric house that revealed Crete's first step out of the stone age into the age of metals, about 3000 B.C. Dr. Evans and others believe that this first copper came from the valley of the Nile.

Copper Comes to Crete

Man's first useful metal had reached Crete by a circuitous route. Sumerian migrants and metalworkers had developed the first use of copper at Gerza near the Nile. Then, after King Menes had united Egypt, the early dynasties launched one of history's first ventures in the mining of copper on a commercial scale in the Sinai peninsula, as we have seen in a previous chapter. Copper's superiority over stone soon induced Egypt to produce important quantities of metal utensils, tools, and weapons. These increased considerably Egypt's store of trade articles, which she used in procuring materials sorely needed in the Nile kingdom.

As early as 3000 B.C., Egypt's many-oared boats were slowly finding their way northward along the Mediterranean coast, past the yawning caves of Carmel, to Byblos in order to trade their wares for highly prized timber from the 'Cedars of Lebanon.' Favored by prevailing wind and current, some ships continued on to nearby Cyprus and even farther westward to Crete. The return leg from Crete to the Nile delta was about 320 miles, marking the route of mankind's earliest seaborne commerce.

As the first great stone pyramids of Egypt were being raised, the refinements of Egyptian culture were being transmitted to Crete; writing, fresco painting, fine pottery making, the carving of stone statuettes, vases, bowls, seals and similar crafts. Egypt's influence upon Cretan art was so pronounced that it led Dr. Evans to believe that the Egyptians had set up a colony in Crete, possibly by many talented Gerzean metalsmiths who were driven from the lower Nile during Menes' conquest of the region.

It was Mesopotamian metallurgy, however, transmitted through the trade and industrial stations of Anatolia, that became the mainstay of

Cretan metal crafts. Distinctly Asiatic traits can be seen in Cretan axe-heads and other metal forms. Nearness to the land mass of Asia Minor, and favorable winds and currents, induced the migration of venturesome peoples from Anatolia to Crete, attracted by the seagirt security and serenity of the lovely isle. Mingling with the indigenous people, the Anatolians acquainted the early Cretans with Asiatic metalmaking techniques, including the all important secrets of the magical bronzesmiths.

The Magical Metalsmiths

These metalsmiths of antiquity, seeking the freedoms of distant frontiers, were an enterprising breed of artisans, and they attained a high level of respect and importance in their societies. R. J. Forbes, in his excellent treatise "Studies in Ancient Technology" devotes a chapter in Volume VIII on "The Evolution of the Smith, His Social and Sacred Status." He states, "Since the first smiths started their craft in the Late Stone Age and since the first metals were used by mankind, this mysterious trade, which was so different from the other Neolithic arts and crafts, formed the center of a wealth of myths and legends, and the smith grew to form a special type encumbered with religious rites and taboos, endowed by a popular feeling with magical potencies in many directions."

The introduction of metals into man's way of life was one of the most influential advancements of all times. The technicians who became a part of that development were specialists in their own field: the prospector who learned in a primitive way to know the surface indications of possible ore deposits and where to look for them; the miner, who might also be the prospector, who developed methods for digging and recovering the ore from shafts and galleries; the metallurgist who by trial and error and continual research had to unlock the secrets of wresting metal from its sometimes complex ores; and finally the smiths who fashioned the metals into the many ornamental forms, implements, utensils and weapons of his society. The greatest scientific perception and magical powers were attributed to the metallurgists, and the most consummate skill and dexterity was credited to the craftsmen.

The early technicians of Sumer, Babylon and Egypt were not free men. They enjoyed a certain religious prestige and were absolved from various obligations, but they were controlled entirely by the temple priests and contributed solely to the temple economy. However, they were such a valuable element in certain countries that invading conquerors made special efforts to carry them off into captivity.

Myths of the Metalworkers

To the ignorant peasants of ancient times, occupied wholly with farming, the herding of cattle and sheep, and the more prosaic segments of everyday life, the methods of the small, exclusive circle of metalsmiths and their mysterious stones were viewed with awesome respect. The mythical legends that arose around the smiths of primitive times were many and highly varied. Often the smith was considered an ingenious magician of supernatural traits, a wise man drawing special powers from his fires, from his tools, from the metals as well, and often invoking the aid of the gods. Many forms of taboos were common. Fires had to be kept pure and constantly purged with offerings in order to propitiate the gods whose invisible power it was to melt and transform the stones into metal. Every operation was governed by a special ritual. Men who worked in the smelting kiln were not allowed to drink water during the operation. The smiths lived in restricted quarters and had to avoid the company of women; pregnant women especially were not allowed in the smithy.

The singing of religious hymns during the work eventually provided a legend of rich and interesting customs. Since some gods were considered the forgers of metals they were thus linked with the metalsmiths. Ptah, the mummy-form Egyptian god of Memphis, worshipped as early as the First Dynasty, was regarded as the shaper of the world, the mountains and precious stones. The hawk-headed god of the rising sun was Horus, and as gold was the metal of the sun, the goldsmiths were smiths-of-Horus.

The Smiths of Antiquity

As metal supplies and demands increased, specialization became a natural outcome. The goldsmith, the coppersmith, the silversmith, the tinsmith, and the bronzesmith each became highly proficient in his art. From earliest times the goldsmith became the most skilled and respected artisan. His works, on display in many of the world's museums, have not been outdone in perfection by any modern craftsman. It was the custom for smiths to hand down their trade secrets and mystical rituals to their kinsmen, especially their sons and brothers. In time, some of these experts became important merchants and traders, village chiefs, priests, or princes. They were clannish and formed guilds or castes, jealously guarding their secrets and profession, perhaps the first trade unions in history.

We owe the diffusion of the knowledge of mineralogy and the many diverse ores, and the science of metallurgy, which exerted such a profound influence upon the material evolution of mankind, to the craftsmanship and the inquisitive wanderings of the smiths of antiquity. Always it seems the frontiers of civilization have lured this breed of men into lands of new opportunity in quest of new resources, new markets and new freedoms, away from the fetters and restraints of more settled, more disciplined communities. We watched them coursing westward through Asia Minor. Now we meet them again on a sunny isle in the Aegean Sea. But this time the blending of supreme Egyptian artistry with advanced Asiatic technology is to produce an amazingly competent and thriving trade economy, and a civilization whose echoes will never die throughout the whole Mediterranean world.

Cretan Commerce

In Crete, as in Sumer, the need for business records introduced the art of writing. Cretans first used picture signs, or hieroglyphs, adopted from Egyptian and Babylonian forms. Then came the phonetic writing of the Cretans about 2000 B.C. Inasmuch as Crete lacked a ready source of paper, the papyrus plant, Cretan records were made in the Mesopotamian manner on clay tablets. Great quantities of these tablets have been recovered, revealing an older form known as Linear A and a younger writing used subsequent to 1400 B.C., known as Linear B. The latter, used for business transactions mainly in the palace of Knossos in Crete and on the mainland at Pylos and Mycenae, represents basically the first Indo-European language in Europe, which was Greek. About 800 B.C. the Greeks would adopt another script taken from the Phoenicians.

The mineral resources of Crete were relatively small. A little copper existed along the west coast of the island but not enough to support the busy metal industries which were to develop. Copper from Cyprus and Anatolia, gold, silver, and lead from Asia Minor and the Grecian mainland, and tin from Anatolia and possibly from Bohemia, came to Crete. Therefore, it was not the posses-

sion of mineral wealth that made Crete great; it was Crete's strategic position astride the safest and easiest routes of trade, the sea routes, of the booming ancient world. As in Sumer, which also lacked mineral resources, it was her trade and expertise in working metals that propelled Crete into the mainstream of ancient world prosperity.

Because of her island isolation, unlike Sumer and Babylon, Crete was free of the depredations of fringe barbarians, and unlike Mesopotamia, the cities of Crete did not fall into ruinous warfare with each other. The palaces which developed in Crete at Knossos and Mallia near the north coast and at Phaestus near the south coast never were fortresses; they were luxuriant, many-roomed abodes and storehouses of the merchant kings.

"A Rich and Lovely Land."

Homer described Crete as "a rich and lovely land . . . boasting ninety cities."

In the salubrious climate of a sun-bathed island, set like a jewel in the blue Aegean Sea, Crete was allowed to formulate and peacefully develop its civilization over a period of a thousand undisturbed years. Island valleys thrived with prosperous farming villages producing excellent olive oil, figs, medicinal herbs and fruits. On or near the coast, convenient to shipping, centers of industry grew into great palaces, workshops and warehouses combined. About 1700 B.C. a great catastrophe leveled all the palaces of Crete. As this is a region of frequent terrestrial disturbances, the cause no doubt was a shattering earthquake followed by devastating fire. But the Cretans vigorously rebuilt new and greater cities upon the ruins, and Crete then emerged upon its most brilliant period during the years 1600-1400 B. C.

The largest and most noted of these centers was Knossos. Surrounding the palace were the craftsmen and members of the community, a city of 80,000 people, occupying one and two storied houses. Beneath the palace was a great maze of corridors which became known as the "Labyrinth." *Labrys* is an Anatolian term used for the double-axe, a symbol often portrayed with the images of the most sacred deity, the mother goddess. As the symbol of the double-axe, or labrys, was found throughout the ruins of the palace its vast passageways acquired the name *Labyrinthos*, from which we derive our word labyrinth.

Minos and The Minotaur

The ruling kings of Crete became known by the

title Minos in the same manner as the name Pharaoh designated the ruler of Egypt. Therefore, the early Cretan civilization has been called Minoan. According to Greek mythology, King Minos kept a horrible monster, half man and half bull in the labyrinth. It was called the Minotaur, combining the king's name Minos with the Greek word tauros, meaning "bull". The Greek legend states that it was the custom of King Minos to demand from Athens a tribute of seven youths and seven maidens every nine years to be sacrificed to the Minotaur. Minos had invoked this custom in order to avenge the death of his son who had been slain by the Athenians. On the third journey to Crete an Athenian hero named Theseus volunteered to join the party intending to slay the Minotaur. At the palace the king's fair haired daughter, Ariadne, fell in love with the handsome Theseus and gave him a dagger and a ball of thread, with which Theseus was able to destroy the Minotaur and find his way safely out of the labyrinth. But the tale ends sadly, for after Theseus fled from Crete with Ariadne he married the maiden and then thanklessly abandoned her on the island of Naxos.

The Artisans of Knossos

Crete enjoyed the fullest impact of the Bronze Age boom. Its bronze ware became widely known and desired due to its excellence. Bronze tools and implements, axe-adzes, double axes, hammers, even razors and mirrors, and weapons such as daggers, swords, spearheads, and helmets were produced for Crete's expanding commerce. The Cretans became famous also for their pottery. Highly creative types and fresh techniques were devised depicting brightly colored scenes, games, processions, animals, and flowers. Nobles all over the ancient world, especially Egypt, prized greatly the new styles developed by Cretan artisans. This marked the first trend toward individuality in design to appear in Europe.

Knossos became the center of Cretan power. Its huge palace of colonnaded halls, grand stairways, and spacious courtyards covered more than six acres. In places three stories high, the palace stepped majestically up the gentle slope of a low hill. It had a commanding panorama of vineyards, olive groves and fruit trees covering a fertile valley. The palace was a magnificent architectural achievement, the first of such structures to be built in Europe. From the limestone hills blocks of stone were cut so precisely they could be fitted together without mortar. Walls were covered with beautiful frescoes depicting colorful scenes of daily life. Niches contained figures reflecting the Egyptian art in glazing.

Numerous bright red pillars, tapered at the bottom, typified Cretan architectural style. These pillars, with their decorated corbels and arches, supported tiers of royal apartments and gardens. Cretan craftsmanship was superb. Their pottery making, realistic forms of painting, sculptures in stone and ivory, and masterpieces in gold, silver, and bronze exerted a marked influence upon the cultures that were dawning in Europe.

Gay, Glorious Knossos

The Cretans were a dark, curly haired Mediterranean race. Unlike the Semites they were clean shaven. They were gay, joyous people, loved celebrations, processions and athletic contests. They worshipped nature, the mountains, the sun and moon, and a mother goddess who represented the forces of reproduction. The Cretans burned incense to ward off evil spirits and buried their dead with food and articles for use in the afterlife, which mirrored the influence of Egypt and Mesopotamia. But contrary to Egyptian and Mesopotamian customs the Cretans erected no overpowering temples. A Cretan ruler was both priest and king and his altar was in the great palace.

Through centuries of rich cultural development Crete reigned as Europe's first civilization. The wide ranging merchant fleets of Cretan kings commanded the sea lanes of the Mediterranean and became the earliest naval power in history. Their ships linked the civilizations of the ancient Middle East to barbarian Europe. The energizing force of Crete's culture and power was its long-lived trade and prosperity, brought about by the remarkable originality of its art and technology and especially its participation in the swelling tide of the Bronze Age boom.

At the height of her supremacy Crete was stricken with catastrophe. About 1400 B.C., Knossos was leveled to the ground and consumed by uncontrollable fire. Only blackened walls and pillars, charred beams and rubble remained. Nearly everything made of metal disappeared from the palace. Disaster must have come swiftly. Jars of alabaster in the throne room at Knossos were found filled with olive oil apparently awaiting a sacred ceremony. Artisans in the workshops of the city had been overcome in the midst of their labors.

Either a sudden and powerful invasion

followed by ruthless looting, or the earth shattering explosion of an ancient volcano 70 miles away, known as Thera, had quickly ended the greatness of Crete. Perhaps after Thera's devastating blast had leveled the Cretan cities a rival maritime power appeared and dealt a death blow to the Cretan navy. Cretan cities had never been fortified. Instead, they had depended upon the protection of their strong merchant fleet. Lacking defenses the Cretan palaces became easy prey to invaders, who then completed the destruction of the cities.

However, the seeds of Crete's imperishable culture already had been planted elsewhere, in what was perhaps the homeland of the conquerors. Two hundred miles northward across the sea the legacy of Crete would live renewed on the mainland of what is now known as Greece. There, two great cities had risen, Tiryns and Mycenae, which were to become the fountainheads of Greek mythology, culture and civilization.

Mycenae, Cradle of Greek Civilization

Northward, 220 miles across the Sea of Crete from Knossos, lies the Plain of Argos, encircled by the mountains of the Peloponnesus on the southern mainland of Greece. A few miles inland stand the ruins of ancient Tiryns, and ten miles farther are the walls of Mycenae. It was here that the glorious and fertile civilization of Greece began. Its earliest days are bathed in legends of Grecian mythology. It was to Mycenae that the dejected Hercules came to do penance. Submitting himself to 12 years of servitude under Eurysthesus, King of Mycenae, Hercules was given 12 impossible tasks. These included killing the indestructible lion of Nemea, slaying a monster swamp serpent of nine heads, called the Hydra, and diverting the course of two rivers into and through the Augean Stables, cleansing the stalls of a thousand cattle in a single day. As a memorial to his feats, at the western end of the Mediterranean, Hercules set up giant rocks called the Pillars of Hercules. Today they are known as the Rocks of Gibraltar. Such were the legends that veiled Mycenae's mythical past.

For the first time in history the worship of gods in the form of bird-beasts, lions and bulls with outstretched wings, and the elements of the sun, moon, earth, and sky were abandoned. The Greeks were the first to make their gods human, in their own image. And, the science of archeology has proved that the epics of Homer were not entirely fictional. Instead, the Iliad seems actually to have been the first written account of Grecian life, glorified to inspire adulation.

Archeology reveals that as far back as the late Neolithic age, from a vast reservoir of Indo-European races beyond the Balkan Mountains and the Caucasus, waves of Aryan nomads swept into India, Iran and Asia Minor, and also into Europe. Into Greece, the Aryans filtered southward through what is now Thrace, Thessaly, and Boetia, and on into the Peloponnesus where they occupied Tiryns and Mycenae.

The Acheans

About 1300 B.C., when the metal merchants of Troy were growing rich with trade, another wave of migrants, known today as Greeks, crossed the Dardanelles and the Aegean into Greece, bringing with them Anatolian culture, including the use of metals. The warlike character of these invaders is shown by the metal remains found in their graves, including bronze daggers, knives, spearheads and other weapons. The newcomers did not destroy the earlier inhabitants. Instead, they assimilated them, became leaders, and accelerated the economy. Then they began to trade with Crete and the islands of the Cyclades. They have been called Acheans, a name derived perhaps from their homeland in Asia Minor.

Astride a main artery of trade linking the Gulf of Argolis to the Isthmus of Corinth, Tiryns and Mycenae grew increasingly prosperous and powerful. Evidently Mycenaean kings prevailed upon Cretan craftsmen to work at their courts. Copying Cretan methods, the Mycenaeans developed their own merchant fleets and were soon venturing forth for the metals and raw materials needed for their workshops. With a booming industry in bronze the Mycenaeans took over the Cretan mercantile trade and soon captured the markets of the Aegean, the Cyclades and the very important island of Cyprus.

The Copper Isle

Cyprus occupies an eminent part in the history of man. Its great storehouse of copper is not only being worked in modern times, it also provided early man with much of the metal which helped him emerge from the stone age. Its ancient renown was such that from Cyprus came our word 'copper', derived from the Latin word *Cyprium*.

Copper metallurgy came to Cyprus as early as 2600 B.C., but it was the demand from Cretan industry that developed the island's copper resources most rapidly, after 1600 B.C. In addition to supplying Cretan workshops, copper ingots were made and distributed to the coppersmiths of Anatolia, Syria and Egypt by the merchant kings of Crete. The ingots were shaped like ox-hides weighing one talent of copper, perhaps representing the value of an ox. Thus shaped they were easier to carry on the shoulders of men or upon packsaddles. Paintings on tombs in Thebes, Egypt show men carrying ingots of copper to Thutmose III about 1450 B.C. The Amarna tablets in the ruins of the Ikhnaton's palace refer to many shipments of copper from Cyprus in exchange for Egyptian gold and fabrics.

In the 13th century the copper deposits of Cyprus received renewed attention when the Mycenaeans sent colonists to exploit the mines. Their settlement at Katydhata worked the rich ore bodies of the now famous Skouriotissa mines, one of the few deposits of proven antiquity to be worked in modern times. The ore body was rediscovered by an adventuresome mining engineer named Charles Gunther, in one of the romantic sagas of the mining world.

A Copper Legend

Like Schliemann who pursued Greek legends in unearthing Troy, and later, Mycenae, Gunther delved into accounts of fabled riches of the past. He first encountered bitter, frustrating hardships in the wilds of South America and Mexico, and then searched the burning wastes of the Sinai Peninsula for King Solomon's legendary mines. Grubstaked by Seeley W. Mudd and Philip Wiseman, prominent mining men of Los Angeles, Gunther finally reached Cyprus and found the end of the rainbow.

There, black slag dumps of ancient smelters and the tell-tale red "iron hat" outcrop of an ore body disclosed the presence of a once great mine of the Mycenaeans. From a later period a marble stone marker bore the inscription of Sergius Paulus, Roman proconsul of 45 A.D. Nearby were the stone houses and earthen ware of the ancient Cretan workers of 1300 B.C. Today the Skouriotissa mine, and the Mavrovouni mine not far away, make the Cyprus Mines Corporation one of the world's greatest producers of pyritic ore, which is mined for its copper and sulphur content.

Bronzewares of Mycenae

Thus, the copper of Cyprus has played its im-

portant role over the ages. Mycenae especially used it to reach the highest peak of perfection in making products of bronze that became famous and desired in nearly every corner of the ancient world. Although exquisite articles of the goldsmiths were also produced, it was in bronze making, particularly weaponry, that the Mycenaeans excelled all other peoples. They developed a new flange-hilted sword that could be carried around the pommel of a saddle. Now, warriors could be armed and mounted on horseback, becoming the first cavalrymen in history.

Along with metalware went other articles from Mycenae, such as pottery, which were exported eastward to Palestine, Syria and Egypt, and westward to Sicily, Italy and Spain. A Mycenaean bronze flange-hilted sword was even found buried with a tribal chief in faraway Cornwall, England. Amber beads unearthed in Mycenaean tombs revealed that the people of the Baltic region were glad to trade their precious amber for the famed bronze wares of Mycenae. Mycenae indeed was riding the crest of the Bronze Age boom.

Powerful Troy

As Mycenae was attaining the peak of its power and spreading its culture, another strong city-state had become a serious competitive threat to Mycenaean domination. That city-state, in the northern Aegean Sea near the entrance of the Dardanelles, was rich and vigorous Troy. We have already visited Troy, known also as Hissarlik, as we watched civilization move westward over the caravan trails of Asia Minor. At Troy, shortly after 1200 B.C., one of the great conflicts of history, immortalized by Homer, took place between the Mycenaean Greeks, or Acheans, and the Trojans.

In Homer's epic, *The Iliad*, it is made clear that the Greeks were driven to destroy Troy because of the abduction of the Achean heiress Helen, by Paris of Troy. The expedition to eliminate a rival was thus clothed by a mythical tale of gallantry. The story, handed down many centuries prior to Homer's time, which was about 800 B.C., had become a national tradition glorifying Grecian gods and heroes, perhaps to justify the aims of conquest.

The Golden Fleece

The real provocation was Troy's strategic position commanding the north-south sea route from the Aegean into the Hellespont and beyond to the rich metal provinces around the Black Sea. This area included the wealth depicted by the saga of the Golden Fleece. Homer knew of this ancient legend and speaks of the ship "Argo" that carried Jason, Hercules and 50 Greek heroes, about 2500 B.C., seeking the Golden Fleece. These argonauts endured terrifying trials endeavoring to reach Colchis, home of the golden ram.

Flying monsters, called Harpies, plagued them; clashing rocks in the Hellespont barred their way; Hercules slew the vultures that were tormenting Prometheus, and Jason was required to plow the field of Ares with dragon's teeth, using fire snorting bulls hooved with bronze. With the aid of the Sorceress Medea, Jason slew the dragon guarding the Golden Fleece and recovered the fabled treasure. Although the venture was glamorized by exploits of the Greek heroes, we know now that gold and other metals were to be found south of the Black Sea in the region of Colchis, and that for ages grains of gold have been washed from river sands and collected in the fibers of woolly blankets, as well as fleece.

Troy was master also of an important east-west overland route from Asia to Europe. From the east came caravans across Asia Minor bringing lead, silver, gold, horses, wild asses, and even jade from distant China. From the Baltic and Danube regions on the west came copper, tin, and amber. Troy also siphoned considerable wealth in taxes which were levied on articles passing through its portals, another source of irritation to the Greeks. Vast stores of mineral wealth, which were becoming increasingly vital to man's economy, were being dominated more and more by a few important trade centers such as Troy. For such a prize kingdoms have fought many times during the history of the world.

The Fall of Troy

Another circumstance lending bitterness to the struggle was the presence in Troy of a Cretan population, whose ancestors had been driven from burning Knossos. Many Cretans had formerly settled in the Troad, as excavations have revealed. Smarting under the loss of their island paradise a few generations before, it is no wonder that Cretan descendants, mixed with Asiatic and Danubian elements, had good reason to defy the mainland Greeks. Therefore, it was not the face of Helen nor the abduction of this fair-haired daughter of Zeus that impelled the Greeks to launch a thousand ships against King Priam's prosperous city of Ilium. It was Troy's glittering

wealth in trade that brought about the fall of the ancient citadel.

Only the cause and outcome of the events recited in Homer's immortal tale have a place here. We can believe him when he says that it was Agamemnon, King of Mycenae, who led the confederated Greek hosts across the Aegean Sea; that the brave commander, in order to calm frightful winds and tides threatening his forces, resigned himself to the demands of the soothsayer Calchas and sacrificed his own daughter Iphigenia; that it was Agamemnon who saw Troy reduced to ashes after ten years of struggle; and that he returned to his faithless wife, Clytaemnestra, in Mycenae, and finally to his own death.

Not long after the fall of Troy, as had all prior kingdoms, Mycenaean supremacy drew to a close. New waves of Indo-Europeans began drifting into Greece. These were Greek tribes, and although their dialects varied, they possessed a common language. The Aeolians settled in the north; the Ionians took possession of such Aegean islands as Chios and Samos and the areas in western Anatolia that became known as Lydia and Caria. The greatest disturbance occurred with the appearance of the Dorians, about 1100 B.C., less than 100 years after the defeat of Troy. But by then the merchant fleets of Crete and Mycenae had performed their vital part in diffusing the first rays of the Aegean civilization among the peoples of barbarian Europe.

Mycenae Today

No classical columns such as are found throughout Greece are to be seen today at Mycenae. Only great massive walls 25 to 50 feet high, made of huge limestone blocks, outline the ruins. According to Greek mythology only that race of Titans having one eye in the center of their foreheads, the Cyclopes, the favorite workmen and forgers of thunderbolts for Zeus, could have set the heavy stones that average 4 feet thick and 5 to 12 feet in length.

Two large rough-cut stone pillars, capped by a triangular shaped stone lintel upon which had been carved two lions facing each other, form the famous 'Lion Gate' entrance to the citadel of Mycenae. Inside the Lion Gate stands a circle of stone slabs about four feet high and 80 feet in diameter. Within this enclosure Heinrich Schliemann uncovered six tombs cut 15 feet into the underlying rock, from which he recovered 16 skeletons and an astonishing array of funerary treasure. During the period 1600 to 1500 B.C.

this had been the sacred burial place of Mycenaean kings.

After Schliemann had shown his faith in Homer by excavating Troy in 1870, he had moved on to Mycenae hoping to find the grave of King Agamemnon and the treasure of King Atreus, Agamemnon's father. Schliemann recovered a great wealth of golden objects and many bronze swords and daggers beautifully inlaid with gold and silver. Cups of gold, seal rings of gold, carved ivory figures, necklaces and diadems of gold, faience beads, vases of alabaster, and necklaces of amber and amethyst form part of the remarkable treasure that may now be seen displayed in the Mycenaean room of the National Museum in Athens. Most extraordinary are the several funerary masks of beaten gold, reflecting one of the finest examples of ancient portraiture ever made.

Impressive and decidedly significant was the profusion of swords and daggers, and although the bronze was heavily corroded, their ornate handles of gold were as bright as the day they were made. The famous 'Lion Hunt Dagger' was marvelously inlaid with gold and silver figures of huntsmen armed with bows and protective shields, locked in combat with three lions. It is easy to see why Mycenaean trade articles won such renown, as the new and popular metal bronze, combined with gold and silver, was produced so lavishly.

From the Lion Gate and beyond the Royal Grave Circle a broad stone-paved ramp ascends to the royal palace atop a hill that made Mycenae impregnable. Up this road once rumbled the chariots of Mycenaean kings. A few low stone walls and paved courts are all that remain of the palace today. Opposite the acropolis of Mycenae Schliemann discovered an amazing structure which he mistook for the tomb of Agamemnon. It is now called the treasury of Atreus.

An open passageway cut into a low hill and lined with Cyclopean stones leads to an imposing portal. The lintel above the entrance is a huge stone 30 feet in length and about 4 feet thick, all in one piece, weighing about 120 tons. One wonders how men managed to raise it into place 3500 years ago, not to mention cutting the stone with bronze chisels and hammers. The tomb is a vaulted chamber, or tholos, 47 feet in diameter built of inwardly overlapping stones. All of these "Bee-Hive" tholos of Mycenae were found empty, plundered of their treasures ages ago.

A similar but smaller tomb nearby was once thought to be the tholos of Clytaemnestra who, with her paramour Aegisthus, plotted and carried out the assassination of her husband Agamemnon after his return from Troy. Orestes, the son of Agamemnon and Clytaemnestra, avenged his father's death by slaying his mother and her lover. Such are the sad as well as heroic legends that whisper to inquisitive visitors who roam among the ancient walls of Mycenae.

Europe, the Bronze Age Frontier

Aboard the Mediterranean merchant ships of Crete and Mycenae, and on the backs of caravan donkeys across Asia Minor, civilizations that had dawned in Sumer, Babylon, and Egypt were carried to the frontiers of Europe. There, traders found the growing peasant population a virgin market for a wide variety of wares: agricultural implements and household utensils for daily use, and battle-axes and spearheads for warring peoples competing for arable land. Europe possessed vast resources in copper and tin as well as gold, silver, and lead, but, until Europeans learned the techniques of metallurgy, they relied upon the finished articles brought to them by Aegean traders. Later, they would mine and smelt their ores and establish their own metal industries.

The red orb of the setting sun has always attracted explorers westward across the sea. In the Mediterranean the stepping stones for mankind's progress were the Aeolian islands and Sicily, the land of smoldering Stromboli and Etna. Prehistoric cemeteries near Syracuse and those of Monte Salia and Castelluccio have yielded bronze swords and daggers of Mycenaean origin. The volcanic islands of Filicudi, Lipari, and Panarea, north of Sicily's mainland, were depots for the Aegean trade ships.

Some of this trade leaped to the Italian mainland. Near Taranto a Bronze Age village yielded a winged axe, bronze sickles, daggers, razors and Mycenaean pottery. Aegean influences pushed up the Tiber and Arno rivers and on into the Po Valley. But there, a greater impact was felt from an advanced bronze culture that was spreading southward from the Danube River region. From the union of these two cultures, coming from the Aegean and the Danube, a rich and versatile Bronze Age developed in Italy.

Spain—Rainbow's End

The end of the rainbow for these adventurers was

the peninsula of Spain, or ancient Iberia. It was a fabulous storehouse of gold, silver, copper, lead and tin. Gradually, as its wealth was revealed, it became one of the richest prizes of the ancient world. Neolithic Iberia was first exposed to Aegean and Anatolian metal culture about 2000 B.C. A few miles up the Andorax River from the modern port of Almeria is the prehistoric site of Los Millares. Excavated materials reveal that this had long been an agricultural center. When the first Aegean traders appeared, they found farmers growing barley, beans, and flax, and using sickles, hammers, axe-heads, and knives of stone. Into the mountains beyond went eastern prospectors seeking metallic ores. In the streambeds they found placer gold, and in the rocks there were veins containing copper, silver and lead.

These first frontiersmen from the cultured cities of the Aegean were not of the sedentary, highly skilled class of artisans. Like wandering prospectors of later days they knew the habitats of the useful ores, how to mine and smelt them, and how to roughly fashion certain metallic wares. They taught the natives the rudiments of their crafts, established workshops in the villages, and made crude castings of axes, knives and other implements. How fascinated these Iberians, barely out of the stone age, must have been with their bright new tools and weapons of metal.

Los Millares arose from its days of primitive farming and acquired a new, stimulated mode of life. Similar settlements were established up the Almanzora River at Almizarque, and at Tabernas and Purchena, as discoveries of more mineral wealth spread across Andalusia. In the Argave province of Portugal and up the Portuguese coast as far north as Torres Vedras, Cintra and Estoril, archeologists later found numerous bronzes, faience beads, and tholos tombs showing distinct Aegean influences. Such were the tide marks of the Bronze Age, which reached Europe across the Mediterranean Sea.

Bronzesmiths on The Danube

Across land, it was in the valley of the Danube River that the Early Bronze Age reached Central Europe between 2400 and 2100 B.C. So outstanding was this culture that some historians call it "The Danubian Civilization." Flowing eastward over 1700 miles from the Black Forest of Germany and on through the modern countries of Austria, Hungary, Yugoslavia, Rumania, and Bulgaria to the Black Sea, the Danube forms a natural water route, which comes nearer to Asia Minor than any other European river.

This was the most widely used European land route of prehistoric times. Over it went traders carrying flint and salt, and the Baltic amber that was so highly prized by Aegean, Mesopotamian and Egyptian rulers. Much of this traffic went through and enriched the ancient gateway of Troy. Soon after the discovery of metallurgy in the Middle East, Anatolian adventurers apparently explored westward following the Danube valley. It was then, about 2400 B.C., that the Anatolians imparted the knowledge of their superior skills to the Europeans, and taught them the rudiments of winning copper metal from the brightly colored ores.

Evidence of these explorations along the Danube is revealed by the early elemental bronzes later excavated at Troy, which show traces of arsenic, nickel, and cobalt, in addition to copper and tin. Nickel and cobalt are minerals particularly characteristic of Bohemian ores in the Danube region, which supports the belief that some of early Troy's raw materials came eastward from central Europe along the Danube. From 2000 to 1400 B.C., while the virgin resources of the Danube valley beckoned eastern metalsmiths, the cities of Crete, Mycenae and the Middle East were growing populous and rich with industrial surpluses, inducing traders to seek new outlets in foreign lands. It was then that a new market westward in undeveloped Europe became an exciting, untapped frontier.

A regular class of traveling merchants began carrying their bronze wares and other articles along the centuries-old Danube route. Many of their hoards and caches, hastily buried when threatened by danger, have been recovered by archeologists. Finds of sample boxes containing amber from the west and faience beads from the east, along with molds, ingots, coiled metal rings known as 'ingot-torques,' gold wire, copper and tin, mark the ancient routes along the Danube and a branch across Brenner Pass to Italy and the Adriatic Sea.

The Ores of Bohemia

The growing use of metal products naturally led Europeans to become more inquisitive concerning metallic ore deposits in their own lands. Aided by superior eastern knowledge, the systematic classification of minerals and the science of prospecting, mining, and smelting, Europeans were stimulated in their search for raw materials. Some historians believe that Europe created its own bronze industries independently, but it has been well established that the eastern development of metallurgy and the Bronze Age preceded European technology by many centuries.

The fortuitous presence of the vast and varied mineral resources of Thuringia, Saxony and Bohemia in present Germany and Czechoslovakia, and in the Hohe Tauern of Austria, no doubt incubated the Danubian Bronze Age. In the "Ore Mountains", or Erzgebirge, of Bohemia were the necessary copper and tin deposits of present Altenberg and Zinnwald, and the silver and copper districts of Schneeberg,. Annaberg, and Joachimsthal. Copper, silver, and lead ores existed in the Harz Mountains near modern Goslar. Southward in Austria were the copper regions of Muhlbach and Bischofshofen, and the gold deposits near Gastein. The metallic needs during the early Bronze Age were relatively small, therefore the first ore producers barely scratched the potential wealth of these regions. But they would play dramatic roles later in the Iron Age, in the Middle Ages and even in modern times.

The Skilled Uneticians

The most prolific and luxuriant of the Danubian bronze cultures developed in the Unetice (Aunjetitz) region northwest of modern Prague, Czechoslovakia. Highly favored by its proximity to the Bohemian Erzgebirge ore deposits on the west, and on the east by another rich mineral belt 100 miles long southwest of Prague, the Unetician culture developed a very proficient and profitable bronze industry along the Saale and Oder rivers about 1600 B.C.

Perfecting a fine degree of core casting, they made socketed spearheads and chisels, daggers, battle axes, swords and bell-shaped helmets with greater skill and originality than even their contemporary smiths of the Aegean. Their bell helmets and newly invented heavier striking swords came into great demand from battle-axe warriors who thereby attained an advantage over their adversaries. For the needs of this busy bronze industry came a generous supply of copper and tin ores from the green hills of the nearby Erzgebirge. The Uneticians were blessed not only with these vast stores of copper and tin, but also with rich deposits of gold close by toward the south.

A region extremely rich in gold and silver existed southwest of modern Prague. Today it contains such well known districts as Jilove, Milesov, Kasejovice, Velhartice, Roudny and others. From the virgin, untouched ore deposits of this area Unetician chieftains obtained an abundance of gold, which was fashioned into articles for adornment and trade. The desire to live, and to be buried, surrounded by golden splendor prevailed among European lords as it did in the ancient east. This symbol of opulence also enlivened the demand and production of metals.

Another circumstance favored the Uneticians. They were located astride the long used amber route from the Baltic southward to Crete, Mycenae and the Adriatic Sea. Thus, with amber from Jutland on the north, and salt from nearby Austria, added to their bountiful supply of metallic ores, the Uneticians were able to establish an expanding network of trade routes, which extended from the Aegean on the east to the British Isles on the west.

The Bell-beaker Folk

Because of their penchant for engaging in widespread trade, it was the Bell-beaker folk, however, who were the most active in diffusing the knowledge of metallurgy and bronze making throughout Europe. The Beaker-folk were well armed bands of aggressive, resourceful merchants, who roamed from Sicily to the North Sea and from the coasts of Spain and Portugal to the lower Danube. In regions of industrial activity and at the junctions of important trade routes they established their trade centers. In their bands were many highly skilled metalsmiths, craftsmen and pottery makers. Their drinking mugs or cups were bell-shaped beakers made of finely tempered pottery, the distinguishing feature that gave them their name.

The exact origin of the Beaker-folk is an unsolved mystery. Were they migrant traders and metalsmiths from Anatolia or Mesopotamia? Possibly they came from the lower Nile, as their dagger and pottery designs seem to indicate. Perhaps they were the more venturesome elements of the Cretan or Mycenaean civilizations who had been attracted first to the metallic wealth of Iberia, and who then spread outward. One thing is certain—the Beaker-folk intensified the Bronze Age boom, and became the trailblazers of commerce and communication throughout Central Europe.

Bands of Beaker-folk seem to have introduced bronze making to the British Isles. Beaker-folk dead have been found buried with their pottery beakers, daggers and axes of bronze, and their customary buttons of amber incised with

V-shaped perforations, along with the stone wrist guards which were commonly worn by their bowmen. Landing on the south and east coasts of Britain the Beaker-folk spread westward. Some crossed to Ireland where they found gold in the streams of County Wicklow.

Mysterious Stonehenge

In Britain they mixed with the pastoral population, increased agricultural production, and engaged in extensive trade. They inaugurated new religious cults and participated in the erection of great circles of stone, or henges, apparently for observing the rising of the summer solstice sun. The most noted of these monuments is Stonehenge in Wiltshire, constructed in several stages over a period of some 400 years. The first stage was begun by late Neolithic people who dug a series of ritual pits known as 'Aubrey Holes.'

About 1500 B.C., during the Early Bronze Age, a circle of huge stones called Sarsens was erected. Some weighed as much as 40 tons. Carved on some of the stones of the Sarsen Circle were outlines of daggers and a bladed axe resembling bronze weapons of Mycenae, in use about 1500 B.C. Were these carvings the trade mark signatures of far roaming Mycenaean artisans, and were they related in some way to the enterprising Beaker-folk who are believed to have taken part in building a portion of Stonehenge?

Warlords of Wessex

The arrival of new warrior chieftains in the Wessex region of southwestern Britain marked a sudden end to the Beaker-folk's domination of the country. These Wessex lords apparently came from the prosperous, productive Unetice culture in the Saale Valley of Saxony. Far flung trade activities had taken Unetician merchants to distant Britain where they had become familiar with the island's metallic wealth and commercial potentialities. Before long the Wessex chiefs had extended their rule westward to Devon and Cornwall.

In possession of the rich copper and tin deposits of Cornwall, and through control of trade, the newcomers attained considerable prosperity and power. Importing expert craftsmen from Saxony and Bohemia, the Wessex rulers were able to develop their own distinctive types of bronze-ware and jewelry, using gold from Ireland and the ores of Cornwall. They made skillfully cast daggers, battle-axes and socketed spearheads of bronze, and a wide variety of jewelry including necklaces of crescent shaped amber discs bound with Irish gold, and gold lunulae collars similar to those worn by Egyptian nobles.

Wessex lords and their ladies were extravagantly adorned with ornaments of gold, Baltic amber, and even faience beads from far away Egypt. By virtue of supplying their own wants and fashioning articles for trade, "Made in Britain" could have been the popular trade mark on the numerous products that were dispersed throughout Central Europe and the eastern Mediterranean. Such was the high state of culture that had at last come to the British Isles, civilization's farthest westward reach, by land and by sea.

Legacies of The Bronze Age

The Bronze Age culture had spread westward from the Middle East across the Mediterranean to Crete, Mycenae, Sicily, Sardinia and to Italy and Spain. Another surge had pushed up the Danube Valley where it blossomed brightly in the hills of Saxony and Bohemia, then continued westward to Brittany and across the English Channel to the British Isles. After attaining new creativity it rebounded eastward with greater vitality and originality to the land in which it had been born. European metalsmiths had reacted to Asiatic concepts of design with an inventiveness of their own, marking new steps forward in the progress of mankind.

The Bronze Age, speaking generally, covered a period of 1500 years, from about 2500 B.C. to 1000 B.C. Although it arrived in Central Europe many centuries after its first appearance in the Middle East, western man had finally emerged from the darkness of the Stone Age into the bright, promising Age of Metals. And what was most important, he had learned at last to find and to utilize the natural resources available within his environment.

Henceforth, as bronze took its prominent place in industry, commerce and art, and such metals as copper, tin, silver, lead and gold came into expanding use, man's desires for betterment would increase and his spirit of adventure would be stirred anew. He would now embark upon countless trails of exploration. In his search for metallic wealth he would discover the earth. Then would come intellectual, artistic, scientific and spiritual advancements never ending. Many generations of the future would follow in the footsteps of these first adventurers who set their faces toward the westward sun during the widening surges of the Bronze Age boom.

Chapter 6

DAWN OF THE IRON AGE

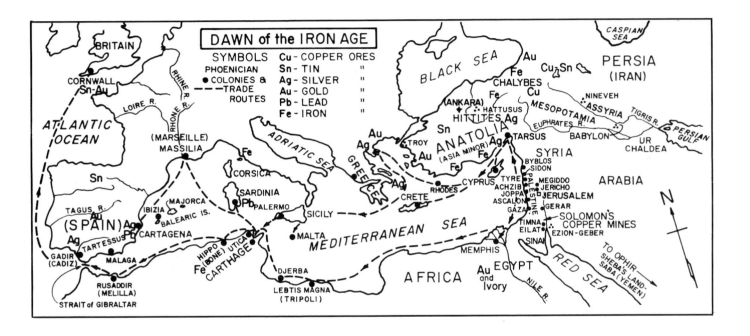

Among the riches of the earth inherited by man, iron became the most useful and invaluable; and, one of his most outstanding discoveries was the science of ironmaking. Iron, and its various forms of steel, today is the keystone of man's material existence. Iron fills a tremendous segment of human needs from the tiniest pin to the loftiest skyscraper; it transports mankind over and beyond the face of the earth; it carries the commerce of the world and provides countless daily necessities and conveniences.

It is fortunate that the ores of this durable metal are so plentiful. About 5 percent by weight of the earth's crust is composed of iron; only aluminum (8%) is a more abundant metal. But this percentage of iron is spread very thinly throughout many forms of rocks. A tiny portion of iron's rusty oxides color the beautiful pink and red sandstones and shales which make up some of the earth's most spectacular scenery. In combination with other elements, iron minerals form various proportions of igneous and metamorphic rocks. Only when iron minerals have become sufficiently concentrated by chemical or mechanical means in certain localities are they rich enough to be of commercial value and become an ore of iron. Fortunately, iron ore deposits are widely scattered over the world.

The Ores of Iron

The earliest form of iron used by man was *meteoric iron*. Objects of iron found in the Great Pyramid at Gizeh, and the iron beads of pre-dynastic El Gerzeh, testify to the metal's early use. Averaging 7 percent in nickel content meteoric iron was usually malleable, fortunately for those who endeavored to shape it. Nickel and cobalt are metals that are usually present in meteorites, but are not commonly found in terrestrial iron ores. This enabled archeologists to establish the celestial origin of most of man's primitive iron ornaments. The ancients recognized the source of their iron material and often called the pieces they found "hard stones from heaven."

Native terrestrial iron is quite rare. Most iron ores are oxides containing from 30 to 60 percent of metallic iron. One of the most common is *hematite*, which the ancients often called "bloodstone" because of its vermilion color. In powdered form it was used as a pigment. *Magnetite* is another important ore of iron. It is

a black, more crystalline oxide of iron, and strongly magnetic. Occasionally it possesses polarity and is known as "lodestone." Needles which were touched to lodestone in order to obtain polarity guided many ships of the world's early explorers. *Limonite* is a brown to yellowish oxide, and in common with hematite it often colors the outcrops of iron ore deposits. When limonite occurs in bogs or swampy places, carried there in solution and deposited by evaporation and chemical reaction with decayed vegetation, it is known as *bog-ore*. A less common ore is the iron carbonate *Siderite*, also known as *Chalybite* or spathic iron. These were the red, black and rusty colored stones that waited for man to discover they contained his hardest and toughest metal, iron.

It seems strange that the purposeful use of iron came more than a thousand years after the development of copper and bronze. But copper had first attracted man's attention because native copper was far more abundant than the very scarce metal, native iron. The bright green and blue surface ores of copper also appealed more to man's sense of curiosity than the less conspicuous oxides of iron. The copper ores were also more amenable to primitive metallurgical treatment than iron ore in producing a workable metal. Iron metal was wrung from its ores only after surmounting many obstacles.

Discovery of Ironmaking

Among the Arundel Marbles now at Oxford, England, is a tablet known as the Parian Chronicle inscribed in 260 B.C. Its 93 lines describe one of the earliest periods of Greek history. One revealing line reads, "From the time when Minos the elder was king of Crete and built Apollonia, and iron was discovered in Ida by the Dactyls and Kelmis during the reign of Pandaion of Athens . . . ." Therein lies one clue as to where and when occurred the momentous discovery of making iron.

The Dactyls of Greek mythology were attendants of Rhea, the Mother Goddess, near Mount Ida in Crete. After the destruction of Crete's great merchant empire some Cretans moved to Asia Minor. Homer refers to a 'Mount Ida' not far from Troy, and there is today a range known as the Ida Mountains southeast of ancient Ilium. Thus there is reason to believe that the Cretans transferred their worship of a holy mountain from Crete to the Troad. With them went their superior knowledge of metal-lurgy, which we have seen displayed in the workshops of Knossos. Since Pandaion, the Athenian king, ruled about 1450 B.C. we have one approximate date for man's first use of iron. However, there were other capable metal-workers in various regions of Asia Minor.

Since Babylonian and Assyrian times caravans had carried their culture and knowledge of metalworking westward into Anatolia, as Asia Minor was once called. Already in the Pontic region south of the Black Sea, there was a tribe known as the Chalybes, believed by some scholars to have been among the earliest and most advanced metalsmiths of the ancient world.

Blooms in The Firepit

Whoever made the discovery, it was a prospector perhaps in either the Troad or Pontic region that gazed with curiosity at an outcrop of red or yellow material which harbored the metal iron. He knew that these rusty stones were used as pigments, but otherwise had been of little value. As his ancestors had first done with copper ores he probably put some of these dull, earthy stones into a firepit containing charcoal, and with the aid of a windy draft endeavored to obtain the highest possible temperature for his fire.

If the fire produced anything it was a scoriaceous mess of slag mixed with dark, lusterless bits of unrecognizable metal. It was not at all like the bright, colorful metal of copper, or the silvery-white metal of tin, which he obtained by customary smelting methods. No wonder that these rusty stones were discarded as useless. But this man unknowingly had made the first *bloom* of iron.

In due time someone thought of reheating and rehammering the drossy mass repeatedly in order to expel the slag. The metal that remained proved to be malleable and workable. It was an ingot of iron which became known as a *bloom*, and these early firepit furnaces, later built of clay or stone, were called *bloomeries*. They provided the simplest and most direct method of producing iron from its ores. Because of the hammering required, the resulting metal became known as *wrought iron*.

Not until man had learned to obtain higher temperatures and a suitable flux to make the melt more fluid was he able to pour the iron into molds to form *cast iron*. When he learned

later to add carbon and such ingredients as manganese, nickel, tungsten or molybdenum to his iron ore, he was able to make *steel*. A form of steel was produced accidentally by the Chalybes because their iron ore contained manganese. The fortuitous combination of various hardening metals occurring in certain iron ores accounts for such famous steels as the blades of Damascus, the Parthian steel of Persia, and the steels of India and China.

Most of the earliest iron produced was of the *wrought iron* type. Bloomeries were built on hillside slopes or in windy places to increase the temperature of the fire. Bellows were later used to force air through holes in the bottom of the furnace. The lava-like slag which formed atop the melt was run off leaving a spongy mass of impure iron, the *bloom*, at the bottom.

Hittite Arms of Iron

Man's discovery that certain red, black and yellowish stones could be made to yield iron launched a great social revolution. An ominous prophesy for future generations also came with the realization that this new metal could be employed to dominate his fellowmen. The first to use iron in warfare, spearheads, battle-axes, swords, and helmets of iron, were the Hittites of Asia Minor. They held the advantage of controlling the peoples, including the Chalybes, who first discovered the secret of making iron.

As early as 2500 B.C. nomadic bands of Hittites, a non-Semitic branch of the Indo-European race, had roamed out of the grassy steppes east of the Caspian Sea and settled in Asia Minor. They chose an area circled by the great bend in the Halys River, a region that became known as Cappadocia. When they entered Asia Minor the Hittites were relatively barbarous, but they finally developed a civilization due to the westward flow of Meso-potamian culture and technology brought by Babylonian traders seeking commerce and metallic ores.

By 2200 B.C. the Hittites had developed a kingdom known as Hatti, with its capital at Hattusas, today called Bogaskoy. Nearly 4000 clay tablets written first in Sumerian, then Babylonian and Hittite script, have been found in the city's archives. These records, including trade invoices, disclose civilization's influence upon a primitive people. By 1750 B.C. the Hittites were powerful enough to raid and destroy Babylon. But back in Hatti, for 300 years thereafter, the Old Hittite Empire languished and was torn with internal strife. Then, out of chaos and the iron bloomeries of newer generations came the period of greatest Hittite achievements and their Second Empire.

The Hittite Empire

About 1385 B.C., significantly coinciding with the discovery of iron making, a brilliant Hittite military leader King Suppiluliumas came to power. With superior weapons of iron and Chalybic steel the Hittites set forth on their horses and chariots to conquer the world. They reached the Euphrates, subdued the Assyrians, penetrated northern Syria and Palestine, then boldly challenged the Egyptians, their one remaining rival, for domination of the ancient world. The warlike and enterprising sons and grandsons of Suppiluliumas went on to establish the Hittite empire as the foremost military and political power in Western Asia. Its influence was felt as far west as Troy and the Aegean Sea. But the very same invention that had been born in their land proved to be the Hittites' undoing.

The processes by which the Hittite metallurgists made iron a new lethal weapon had been jealously guarded due to its great military importance. Although the ironsmiths were forbidden to migrate or reveal their techniques, the secret of ironmaking soon leaked to other parts of the ancient world. That marked the beginning of the end of Hittite supremacy. A growing number of hostile and competitive peoples acquired the process for making iron, signalling the disintegration of the great Hittite Empire. Its glory faded forever.

Hittite Legacies

During the periods of Hittite eminence, their contributions to the advancement of mankind were many. New codes of law became more humane than those of Egypt and Mesopotamia. New forms of columned architecture, and monumental sculptures of lion heads combined with outspread wings of the eagle carved with iron tools, were introduced. Old Babylonian legends including the Epic of Gilgamesh and The Great Flood were copied and preserved for posterity by the Hittites. While it lived, the empire of the Hittites was one of the greatest of the ancient world.

Occupying a geographical bridgehead from western Asia to the Aegean, the Hittite civilization served as an important cultural link between the Middle East and Europe. Hittite art, language, science and technology were added to gifts emanating from the Euphrates and the Nile, and were transmitted westward to benefit mankind. In their employment of iron-making the Hittites opened the door to an amazing new age, The Iron Age. Articles of iron would stimulate trade and communication in all directions and propel mankind forward with increasing momentum. Unfortunately, weapons of iron would tempt many peoples to set forth on trails of conquest. Centuries later Pliny would be moved to say, "the ores of iron provide a metal which is at once the best and the worst servant of mankind . . . but the blame for death must be credited to man and not to nature."

Canaan, Crossroads of History

Situated between two of man's earliest civilizations, Egypt and Mesopotamia, the land of Canaan became an all important corridor through which trade caravans plodded and armies often marched. Its earliest inhabitants had been Semitic nomads who had wandered out of the Arabian deserts ever since 4500 B.C. Some tribes went on to Kish and Babylon on the Euphrates, while others known as Canaanites settled in a land we know today as Palestine.

Lacking mineral resources of their own and being inured to hardships of the trail, the Canaanites turned to trade. They appeared in the bustling market places of Egypt and Mesopotamia and gazed with awe upon the fine cloths and gleaming articles of gold, silver and bronze. Eventually, the Canaanites established industries of their own which produced wares of superb craftsmanship. Opulent cities developed at Jericho, Hazor, Megiddo, Jerusalem, Ascalon and Gaza. Their glittering wealth soon caught the eyes of foreign conquerors.

First came the Egyptians. One of them was Thutmose III. Dressed in gold and leather armor and standing in his chariot of shining electrum, in 1479 B.C. Thutmose overpowered Megiddo and made Canaan subject to Egypt. But 193 years later a rising tide of Hittite power ended Egypt's domination of the region and Canaan again became free—but not for long. A kindred tribe, known as the Israelites, appeared to take possession of their Promised Land.

As early as 2000 B.C., Abraham, the first of the Patriarchs, had led his Hebrew followers from Ur of Chaldea into Canaan taking with him his religious beliefs and the legends of Mesopotamia. The latter included the stories of Creation, The Great Flood, The Garden of Eden and the Tower of Babel. When famine threatened Canaan, Abraham's descendants, known by the tribal name of Israel, moved to Egypt and settled in Goshen in the Nile Delta. There they lived from 1700 to 1300 B.C.

After Ramses II endeavored to enslave the Israelites, Moses led the tribe out of Egypt, crossed the Red Sea and spent 40 years in the blistering wastes of the Sinai peninsula. In an amazing feat of survival and steadfast purpose, the children of Israel followed trails across the Sinai that had carried copper and turquoise to Egypt a thousand years before the Exodus.

Upon reaching Canaan Moses died and was replaced by Joshua, a strong religious and military leader. With the help of other rough Hebrew tribes whose one and only god was Yahweh, or Jehovah, after centuries of conflict Canaan was finally conquered. By 1200 B.C. an intermingling of Canaanites and Hebrews had produced a religious, political, and cultural entity known as the Kingdom of Israel. Hardly had this occurred, however, when a new menace came to the harassed land. On the nearby shore of the Mediterranean Sea appeared the Philistines armed with weapons of Iron.

The Philistines Bring Iron to Canaan

About 1200 B.C. the entire central and eastern Mediterranean world was disturbed by a revolutionary wave of Indo-Europeans sweeping out of the north replacing the older populations. Immigrants from the ruined civilization of Crete, as we have seen, already had settled in Asia Minor. Now, under the pressure of fresh invasions they were being uprooted again.

A certain group, apparently displaced Cretans, sought refuge and new opportunities southward along the eastern Mediterranean shore. In sturdy, many-oared vessels they launched an attack upon Egypt near the mouth of the Nile about 1175 B.C. Heroic carvings on the walls of Egyptian temples depict how Ramses III managed to defeat these "Raiding Sea Peoples."

The Sea Peoples then turned their ships toward Canaan's coast and soon were swarming upon the beaches. They disdained the bows and arrows of the gallant defenders, for these latest invaders were armed with new implements of warfare, great broadswords, spears, and large protective shields of iron. The newcomers succeeded in seizing a rich section of Canaan's coastal plain. It was an important turning point in the fortunes of this strategic land. To Canaan had come the Philistines and The Iron Age.

Egypt had called the sea raiders "Purasati"; the Old Testament referred to them as "Philistines" and the Greeks subsequently named them "Palaestina." It is ironic that this land received the name Palestine not from its original settlers, the Canaanites or the Israelites, but from these venturesome Philistines. Over 3000 years later the land would receive its modern name, Israel.

A highly civilized but warlike people, the Philistines took over the plain bordering the Mediterranean, which now includes the cities of Gaza, Gerar, Ascalon, and Joppa (Jaffa). They specialized as blacksmiths who fashioned their wares from ingots of iron imported from outlying regions, for Palestine was poor in iron ores.

The introduction of the Iron Age brought notable economic advancements to Palestine. The workshops of Joppa and Gerar soon hummed with activity. At Gerar, Sir Flinders Petri unearthed furnaces used for case-hardening and forging iron, and a large store of picks, adzes, ploughshares, and hoes, perhaps the oldest man-made objects of iron ever recovered.

Emulating the Hittites, the Philistines also monopolized the manufacture and care of iron wares. Biblical accounts reflect the plight of the Israelites who complained, "Now there is no smith found throughout the land of Israel, for the Philistines have said, Lest the Hebrews make their own swords and spears. But all the Israelites went down to the Philistines to sharpen every man his share, his axe, and his mattock."

The Israelites Subdue The Philistines

If these Cretan descendants were first of non-Semitic Indo-European stock it was not long before they had become a Semitized people. Eventually they were overcome by an able Hebrew warrior named Saul, who united the tribes of Israel and ended Philistine domination. After Saul died in battle his son-in-law David seized the Canaanite citadel of Jerusalem and made the city his residence and the religious capital of the Kingdom. A heroic soldier, slayer of Goliath, poet, singer and brilliant statesman, David created a small pastoral empire from the Sinai to Syria, and enjoyed a long prosperous reign from 1013 to 973 B.C. Under David's rule both the Canaanites and the Philistines ceased to be a threat to the Kingdom of Israel.

David's son, Solomon, inherited the throne, receiving his name from the Hebrew word "Shalom" symbolizing peace. Both David and Solomon had established close relationships with a new class of merchants who had come into prominence on the coast of Palestine. Known today as Phoenicians, these people were to carry civilization into the farthest corners of the known world. Among their many skills in fashioning metal wares they would make good use of iron-making which they had inherited from the Philistines.

Some scholars believe that the Phoenicians were dispossessed Canaanites who turned to industry and trade after losing leadership of the land. However, Herodotus reported that the Phoenicians had migrated from the Persian Gulf or Babylonia as early as 2750 B.C. For certain, they were highly accomplished metalsmiths and traders who established thriving seaports such as Byblos, Beirut, Sidon, and Tyre on the present coast of Lebanon, and at Achzib and Acre on the coast of modern Israel.

The Wily Phoenicians

The name Phoenician was derived from the Greek word *phoinix* which referred to either the red purple dye used in their renowned fabrics, or to their coppery-red skin tanned by the Mediterranean sun. Using timbers brought down from the Cedars of Lebanon in the mountains above Byblos, the Phoenicians became expert ship-builders. To spread their trade and to defend their harbors and sea lanes they created the most powerful fleets of the ancient world. Rowed by many slaves and assisted by large square sails, these vessels were hailed everywhere with great anticipation.

Having assimilated the best of Egyptian and Babylonian techniques, the Phoenicians attained a magnificent degree of perfection in their craftsmanship. People lined the shore and gazed in amazement at the luxurious displays of gold and silver jewelry, the elaborately scrolled plates and bowls of silver and bronze, and the ornate bottles of colored glass and alabaster filled with unguents and rare perfumes.

The Phoenicians won great renown for their gorgeous purple fabrics which were colored with dyes obtained laboriously from the murex shell-fish found on their shores. The expensive cloths were sought by rulers of every land and became a widely known symbol of royalty. There were also large displays of daggers, swords, helmets and shields of bronze, but most intriguing to the natives were the implements and weapons of iron that were now coming into vogue.

Arriving on the coast of Asia Minor and Cyprus the Phoenicians exchanged their merchandise for ingots of silver, copper and gold to be used by the metalsmiths of Tyre, Sidon and Byblos. Farther westward, beyond the Strait of Gibraltar, went the Phoenicians to obtain tin in far away Cornwall, Britain. According to Herodotus, the Phoenicians even circumnavigated the continent of Africa as early as 700 B.C., which would have been 2000 years before Vasco da Gama reached the Cape of Good Hope. The Phoenicians, however, concealed their routes of trade in order to discourage competition.

The Silver of Tartessus

At the mouth of the Guadalquivir River on the coast of Spain the Phoenicians founded the important colony of Gadir, now known as Cadiz, about 1100 B.C. They had seen natives using common drinking mugs made of silver, which led them to seek the metal's source northward up the valley of the Guadalquivir. Rich in silver, copper, and gold, this region became known as Tartessus, probably the Biblical Land of Tarshish. It was there that the Phoenicians found the greatest mineral wealth. Later, it would lead to colonization of the region.

Silver was so plentiful, said Diodorus, the Greek historian, that the Phoenicians replaced their customary iron anchors with ingots of silver. The Phoenicians themselves were neither miners nor prospectors; they were unrivaled mariners and shrewd, unscrupulous traders. When not engaged in disposal of their wares they attacked villages and seized the able-bodied men and attractive females and sold them in the slave markets of the world. Others were used to exploit the immense, untapped ore deposits of Spain.

To the ever hopeful metal seekers of antiquity, the first great bonanza-heaven found in the western Mediterranean was fabled

Tartessus, now the province of Andalusia of modern Spain. In ancient times it was the richest mineralized region in the world. It was the light that beckoned treasure seekers and civilizations ever westward. It was the goldfield of California, the Yukon, the Klondike, and all other Eldorados rolled into one. It would play many stirring roles in the history of Europe.

Paper from Byblos

At the Phoenician seaport of Byblos, the papyrus plant, imported in large quantities from Egypt, was used for making records of their transactions. Paper replaced clumsy tablets of clay. As in the past, the complexities of commerce led the Phoenicians to develop a rudimentary alphabet containing 22 letters, but without vowels to match the sounds of their language. Later, the Greeks would adopt this script and add letters for the vowel sounds, the first being "alpha" and the second "beta", hence our word alphabet. As navigators and explorers the Phoenicians had few equals in history, but their greatest contribution to mankind was in originating the alphabet and in transmitting eastern culture to the western world.

Byblos, Sidon and opulent Tyre became noted Phoenician city-states. Both King David and his son Solomon entered into friendly and profitable trade relations with Tyre's powerful and astute King Hiram. Since Hebrew law forbade the making of graven images there were few artisans among the Israelites. When Solomon resolved to have a great temple worthy of Yahweh, and a magnificent palace for himself, he called upon his good friend Hiram to provide the craftsmen and the materials. On a low knoll in Jerusalem, now occupied by the Moslem shrine Al-Haram-Al-Sharif, the Phoenicians built Solomon's Temple, using huge blocks of limestone cut in the nearby hills.

The Riches of Solomon

Prominent bronze pillars flanked the entrance to Solomon's great temple. In the courtyard an enormous bronze vat upheld by huge bronze bulls contained holy water. The interior of the temple was of carved cedarwood overlaid with gold. Two large gold plated cherubim guarded the Ark of the Covenant. Solomon's palace, many times larger than the temple, contained great halls lined with statuary, and its walls and

ceilings were ornately carved cedar decorated with bright colors and gold leaf. Nothing remains of these structures, but one wonders, where was the fountainhead of Solomon's vast wealth?

Southward from the Dead Sea to the Gulf of Aqaba a narrow valley cleaves the barren, torrid landscape which forms the strife-torn boundary between Israel's Negev desert and Jordan. The Israelites first saw this region during the ordeals of the Exodus. En route they had passed the copper-bearing sandstones and Egyptian mines of the Sinai. When they reached Wadi Araba they noticed that the outcrops of green malachite resembled those of the Sinai. The Bible called this the Wilderness of Zin "in whose hills thou canst dig for copper."

It was here on the western edge of Wadi Araba, some 15 miles north of modern Eilat, that Solomon found the wealth that enabled him to launch his era of trade and prosperity. Today, many of the colorful green stones of copper from this same region are made into jewelry in modern Tel Aviv. These stones were a blessing not only to Solomon, they are today providing wealth to Israel from a modern open pit mine named Timna Copper Company.

Solomon's Mines

Towering red sandstone cliffs called "The Pillars of Solomon" today greet tourists who visit "Solomon's Mines." But one must go much farther in order to penetrate this eerie area. Curious formations resembling sphinxes, prows of ships and lofty spires, stand in hushed solitude under a blue sky. Here and there over the parched desert terrain are piles of black slag. Mutely they mark the ancient mining and smelting sites. One slag pile is larger than the rest. Surrounded by a wall of fallen stones it is known as the "slave circle." Here, captives worked in the broiling sun, reducing the green copper ore to crude metal in small earthen pits.

The Old Testament called this place "The Valley of Blacksmiths." In Chronicles it was reported that there were 80,000 miners in these royal mines. They apparently worked numerous but small surface exposures of rich copper ore, as did the Egyptians in the Sinai Peninsula. Where horny human hands labored 3000 years ago, giant power shovels in a large open pit now lay bare the green and blue copper minerals that occur scattered through the sandstone strata. Otherwise the surrounding landscape of serrated cliffs and flat topped mesas, horizontally banded with layers of red and buff hued sandstone and shale, remains indifferent to change.

Strategic Ezion-geber

Eastward from Timna, across the barren Wadi Araba covered with sand and tamish bush, rise the red tinted mountains of Jordan. Where these mountains dip their burning feet into the blue Gulf of Aqaba a few miles from Eilat stands the ruin of King Solomon's ancient copper smelter, known as Ezion-geber. It belonged to Solomon, but it was operated by Phoenician metallurgists. Copper produced here was used as barter for materials which Solomon desired from other lands, gold from Ophir, perfumes, spices and incense from Arabia and India.

Ezion-geber was no less important as a fortress on one of the most important commercial highways of history. As early as 2500 B.C., it was on a caravan trail that carried ivory and spices from India. And, as an outlet to the Red Sea and the Indian Ocean, Ezion-geber became a vital naval base for King Solomon and his Phoenician cohorts. The Bible says, "And King Solomon made a navy at Ezion-geber on the shore of the Red Sea in the land of Edom. And Hiram of Tyre sent in the navy his shipmen that had knowledge of the sea. And they came to Ophir and fetched from thence four hundred talents of gold, and brought it to Solomon ... for the King had the navy of Tarshish, bringing gold, silver, almug trees (sandalwood), ivory, apes and peacocks."

Where is Ophir?

Where was this fabulous land of Ophir? So undimmed has been its legendary wealth that optimistic prospectors throughout the ages have endeavored to bless their finds with the magical name of Solomon's bonanza. It is fascinating to see the number of mines over the world that bear the name "Ophir." In trying to determine ancient Ophir's location, the three years required to reach the land and return eliminates such nearby places as Egypt's Wadi Allaqi where gold occurred abundantly. Solomon married a Pharaoh's daughter, but it is unlikely that Egyptian gold was included in the dowry.

The Pharaoh's Land of Punt in Africa can also be discarded because the gold of Punt was noted for its greenish cast due to its being alloyed with antimony or copper. Ophir's gold, however, was celebrated for its pure, yellow color. The Bible makes several references concerning the rich, yellow character of Solomon's Ophir gold, a purity which today is expressed in parts per thousand of gold, termed 'fineness.'

We are led to Arabia to look for Ophir and for gold of such fineness. In ancient times, gold had been produced in several meandering wadis of this vast desertland, such as the Wadi ar-Rima and Wadi Dawasir. Other known gold regions existed not far from Arabia's western coast, including Asir. A well known mine of antiquity is the Mahd Dhahab southeast of Medina. Farther south in present Yemen was the land of Sheba, or Saba. It was a fabled source of ancient gold.

According to the Bible the Queen of Sheba was one of the rulers of Saba. The capital was Marib, 60 miles northeast of modern San'a. Marib was a great trade center on the famous overland route from southern Arabia to Egypt, Canaan and Mesopotamia by way of Ezion-geber. It was probably to seek assurance of the continued use of this land route that caused the Queen of Sheba to visit Solomon, bearing "very much gold and precious stones," and not the fabled purpose of testing the King's wisdom. The mainstay of Sabaean livelihood was at stake when the Phoenician trade ships on the sea began to compete with this established overland route of commerce.

Sheba's Golden Land

Ancient writers such as Strabo later described the land of Sheba, saying, "They exceed the neighboring countries in wealth. All the people seem to flow in streams of gold and silver. Their vessels and cups are of gold and silver. Their beds and chairs have feet of silver. Gold was obtained not as gold dust but as nuggets. They make collars of these nuggets which are the size of olive stones and walnuts, and they string them alternately with transparent stones and sell them cheaply. Copper is worth thrice, iron double, and silver ten times its weight in gold."

In 738 B.C., according to Assyrian records, the great militarist and empire builder Tiglath Pileser III received gold, silver and incense from the Queen of Arabia, and about 700 B.C. Sargon II obtained gold and camels from the

King of Sheba. As late as 600 A.D. a Sabaean king boasted to the Persian conqueror Khosrau that in his land "the hills are of gold and its dust silver." Allowing for excessive enthusiasm in all these reports, it must be considered nevertheless that Saba was rich in precious metals.

The lack of modern gold production has discouraged some scholars from seeing Arabia as the land of Ophir. It should be remembered, however, that most mining districts eventually become depleted. Many great gold deposits in America, including the far famed and prolific gold bearing streams and veins of California's Mother Lode, are now virtually abandoned. It is not surprising that Sheba's golden land, famed 3000 years ago, is today only a Biblical memory.

The Ships of Tarshish

A voyage of three years, reaching out 4000 miles, would have taken the ships of Hiram and Solomon to Bahrein on the Persian Gulf where Mesopotamians had once secured pearls and precious metals. The Phoenician ships of Tarshish, largest yet to sail far-off waters, could have continued to the coast of India to be loaded with spices, sandalwood, ivory, peacocks and gem stones. Homeward bound these traders could have brought incense from the Hadramaut region of present Aden. Then, the final and richest cargo would have been collected in Saba, the land of Sheba.

The silver, copper and tin of Tartessus in the far west, and the exotic resources of India far to the east, had lured men in their primitive vessels upon the longest sea voyages of early commerce. Among the tempting articles of barter fashioned in Phoenician workshops, there was an exciting array of implements made of iron, man's newest metal. As a result, the Iron Age was diffused much more rapidly than the Bronze Age had been in the previous thousand years.

But the shining splendor of Solomon's throne of ivory and Ophir gold and the aura of wealth emanating from Tyre, whose streets were said to be rich with the dust of silver and gold, already had attracted envious aggressors. The disintegration of Solomon's kingdom and the power of Phoenician cities in Palestine was near. And, it would be arms made of iron that would hasten their downfall.

The Iron-girt Hordes of Assyria

With the aid of new and powerful weapons of destruction, man's next wave of pillage and conquest was launched by the Assyrians who had long yearned for an outlet to the Mediterranean Sea. Only the strong and opulent cities of Phoenicia and Israel stood in the way. Then, after Assyria acquired the secret of ironmaking from the Hittites she devised the first blitzkrieg military force, an army protected by armor of iron and spearheaded by siege engines equipped with battering rams tipped with iron. Cavalry units and swift charioteers bearing iron tipped lances, archers and pikemen carrying huge shields, cutlasses, maces and battle-axes of iron, swept all opposition before them.

A sadistic system rewarded Assyrian soldiers with booty in proportion to the number of severed heads brought in from the battlefield. Fallen foes were decapitated on the spot. Only craftsmen and metalsmiths needed in Nineveh, the Assyrian capital, were taken as prisoners. Intoxicated by their irresistible power the Assyrians struck terror in the hearts of everyone in their path. Desolation everywhere followed in the wake of the armies from Nineveh. Man had made shameful use of one of earth's most bountiful blessings, the reddish stone of iron, which fittingly he had named 'bloodstone.'

With the news of their ruthlessness traveling before them, one Assyrian conqueror after another descended upon the Phoenicians and the Israelites. In 853 B.C. came Shalmaneser III, followed by Tiglath-Pileser III in 734 B.C. Ten years later it was Sargon II. When archeologists excavated Sargon's sumptuous palace they found 200 tons of iron bars and countless weapons, chains, ploughshares and other implements of iron, showing how completely the Iron Age had come to Assyria.

When Sargon's son Sennacherib became king of Assyria he vented his hatred of ancient Babylon, the old Assyrian rival, by destroying the city. Wholesale massacre, consuming fire and flooding obliterated a civilization that was a thousand years older than Nineveh. In 648 B.C. Ashurbanipal extended raids into Egypt, sacked Thebes and carried off immense plunder in gold and precious stones and thousands of captives. But Assyria was nearing the end of her bloody trail of oppression. Another Semitic people, the Chaldeans who had long occupied the southern part of Babylonia, had risen and were ready to challenge Nineveh and restore Babylon to power.

Nebuchadnezzar, King of Babylon

Nineveh was seized and destroyed in 612 B.C., never to rise again, by Nabopolassar who then founded a new Babylonian empire. Israel and Phoenicia had barely sighed with relief at the destruction of Assyrian despotism before they were assailed again, this time by Nabopolassar's son Nebuchadnezzar. In 586 B.C., after 16 months of seige, the Chaldean entered Jerusalem amid a hurricane of fire and devastated the city, including the Temple of Solomon. He extinguished what had remained of the kingdoms of Israel and Judea and led 10,000 Hebrews in chains across the dusty deserts to Babylon. There, these captives, along with thousands of Phoenician craftsmen, were used to further embellish the great palace and public buildings of Babylon.

With enormous wealth in confiscated metals and an unending procession of captives pouring into Nebuchadnezzar's capital, Babylon had regained her prestige and splendor after centuries of oblivion. Archeological discoveries confirm many of the vivid descriptions furnished by Herodotus, who visited Babylon in the 5th century B.C. A great outer wall eleven miles long crowned with hundreds of towers encircled the city. The most famous entrance was the Ishtar Gate. It was completely covered with bright blue glazed tile upon which 500 red and yellow enameled emblems and bulls stood out in relief on the blue background.

Through the Ishtar Gate passed the principal thoroughfare, the Processional Way. It led to the great 300 foot high ziggurat of Babylon, known in the Bible as The Tower of Babel. It was a man-made mountain built of stones and dirt covered with burnt brick cemented with bitumen obtained from the surface seepages of oil pools then unknown. Farther on was the lofty Temple of Marduk the supreme god of Babylon. Its shining pinnacle of gold was visible for miles around.

Mighty Babylon Has No Rival

Nebuchadnezzar's palace and Hanging Gardens were famed worldwide. The palace was a walled citadel encompassing five large courtyards which bustled with the commercial activities of the king. The interior of the palace was magnificent. A symbol of regal power was the throne room and audience hall 160 feet long and 60 feet wide, scene of the famed feast of Belshazzar. Walls and stately columns were covered with blue glazed brick elaborately decorated with gold and enameled garlands of yellow, white

and red lotus petals. Doors were made of cypress and cedar inlaid with ivory, gold and silver. Hinges and thresholds were of gleaming bronze. This lavish display of metals exemplified man's exuberant enjoyment of the wealth in natural resources that were being unearthed throughout his domain.

Above the palace, supported by a vast system of columns, were the celebrated 'Hanging Gardens of Babylon.' Palms, ferns, flowers and exotic plants imported from all parts of the empire were planted in many feet of topsoil, providing deep, cooling shade for members of the royal court. Water was pumped to irrigate the gardens by means of buckets attached to treadmills operated by slaves working day and night.

Trade routes converged upon Babylon ranging from the Caspian Sea to India, from Persia to Palestine and Arabia, and from Egypt to Asia Minor. Over these routes Babylon collected immense quantities of metals by exploiting the ore deposits of other lands and by seizing riches won by conquests. Using thousands of captive craftsmen brought from every land Babylon converted these metals into articles of trade and made the city the commercial center of the world. Rich, powerful Babylon had no rival.

The Wealth of Carthage

Although weapons of iron had enabled the Assyrians and the Babylonians to devastate Israel, Judea, and Phoenicia, a hidden windfall awaited mankind. The center of man's future development would be forced toward the central and western Mediterranean. The first significant step was the transfer of Phoenician enterprise to their recently established colonies of Carthage and Utica on the northern coast of Africa near modern Tunis.

After Nebuchadnezzar destroyed Jerusalem and seized Tyre the Phoenician cities on the eastern Mediterranean coast lost their independence. Their navies, however, survived and remained intact. Attracted by strategically located twin harbors capable of berthing over 200 ships the Phoenicians had founded Carthage about 814 B.C. Turning to the enormous undeveloped metallic wealth of Spain, known to the Phoenicians for 300 years as Tartessus, and utilizing her favorably situated trade center, Carthage grew to a flourishing city of 700,000 people.

Ruling the sea with undisputed power, the ships of Carthage brought materials from all directions to supply the workshops and to fill the warehouses of the great industrial complex. From Egypt came ceramics, flax, and papyrus; through an Egyptian canal that connected the Red Sea and the Nile with the Mediterranean vessels carried spices, incense, pearls, precious stones, and gold from Arabia and India; lion and leopard skins and ivory came from Africa, and from Tyre came the purple fabrics for which the Phoenicians were renowned.

Carthage—Master of The Seas

Spreading her control of the Mediterranean, Carthage established colonies on the island of Malta and at Motya on the western tip of Sicily. On Sardinia a colony was formed at Caralis, the modern port of Cagliari. Farther west, in about 650 B.C., Carthage planted colonies in the Balearic Islands. Later, she founded the important colonies of Carthago Nova, today's Cartagena, as well as Malaga and Sexi (modern Almunecar) on the southern coast of what is now Spain. These were seaports for a hinterland rich in mineral deposits.

By 500 B.C. Carthage had taken on the mantle of the richest city on earth. As a maritime commercial power and colonizer she spread the arts, sciences and culture of the Middle East to the shores of Barbarian Europe. Of all the resources at her command, Carthage's most abundant storehouse of wealth came from her exploitation of Spain's ore deposits. Strabo, the Greek traveler and geographer, stated that Carthage owed her rise to power to the silver riches of Tartessus. It was with Spain's silver that Carthage paid her soldiers and seamen and maintained the forces that dominated the Mediterranean Sea.

Carthage was soon to desperately need these resources to prosecute her wars with threatening rivals, for new powers were rising in the central Mediterranean. They too, had their eyes on the mineral wealth of Spain, and already were embarking on campaigns of colonization. Among these were the Greeks who were about to take the center of the world stage.

Chapter 7

THE GREEK CIVILIZATION

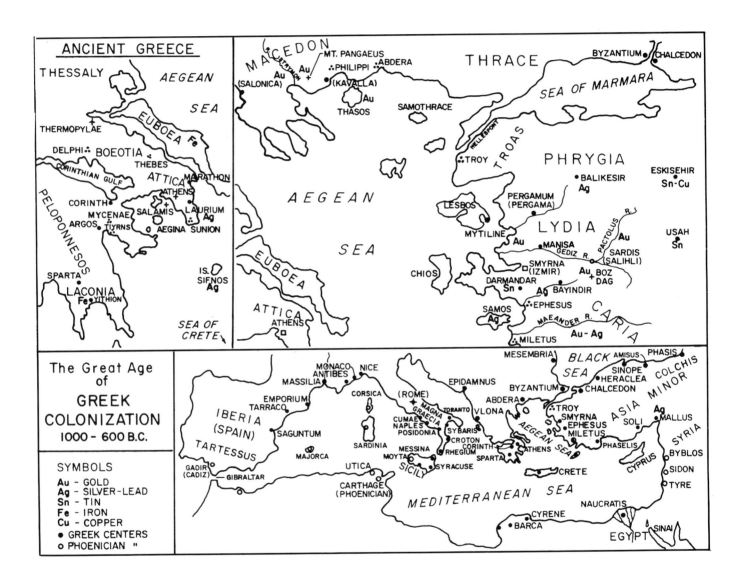

ANCIENT GREECE

THESSALY — AEGEAN SEA — EUBOEA Fe — THERMOPYLAE — DELPHI — BOEOTIA — THEBES — CORINTHIAN GULF — ATTICA — MARATHON — ATHENS — PELOPONNESOS — CORINTH — MYCENAE — SALAMIS — LAURIUM Ag — ARGOS — TIYRNS — AEGINA SUNION — SPARTA — LACONIA Fe — YITHION — IS. SIFNOS Ag — SEA OF CRETE

MACEDON — MT. PANGAEUS — PHILIPPI — ABDERA — Au (SALONICA) — Au (KAVALLA) — Au THASOS — SAMOTHRACE — THRACE — BYZANTIUM — CHALCEDON — SEA OF MARMARA — HELLESPORT — TROAS — TROY — PHRYGIA — BALIKESIR — ESKISEHIR Sn-Cu — PERGAMUM (PERGAMA) Ag — LESBOS — MYTILINE Au — MANISA — GEDIZ R. — PACTOLUS R. — SARDIS (SALIHLI) Au — USAH Sn — SMYRNA (IZMIR) — DARMANDAR Sn — Au BOZ DAG — Ag BAYINDIR — CHIOS — EPHESUS — SAMOS Ag — MAEANDER R. — CARIA — MILETUS Au-Ag — AEGEAN SEA — EUBOEA — ATTICA ATHENS

The Great Age of GREEK COLONIZATION 1000 - 600 B.C.

SYMBOLS
Au - GOLD
Ag - SILVER-LEAD
Sn - TIN
Fe - IRON
Cu - COPPER
● GREEK CENTERS
○ PHOENICIAN "

MONACO — ANTIBES — NICE — MASSILIA — EMPORIUM TARRACO — IBERIA (SPAIN) — SAGUNTUM — TARTESSUS — MAJORCA — GADIR (CADIZ) — GIBRALTAR — UTICA — CARTHAGE (PHOENICIAN) — CORSICA — SARDINIA — (ROME) — MAGNA GRAECIA — CUMAE — NAPLES — POSIDONIA — TORANTO — SYBARIS — CROTON — RHEGIUM — MESSINA — MOYTA — SICILY — SYRACUSE — EPIDAMNUS — VLONA — BYZANTIUM — ABDERA — CHALCEDON — TROY — SMYRNA — EPHESUS — MILETUS — CORINTH — SPARTA — ATHENS — AEGEAN SEA — CRETE — PHASELIS — CYPRUS — MESEMBRIA — BLACK SEA — AMISUS — PHASIS — SINOPE — HERACLEA — COLCHIS — ASIA MINOR — SOLI — Ag MALLUS — SYRIA — BYBLOS — SIDON — TYRE — MEDITERRANEAN SEA — NAUCRATIS — CYRENE — BARCA — EGYPT — SINAI

Plate 51 The *"Owls of Athens"* became the supreme commercial currency of the 5th century B.C.   p. 88

Plate 52 *Coins of antiquity* disclose national prosperity, extent of commerce and portraits of historic leaders.   p. 88

Plate 53 Near *the Greek theater at Thoricus* Cretan and Mycenaean miners dug for silver 3,500 years ago.   p. 88

Plate 54 *The ancient mine pits of Maronea* in Laurium's hills supplied silver for the defense of Greece.   p. 88

Plate 55 In *the cisterns of Soureza*, a mining camp of 483 B.C., water was stored for the concentrating tables.   p. 88

84

Land of Hellas

According to tradition, King Deucalion and Queen Pyrrha of Thessaly were the only human pair to survive a great flood in an ark which came to rest upon Mount Parnassus. Apparently this Sumerian legend of the Great Flood had been carried by traders westward across Asia Minor and repeated in the land of Hellas. It was from the survivors' son Hellen that all the Greek speaking peoples received their common name, Hellenes. Achaeus, Aeolis, Dorus and Ion, descendants of Hellen, thus became the progenitors of the principal Greek tribes, the Achaeans, Aeolians, Dorians and Ionians.

Homer alluded to the confederated Greek heroes, who crossed the Aegean Sea to attack and defeat the wealthy citadel of Troy shortly after 1200 B.C., as Achaeans. These Achaeans appear to have invaded Greece about two centuries earlier armed with long swords and huge, round shields of bronze. Their origin is somewhat obscure, although Hittite inscriptions of 1300 B.C. refer to the "Ahhijava" a progressive, warlike tribe who inhabited western Anatolia, a land known for its expert metalworkers. A glimmer of tradition also connects these people with the ancient "Raiding Sea Peoples," possibly of Cretan origin, whose kinfolk invaded Egypt. One thing is certain, Homer's Achaeans were highly accomplished in the fashioning of gold, silver, copper and bronzeware, and they contributed greatly to the brilliant culture of Mycenae.

The Dorian Conquest

Less than a century after Agamemnon led the Achaeans against Troy, a new race of invaders swept into Greece, destroyed Mycenae and brought that splendid civilization to an end. The newcomers were the Dorians, a kindred tribe of the Greek or Hellenic race but crude and less civilized than the Achaeans. The spears, swords, and shields of bronze raised in defense by the Mycenaeans were decidedly inferior to the sturdy weapons of iron carried by the invaders.

The Dorian conquest was to effect great changes in the course of Greek development. After ravaging the Mycenaean cities, the Dorians crossed the sea to Crete and dealt a final blow to Knossos. They failed to subdue Attica because the Acropolis of Athens was a natural rock-ribbed citadel able to stave off attack. Settling in the Peloponnesus the Dorians established a city-state and made Sparta its capital.

The origin of the Dorians is also obscure. Possibly they came southward from the Salzkammergut region of Austria where an iron culture was rising around Hallstatt. A similarity in weapons from this area supports such a belief. It appears more likely that the Dorians came westward from Asia Minor, the birthplace of ironmaking, but whichever was their original homeland they were well supplied with crude but more effective weapons of iron. Hesiod called this period the 'Age of Iron' and deplored its use in the destruction of man.

The Iron Age had indeed come to Hellas in the wake of the Dorian conquest. Iron ores were plentiful in several areas of Greece. Deposits occurred in Boetia, Euboea and in the Taygetas Range near Porto Kayio in Laconia, not far from Sparta. Gythion, modern Yithion on the Gulf of Laconia, became an early arsenal and seaport of Sparta. Laconia eventually became famous for its steel.

The Great Greek Migration

A decisive moment in the dawn of the Greek civilization was marked by the appearance of the Dorians. Scattering before the invader's merciless spirit and hard metal swords, the Achaeans sought sanctuary in many places. But there was a hidden blessing in this dark period of Greek history, for this dispersal was to have a salutary effect upon the future progress of all mankind. It started the most significant era of migration and colonization ever known, and gave birth to the incomparable age of Greek expansion. Fortunately, these exiles were determined to preserve their glorious Mycenaean heritage. It was this dedication to ideals, and the freedom, wealth and opportunity encountered on new frontiers, that nourished Greece's gifts to the world in literature, philosophy, science, art and architecture.

As the dispossessed societies fled before the Dorians, some of the Mycenaean migrants gathered around the little town of Athens; others continued eastward to settle on the coast of Asia Minor where they established the Ionian League of twelve cities including Ephesus and Miletus. Another group formed the Aeolian League, which included the Island of Lesbos and the city of Mytilene.

Wondrous Ephesus

After Athens became overcrowded, colonists left the city and founded Ephesus about 1000 B.C. Fortune had favored these new settlers, for in all directions there were deposits of metallic ores to be developed. Northeast of Ephesus near modern Bayindir was the 'silver mountain' of Gumush Dag. To the northeast were more silver deposits near Seferihissar. Tin ores occurred near Darmandar. Off the coast there were silver ores on the Island of Samos where, even in modern times, mines were worked by a Belgian company.

Due to her strategic location astride an important trade route which terminated at the mouth of the river Cayster, and the providential presence of nearby ore deposits, Ephesus became a flourishing center of commerce. Blessed with an abundance of metals, the Ionians became renowned for their silver craftsmen. Overflowing with wealth and resultant leisure, the great Ionian city expressed its exuberance in luxuriant living, expensively dressed citizens, and stately buildings. Ephesus became the birthplace of superb Ionic architecture, and its great temple became one of the Seven Wonders of The World. Noted philosophers, such as Heraclitus, an early metaphysician, were motivated by the stimulating environment of the famed city.

Some 60 miles north of Ephesus the ancient city of Smyrna, now known as Izmir, was founded originally by an Aeolian colony about 1015 B.C., and was later occupied by the Ionians. Located on an arm of the Aegean that reached far eastward into the Asiatic mainland, for ages Smyrna had been the terminus of one of the great trade routes coursing across Anatolia westward into a kingdom that came to be known as Lydia. Descending the Hermus (Gediz) River, the route passed ancient Sardis (modern Salihli), thence over a mountain pass to Smyrna. Opposite Sardis, the famed capital of Lydia, the legendary waters of the river Pactolus joined the Hermus.

Midas, Croesus and Pactolus Gold

According to mythology, King Midas of nearby Phrygia made the wish that everything he touched might be turned to gold. Starving to death when even food and drink turned to gold, Midas prayed for relief. Dionysus told Midas to bathe in the waters of the Pactolus and the fateful gift would then be removed. The king immersed himself in the river with the result that the sands of the Pactolus turned to gold.

The myth may have contained grains of truth, for it was from the Pactolus that Croesus, King ot Lydia in 560 B.C., is said to have gathered his fabulous wealth. No evidence of gold exists in the river's sands today, but remains of very old mines have been found on the slopes of Mount Tmolus (Boz Dag) south of Sardis. Beyond any doubt, the trade that crossed Lydia and passed through Sardis on the way to Smyrna must have heaped the coffers of Croesus high with gold. Significantly, the main street of Smyrna was named 'Golden.'

Invention of Coinage

It was Lydia's abundant supply of metals that inspired her great contribution to world progress, the invention of coinage. Having attained a position of wealth, culture and industrial power, Lydia and all mankind needed a common, convenient medium of exchange having standardized weight and purity guaranteed by the state. The clumsy old system of bartering article for article or exchanging ingots of metal for quantities of food, animals or other commodities, was being outdated by the expansion of world commerce.

About 680 B.C. Lydia became the first to strike coins crudely stamped upon electrum, a pale, natural mixture of gold and silver. About 560 B.C. Croesus issued coins of pure gold and silver backed by state authority, which greatly

PLATE 45. "Solomon's Pillars" on the edge of the area covering Solomon's copper mines.

PLATE 46. Fallen walls surround slag mounds where slaves labored to smelt copper for Solomon.

PLATE 47. Typical copper ore of the Solomon region, now being mined by a modern company.

PLATE 48. The Timna mine now wins copper, as did Solomon, from a district near Eilat, Israel.

PLATE 49. Beyond Eilat and the Gulf of Aqaba, below the Jordan Mountains, lies Ezion-geber, site of Solomon's smelter.

PLATE 50. On Assyrian wheels of iron rode the ruthless conquerors of Judea and Israel.

PLATE 51. The "Owls of Athens" became the supreme commercial currency of the 5th century B.C.

PLATE 52. Coins of antiquity disclose national prosperity, extent of commerce and portraits of historic leaders.

PLATE 53. Near the Greek theater at Thoricus, Cretan and Mycenaean miners dug for silver 3500 years ago.

PLATE 54. The ancient mine pits of Maronea in Laurium's hills supplied silver for the defense of Greece.

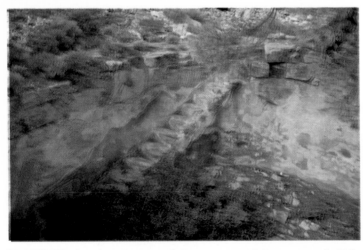

PLATE 55. In the cisterns of Soureza, a mining camp of 483 B.C., water was stored for the concentrating tables.

PLATE 56. One of the wash tables that concentrated the silver used to finance additions to Athens' navy.

PLATE 57. A modern mine at Kamareza. Here, in 551 B.C., Peisistratus procured silver to stimulate Greek commerce.

PLATE 58. The Soros at Marathon. Here lie the ashes of the Greek heroes who defeated a Persian horde in 490 B.C.

PLATE 59. The Bay of Salamis where Greek ships defeated Xerxes' fleet in 480 B.C.

PLATE 60. Known as the Theseum, it is actually the temple of Hephaistos, god of the metalworkers.

PLATE 61. The Agora, or market place, in Athens. Here walked Themistocles, Pericles, Socrates, Aristotle and others.

PLATE 62. The Parthenon was completed in 432 B.C., superbly reflecting the glory of ancient Greece.

PLATE 63. These temple decorations of Etruria depict the delicately modeled features of the Etruscans.

PLATE 64. This bronze incense urn reveals the Etruscans' mastery of metals which won them wealth and power.

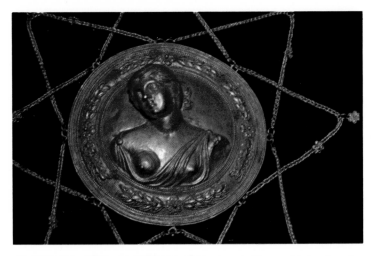

PLATE 65. This magnificent Etruscan gold pendant, showing Greek influence, reveals the extent of their trade.

PLATE 66. The Fabricio Bridge across the Tiber River marks the site of Rome's beginning.

PLATE 67. A silver mine in Spain, one of the sources of Rome's earliest mineral wealth.

PLATE 68. Cadiz, Spain, founded about 1100 B.C., was a rich mineral outlet for both Phoenicians and Romans.

PLATE 69. The red mountain of the Rio Tinto mine first attracted the Phoenicians and later the Romans.

PLATE 70. Below the red oxidized surface deeper workings encountered brassy pyrite containing copper.

PLATE 71. Today, huge open pits have replaced the mountain. Worked for 2500 years, the Rio Tinto mine is world famous.

PLATE 72. Roman-Syrian goldwork of 200 B.C. testifies to Rome's skill in metalworking as rich resources were won.

PLATE 73. The Roman Forum took shape as distant metal-rich provinces were added to Rome's possessions.

PLATE 74. The Temple of Jupiter in Baalbek arose after Roman colonization spread from Britain to Syria.

PLATE 75. Emperor Augustus ruled an empire that possessed all the known mineral wealth in the world.

PLATE 76. Augustus not only beautified Rome; his great palace on the Palatine became the model for imperial living.

PLATE 77. Trajan's column honors the emperor's capture of the rich province of Dacia and an immense booty in gold.

PLATE 78. Hadrian, Trajan's nephew, built his tomb beside the Tiber. He was a great emperor.

PLATE 79. To the Colosseum came the pleasure-bent thrill seekers and maniac rulers to witness contests and human slaughter.

PLATE 80. Emperor Marcus Aurelius' reign ended 200 years of Rome's golden age of peace and prosperity.

PLATE 81. The basilica, St. Sophia, was completed A.D. 537 after Emperor Constantine established his capital on the Bosporus.

PLATE 82. The Arch of Constantine, archetype of honorary structures everywhere, is only one of Rome's legacies.

PLATE 83. The famous aqueduct, Pont du Gard, near Nimes, France exemplifies a rich heritage in engineering.

PLATE 84. The Roman arena in Arles, France, has been reproduced the world over, a type widely used today.

PLATE 85. Along the shore of Monaco harbor once strode Roman legions on their way to conquer Spain and Gaul.

PLATE 86. Paris' Ile de la Cité in the River Seine is the site of Rome's colony, Lutetia, founded 52 B.C.

PLATE 87. Rothenburg, Germany, is typical of the medieval towns that became walled cities during the barbarian invasions.

PLATE 88. Charlemagne The Great, after the "Dark Ages," revived mining and established a stable currency.

PLATE 89. The Rammelsberg mine, discovered in 938 near Goslar, Germany, started an eastward rush of pioneers.

PLATE 90. Rammelsberg's copper, lead, and silver ores have supplied Europe with metals for 1000 years.

PLATE 91. Jewels of the Orient aroused in Holy Land Crusaders desires that awakened Europe's industry and commerce.

PLATE 92. The famed emerald and diamond dagger of the Topaki Museum is a sample of Oriental splendor.

stimulated trade and banking. The standard was the silver mina of Carchemish of Babylonian origin, which had been passed on across Asia Minor.

The coinage ideas of Lydia spread quickly to Greece. Aegina, an important maritime island west of Athens, became the first to coin money in Greece proper. Corinth's thriving commerce was bolstered when it struck staters having an image of Pegasus. It was the coinage of Athens, however, that became the greatest commercial currency of the 5th century B.C. Fortunately, Athens possessed prolific silver mines at nearby Laurium.

The "Owls of Athens"

Athenian coinage had a far reaching effect upon coin types. They were the first to show in perfection a human head, clearly depicting the goddess Athena. On the reverse side was a big-eyed owl, which earned the coins the famous name of the "owls of Athens." In addition to being an inestimable boon to trade, coins were imperishable records of their times. They indicated the relative importance and wealth of ancient city-states, and the extent of their commerce. Even in ancient times inflation was often a threat. The resultant debasement of coins with cheaper metals has disclosed various periods of economic stress.

Portraits on coins of gold, silver, copper, and bronze have given us glimpses of historic personalities, ancient myths and religions. But the most important effect which coinage exerted upon mankind was the world-wide search and human struggle generated to obtain metallic resources necessary for coinage production. As money became the recognized symbol of wealth and power and an absolute requisite for trade, precious metals assumed the position of man's most coveted treasure.

Fascinated by the convenience and flexibility which money gave to purchasing power and banking operations, consumer demand increased, bringing greater growth to industry and commerce. In turn, new lands and new economic resources were sought, with the result that the greatest age of expansion the world had ever known was set in motion. In the vanguard were the prospectors seeking deposits of useful and precious metals. Many of their finds would play dramatic roles in the history of mankind.

Expansion of Greek Culture

The invention of coinage and the development of the Greek alphabet, which had been borrowed from Phoenician traders and then improved, were tremendous stimulants to trade and industry. Now, with an efficient medium of exchange and a better system of writing, the Greeks were ready to spread their booming commerce and their blossoming culture across the Mediterranean world. Colonies on the coast of Asia Minor, and their parent cities on the Greek mainland, began to multiply the number of colonists sent to explore and settle distant lands.

Upon the site of a former Cretan settlement at the mouth of the fertile valley of the Maeander River, Ionian colonists had founded the city of Miletus about 1000 B.C. Like Ephesus, the hinterland beyond Miletus was rich in mineral resources. To the Aegean coast the Maeander River brought metals from the mines and wool from the pastures of the interior of Asia Minor. The stage was set for Miletus to play her destined role in the affairs of mankind.

There seems to be no greater energizer that can excite man's imagination and creative efforts than the vision of new frontiers to explore and conquer. So it was with the men of Miletus. Flushed with prosperity and the spirit of adventure, Miletus sent out traders and colonizers in every direction. Along the Hellespont, the Sea of Marmora and the Black Sea to the north, Miletus settlers founded over 60 cities. As the main seaport for the fabulously rich mineral region of the Pontus, Sinope became the most flourishing Greek settlement on the south shore of the Black Sea.

Trapezus, now Trabzon, became the central outlet for another rich area containing gold, silver, copper and tin. It was also the doorway to legendary Colchis, the land of the Golden Fleece where gold was collected on sheep skins. From this northern realm, formerly guarded so carefully by ancient Troy, Miletus gathered immense wealth. Turning eastward to the lower Nile, Milesians who had founded Naucratis in 640 B.C., exchanged Greek handicrafts for Egyptian wares, and African ivory and incense. By the 6th century B.C. Miletus had become the richest city in the Greek world.

With great riches came luxury and leisure, and a yearning for refinement. Wealthy merchants and money-lenders sponsored art and freedom of inquiry, and turned to the cultures of Babylon and Egypt for inspiration. While these legacies of the Middle East were thus being transmitted to the western world, the opulent climate of Miletus was giving birth to Greek philosophy and science. Miletus gave to mankind the great scientist Thales, one of the Seven Wise Men of Greece. In 585 B.C. Thales predicted an eclipse of the sun.

Thales' pupil Anaximander taught the principle of primary matter, eternal, infinite and indestructible, and that the universe had been created through elements of heat and moisture; that earth's first organisms arose from the sea and primary moisture, and that man too evolved from the sea. He was well in accord with modern concepts of creation. Thus did new horizons challenge and inspire the minds of men.

Greek Colonization Westward

It was the great westward colonization of the Greeks, seeking new lands and new resources, that laid the foundation for the sweep of civilization into Europe. Along the now famous French Riviera Greek colonies were founded at present day Nice, Monaco and Antibes. About 750 B.C. colonists settled in Sicily and southern Italy. Cumae, 12 miles west of modern Naples, was the first settlement in Italy. The Cumaeans amassed great wealth selling the civilized wares of eastern Greece. Their philosophy, ideas and art were spread throughout the region, and would greatly influence the culture of Etruria and Rome to the north in days to come.

About 600 B.C. Ionian Greeks from Phocaea founded a settlement called Massilia, now known as Marseille, which became the terminus of an important trade route leading up the Rhone River into Gaul, continuing along the Loire to the coast and ending in the fabled tin lands of Cornwall, England. These indeed were far-flung explorations for such ancient times.

On the southeastern coast of Spain, which they named Iberia after the Iberus River (now the Ebro), the Greeks established the colonies of Tarraco (50 miles southwest of modern Barcelona), and Saguntum near present Valencia. Endeavoring to exploit the silver wealth of Tartessus, the colonists intruded dangerously close to the private domain of the powerful Phoenicians of Carthage. Before long this encroachment would lead to serious trouble, and mineral wealth would become the prize of the conflict.

Taking full advantage of the natural resources found on new frontiers, which equalled or exceeded those of their native lands, the Greeks became true colonizers. They did not confine their efforts merely to trade, as did the Phoenicians. Replanting their way of life among the indigenous peoples, the benefits of Greek literature, philosophy, art, science and architecture became firmly embedded in European culture. And, it was in these far-off independent city-states that some of the greatest cultural accomplishments of Greece were born.

Leaving the comforts and protection of their civilized homelands and surmounting the hardships and dangers of strange, unknown lands, true to the spirit of all adventurers of history, this great colonization movement became one of Greece's most beneficent attainments. It marked a momentous milestone in the advancement of mankind, for it dispersed and bequeathed an incomparable legacy to the western world and laid the foundation of our present civilization.

The Rise of Athens

While the colonies of Greece were spreading the fruits of their civilization throughout the Mediterranean, the city-states of their homeland were vying for supremacy. Militant, disciplined Sparta, living in rugged simplicity, competed for Hellenic leadership with talented and aristocratic Athens of Attica. Sparta, Athens, Corinth and Thebes, isolated by geographical barriers, were entities unto themselves. They seldom united in a common cause, always considering that their city-state, rather than Hellas, was their true homeland. With her Achaean and Mycenaean heritage Athens eventually came to play the dominant role in Greek culture.

Earliest rule of the city-states was under kings, or monarchies, followed by oligarchies consisting of landed nobles. Unrest among the common people induced the rise of dominant personalities who, although termed "tyrants," were often public benefactors. Solon became archon or chief magistrate of Athens in 594 B.C. during a period of acute economic distress. He instituted many democratic reforms and became known as one of the Seven Wise Men of Greece.

The development of democracy has been attributed to the Greeks, but their form of government was not democracy as we know it today. The Athenian constitution granted participation in lawmaking to all adult free men and citizens of Athens. However, the population was not composed to any large degree of citizens. Slaves and even free men living out of the city, or men born of parents beyond the city, and those without property, were excluded from citizenship. But poorer citizens as well as the rich finally acquired a voice in government affairs. No longer could autocracy rule the land. Democracy had at least taken its first step toward the equality of man.

Peisistratus

In 561 B.C., the eloquent and popular general, Peisistratus, by championing the cause of the working class, seized the Acropolis and established himself as Tyrant of Athens. But he was soon ousted from office. Retiring to Macedonia he gained control of the silver mines of Mt. Pangaeus and the placer gold deposits of the River Strymon. With the wealth thus acquired Peisistratus was able to raise an army of mercenaries. Landing upon Attic soil near his family estate at Marathon, the determined warrior regained his leadership as Tyrant of Athens in 541 B.C. And it was fortunate for Athens that he appeared on the scene at this moment in history.

Peisistratus encouraged the arts, beautified Athens by building the first Parthenon and brought the city into its first architectural prominence. By using the wealth of the Pangaeus mines in the north and the rich, promising silver deposits of nearby Laurium, Peisistratus was able to issue a new, stabilized Athenian currency, which greatly stimulated commerce. Aided in no small measure by the mineral resources at her command with the stability thus attained under Peisistratus, Athens was preparing for a crisis.

The Persian Threat

While Athens and Sparta conducted their long feud over domination of Hellas, Cyrus the Great, King of Persia, was forming a mighty empire in the east. He already had subjugated the Medes and Assyrians. But the prize that most attracted him was located in the west, land of the river Pactolus, with its legendary sands of gold, and the realm of the Lydian king Croesus, richest monarch of his time. Adding to the luster were the opulent cities of industry and commerce such as Sardis and Miletus.

In 546 B.C. Cyrus stormed the city of Sardis and defeated Croesus and his Lydian forces.

Croesus became a wretched prisoner pleading for his life. The Persian shadow had begun to fall across the threshold of The Greek mainland.

In 521 B.C. Darius I succeeded to the Persian throne and became ruler over the greatest empire the world had yet known. In addition to Persia it included Egypt, northern India, Mesopotamia, Palestine, Asia Minor and now Lydia and Ionia. Hordes of allies were included in Darius' forces, but the core of his vast army was formed by the Medes, those daring, well-armored horsemen from the highlands of metal-rich Kurdistan.

When Miletus and other Greek cities of Ionia revolted against Persian rule in 499 B.C. they appealed to Athens for help. The Athenians sent 20 ships but the revolt failed. In reprisal the Persians plundered Miletus and burned the city, leaving hardly a trace of its former greatness. The failure of the Athenians to free their Ionian brothers seemed an indication of weakness and convinced Darius that the time had come to reach out and conquer the Greek mainland.

The Persian Invasion

Darius made his first move against Greece in 492 B.C. He sent Mardonius with a large force of men and ships to subdue Thrace and Macedonia. That attempt succeeded, but when Mardonius endeavored to move into southern Greece the Persian fleet was wrecked in a stormy sea while rounding a promontory near Mt. Athos. Failure forced Mardonius to return home. However, a crucial moment in history was getting closer. The fate of Western civilization hung in the balance. A decisive conflict was brewing between the regimented armies of an Oriental power and the heavily outnumbered forces, composed mostly of free men, fighting in defense of their ideals, homes and country.

The next attack upon Attica came in 490 B.C. A fleet of 600 ships, built by Phoenicians, sailed westward across the Aegean Sea. Landing on the south coast of Euboea the Persians quickly and easily seized Eretria near Chalcis, then crossed the gulf to Attica. When the news of Eretria's fall reached Athens a courier named Pheidippides was dispatched to Sparta for aid. He ran the distance in less than 48 hours. Today's road map indicates that he ran about 160 miles. The heroic deed was in vain, however, for the Spartans would arrive too late. Persian ships were already rounding a headland a few miles from the village of Marathon perilously close to Athens.

The Battle of Marathon

The plain of Marathon is about 4 miles long and 2 miles wide. It is encircled by low mountains and fronts on a crescent shaped beach. Upon that beach Persian ships were disgorging their famed cavalry and fighting men. Miltiades, a Thracian familiar with Persian tactics, led an army of hastily assembled Athenians and some volunteers from little Platea on a forced march from Athens to Marathon. The Greeks moved hurriedly through a mountain pass and out onto the plain. There they grimly took their positions before the formidable Persians. Many figures have been given about the size of the relative forces, but it appears that about 20,000 Persians stood ready to crush 9,000 Athenians and 1,000 Plateans. The Spartans were on the way but had come no nearer than the Isthmus of Corinth.

A mile from the Persian line Miltiades ordered his foot soldiers to close ranks and advance on the run in a mass attack. It was a tactic new to the Persians. Astonished at the cool, reckless abandon of the Greek onslaught, the Persian ranks gave way. Overpowered, they fled in confusion into the sea, desperately trying to reach their ships. The Persian fleet took aboard the survivors, departed and rounded Cape Sunion, planning to attack Athens from the Bay of Phaleron. Unable to land in the face of fierce Athenian resistance, the Persians abandoned the campaign and sailed for home.

The end of the battle of Marathon marked one of the most incredible encounters in history. Relatively untrained Greeks had routed a superior force of Persian veterans famed for their invincibility. Miltiades sent a messenger to Athens with news of the victory. After running non-stop 22 miles the messenger gasped, "We have been victorious," then fell dead.

The Soros of Marathon

Herodotus said that 6,400 Persians were slain in the battle and that the Athenians lost 192. Those 192 warriors were cremated together on the battlefield of Marathon, and their ashes were covered with a Soros, a sepulchral mound 39 feet high. Today one may stand at the top and obtain a panoramic view of the historic battlefield.

At the foot of the Soros is a copy of the stele or marble shaft which was erected after the battle, commemorating the names of the dead arranged by tribes. The original is in the National Museum in Athens. The plain is now peaceful and silent, but according to a legend related by Pausanias "Every night at Marathon are heard the neighing of horses and noises similar to that made by combatants." Here the spirit of freedom and independence, for the first time, had overcome the forces of oppression and despotism.

For 10 years the threat of further invasion lay smoldering. The death of Darius and a revolt in Egypt kept Persia busy elsewhere. Meanwhile, Athens had become involved in a war with the nearby island of Aegina; Athenian leaders were vying for political power and more people were being given voting rights. The Persian problem was of secondary concern.

Themistocles

There were some, however, who were more far sighted about the ultimate safety of Attica. The most anti-Persian was a man who was far from being an aristocrat. His name was Themistocles. According to some of his contemporaries, he lacked the typical polish of the Periclean Age, was ambitious and unscrupulously pursued his aims. But as a soldier and statesman he possessed rare ability in analyzing complex problems and arriving at quick, accurate decisions.

Overcoming the rivalry of other politicians, Themistocles became the leading voice in the Athenian democracy. He relentlessly advocated a policy of naval expansion by playing upon the public concern over the increasing threat from Aegina, whose naval power was already equal to or superior to Athens. But his veiled intention was to prepare for another Persian invasion which he felt was sure to come.

Acutely aware of Athens' jeopardy, Themistocles urged his countrymen to begin fortifying the three natural harbors at Piraeus and to abandon the open, vulnerable roadstead then in use at Phaleron. Of greatest importance to Athens, indeed to all Greece, was Themistocles' proposal to expand the Athenian navy by building 200 fighting triremes.

At this critical point in his country's history, Themistocles turned to one of the world's most noted storehouses of mineral wealth, the silver mines of Laurium. In 483 B.C. the treasury of Athens was about to distribute to its citizens their annual share of revenue from the state owned mines of Laurium. The mines were then producing silver bullion equivalent in value to about $600,000 per year, but its purchasing power was far greater than it would be today. Themistocles induced his fellowmen to heed the oracle of Delphi who advised building "a wooden wall" for the defense of Athens, taken to mean a fleet of ships.

Laurium, Bulwark of Silver

Over a period of a thousand years prior to the time of Themistocles, riches from the Laurium hills, located 30 miles south of Athens, had been a bounteous boon to the Greeks. Mycenaeans and probably Cretans had been the first to dig into the reddish slopes of a cone-shaped hill called Velatouri, which overlooks the Aegean waters at a hamlet known as Thoricus, one of the oldest inhabited places in Attica. A few miles to the south is the present seaport village of Laurium, itself an ancient smelting site.

In later centuries the silver veins were traced southward from Thoricus along the crest of a pine-clad mountain ridge above Laurium. More ore deposits were found at a place named Kamareza. It was there that Peisistratus had obtained the silver used to mint the famed "owls of Athens," which bolstered Greece's economy and became the greatest commercial currency of ancient times. Continuing farther southward atop the ridge, a vast silver-rich region was gradually uncovered as miners delved into the reddish streaks of silver-bearing galena ore that lay buried in the gray limestone hills of the Laurium massif.

Only a few years prior to 483 B.C., the year that Themistocles appealed to the citizens of Athens to use Laurium's wealth for the city's defense, an extremely rich deeper zone of silver ore was fortunately discovered amid the pines at a place named Maronea a few miles south of Kamareza. Here, one of earth's greatest treasures stood ready to help stem an onrushing national calamity.

It is no wonder that Themistocles saw in the mines of Laurium the realization of his ambitious plan to "build a wall of wood," a grand fleet of ships to bolster the might of Athens not only against her Aegean rival, but

more essentially against the approaching menace from the Orient. The Athenian navy then possessed 70 fighting galleys having three banks of oars, known as triremes. Using the silver from Laurium, 130 more ships were built and added to the fleet.

Xerxes' Mighty Horde

The wealth obtained from Laurium's mines had reinforced the Athenian navy barely before Xerxes I, who had succeeded Darius, was on his way toward Greece with the most powerful force ever assembled. His mighty army and navy were composed of Persians, Medes, Assyrians, Babylonians, Indians, Arabians, Egyptians, Phoenicians, Ionians, Lydians and Thracians. Several hundred thousand fighting men (Herodotus said there were over 2½ million) and a fleet of over 800 ships made up the Persian expedition. Xerxes was confident that when the news of this oncoming irresistible juggernaut of footmen, cavalrymen, chariots, elephants and fighting triremes reached the Greek mainland, all Greece would quickly capitulate.

Xerxes had his engineers build a bridge across the Hellespont, now the Dardanelles, near Abydos. When the first bridge was destroyed by a storm Xerxes ordered that the Hellespont be chastised with 300 lashes. In one of the great engineering feats of antiquity, two more bridges were built consisting of 674 war galleys lashed together 10 feet apart with flax and papyrus cables. A roadway, and bulwark of planks along the sides completed the bridge, floating securely on the waters. For seven days and nights the roadway planks resounded to the rumble of the Persians breaching the mile and one-half wide Hellespont.

Westward through Thrace and on into Macedonia and Thessaly marched Xerxes and his army, following closely the shore while the fleet kept nearby to furnish support and supplies. Across an isthmus near Mt. Athos a canal was dug to shorten the route by sea and to avoid the stormy promontory. All through the north the Greeks were forced to surrender in the face of the invincible army—until the Persians arrived at Thermopylae.

Thermopylae

A narrow defile then separated a mountainous shoreline from the sea at Thermopylae. There the Persians came upon 300 Spartan warriors under the command of their king Leonidas, and 6,000 more Greeks who had joined the march northward. Xerxes launched several savage attacks against the determined defenders, but his assaults failed. Xerxes was about to abandon the battle when a Greek traitor undertook to guide the Persians over a mountain path, enabling them to attack the Greeks from the rear.

Becoming aware of impending disaster, Leonidas sent his main force back to safety. Keeping his 300 Spartans and 700 hand-picked Thebans, Leonidas was determined to hold the pass or die in the attempt. In an audacious countercharge Leonidas was killed. Four times the Persians tried in vain to seize the Spartan king's body. Bearing their fallen leader, the Greeks dropped back. When they were besieged from the rear they retreated to ramparts in the narrowest part of the pass. With their spears broken they stood and fought, using short swords and their bare hands, until not a single man remained alive. They were buried where they fell. Over their tomb was inscribed this epitaph, "O stranger, go and tell the Lacedaemonians that we lie here after obeying their laws."

Xerxes Burns Athens

After Thermopylae Xerxes moved unopposed southward into central Greece. With the fate of all Greece at stake the plan of defense called for a stand upon the narrow Isthmus of Corinth, leaving the beautiful and cultured city of Athens to be abandoned to the mercy of the invaders. Families, with such possessions as they could carry, fled to the nearby islands of Aegina and Salamis. Many of the elderly, tame animals and pets, had to be left behind. When Xerxes rode triumphantly into the city it was almost deserted. Athens was promptly pillaged and set afire.

The Peloponnesian commanders favored assembling the combined Greek naval forces in the Saronic Gulf near the Isthmus of Corinth. But Themistocles successfully resisted the plan, determined to engage the Persian fleet in the narrow bay between the mainland and the island of Salamis. Here, thought Thermistocles, his greatly outnumbered triremes might have a tactical advantage. Herodotus placed the number of Persian ships at 1,207. They probably had nearer 800. The Greek fleet totaled 317, of which 200 were Athenian ships. 130 of these had been built with funds provided by the Laurium mines.

Decision at Salamis

While his navy assembled in the Bay of Salamis west of Piraeus, Themistocles sent a trusted slave, who pretended loyalty to Xerxes, with a message that the frightened Greek fleet was about to flee. Thus duped, Xerxes launched his attack and seated himself upon a throne overlooking the scene to witness the destruction of the Greek navy. It was at dawn on a late September day in 480 B.C. when the Persian fleet left the Bay of Phaleron near Athens and deployed westward along the coast which then was being held by Persian troops. From his vantage point at the foot of Mt. Aegaleus on the shore Xerxes saw his ships enter the narrows between Kamatero and Salamis. It was there that the battle began.

The Greek ships were smaller and outnumbered three to one. But they were easier to maneuver and were fitted with rams. They were also manned by free men fighting desperately for their homes. With supreme audacity and expert seamanship the Greeks darted among the Persian ships, rammed their bows, sheared off their oars and left them helpless. First the Phoenician ships were driven onto the Attic shore, then the Athenians turned upon their brother Ionians, questionable allies of the Persian king, and dispersed them in wild confusion. Xerxes looked with dismay upon the scene—his ships crippled, floundering in the water or in flight, the sea choked with wreckage and dying men. That night the battered remnants of the Persian navy tottered back to Phaleron, broken and defeated. The momentous battle of Salamis was over. Athens was free.

Xerxes was forced to withdraw his fleet and his army from Attica. Leaving 300,000 men under his capable general, Mardonius, to retreat northward and occupy Thessaly, Xerxes took his main force to the Hellespont homeward bound for Sardis. A year later a Spartan king drove Mardonius' army from Greece, and a Greek squadron defeated a Persian fleet, freeing the Ionian cities from Persian rule. The Battle of Salamis marked the end of Persian encroachment upon the western world. It was one of the most crucial battles in world history, for it opened the way for the continued development of European civilization under the aegis of Greek culture, whose ideals of liberty, government and economics control our lives today.

The paramount contribution to victory, of course, was the unquenchable spirit of the brave, resolute Greeks who met the challenge. But without Laurium's bulwark of silver there would have been no fleet of sufficient strength to stem the Persian tide. Historians credit the wealth of the Laurium mines and the ships that were built with the silver of Maronea for the Persian defeat.

Athens' Economic Supremacy

The Athenian fleet that Themistocles had created became undisputed master of the seas and established Athens as a naval and commercial power. Every port in the Mediterranean region was open to Greek trade. With the mines of Laurium, Athens developed a monopoly on silver coinage throughout the world. The 'owls of Athens' were known and gladly accepted everywhere. Athens expanded its sway to include the island of Thasos and its gold mines, and the rich silver mines on the island of Siphnos. On the mainland north of Thasos the mines of Scapte Hyle and the Crenides and Mt. Pangaeus added also to Attica's economic supremacy.

Little Attica, David among the giants of world empires, proud of its victories, fired with idealism and rich in natural resources, after a thousand years of maturation was ready now to bestow its great cultural legacy upon mankind. Wealth brought added leisure and stimulated the Greek spirit of creativity. Poets, inspired by the heroic deeds of Marathon, Thermopylae, Salamis and Platea, glorified them in epics of literature. Greek legends of momentous encounters and valiant warriors became synonymous with the Greek ideals of freedom and adventure. Such were the great days when the silver of Laurium played a memorable prelude to the Golden Age of Greece.

The Golden Age of Greece

The century following the Battle of Salamis saw Greece embarked upon its Golden Age, perhaps the most enlightened period in world history. It was during the ascendancy of Pericles that Athens became the world center of art, literature and philosophy. Pericles inspired his fellowmen to make Athens an architectural masterpiece that would live forever in the minds of men. On the Acropolis, Pericles chose to erect the noblest monument in Athens, a new Parthenon.

An abundant supply of excellent marble fortunately was available on Mt. Pentelicus a few miles north of the city. Aided by the wealth of Laurium, widespread commerce, and the treasury of the Delian League, Pericles had at his disposal seemingly unlimited funds for his vast construction projects. Also at hand was a large work force inspired with the challenge of exalting their city. Sculptors, artists, metalworkers and stoneworkers of rare genius contributed their talents.

Built to glorify Athen's tutelary goddess Athena, the Parthenon was begun in 447 B.C. and completed in 432 B.C. At one end of the temple stood the 39 foot high statue of Athena. Its crown, shield, and flowing robes were made of 2500 pounds of gold; ivory was used for the flesh. It was the work of Phidias, greatest of Greek sculptors. No trace of the statue exists today.

After completion of the Parthenon, the Propylaea was built by Pericles to form an impressive entrance on the west face of the Acropolis. Its dignified columns of Ionic and Doric style represent the prototype of grand gateways the world over. On the rim of the Acropolis and north of the Parthenon stand the remains of the Erechtheum. Its celebrated Porch of the Maidens, or the Caryatids, appears to be a funerary canopy over the burial sites of Crecrops and Erechtheus, legendary founders of Athens.

According to mythology it was here on the site of the Erechtheum that Poseidon, god of the sea, with a blow of his trident made water flow from the rock, and Athena the goddess caused the first olive tree to grow. Occupied since Neolithic and Mycenaean times, the Acropolis formed a natural citadel upon which 10 ancient shrines of great beauty were built, the most remarkable collection of monuments ever produced by the Greek civilization.

Symbolizing Greece's Golden Age, these magnificent structures have been standing majestically for nearly 2500 years. Few visitors realize the part nature has played in preserving this treasure. Many marble buildings elsewhere in the world, little more than a century old, gradually have been flaking away into ruin. When composed of nearly pure calcite, as are many famed national buildings, the stone is fairly soluble under certain atmospheric conditions. The marble of Mt. Pentelicus, however, is fine textured and contains a small percentage of iron and silica, or silicates, which cement the calcite grains. The iron gives this Pentelic marble its honey colored glow so apparent at sunset, and the silica content makes the marble especially resistant to wear. How fortunate that the everlasting stone of Mt. Pentelicus was available to keep alive the classical beauty of Greek design.

Our Imperishable Greek Heritage

As Greek architecture and art blossomed to the fullest, so did philosophy, poetry, drama, painting, sculpturing, history, science and medicine. Animated by widespread affluence and independence, all Greece yearned for expansion of knowledge and artistic betterment. Epochal volumes unending have been written describing the rich variety of Greek achievements and the genius of her famed citizens. In a volume such as this there is room to name only a few of the great philosophers, poets, scientists and statesmen of Greece.

Still preserved in stone and bronze are the immortal works of such men as Ictinus, architect of the Parthenon, and Callicrates its master builder, and Phidias the designer and sculptor of its friezes and statues. Famed for their perfect and realistic statues in bronze are Polycritus, Myron and Praxiteles. Recorded indelibly in the halls of time are the deeds of such statesmen as Solon, Peisistratus, Cleisthenes, Themistocles and Pericles.

Everliving are the words of such poets and historians as Homer, Hesiod, Pindar, Sophocles, Herodotus, Thucydides and Aristophanes. Among those who have contributed immeasurably to man's well being, learning and achievement are such philosophers, mathematicians and scientists as Thales, Pythagoras, Anaximander, Anaxagoras, Hippocrates, Socrates and his pupil Plato, who was a teacher of Aristotle. Unforgettable are the orations of such men as Protagoras, Isocrates and Demosthenes. These are but a few of the gifted Greek thinkers, dreamers, and doers, whose brilliance is reflected in nearly every aspect of western civilization.

The Golden Age of Greece marked the greatest advancements in intellectual and cultural attainments the world had ever seen. But the era of Athenian supremacy at last came to an end. The precarious bonds between Greek city-states had been periled for ages by constant dissension, small wars and opposite political viewpoints. The time came when it was Greek against Greek. In 431 B.C. the storm broke with the Peloponnesian War between the two main protagonists, Athens and Sparta. Those who wish first-hand details should consult Thucydides, the Greek historian, who tells the story superbly.

The Decline of Athens

Upon the advice of a traitorous Athenian general, Alcibiades, Sparta seized control of southern Attica and prevented operation of the Laurium mines. It was a fatal blow to Athens, for the financing of Athenian resistance depended considerably upon the silver from Laurium. By 407 B.C. the Athenian treasury was so depleted that the gold and silver statues on the Acropolis were melted to furnish coinage. The next year Athens issued copper coins for the first time.

A Spartan navy, built with Persian aid and led by the audacious Lysander, dealt the death blow to Athens. Athens was forced to surrender in April 404 B.C. She lost nearly all her navy, all of her foreign possessions, and was forced to become an ally of Sparta. Under her militant policies, however, Sparta was unable to unite the Greeks. In 371 B.C. it was Thebes, after defeating Sparta, who became leader of the Hellenic people.

As for Laurium, in those unsettled times very few people were disposed to work in the mines or risk prospecting for new ore bodies. But when conditions bettered for Athens, mining was slowly resumed. By 355 B.C. revenues had again attained such proportions that Xenophon, a Greek general, was tempted to make his infamous proposal requesting the state to acquire slaves and lease them to the mine operators for the enrichment of the Athenian treasury. The plan was never carried out. A few years later a private lessee was condemned to death for mining the rock pillars left in the mines to support the openings. This indicates that the famed Laurium ore bodies were nearing depletion after centuries of production.

Demetrius Phalereus, in the second century B.C., referred to those "who mined with much eagerness" at Laurium, but reaped only discouraging rewards. In the first century A.D., Strabo disclosed that Laurium miners were forced to rework the discarded rock on the waste dumps and to resmelt the old slag heaps. This was the customary epitaph of many exhausted mining districts. Pausanias, the Greek traveler and geographer of the second century A.D. mentions with melancholy retrospection that Laurium had once been the main source of Athens' great wealth. Its former glory was recalled by the Greek tragic dramatist Aeschylus, who had called Laurium "a fountain of silver, a treasure to the land." Heeding Pausanias' obituary, it becomes clear that the fountain had run dry.

Edouard Ardaillon, the most reliable authority on Laurium, in his "Les Mines du Laurion dans l'Antiquite" published in Paris, 1897, stated that the old Laurium mine dumps in 1869 contained about seven million tons of discarded waste rock averaging 8 to 10 percent lead which contained 40 to 120 ounces of silver per ton. A. Cordella, a Greek engineer (1871) estimated that Laurium had produced over two million tons of metallic lead which, with its silver content, would be equivalent in value to about one billion dollars. Such was the bulwark of silver that contributed to the salvation and nourishment of the Greek civilization.

Laurium in Its Heyday

Although Laurium became noted as a silver producing district it was a mineral compound of lead and sulphur known as galena, richly inter-mixed with silver, that formed the principal ore. Associated with this argentiferous lead were other minerals, the zinc sulphide sphalerite and the iron sulphide pyrite. These sulphides were found impregnating the limestone host rock, often in tabular shaped masses up to 35 feet in thickness.

If the discarded waste rock contained 8 to 10 percent lead, as reported by Ardaillon, the ore underground must have been rich indeed. The ratio of silver was supposedly 40 to 300 ounces per ton of lead. At the surface some of the galena was altered to the gray, glassy lead carbonate, cerussite. Decomposition of the iron pyrite gave the outcrops their characteristic red hue.

Compared with many mining districts the workings of Laurium were shallow, rarely over 350 feet deep. The three principal layers of limestone contained the ore bodies and lay fairly close and parallel to the mountaintop, which made the ore conveniently accessible by means of shallow shafts or short passages all along the ridge. Many of the ore bodies were mined by digging underfoot, a method called underhand stoping. The walls and roofs of these rooms or

"stopes" were supported by pillars of lower grade rock left in place, or by "drywall" pillars built of stone blocks.

Slavery in The Mines

Laurium's mines were owned but not operated by the city-state of Athens. Various sections along the ore belt were leased to citizens who paid a royalty in bullion of about 4 percent. Slaves, war captives, condemned criminals and other unfortunates composed the work force. Slave owners often bought slaves for about $150 and leased them to mine operators for one obal, or 17 cents, per day. Some slave owners, possessing as many as 1200 slaves, grew rich trafficking in slaves. Nicias, the famed Athenian general, and Hipponicus, renowned for his wealth, derived large sums from slave rentals.

Iron chains found occasionally in the mines testify to the discipline imposed upon rebellious workers. A miner often toiled on his knees or prone on his back in cramped, twisting passages barely large enough for his body, picking at the reddish rock with iron chisels and hammers in the dim light of a small, noxious oil lamp. The gleaming galena ore and intermixed rock waste were placed in bags made of ox hides or woven grass and passed from hand to hand or carried on the backs of slaves to the surface. Sometimes the ore was hoisted to the top by means of a windlass.

On the surface more slaves sorted the ore, discarding the rock waste. Wielding iron pestles in large stone mortars the ore was crushed by hand, or in stone rolling mills operated by several slaves. The crushed mixture, containing grains of shiny, heavy galena and dull, barren rock waste was then spread upon slightly slop-ing, rough-surfaced stone slabs or washing tables known as laveries. As water was gently washed across the slabs the lighter worthless particles were flooded away, leaving a "concentrate" of the heavier silver-bearing galena.

Separating the Silver

The concentrates were dried and taken to the smelting furnaces, small round cupolas built of rock and lined with fire resistant clay, where the lead sulphide, galena, was heated and roasted to expel the sulphur. Using charcoal as a fuel, and a bellows made of goat skins to provide a forced draft and high temperature, the roasted concentrates were reduced to a mass of metallic lead, which then contained a high proportion of silver.

Silver was separated from the lead by a process known as cupellation, one of great antiquity and in common use even today. The metallic lead was placed in a cupel, a shallow porous dish made of bone ash, and heated to a high temperature. Since lead volatilizes at low temperatures, the lead was driven off as a red oxide vapor known as litharge, which was collected for later treatment. After cupellation only metallic silver remained in the cupel. The silver was then melted, cast into bars and sent to jewelers or to the mint to be used for coinage.

Now freed of its silver, the metallic lead was recovered by smelting the accumulating litharge with charcoal. Lead was widely used in ancient times. In fastening the heavy stones of their classical structures with metal instead of mortar, the Athenians used considerable quantities of lead to seal and tighten the iron dowels and rods imbedded in the stonework.

The Riches of Macedonia

Rich resources in gold and silver again played an influential role in history; they provided the sinews of war for the early armies of King Philip and Alexander The Great. In 359 B.C. Philip became the ruler of a hardy mountain folk in northern Greece, a region known as Macedonia. A year later, expanding his power eastward into Thrace, Philip seized the Athenian colony of Amphibolis which controlled a region immensely rich in gold and silver centered about famed Mount Pangaeus.

A few miles to the west were the gold bearing sands of the River Strymon, emptying into the sea near present day Amphibolis. On the slopes of Mount Pangaeus near the village of Eleftheoupolis were the rich silver veins of Crenides, a district founded by colonists from the nearby island of Thasos, itself a famed producer of gold. According to Pliny, a legendary Cretan or Phoenician king named Cadmus, founder of Thebes, had discovered and worked the silver lodes of Mount Pangaeus as early as 1300 B.C.

One of Philip's first moves was to seize and fortify the town of Crenides in 356 B.C. He renamed it Philippi. Its ruins may be seen 8 miles northwest of modern Kavalla. From the Crenides mines and others around Mount Pangaeus, Philip drew 1000 talents in gold per year, equivalent to about six million dollars. With wealth pouring in from the sands of the Strymon and the veins of Mount Pangaeus, from nearby Thasos and as far west as Paeonia, Philip amassed a great fortune. As did other ambitious leaders, including Peisistratus, Philip used this wealth to hire and train a professional army. While doing so he developed a dramatic new art in warfare, the phalanx, a solid body of infantrymen armed with spears to open the way to future conquests.

Leading his massed armies southward, Philip defeated the Thebans and Athenians at Chaeronea, set up the League of Corinth (without Sparta) and established his control over Hellas. He was ready now to lead the united Greeks against their common enemy, the Persians. But in 336 B.C., while celebrating his daughter's marriage, Philip was murdered. His 20 year old son inherited the wealth, military machine and the ambition of his father, and promptly prepared to conquer the world. He became known as Alexander The Great.

Alexander The Great

Philip had prepared his son well to rule his budding empire. Aristotle was one of Alexander's many tutors. Young, dashing, extremely athletic, wildly energetic, with his auburn hair and blue eyes Alexander was a handsome king. He was acutely aware of his royal blood, for his mother Olympias claimed descent from Achilles, and Alexander bore himself accordingly. His impetuous bravery and eagerness to share the perils of battle endeared him to his soldiers and generals. On occasions he was a compassionate conqueror, but often gave vent to cruel outbursts of savagery. Abstinent in earlier years he later succumbed to dissipation and drunkenness. Nevertheless he was a brilliant military strategist and political administrator, ardently interested in fostering the arts and science. His chief aim was to spread the greatness of Greek culture everywhere.

The rich mines of Thrace and Macedonia not only financed the conquests of his father, they also started Alexander on the road to accomplish his dream to Hellenize the world. But it would be booty collected in foreign lands and divided among his followers that would keep his small but potent army on the move.

Alexander's first step was to master Greece from Thrace to Illyria. His ruthless destruction of Thebes, who dared to withhold her loyalty, his crossing of the Hellespont into Asia Minor and his defeat of the Persian army under Darius III are well known to students of history. Liberating Egypt from Persian rule, Alexander founded the great intellectual city of Alexandria in 332 B.C. It became the center of Hellenistic Greece. While in Egypt, Alexander visited the Oracle of Ammon at Siwa and wondered if it could be true that he himself was a descendant of the god Zeus-Ammon.

The Wealth of Persepolis

Moving into Mesopotamia Alexander received wild acclaim in Babylon, and then in 331 B.C. he captured ancient Susa, seizing 40,000 talents in gold and silver bullion, worth about $250,000,000. Pushing on to Persepolis the Macedonians seized the Persian royal treasury. According to Plutarch, 20,000 mules and 5,000 camels were required to remove the loot. Alexander spared Babylon, even restored some of its shrines, but in a drunken mood of revenge he sacked and burned Persepolis unmercifully. He had retaliated for the Persian attacks upon his native land.

Alexander's long, wandering campaigns of conquest through Parthia, Afghanistan and over Khyber Pass into India have been told fully by many historians. After nine years of tramping and battling, Alexander's tired, valiant comrades insisted upon returning home. Along the bleak wastes of Baluchistan and Iran, 10,000 died of thirst and exhaustion in the insufferable desert heat.

In 323 B.C. Alexander returned to Babylon, nearly insane with fatigue, disease and wounds received in India. On the 13th of June Alexander died—at the age of 33. His empire soon fell apart and was divided among his generals. Ptolemy seized Egypt, beginning the dynasties of the Ptolemies. Sparta and Athens resumed their status as independent city-states. Alexander's great gift to the world was the dissemination of classical Greek culture, introducing a new era, the Hellenistic Age.

The Hellenistic Age

The immense wealth in gold and silver bullion, which had so long accumulated in eastern empires, was sent to the western world where it was transformed into standardized coinage to be used in Alexander's vast domain. Commerce flourished, traders and foreign ministers amassed great fortunes, and levels of opulence were attained in a new, rich stratum of society as never before.

Macedonian rulers and citizens in far away lands proudly championed their Hellenic legacy. The language and customs of their courts were Greek. Kings everywhere patronized Greek arts and letters. Buildings, furnishings and dress were Greek in design. Greek sculpture, more expressive of human emotions and anatomy, became greatly in demand. New cities in Asia Minor, Syria and Egypt adorned their temples and streets with Greek statuary. Quarries and factories could hardly keep up with the demand.

The new cities of the Hellenistic Age became marvelous examples of Greek architecture. Forsaking mostly the severity of Doric and Ionic styles, the more elaborate Corinthian columns now graced stately temples and public buildings. Art, literature and science continued to flourish but now fell largely under the patronage of kings. Medical schools and libraries, especially at Alexandria, became features of the age.

Greek culture was more and more changing the face of the world. However, the Hellenistic Age also reached its zenith of achievement, fame and power. The twilight of Grecian greatness grew darker. The suicidal Peloponnesian War had marked a beginning. Hopelessly divided, Greece lay exhausted by the many fratricidal conflicts between its quarrelsome city-states.

End of Grecian Glory

With its soil impoverished by endless raids and devastations, its mineral resources nearly depleted, its trade and navy decimated, its treasury emptied and its morals and democratic principles impaired, the great civilization of Greece crumbled, destroyed from within.

But the cyclic evolution of man's civilizations marched on. As one rose to the heights and fell into decay, another more virile was ready to take its place. Again, resurgence would come from the west. By 146 B.C. Greece and Macedonia would become provinces of Rome, and Roman legions would be tramping over the hallowed shrines of Hellas. And, a great new empire would arise and inherit from the Greeks their incomparable legacies and spread them into many distant and undeveloped frontiers of uncivilized Europe.

One cannot help but wonder. Without the silver of Laurium and the gold of Pangaeus would all of these momentous events have taken place? What would have been the history of the Greeks if they had been deprived of Laurium's timely assistance, first to Peisistratus in the development of coinage and the invigoration of commerce in the 6th century B.C., and again to Themistocles in the crucial defense of Athens in 480 B.C.? And then, at the opportune moment, in 345 B.C. came the gold and silver of Pangaeus to smooth the way for the ambitious plans of Philip and Alexander. Perhaps, more than is generally realized, these shiny inarticulate metals have had a voice in the destiny of mankind.

Chapter 8

THE ROMAN WORLD

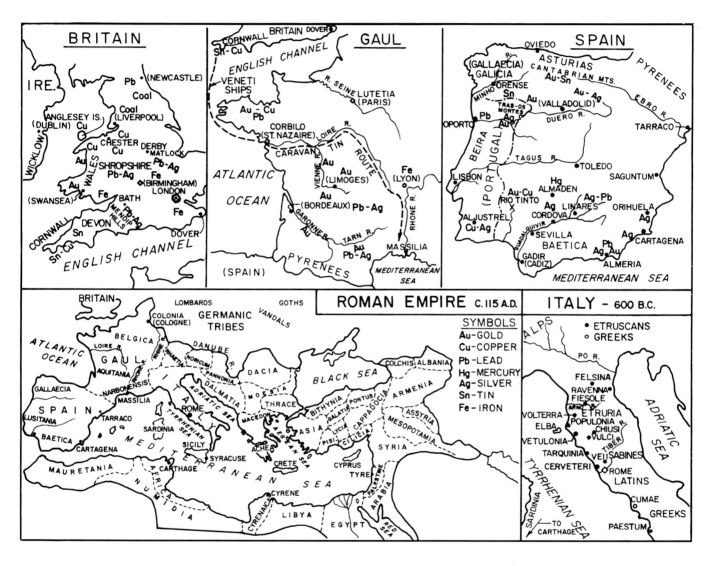

Plate 63   These *temple decorations of Etruria* depict the delicately modeled features of the Etruscans.   p. 90

Plate 64   This *bronze incense urn* reveals the Etruscans' mastery of metals which won them wealth and power.   p. 90

Plate 65   This magnificent *Etruscan gold pendant*, showing Greek influence, reveals the extent of their trade.   p. 90

Plate 66   The *Fabricio Bridge* across the *Tiber River* marks the site of Rome's beginning.   p. 90

Plate 67   *A silver mine in Spain*, one of the sources of Rome's earliest mineral wealth.   p. 90

Plate 68   Cadiz, Spain, founded about 1100 B.C., was a rich mineral outlet for both Phoenicians and Romans.   p. 90

The Greek Colonies

While the Greeks were spreading their colonies throughout the Mediterranean and approaching their Golden Age, other races in central and western Europe were preparing to step into the mainstream of history. As in the past, the rise of new civilizations would be preceded by the development of industry and commerce, and conflicts over territorial supremacy would decide national destiny. One of these peoples, charged with creative energy and competitive impulses, would rule the world.

Already established in southern Italy, as a result of an amazing program of Greek colonization, were the strong, prosperous city-states such as Cumae, Tarentum, Rhegium, and rose-bedecked Poseidonia (Paestum) whose beautiful Doric temples, now standing alone and deserted, testify to Greece's prestige in ancient Italy.

Across the Strait of Messina basked fertile Sicily. In 734 B.C., settlers from Corinth founded Syracuse. The Island's rich volcanic soil, nourished by a warm climate and plentiful rainfall, made Sicily's vineyards and olive groves far more productive than the sparse lands of continental Greece. To the Greeks, Sicily was an island paradise. Syracuse became wealthy and powerful.

West of Sicily, across the Mediterranean and on the northern coast of Africa, the Phoenicians founded Carthage in 814 B.C. Carthage thrived with trade and soon became the dominant force in the Mediterranean. Ruthless and aggressive, and considerably disturbed over the rise of Greek city-states and the threat to her commerce, Carthage stood ready to check Greek expansion.

The Mysterious Etruscans

This, indeed, was a land of promising opportunity. Rich in natural resources and a virgin market for civilized wares, it had attracted another group of colonizers, a people we know today as the Etruscans. They were a mysterious, vigorous race. As skilled mariners and expert metalworkers they had few equals. Their appearance on the scene about 800 B.C. marked the beginning of a bitter three-cornered struggle for domination of the western Mediterranean. In their hands rested the destiny of Europe, for they were to become the forerunners of a world empire.

Who were these talented people? According to Herodotus, the Etruscans migrated from the rich metal province of Lydia in Asia Minor, acting upon the command of their king Atys who was endeavoring to relieve a famine which had ravaged his over-populated land for 18 years. These emigrants knew themselves as 'Rasenna', but were named Tyrrheni by the Greeks, after 'Tyrrhenos' the Lydian king's son who led them into exile. Today, the water off the coast of Italy is known as the Tyrrhenian Sea. Later, the Romans would call them 'Etrusci', giving them the name Etruscan.

After temporary sojourns in the Aegean region, apparently seeking new sources of raw materials and trade, their quest led them to the western coast of Italy, no doubt attracted by rumors of its metallic wealth. Their choice had been wise, for there they found a region rich in the resources they had sought, and there they built Italy's first cities.

The Metals of Tuscany

It is significant that opposite the Island of Elba, which contained abundant supplies of specularite iron ore, one of their earliest cities was Populonia, near modern Piombino. Layer upon layer of black, crusty slag, which accumulated over an immense area, reveals that Populonia became a thriving Etruscan smelting center. In the mountains northeast of Populonia, copper ores were found at Montecatini, Montanto and Monte Calve. Minor tin deposits were available for use in making the celebrated Etruscan bronzes, although most of the tin was later imported.

With their superior technical skills the Etruscans took full advantage of the metallic ores of Etruria, or Tuscany as it is known today. The Etruscans became the first in Europe to introduce the use of iron and other metals on a prominent and widespread scale. It is well known that the wealth and power of the Etruscans, and their amazingly fertile and influential civilization, sprang from the expert use of the metals employed in warfare and trade.

After Populonia the Etruscans founded Volterra, Vetulonia, Tarquinia and Vulci, Cerveteri, Chiusi and others until there were twelve cities, ruled by leading families or monarchs, forming a loose confederation known as the Etruscan League. These independent city-states grew to number 42 when Etruscan domination expanded northward to the Po Valley, eastward to the upper Adriatic and into southern Italy.

Master Artisans of Etruria

From the cemeteries of ancient Etruria archeologists have recovered a remarkable record of Etruscan art and craftsmanship. Numerous grave mounds and tomb chambers, carved in volcanic tuff, have yielded ornate funerary urns of bronze and alabaster, magnificent pottery and ornaments of gold, silver and ivory. The Etruscans were master artisans in producing realistic statuary of their people and animals cast in bronze. They were especially adept in fashioning elaborately engraved armor of iron and bronze, adorned with figures depicting scenes in battle. Their shields, lances, battle-axes and helmets were by far the best of their times. Etruscan bronzes are famous and may be seen today in highly prized exhibits of many museums throughout the world.

End of Etruscan Power

Etruria's metal industries formed the basis of an extensive maritime trade. Etruscan ships plied the Mediterranean as far away as Egypt, the Levant and Africa, to the coasts of France and Spain. Imports from Greece exerted considerable influence upon Etruscan arts. In fields of battle the Etruscans, with their well armored warriors and horse-drawn chariots, were supreme. Although they were fearless fighters, they were also a gay, joyous and musical people. But so aggressive and piratical were the maritime practices of the Etruscans that they earned a reputation for being the scourge of the sea.

Eventually the Etruscans were bound to meet resistance from the Greeks whose colonies were so numerous in southern Italy that the region was known as Magna Graecia. Endeavoring to check Greek expansion, the Etruscans allied themselves with the Phoenicians of powerful Carthage, who were also disturbed over Greek activities. But in the naval battle of 540 B.C., they were unable to defeat the Greek navy.

When the Etruscans moved into southern Italy the Greeks won a decisive victory at Cumae in 524 B.C. Then came a crippling blow from the north, as the barbarian Gauls launched a raid into northern Italy and devastated all Etruria. The days of Etruscan domination were coming to an end. The city-states of Etruria, jealous of their separate independence and seldom united against a common foe, would be unable to match the surge of a new race, the Romans, rising to power on the Tiber River.

When the Etruscans made their first appearance, about 800 B.C., the land was already peopled by Italic or Latin tribes around Mount Alban and the Tiber River. In a village located at a strategic ford on the Tiber, towns of the Latin League found a leader. That village became known as Rome. The Latins possessed no 2000 year old heritage in metalworking, painting, sculpturing and architecture, as did the Etruscans. The Romans were crude and barbaric compared with the talented newcomers from Asia Minor. But they were a stoic, self-disciplined and virile people, whose spirit of patriotic unity would eventually enable them to create a world empire of such grandeur and power that its fame would never die.

The Rise of Rome

Despite the fanciful legends that surround the founding of Rome, burial grounds found beneath the ruins of the Forum, and the remains of iron-age huts on the Palatine hill above, clearly reveal the Etruscan influence over the development of early Rome. Perhaps even the city's name *Roma* stems from the Etruscan word *ruma*, which means river.

Latium, including Rome, was first ruled by the Tarquin kings of Etruria, including Tarquinius Priscus "the ancient," a Corinthian adventurer and great builder who started the Capitoline Temple of Jupiter in Rome. The seventh and last king, Tarquin The Proud, was driven from the throne in 509 B.C., which marked the beginning of the Republic of Rome. Each year thereafter, the *imperium* or power was held by two Roman consuls, called Praetors, elected by the patrician class.

In 396 B.C., Veii, the last Etruscan stronghold, only 12 miles north of Rome, was captured and annexed to the city on the Tiber, which made Rome the leader of the Latin League. During the following century Rome was busily engaged in maintaining supremacy over her neighboring tribes, overcoming the raiding Celts, or Gauls as the Romans called them, and extending her sway southward by occupying the Greek cities of Crotona and Thurii.

In 272 B.C. the important Greek ports of Tarentum and Rhegium fell to the Romans. With the capitulation of these two leading cities of Magna Graecia came a great change in Rome's intellectual development. Looking upon centuries of Greek achievement in literature, philosophy, art and architecture, as well as science and commerce, the rough Roman conquerors were filled with awe and admiration. While reaping the spoils of war, the Romans were gathering the seeds of Greek culture and preparing to plant them soon on fertile Roman soil.

The crude little village on the Tiber River had come a long way since 509 B.C., when it over-

came Etruscan rule and set up the Roman Republic. Standing on the threshold of enlightenment, by 270 B.C. it had become master of all Italy south of the Po valley, and was now a first class world power. Only the wealthy and powerful Phoenician city of Carthage, supreme in the western Mediterranean, stood in the way of Rome's ambitions and destiny.

The Punic Wars

An appetite for plunder, whetted by the captured wealth of Tarentum and other Greek cities, induced Rome to covet the lush island of Sicily and its rich city, Syracuse. When the Romans crossed the Strait of Messina and endeavored to seize the Sicilian seaport of Messina, Carthage sent a counter force to defend the city. This clash of desires to dominate Siciliy, and to expand territorial supremacy, brought on the First Punic War, followed by more wars spanning 120 years of relentless conflict. *Punicus* was the Latin word for the reddish skinned Phoenicians, hence the term *Punic*.

The Romans lacked a navy to match the mighty Phoenician fleet, but they managed to seize a stranded Carthaginian quinquereme, a huge warship with five banks of oars, and quickly reproduced 100 copies of the fighting ship. Since the Romans' forte was hand to hand combat, rather than maritime warfare, they added a drawbridge, or corvus, to the ships which enabled them to land their warriors upon the decks of the Carthaginian vessels. The method was a complete success. In 241 B.C. Carthage sued for peace, agreeing to pay an indemnity of 3200 talents of silver. Rome annexed Sicily and mineral rich Sardinia, the first of her galaxy of conquered provinces. But the struggle for control of the western Mediterranean was not over.

Founded in 814 B.C. by Phoenician colonists, after 500 years of undisputed supremacy, Carthage had grown to a city of 700,000 people; and it was far more affluent and powerful than Rome. But the wealthy citizens and aristocracy, unlike Rome's loyal body of free men, escaped military service by hiring barbarians to fill the ranks of their army and navy. Gold and silver built the magnificent vessels of war and commerce, and paid the hordes of mercenaries who manned the ships and fought the wars. When mutiny arose from lack of funds, Carthage became hard pressed for metallic resources to maintain her power and to pay the indemnity owed to Rome.

Carthage Turns to Spain

Since Tartessus of southern Spain had long been a source of Phoenician wealth, Carthage turned to this ancient Eldorado for relief. The only threat to her plans was the presence of the Greek colonies Saguntum (near modern Valencia), Tarraco (Tarragona) and Emporium on the northeast coast of Spain. Hamilcar Barcas undertook to go to Spain, develop the great potentialities of the Spanish Peninsula, avail himself of the land's resources, and establish a base for continuing the war against Rome. Carthago Nova (Cartagena) was founded in 225 B.C. and soon became a thriving, prosperous city. Its hinterland proved extremely rich in gold, silver and lead, a bonanza of great economic value to Carthage.

Noting the wealth being unearthed in Spain, Rome became concerned with this new sign of Carthage's rejuvenation. Rome warned Carthage to confine her activities south of the Ebro River, a natural line separating their spheres of influence. Rome's aim was to protect her ally Emporium, and especially Massilia (Marseille) which lay north of the Ebro. Massilia had long been a vital outlet and port for the Mediterranean tin trade. Since Carthage had blocked Massilia's use of the Strait of Gibraltar for importing tin from Britain, the metal had to be shipped across the English Channel to Gaul, and then carried by pack train up the Loire Valley and down the Rhone to the port of Massilia.

After Hamilcar died and his successor Hasdrubal was assassinated, a new and dramatic figure appeared upon the stage of history. His name was Hannibal. As a nine year old boy he had accompanied his father, Hamilcar, to Spain. Pledged to seek vengeance against Rome and to restore the glory of Carthage, at the age of 28 Hannibal was placed in command of the army and the province of Spain. Emboldened by the wealth, materials and men that had been gathered over the previous years, Hannibal scornfully rejected Rome's warnings to stay south of the Ebro. Instead, in 219 B.C. he attacked and captured Saguntum and launched his famed campaign against Rome. Thus began the Second Punic War.

Hannibal Crosses The Alps

Dashing young Hannibal, revered by his troops for his audacity in battle, commanding presence, and democratic concern for his men, led 50,000 loyal soldiers, none of them mercenaries, and 9,000 cavalry over the Pyrenees and through southern France. He then crossed the Alps into Italy, sweeping all opposition before him. At the Tincino River and Lake Trasimeno in northern Italy and at Cannae and Tarentum in the south, the Romans were thrown into panic-stricken routs. Only well fortified positions saved the city of Rome. But after 15 years of unparalleled campaigning in a foreign, hostile land, Hannibal was forced to return to Africa and defend Carthage against Roman attack. There, Scipio Africanus defeated Hannibal, ending the Second Punic War.

It was a crushing blow to Carthage. She surrendered all her islands in the Mediterranean, agreed to pay an indemnity of 10,000 talents of silver, and gave up Spain, her age-old treasure chest. The metallic resources of the Spanish Peninsula proved to be the real prize of victory, for there Rome would exploit the wealth and develop the sinews for her future conquests. It was a very decisive moment in Roman history.

The Third and last Punic War was provoked needlessly by Rome's jealousy over the resurgence of Carthaginian trade and prosperity. Marcus P. Cato, Roman Censor, visited Carthage and noted with concern the increasing vitality of the city. Under pretext of Carthaginian treaty violations, Cato returned to Rome and launched a bitter campaign to eliminate Carthage, ending every speech in the senate with the words, "Delenda est Carthago"—"Carthage must be destroyed."

Carthage Destroyed

Rome declared war in 149 B.C., attacked Carthage and starved the city into submission. Of the city's population of over one-half million people, only 50,000 survived. They were corralled and sold into slavery. The ancient city was burned to the ground, ploughed under, seeded with salt, cursed, and made unfit for human habitation. The surrounding region became the Roman province of Africa, and Carthage became but a memory.

Meanwhile, after the Second Punic War, Rome had turned eastward in answer to appeals from Greek cities for protection against the threats of Philip V of Macedon. Fearing the rising power of Rome, Philip had earlier sought to aid Hannibal. This brought Rome and Macedon into conflict, the First Macedonian War. As Rome continued to war with Philip, Scipio Africanus crossed the Hellespont into Asia Minor in order to subdue Philip's ally, the Syrian king Antiochus III. A Roman victory brought to the growing empire the mineral-rich territory of Anatolia and an indemnity of 15,000 talents. In 168 B.C., under Paullus, the Romans again defeated Macedon, took 1000 prisoners to Rome and gathered so much booty in tribute that Roman citizens were relieved of taxation on their lands.

Macedon persisted in her attempts to arouse the Greeks to the Roman peril, even allying herself with Carthage to stave off the ruthless intruder from the west. But the Greek city-states remained divided in their hopes and their fears, unable to agree whether Rome or Macedon constituted the greater threat to their liberty.

Greece Bows to Rome

After Rome quelled the Third and Fourth Macedonian uprisings and took Corinth in 146 B.C., Roman oppression became a stark and terrible reality. Corinth was sacked and burned, its treasures were seized and sent to Rome, its men were massacred and its women and children sold as slaves. Macedonia and all Greece then became a single province of Rome. The Romans had come as friends and protectors and had left as conquerors and despoilers. The great and glorious civilization of Greece faded into the past as Greece became simply a vassal state of Rome.

Greece really died from within, of its own failures. At the moment of her greatest crisis, lack of unity among the Greek cities, their perennial weakness, left the world's most magnificent culture bereft of defense. As the ancient treasure chests of Greece and the Hellenized world were being emptied, the vaults of Rome were being filled with the spoils of war and riches from many storehouses of mineral wealth. As Greece became materially poorer, the rude villagers from the Tiber became wealthier, which added to their vigor and power. But the heritage of Greece would survive, to be transmitted to the western world through the greatness of the Roman Empire.

The Fabulous Riches of Spain

As the domination of the Mediterranean world passed to Rome, she undertook to exploit her prizes of victory, Sicily, Sardinia and especially Spain. The latter was the most highly mineralized region then known in the world, a vast storehouse of metallic ores waiting to be discovered and developed. To the early Greeks the Spanish Peninsula was known as Iberia, named after the people who dwelt along the river Iberus (now the Ebro), but the Phoenicians labeled the land *Spania*, believed to be their word for burrowing or mining. To the Romans, the area including the Ebro Valley, Saguntum and Carthago Nova (Cartagena), Hannibal's source of power, was called Hither Spain. Farther Spain encompassed the southern coast and the region tributary to the Guadalquivir River.

It was one of those singular acts of fate in the unfolding development of mankind that delivered the metallic wealth of Spain into Roman hands. Neither the Phoenicians of Carthage, concerned solely with the rewards of trade rather than colonization, nor the quarreling, disunited Greeks, would have been disposed to utilize Spain's resources as did the Romans. It required Roman vitality, organizing skill, solidarity, military genius, and statesmanship to first conquer, then settle, civilize and develop barbaric lands. Momentous indeed was the timely presence of Spain's vast mineral resources, for they supported Rome's dreams of expansion, which in the end so benefited mankind.

Metals for Rome's Legions

The first requisite for the enhancement of Roman power was a reliable currency, backed by an ample metal supply, to maintain Rome's armies and to stimulate her trade. The use of currency had come to Rome comparatively late. Bronze, in the form of heavy, clumsy lumps, was the first metal used as a medium of exchange, indicating that early Latium was poor in precious metals. After the Second Punic War, expansion of the Roman currency system became imperative owing to Rome's increased responsibility of world leadership and the change that occurred in recruiting her armies.

Until the defeat of Carthage, Roman troops had been drawn from the ranks of free citizens, mostly farmers who "enlisted" for short campaigns and then returned to their homes. As Rome's involvement grew more extensive, larger and better trained armies became necessary. Then for the first time the Roman soldier became a professional and was paid for his services. Under the early Republic, Rome's gains had been achieved by dutiful citizens whose commander was the consul of the year. As military operations were enlarged the legions of Rome became subservient to their leaders in the field. This had a significant effect upon both Rome's system of currency and the allegiance of the armies.

The governors of new provinces, or the generals who conquered them, were permitted to establish local mints and coin their own money to pay the troops. This served to increase the loyalty of the legions to the generals who led them to victory, and often to spoils of war.

Silver For Coinage

To meet her crucial need for currency, Rome was able to turn to the Phoenician *Spania* which she had won from Carthage. Spain's potential wealth had been revealed dramatically to all Rome when her generals returned in triumph from Spanish conquests loaded with booty. Scipio's procession alone displayed 120,000 pounds of silver on litters borne by slaves through Rome's roaring, excited streets. By 180 B.C. there had been added to the loot 216,000 pounds of silver and 3800 ounces of gold.

For a long time silver formed the mainstay of Roman coinage and it was Spanish silver that performed this vital function. The denarius became the principal coin, roughly equivalent to forty cents in American money. A talent varied according to economic circumstances from $1200 to $4,000 in value. The abundance of coins obtained by Rome in her eastern conquests, including the silver tetradrachms of Athens and the gold staters of Macedon, were used in the east in place of Roman money.

During the period of Rome's early growth, except for iron, her own reserves of metallic ores were being depleted. New sources of mineral wealth were essential, not only to meet increasing demands for currency, but also for armor and weapons of war, and for the growing metal crafts which were required for the expansion of trade. The arts and crafts of the Greeks, and of the Phoenicians, were already exerting their beneficial influences upon the industries of Rome.

The most accessible metal deposits were those of Spain, made known by ages of Phoenician exploitation. Spain had long been the land of promise for the ancient world. It was also its wild, western frontier. With its aversion to foreigners it was not an easy land to conquer and settle. Scipio, Cato and Tiberius were largely responsible for bringing the tribes of Spain under control.

Spain—The Prodigal Land

After the Romans pacified the region, the primitive landscape of Spain presented a vista of unending lure to the seekers of metallic wealth. Basking under the blue skies of southern Spain, and nestled amongst wooded canyons and upon undulating hillside slopes covered with evergreen shrubs, rock roses, Spanish Broom, sage brush and fragrant ladanum, there were innumerable ore deposits of silver, lead, copper and gold.

Many of these deposits already had been worked by the Greeks and Phoenicians, but many more lay half-concealed by vegetation waiting to be discovered. Although the Romans first came as exploiters, seized the ancient mines as spoils of war and forced captives to work them, it was Rome who developed the mineral resources of Spain with greatest vigor and reaped the most significant benefits.

Referring to the richness of Spain's metallic wealth, Posidonius stated, "When the forests burned, the soil composed of gold and silver, melted and boiled out over the surface, because every mountain and hill is bullion heaped up in some prodigal fortune ... some private adventurers pick up a Euboean talent (62 lbs.Avoirdp.) of silver per day ... among the Artabrians who live farthest in northwest Lusitania (Gallaecia) the soil "effloresces" with silver, tin and white gold." This has the ring of a florid prospectus of ancient times, but it does reflect the esteem in which was held the Eldorado of Spain.

The richest region of Spain, indeed of the ancient world, was the territory drained by the Guadalquivir River. The Romans named the river, Baetis. The territory was called Baetica, and included the Phoenician land of Tartessus. Today we call it Andalusia. For a distance of 200 miles across Andalusia from east to west along the Sierra Morena, which the Romans called Montes Mariani, mines dotted the landscape. Strabo claimed that this region was the greatest storehouse of silver, lead, gold, copper and iron ores ever discovered.

Rome's Spanish Mines

At the eastern end of the Sierra the mines of Castulo, now Cazlona in the noted mining district of Linares, were worked by the Carthaginians and provided Hannibal with the means for launching his campaign against Rome. Pliny stated, "the Baebelo mine alone furnished Hannibal with 300 pounds of silver per day ... the mountain is excavated for a distance of 1500 paces ... water-bearers lighted by torches stand night and day bailing out the water." In 208 B.C. the elder

Scipio defeated the Carthaginians and took possession of this rich region. The Romans worked it long and prodigiously. Coins have been found there dating from the 1st century B.C. to 380 A.D. In the hills near Linares the mines are still known as Los Pozos de Anibal, named after Hannibal.

Ore bodies in the Centinillo mine were worked by shafts 600 feet deep, and by adits 2,000 feet long driven into the hillside to reach the downward extension of the ore zones. Drifts 3,000 feet long were advanced in the ore by using the ancient method of fire-setting to crack the rock. The magnitude of these workings reveals that the Romans used considerable skill in their mining operations.

Some of these mines have been found sufficiently rich to warrant reopening in modern times. German engineers discovered, among other mining relics, the primitive Archimedes screw-pumps used to lift water from the Roman levels. The pumps were wooden cylinders about 14 feet long and 20 inches in diameter, enclosing long, spiral-shaped vanes, or screws, made of copper. When the lower portion of the pump was placed on an incline in the water and rotated by hand or foot power, water was raised vertically about six feet. By using a number of these pumps, one set above the other, water could be lifted from the deeper levels. Named after its inventor, Archimedes of Syracuse (240 B.C.), the pump became widely used over the world. Even today, on the banks of the Nile in Egypt, natives use them to irrigate their fields.

The Silver of Cartagena

Carthago Nova, or New Carthage, founded by Hannibal's brother Hasdrubal, and captured by the Romans under Scipio Africanus in 208 B.C., was a thriving outlet for a hinterland rich and diverse in metallic wealth. Strabo, quoting Polybius, described the district, stating "The silver mines of New Carthage are very large, about 20 stadia (2½ miles) from the city, and embrace in circuit 400 stadia (45 miles). 40,000 men are employed, bringing into the Roman treasury 25,000 drachmae (about $5500) per day."

West of New Carthage, or Cartagena, mines were worked extensively at Mazarron and to the northeast at Orihuela. Since the argentiferous lead ores were the most abundant sources of silver in Baetica, a considerable quantity of lead was produced in the districts of Linares, Cartagena

and Gata. Over 50 ancient lead furnaces have been found at Gata near Almeria. At Coto Fortuna, workings extended over a distance of five miles and included a mile long adit driven into the hillside to drain water from the overhead workings. Roman coins have been found there dated from 200 B.C. to the 5th century A.D., denoting the very long period of mine production that furnished wealth to the Romans. Lead, as well as silver, was important to Roman economy. Lead was used for many purposes, especially for lead pipes in the vast water systems of Rome and other large centers.

Strabo referred to the mountain ridges north of Corduba (Cordova) as being "full of mines," and added that "silver is the most plentiful in the regions above Ilipa, and in those about Sisapo." Situated about 75 miles northwest of Linares, Sisapo is the site of the world's most prolific deposit of cinnabar, an ore of mercury, which the ancients often called "minium." This single mine gave Rome a virtual monopoly of this important mineral. Pliny stated, "This minium mine furnishes revenue to the Roman state; no other property is guarded with greater care." Today the mine is known as the Almaden and still supplies the world with a large share of its mercury. Many mercury mines of all countries have endeavored to add luster to their properties by naming them Almaden.

The Fame of Rio Tinto

Copper was produced in great quantity, coming from a mine that became known as the Rio Tinto located in the province of Huelva west of modern Seville, which the Romans called Hispalis. The Rio Tinto even today is one of the largest, most productive and most famous mines in the world. Since 900 B.C., beginning with the Phoenicians, continuing throughout Roman times and on into our present era, the Rio Tinto has produced great wealth in gold and copper. Said Strabo, "For the Turdetani (in the land of Tartessus) mining is profitable beyond measure since one-fourth of the ore brought out is pure copper." This indicates that the early surface ores were rich in native copper. The mines are today owned by the Compania Espanola de Minas de Rio Tinto, and operated under a British Company leasehold. Active over a period of 3000 years, the Rio Tinto is perhaps the most extensively worked deposit in the world. It also possesses a most fascinating history.

No doubt the Phoenicians were the first metal

seekers to be attracted to that extraordinary river, now called the Rio Tinto, whose blood-red waters empty into an estuary of the Mediterranean near present day Huelva. Never had they, nor has anyone who visits it today, seen a stream so deeply and brilliantly tinted with red, the feature which gives the river its name. Over its entire length of 60 miles it runs like a bleeding wound from its source in the Sierra Morena Mountains to mingle with the blue waters of the Mediterranean.

The Scarlet Mountain

Following this curious phenomenon northward into the highlands, the earliest prospectors came to the secret of the river's color, and there like a pot of gold at the end of the rainbow they found a fabulous bonanza. A dome-shaped mountain, flaming red and saturated with oxides of iron, standing boldly forth against a deep blue sky, greeted the first adventurers.

Seasonal rains, washing its slopes over aeons of the past, had leached the mountain's scarlet colors and carried them downward into the headwaters of the stream and on to the sea. The bright red "iron-hat," always a welcome sign of mineralization to prospectors, was the oxidized outcrop of a huge sulphide deposit of copper and iron, now famed over the world as the Rio Tinto mine.

The Phoenicians and later the Romans who attacked this red mountain with their picks and shovels first reaped a harvest of gold, which was mixed with the native and carbonate ores of copper. Far below the "iron-hat" lay an immense deposit of brassy hued sulphides of iron and copper. As the Romans, and later the modern miners, dug deeper, a huge hole appeared where the red mountain once stood.

The Rio Tinto Today

Today the Rio Tinto mine, after centuries of digging, consists of three enormous open-cast pits, the Corta Atalya, Corta F. Sur, and Corta F. Norte, The latter is three-quarters of a mile wide and over 800 feet deep. Around each pit is a rim of the original ruby-red outcrop from which the Phoenicians won rich rewards in gold, silver, lead and copper. Great splashes of the green and blue colors of copper carbonates on walls of the pits cascade downward beneath the red rims.

Here and there exposed in the walls are the exhumed workings of the Romans, small cramped tunnels and shafts. Crude notches cut in the rock reveal the footholes used by miners to descend the shafts to lower levels. Among the ancient mining tools and equipment recovered by modern miners were numerous water wheels 14 feet in diameter used to lift and drain water from the workings. Axle shafts were made of bronze and connected to treadmills operated continuously by slaves. Far beneath the red rim the great pits are delving into the unaltered, primary ores, the brassy sulphides which are now being mined for their copper and sulphur content. Huge power shovels and steel headframes in the pit bottoms look like miniature toys cast into the void by some errant boys.

A visitor today may walk among groups of fragrant umbrella-shaped pine trees that now grow upon a wide expanse of black slag which the Romans accumulated over centuries of smelting operations. Occasional patches of older slag, perhaps Phoenician, are visible together with remnants of small rock huts used by miners who occupied them nearly 3000 years ago. The slag still contains small amounts of lead, silver and gold, disclosing that earliest mining was directed toward recovery of the precious metals. Even after furnishing the ballast for a railroad built in 1873, running 50 miles from the mines to the coastal port of Huelva, there are 15 million tons of slag remaining beneath the covering of pine trees. Such was the incredible extent of Rio Tinto's treasure chest of metals, which even today still continues to yield its wealth.

Gold of The Tagus

West and north of Baetica, toward the border of Portugal, the district of Metallum Vipascense at Aljustrel became a famous producer of copper and silver. Farther north gold came from the Tagus River which flows from the highlands of central Spain across Lusitania (modern Portugal) to the sea at Olisipo, now Lisbon. Pliny stated, "in the sediments of the Tagus no gold is found more free of impurities ... the gold bearing sand is carried down by the rivers and torrents ... and in the dust, nuggets weighing as much as half a pound are sometimes found."

It is easy to understand why the Roman Emperor Augustus would later lay such stress upon the last stronghold of Iberian independence, the northwest corner of the peninsula. In the remarkable systems of roads developed by Rome to reach her treasures in distant lands, one of the early and important arteries given priority by

Augustus reached into a prodigiously rich territory that included Minho, Tras-os-Montes and Beira. Later, this area became known as Portugal. Farther north, in the northwest corner of the peninsula, were other important regions known as Gallaecia and Asturia. All were flourishing producers of silver, gold, lead and tin. Pliny stated that Lusitania, Gallaecia and Asturia furnished Rome with 20,000 pounds (weight) of gold annually.

But most important were Gallaecia's rich resources in tin. Within 20 miles of Orense were the celebrated lode and placer deposits of tin at Carballino and Allariz. Another productive tin region was in the Cantabrian Mountains. According to Strabo, the Romans built elaborate aqueducts to provide water for washing the heavy tin mineral, which we know today as cassiterite.

The Wealthy Publicani

As provincial mining activity increased, the system of working state-owned mines by captive labor was replaced by leaseholds granted to individuals. Bribery, or the repayment of favors formerly received, often entered into the allocation of these leases. As colonization and Romanization of Spain progressed, many retired Roman and Spanish soldiers became leaseholders and profited handsomely on this new frontier of opportunity.

Greatest exploitation of the mines came from a wealthy class of financiers who, because of their possession of horses and service in the patrician cavalry corps, were known as *equestrians*. Leases were often auctioned by Roman officials to the highest bidder, known as a *publicanus*, who profited by subleasing the property and collecting taxes from the actual miners. Many Roman officials, through corrupt practices, acquired great wealth. Provincial governors grew to resent the growing independence of the *publicani* or businessmen. But credit must be given to these bankers and traders for developing the natural resources of the Roman empire. They started such a flow of wealth into the imperial treasury that the state was able, during certain periods, to dispense with direct taxation of its citizens.

The acquisition by conquest of the vast resources of Spain, and the seizure of fabulous treasures throughout the East, caused a rapid rise in the standard of living and distribution of Roman wealth. Political leaders, businessmen, and bankers and traders grew immensely rich and self-indulgent. Everyone became fascinated with the flexibility and power of money as a means of satisfying their desires and achieving fantastic economic manipulations. As the appetite for opulence grew stronger, the need for the resources of new territories became greater. As a means for satisfying these desires, pathways were about to be explored by a man named Julius Caesar.

The Fortunes of Julius Caesar

It was a fortune gathered on the Spanish frontier that enabled Julius Caesar to establish his popularity in Rome and launch his extraordinary career. In 69 B.C., at the age of 30, he served as quaestor in Farther Spain, a region that comprised the burgeoning riches of Baetica, which included Corduba (the capital), Castula, Sisapo, Huelva and Gades. As quaestor he became custodian of the treasury and assistant to Antistius Vetus, the provincial governor. Very few details have survived concerning Caesar's quaestorship, except that in less than one year he returned to Rome a rich man.

In Rome, alive with ambition, Caesar became champion of democratic traditions and plebeian rights, which won him the support of the Populares, the People's party. But his tastes for lavish living and grandiose expenditures, catering to public favor, led him into debt, until he owed 830 talents, about $3,000,000. With a large loan from one of Rome's richest financiers, Marcus Crassus, who owned silver mines and hordes of slaves in Spain, Caesar was able to forestall his creditors. In 61 B.C. Caesar managed to return to Spain as a propraetor, or governor, of his former province, apparently resolved to thereby extricate himself from his financial difficulties.

Nourished by the thriving economy of Farther Spain, and the rebellious tribes whom he raided and subjugated, Caesar amassed a great fortune. Setting out from Corduba, he campaigned northward against towns in Lusitania (Portugal) and Gallaecia. From these operations Caesar wrung vast amounts of money and booty, plundering communities and accepting huge tributes from local chiefs. When he returned to Rome Caesar's wealth was such that he not only repaid his debts, he also tendered so much booty to the imperial treasury that the senate accorded him a magnificent triumph in the streets of Rome.

The First Triumvirate

Having thus attained a position of affluence,

popularity and power, Caesar was now able to bring about an alliance between Crassus, Pompey and himself, forming the First Triumvirate. Acting as Consul, Caesar arranged to have placed under his control the provinces of Cisalpine Gaul in northern Italy, and Gallia Narbonensis, part of which is now known as Provence in southern France.

When Caesar took over command of these provinces he acquired the right to forge his own army, a step that permitted him to launch the plan to fulfill his ambitions. In order to enhance his political standing, Caesar's aims were to surpass the military reputation of his upcoming rival, Pompey, and to add further to his fortune and fields of conquest. It naturally occurred to him that there might be other lands beyond Rome's frontiers as rich as Spain's Eldorado. The untrod, unconquered land of Gaul to the north might well be such a country. A logical pretext for Caesar's invasion of Gaul was soon forthcoming.

North of Narbonensis, numerous tribes were in restless migration. Over 300,000 Helvetii were swarming southward from Switzerland toward Narbonensis. Moving into northern Gaul, there were 120,000 Germans led by their arrogant tribal chief, Ariovistus. Certain Gallic chiefs, seemingly unable to stem the tide, appealed to Caesar for protection. Caesar accepted the call not only to save Gaul and safeguard Rome's northern frontier; he was also responding to the inherent urge to seek the riches of distant lands.

In 58 B.C. Caesar's legions defeated the Helvetii at Bibracte (modern Autun), and in a long, bloody battle on the plain of Alsace, the "Ochsenfeld" between Mulhouse and Rouffach, Ariovistus and his barbarian forces were nearly annihilated. The next year the Aquitani were subjugated. But on the northwestern coast of Gaul, the Veneti chose to stand and resist the Romans. Possessing a centuries old maritime monopoly of the tin trade, the Veneti were ready to fight for survival. Information gained from the Veneti would tempt Caesar to invade and seek the fabled wealth of Britain.

Until his battle with the Veneti, Caesar had little knowledge of Britain. He knew that for centuries Phoenician and Carthaginian traders had supplied the Mediterranean region with tin. But these canny mariners had deliberately concealed the source, and even devised misleading concepts as to the whereabouts of the "tin islands", vaguely known as the 'Cassiterides.' The name stemmed from *Cassiteros*, the Greek word for tin.

In his masterful and well known Commentaries, De Bello Gallico, written during his invasion of Gaul, Caesar bemoaned the futility of soliciting information from Gallic merchants concerning Britain. He had even sent an investigator into Gaul to report on the source of the age-old tin trade. Since the report was inconclusive, Caesar was compelled to rely upon rumors, legends and suppositions of ancient writers as to the location of the mysterious 'Cassiterides.' Gold and pearls, as well as tin, were said to abound in the land.

The Cassiterides

As early as 430 B.C. Herodotus, the Greek historian, had referred to the 'Cassiterides from where we get our tin.' But as Caesar knew, Herodotus had only said that both tin and amber came from a region in the remote north. In the first century B.C. Strabo endeavored to prove that the Cassiterides lay in the latitude of Britain, but he conceived them to be islands 400 miles west of Lands End. In 90 B.C. Posidonius, a Greek geographer, ventured past the Pillars of Hercules and up the coast to Belerium, his name for the land where tin was mined. Posidonius described the Belerium promontory, which we now recognize as the Cornish peninsula, terminating in Britain's most westward point, Lands End. Posidonius mentioned the 'veins', meaning the streambeds, which were worked skillfully for tin. Today we know the tin mineral as cassiterite, and that the fabled Cassiterides in reality was the land of Cornwall, England.

Throughout geologic ages, grains of heavy, black tin oxide had been eroded from the veins and pink granite rocks of Cornwall and washed into the streambeds below, where they were gathered as placer tin in sluice boxes by the native miners. Using charcoal and bellows, the cassiterite concentrates were then smelted, producing ingots of white, metallic tin.

Posidonius stated that the tin ingots were transported at low tide to an island called 'Ictis' located close to the shore. After eliminating several possible sites we find that 'Ictis' is none other than an island now known as St. Michael's Mount across the picturesque bay from Penzance, Cornwall. Crowned now by a 13th century castle, the island rises majestically above a tide-swept flat directly opposite the present town of Marazion. In a museum at nearby Truro, one may see the tin ingot of St. Mawes that was dredged from the harbor.

The Tin Merchants of Carbilo

The ancient miners of Cornwall took their tin to maritime merchants who maintained a port on the island of Ictis. There, the ingots were loaded aboard strong, high-prowed boats and taken across the English channel to the shore of Gaul. At the mouth of the Liger, or Loire River, the ingots were unloaded at a trade emporium known as Carbilo, the present city of St. Nazaire, where they were transferred to pack trains. The valuable cargo was then carried eastward up the Loire Valley and southward down the Rhone to the Mediterranean seaport of Massilia, now known as Marseille.

These hardy merchant mariners of Carbilo, whom we left a few pages back preparing to battle Caesar in 56 B.C., were the Veneti. Their high-prowed vessels, knowledge of metals, skilled seamanship and instincts for trade suggest that they may have come originally from the Middle East. Settling here on the coast of Brittany, they had become the most powerful maritime people of the North Atlantic region. Caesar's invasion, and the threat of Roman control, placed the Veneti's monopoly of Britain trade in serious jeopardy. Without hesitation, the Veneti took up arms against the Romans.

Both Strabo and Caesar have described the critical and ferocious naval battle that took place on the southwest coast of Brittany. In order to drive the Veneti from the sea, exerting superhuman efforts Caesar's men managed to construct and launch a fleet near the mouth of the Loire. Only by using overwhelming numbers were Caesar's forces able to destroy the sturdy oak vessels of the Veneti. With this amazing victory Caesar learned the magnitude of the Veneti's prosperous maritime trade with Britain. That was enough to whet the appetite of any conqueror in search of riches.

The Gallic Frontier

After Caesar's victory over the Veneti he was forced to delay his invasion of Britain because of a rising tide of Gallic rebellion. Germanic tribes east of the Rhine, infiltrating west of the river, posed a threat against Roman control of Gaul. Caesar had his engineers build a long wooden bridge across the Rhine near present Coblenz, sent punitive forces against the Sugambri "to fill

the Germans with fear," and then two weeks later discreetly withdrew, destroyed the bridge and sent word to Rome of his victory over "500,000 Germans." In Rome, Cato and other members of the senate accused Caesar of endangering an army of the Republic. These imputations worried Gaul's conqueror. He became aware that to attain a change of fortune a new conquest was required. Caesar had in mind the incalculable wealth of Britain.

There were many among Caesar's followers whose main purpose was to find a fortune along the trails of invasion. In the three years of tramping through barbarian Gaul the Romans saw but few signs of riches. No Phoenician exploiters had previously exposed the land's rich mines, as they had in Spain. Compared with the fabulous wealth of Spain, the mineral resources of Gaul were found to be far short of expectations.

Gold had been mined in pre-Roman times in various placer deposits, and had enriched the shrines and treasuries of certain tribal chiefs. Among the Tectosages between Carcassone and Toulouse considerable gold had accumulated in temple coffers. Gold had also been collected in the valleys of the Garonne and Ariege rivers, fed by waters from the Pyrenees, and gold had long been won from the sands of the Vienne, Creuse and Tarn rivers. From these and other districts Caesar was able to gather considerable quantities of gold as the spoils of war.*

Caesar Invades Britain

After being disappointed with Gaul's apparent lack of mineral bonanzas, the convincing evidence of the Veneti's prosperous trade with the tin miners of Cornwall greatly rejuvenated the dreams of the treasure-seeking Romans. Following the surrender of the Veneti, the Romans looked with high hopes to Britain as their next

*Pre-Roman gold also was available in placers and surface croppings near the modern mining district of Chale-let southwest of Montlucan in central France. North of St. Yrieix and south of Limoges gold could be found in districts where modern mines have since operated, such as Cheni, Ladignac, La Tournerie, Fagassierie and Champvert. Lead and silver ores were found among the Ruteni and Arveri (Auverne) near Gevandan, and at Rodez east of the Tarn River. Caesar was impressed with the iron works of Avaricum (Bourges) and recognized iron deposits which later supplied the needs of noted iron industries such as Lugdunum, the modern city of Lyons. In what is now Brittany, some tin occurred in the sands of the Villaine near Ploermel, but it was Cornish tin that had supplied the Phoenicians and Carthaginians for centuries.

Eldorado. In 55 B.C., shortly after the Veneti conquest, Caesar made his first attempt to invade Britain.

The effort was brief and unsuccessful. A year later Caesar tried again and defeated King Cassivelaunus north of the Thames, probably near St. Albans. Caesar was campaigning in eastern Britain, a long, long way from Cornwall, or the Cassiterides, far to the west. He managed to exact promises of tribute, but otherwise made little headway. When revolts in Gaul again demanded his attention, Caesar left the island, leaving the search for Britain's wealth to conquerors of a later date.

It was Caesar's victory over the Veneti, however, that solved the mystery of the location of the Cassiterides. His findings confirmed the tales of antiquity concerning the riches of that land, and provided the incentive for the future conquests and settlement of Britain. But mounting pressures in Gaul, and in Rome, would delay any immediate attention to Britain. In 53 B.C. Caesar was forced again to cross the Rhine and suppress the Germanic tribes. The next year, with nearly all of Gaul flaring in rebellion, Caesar cornered the able and dauntless Gallic leader, Vercingetorix, at Alesia (Mont-Auxois northwest of Dijon). The surrender of Vercingetorix marked the end of Gallic independence, and added to the Roman Empire a province twice the size of Italy.

Caesar's quest for riches and power led him to the conquest he had clearly envisioned, and marked a momentous turning point in the rise of civilization in western Europe. Under the beneficent influence of Roman authority and protection, Gaul would become the seedbed of the French nation.

Caesar Crosses The Rubicon

As for Caesar, he was approaching the apex of his meteoric career. Disturbed by the intrigues of his enemies in the capital, including Pompey who was maneuvering to become the master of Rome, Caesar headed his powerful, well-trained legions homeward. The Roman senate warned Caesar to disband his army before entering the city, as was the custom. Instead, Caesar crossed the Rubicon River and defiantly marched into Rome.

The ensuing events, so prominent in the annals of history, can be traced only briefly here. When Pompey fled from Italy, Caesar pursued and defeated him, and then went on to Egypt where for nine months he enjoyed the charms of Cleopatra. Hearing that Pharnaces, the Parthian

king, had recaptured the mineral-rich regions of Pontus and Cappadocia, Caesar hurriedly left Egypt, met and defeated Pharnaces at Zela, and dispatched to Rome his famous message, *Veni, Vidi, Vici*–"I came, I saw, I conquered."

Returning in 45 B.C., Caesar was accorded the greatest triumph ever seen in the streets of Rome. From the huge booty he had gathered, he paid 5,000 drachmas (about $3,000) each to thousands of his soldiers, and grandly expended immense sums on public feasts and games. The next year he was elected consul for a period of 10 years, and one year later was made dictator for life. Only five months had passed when, on the Ides of March, Caesar's rule ended. He was assassinated by conspirators who feared Caesar's lust for power.

Although his dictatorship brought the Roman Republic to an end, Caesar instituted many far-reaching reforms. He ended profiteering by tax collectors, reduced debts, sent thousands of colonists into the provinces, spent huge sums on public improvements and conceived the empire's vast system of roads. In modifying the Egyptian solar calendar Caesar established basically the "Julian" calendar in use today. His most constructive act was the granting of Roman citizenship to the provinces, thus welding the members of the empire to a common cause.

Twenty years of turmoil and civil war followed Caesar's assassination. His grand-nephew and legal heir, eighteen year old Octavian, rescued the nation from the brink of disaster. Octavian took upon himself the title "Augustus", or revered one. Although he ruled with undisputed authority as the first Roman emperor, Augustus preserved many democratic principles of government. His reign marked the beginning of the Roman Empire, and with it came 200 years of peace, the Pax Romana, and Rome's Golden Age.

The Pax Romana

Augustus cancelled all tax arrears on property, provided spectacular public games at his own expense, generously distributed spoils to his generals and soldiers, all of which enhanced his popularity. He launched an inspiring program of public building planned to make Rome the grandest and most beautiful city in the world. A new forum, a senate building, 82 magnificent temples, and a huge basilica designed to house an array of markets and civil courts, were built. Said Augustus, "I found Rome a city of brick and left it a city of marble." His son-in-law Agrippa,

Rome's noted engineer, built over 150 elaborate public baths, added the Julian aqueduct and hundreds of fountains to Rome's marvelous water system.

It was during the reigns of Caesar and Augustus that coinage was established on the greatest scale, benefiting the empire's world-wide trade; About 19 B.C. a new gold and silver currency was issued in unprecedented quantity by the three great mints of Rome, Pergamum and Lugdunum (Lyons, France). Garrisons of the empire had to be maintained, new conquests had to be financed, and trade was increasing on a grand scale.

The cities of Campania in the south became the industrial heartland of Italy. Using techniques borrowed from the craftsmen of Tyre, Sidon and Egypt, the art of glass blowing was raised to its highest peak by the Romans. Magnificent wares of polychrome hues, blue, purple and especially red, were eagerly sought by the wealthy class, even as they are today by collectors and prominent museums. Particularly famous were the bronze and silver products made in the workshops of Capua. An abundant supply of silver from Spanish mines made silver services available to even the moderately well-to-do. The empire's increasing harvest of metals from its provinces provided the means of support for its armies, its trade supremacy and its affluent society. Upon this metallic base was erected the prosperity and power of the Roman Empire.

Rome's Search for Riches

Under Augustus a vast system of roads was spread across the empire. Colonial settlement was accelerated, and new areas of mineral wealth were exploited. Highways were extended into northwestern Spain where the celebrated tin deposits of Cantabria, Allariz and Carballino in Gallaecia were discovered and worked. North of the Alps new colonies were established in Raetia at Augusta Vindelicorum (Augsburg, Germany) and at Juvavum (Salzburg, Austria) near Hallstatt in iron-rich Noricum, and at Vindobona (Vienna) in Pannonia. On the continent of Europe, only the German barbarians north of the Danube and east of the Rhine remained beyond the reach of the empire.

Rome's expansion was nearly always an effort to bolster the material resources of the empire. Invasions were directed toward regions of supposed metallic riches. This view has been held by many historians. Especially pertinent are the observations of such an eminent authority as Herbert Clark Hoover, one of the world's foremost mining engineers, and 31st president of the United States. Mr. Hoover, and his wife Lou Henry Hoover, in their scientific classic, the translation from the Latin of Agricola's "De Re Metallica," among their many explanatory notes offered this comment:

"The Romans were the most intensive miners and searchers after metallic wealth already mined. The latter was obviously the objective of most Roman conquests, and those nations rich in these commodities at that time necessarily possessed their own mines. Thus a map showing the extensions of the Empire coincides in an extraordinary manner with the metal districts of Europe, Asia and North Africa."

Many examples of the search for foreign wealth by the Romans have been recorded. Aelius Gallus, under orders of Augustus, in 25 B.C. tried to subjugate Arabia while seeking its gold mines, probably lured by the Queen of Sheba's fabled gold. Nero sent an expedition to find the sources of the Nile, which no doubt he believed would lead to the fabulous Land of Punt. As one follows the Romans it becomes apparent that the lands they chose to invade were frontiers of legendary wealth.

When Augustus died in A.D. 14 he already had appointed his step-son Tiberius to succeed him. Tiberius was a great general, and campaigned in the mineral-rich lands of Dalmatia and Pannonia. As the second Emperor of Rome, he was one of the empire's most able rulers. The next emperor was Caligula whose rule became one of insane brutality and depravity. He was murdered by his own troops, the Praetorian Guard, who then took it upon themselves to appoint Claudius, the 50 year old uncle of Caligula, to the principate. Attracted by smoldering tales of the past, it was Claudius who, in A.D. 43, decided that the time had come to follow in Caesar's footsteps by seeking the fabled riches of Britain.

The Prizes of Victory

Tacitus, the Roman historian, echoed the sentiments of this period when he wrote that the mineral wealth of Britain was the "Prize of Victory" to be sought. And in Britain, as in Spain, the Romans first had to subdue the native tribes. Caesar had been the first to experience their fierce resistance. He had found that the inhabitants were mainly Celts who, centuries earlier, had invaded Britain and absorbed the previous bronze age and iron age cultures. Some of the tribal towns already had become marketing centers when the Romans first appeared. Caesar had recorded in his Commentaries that gold and bronze coins, and iron bars of standard weights, were used as currency. He also confirmed that tin was found in "the inland regions of Britain."

When Claudius invaded Britain he embarked at Portius Itius near modern Boulogne, as had Caesar, leading 40,000 men across the Strait of Dover. Landing in Kent, Claudius moved northward and captured a native settlement which he named Camulodunum. Today it is known as Colchester. Later, the Romans founded another base called Londinium, now the city of London. As further legionary fortresses were established, Britain was brought under Roman control.

A serious revolt occurred in A.D. 61 when Boadicea, a brave tribal queen, standing in a chariot beside her daughters, led fierce attacks upon Camulodunum and Londinium, burned and sacked the cities and killed thousands of Romans. Order was restored by the legions of Paulinus. In A.D. 78 Gnaeus Agricola was made governor of Britain, established schools, introduced the use of Latin and encouraged the building of public works, bringing the first rays of civilization to the warlike tribes of Britain.

The Romans lost no time seeking their "Prize of Victory." Men familiar with the characteristics of Spain's mineral deposits eagerly combed the hills for similar riches. They found gold at Dolgelly, Dolaucothy and Golofau in Carmarthenshire, South Wales, where an aqueduct was built to carry water for washing the ore. Copper deposits were found at Alderly Edge east of modern Chester, and near Criccieth in Caernarvon and upon the island of Anglesey as well as at Great Ormes Head west of modern Liverpool. But if it was precious metal that the Romans first sought, they were disappointed.

The Bonanzas of Britain

Britain's bonanzas were not to be in gold or copper; instead they were in vast, easily worked deposits of lead, which also contained some silver. Less than six years after the invasion of Claudius, an immense storehouse of lead ore was opened in the limestone strata of the Mendip Hills east of modern Cheddar, in northeast Somerset.

North of the Mendip Hills there was another important lead mining district in southwest Shropshire, about 11 miles southwest of Shrewsbury. Near Shelve Hill and Minsterly, the Romans dug shallow open-cuts and trenches over an area nine miles long and five miles wide to work the rich surface ores of lead. Several lead ingots bearing the name of Hadrian, and coins issued in the reign of Pius, have been found in the old slag and refuse piles. Farther west near Llanidloes more lead deposits were worked, and their ruins also yielded Roman coins.

Among the Derbyshire hills the Romans found perhaps their most prolific lead supply. The chief mines were near Matlock at Dovedale, and southward to Wirksworth and Castleton. Ingots found there bear the name of Hadrian, as well as the names of private operators, or *conductores*. Many of the Roman mines were worked by the state, guarded by soldiers. In later years private lessees were given the opportunity to work the mines. Slave labor provided most of the work force.

A few miles west of Chester in Flintshire, lead smelters operated at Pentre near Flint. Over 20 ingots of lead were found in this area, mostly on the shore of the Mersey, apparently lost in the wreck of a freighting barge near Runcon. The ingots bore the name of Vespasian, dated about A.D. 70, indicating the early period during which the Romans pushed into this territory in search of mineral treasure.

No less than 70 lead ingots of the Roman period have been recovered throughout Britain. They have been found in many mining districts and upon main routes of transportation, either as hidden hoards or perhaps as discarded burdens along the roadsides. Most of them, weighing from 125 to 230 pounds, were stamped with the names of the emperors under whose reigns the ingots were cast, from Claudius to Constantine, bearing witness to the long period of Roman lead production.

The Romans, however, were not the first to work the Mendip, or mine-deeps, on the limestone plateau of Somerset. Brooches, or fibulae, and other artifacts found in Celtic ruins of the La Tene iron period show that the lead mines had been used centuries prior to the arrival of Claudius. As was their custom, the Romans took over the mines, and with their usual efficiency and energy, rapidly increased production.

Entertainment for the residents of this flourishing camp was not overlooked, for atop a hill the Romans built an amphitheater whose ruins may be seen today. Since the mines have also been operated in the late 19th century, it is apparent that the Mendip deposits have been productive over a period of more than 2000 years.

Lead—The Prize of Victory

Britain's bonanza of lead was a timely and invaluable "Prize of Victory" for the Romans. Everywhere in Britain, Gaul, Spain and Italy, and especially in Rome, metallic lead was being used in roofing the increasing numbers of ornate public buildings and temples. Lead pipes served as conduits for the water systems of growing towns and cities. Even burial urns and coffins, often bearing elaborate designs and figures, were fashioned in lead.

Pewter, an alloy of tin and lead, and sometimes of tin and copper, came into general use in Romanized centers of the Empire. Usually the alloy consisted of 3 to 6 parts of lead to one of tin. Pewter was popularly used in fancy dining services, dishes, tankards and other domestic utensils. As the mode of Roman living grew more affluent, charming pewter dinner sets became widely used by those who were not quite able to afford silver plate.

Not far to the northeast of the Mendip mines, the Romans built their celebrated spa at Bath. Fascinated with the curative powers of the 120 degree mineral hot springs they built magnificent baths and a temple to the native deity, Sul, and named the place Aquae Sulis. The Romans considered Sul to be the counterpart of their Minerva, who was primarily a goddess of the handicrafts. Minerva's temple was the center of worship for the Roman guilds.

Making profuse use of lead, the baths and the conduits that carried the water from the hot springs were lined with metal from the Mendip mines. One of the present baths still receives its water through the original lead conduit. The excavated remains of the baths and the temple form one of the finest examples of Roman antiquities in western Europe. While viewing these relics of Roman opulence, one can picture rich merchants and high citizens enjoying their wealthy provincial city of Aquae Sulis, now known as Bath, nearly 1900 years ago.

Comparing other lead deposits of the Empire with those of Britain, Pliny stated that while the lead in Spain was plentiful, it was extracted with great labor from the deeper veins. The ore in Britain, however, was not only found in abundance, it occurred so near the surface and was so easily mined that a law became necessary to limit lead production. This was probably done to avoid needless damage to the workings by over-zealous operators. The oxidized ores were so soft and exposed that in places they could be mined by the simple process of sluicing the ground with jets of water released from dams which were built for that purpose. Elsewhere only shallow workings were required to mine huge amounts of ore.

Britain's lead deposits also supplied Rome with considerable amounts of silver. Metallic lead was first obtained from the ore by smelting, and then subjected to the process of cupellation which released the silver. The very low silver content of the many lead ingots recovered throughout Britain reflects the high degree of Roman smelting efficiency, especially in their cupellation process.

Britain's Iron Deposits

In Britain's iron deposits the Romans uncovered a natural resource of immense future significance to the nation. As Caesar had noted, the natives were armed with iron swords and spears, and used scythes and other implements of iron, as well as iron bars which formed a medium of exchange. At first the iron deposits were less important than the continental iron fields, but according to Strabo the Romans eventually exported iron to the continent.

A district once luxuriantly wooded with huge oaks, known as the Weald, situated in Kent, Surrey and Sussex counties, was an important source of Roman iron. Since then the forests have been reduced considerably in order to obtain charcoal for smelting. At Beauport Park, near the town of Battle where William The Conqueror, in 1066, would defeat King Harold's Anglo-Saxon army, slag and cinder piles 50 feet high cover a Roman iron making site of about two acres. A number of such sites in the Weald have yielded coins dating from Nero's reign in A.D. 54 to and including the reigns of Vespasian, Trajan and Hadrian.

Thanks to the persistence of the Romans in exploiting the mineral resources of Britain, and the genius of later day English inventors, England would become a leader in the world's production of iron and steel. Her vast iron and coal deposits would form the basis of England's great Industrial Revolution of the 18th century, which would later spread over the world with attendant blessings for all mankind.

The Tin of Cornwall

What happened to the tin of Cornwall, the 'Cassiterides' of antiquity, whose secret location Caesar had discovered when his forces defeated the Veneti? Its importance diminished when sources nearer Rome were discovered. By the time Claudius had subdued Britain, Emperor Augustus had pacified the northwestern Spanish peninsula. This led to the energetic exploitation of the great tin regions of Gallaecia, which were more convenient to the Mediterranean trade route.

With an ample supply available from Gallaecia, the Cornish tin trade was neglected for 200 years. Strabo, Pliny and Tacitus made no mention of tin being exported from Britain during this period. But in Britain, with the development of prosperous, well governed Romanized cities, the need arose for a local tin supply. Late in the first century attempts were made to revive Cornish mining, as the remains of a Roman fort found near Bodmin would indicate. But it was not until the middle of the third century that mining in Cornwall rapidly increased. Excellent Roman roads, extending far westward into Cornwall, marked by the milestones of Gallus, Lininius and Constantine, then began to hum with trade.

The streambeds of Cornwall continued as prolific producers of tin until 410 A.D. It was then that the Romans were forced to withdraw their legions from Britain in order to defend the frontiers of Italy against marauding barbarians. The Romanized population, however, consisting of Britons and Roman merchants and artisans, remained in the centers to which they had grown attached. Rome's exodus was purely a military one.

The period that followed was one of turmoil. Over the sea from the east came new elements, the Angles, Saxons and others. Before long, kingdoms were being formed in Kent and southern Hampshire by the Jutes from Jutland, and in Sussex, Essex, and Wessex by the Saxons, and along the northeastern coast by the Angli. In Cornwall, last to submit to the Saxons, descendants of the earlier Celts and traces of their language have survived to this day.

Romanization of Britain

It was Rome's crossing of the English Channel, inspired by the search for riches, that brought enlightenment to a long darkened land. After 400 years of Romanization, Britain emerged from its primitive isolation to become a civilized country, as it thrived under the Roman system of law and order. Schools were established, and Latin became the language of government, business, the military, the law and the literate class. As Latin words and derivations crept into native speech, the Anglo-Saxon tongue became the mother of modern English.

In addition to Roman culture, when the legions of Rome withdrew they left behind great cities protected by stout walls, elaborate villas, ornate public baths, temples, and edifices of commerce. Over durable Roman highways stretching across the land, coursed an abundance of agricultural products, livestock, wool, and textiles. And from the quarries and mines came the stone and metals which were used to create cities that even today reflect the glory of the Roman Empire. The everwidening wave of civilization, which had sprung millennia earlier in the Middle East, had at last attained its farthest westward reach in Europe as it broke upon the shores of Britain.

Rainbows Along The Danube

The picturesque region tributary to the Danube River was and still is a land of rich and varied forms of mineral wealth. It had witnessed the birth of the Bronze Age and the Iron Age in Europe. In Roman times it became another "Prize of Victory." During the reigns of Augustus and Tiberius, from west to east along the Danube lands were invaded and annexed in Raetia, now parts of Switzerland and western Austria; in iron-rich Noricum of present Austria; in Pannonia and Dalmatia in modern Hungary and Yugoslavia; and in Moesia, now a part of Bulgaria.

Rome's attention had been drawn northward in the direction of the Danube as early as 130 B.C. when a Roman general, Gaius Marius, returned to Rome with rich spoils of gold won from the Cimbri tribes near Vercellae (about 40 miles east of Milan). Thereafter, Vercellae became an early producer of Roman gold. In A.D. 75 Pliny the Elder wrote that there was a law prohibiting the employment of more than 5000 men at the gold placers of Vercellae. Apparently this action was to prevent cheapening the price of gold. Aquileia, 25 miles north of modern Trieste, was another rich source of Roman gold. Strabo quoted Polybius who said that in his time (170 B.C.) the over-production of gold was so great at Aquileia it caused the value of gold in Italy to be reduced by one-third. It had become clear to the Romans that regions northward toward the Danube held forth promise of great metallic wealth.

In Noricum, the same iron ore deposits that fostered the Hallstatt culture now proved of immense value to the Romans. Some of these Noricum iron ores contained a small percentage of titanium, which gave the metallic iron a tougher quality, a fortuitous circumstance for the armor makers of Italy. At Hultenberg and in the mountains around Eisenerz, about 70 miles east of Hallstatt, Roman coins, dated A.D. 316, found among the mines reveal the extended period during which Noricum contributed to the strength of the Empire.

Dacia

In their constant chasing of the rainbow, the Romans found the brightest pot of gold in a land they called Dacia. Today it comprises Romania and the Transylvanian Alps and a part of Hungary. The land was originally inhabited by people of Thracian stock who were called Getae by the Greeks, and Daci by the Romans. These natives attained a notable degree of civilization even before the Romans appeared. Agriculture, cattle-breeding, and an active trade in metals taken from their abundant storehouse of gold and silver in Transylvania brought them prosperity— and the usual attention of envious outsiders.

Even Caesar contemplated an expedition against the Dacians, ostensibly to remove a threat to Roman security, but more likely it was the distant glitter of Dacian gold that caught his eye. Later Augustus considered it an advantage to betroth his five-year-old daughter Julia to Cotiso, one of the Dacian rulers, who thereafter willingly recognized Roman suzerainty. But from A.D. 85 to 89 the Romans had to fight two wars to keep the Dacians quiet.

It remained for Marcus Trajan to put an end to Dacian annoyances, and to further increase the growing wealth of the Roman Empire in the process. Born near Seville, Spain, he was the first provincial to become emperor. In a brilliantly executed campaign he led his legions northward and eastward along the Danube and seized the Dacian capital of Sarmizegetusa in A.D. 101. The conquest was short lived, however, for in a few years Trajan was forced to return to Dacia. He bridged the Danube, evidence of which still remains, and again subdued the Dacians, this time permanently.

Gold Rush To Dacia

Leaving a large garrison in defense of Sarmizegetusa, Trajan then returned to Rome with 10,000 captives, a million pounds of silver and a half-million pounds of gold. When this fabulous booty was displayed in Rome it started a gold stampede to Dacia that must have outshone the combined excitement of the California Gold Rush and the epical trek to the Klondike of later years.

Into the new province poured hopeful Roman colonists to cultivate the fertile fields and to work the rich mines. Forts were erected to protect their newly found Eldorado from foreign intruders. Three great military roads were built to connect the main settlements. A fourth road, named after Trajan, followed the Oltul River and threaded the Turnu Rosul Pass in order to reach Apulum, one of the principal towns. Nearby were the rich gold districts of the Monts Apuseni.

It is difficult to appraise the amount of gold that the Romans acquired from Dacia. Like the Phoenicians of old who purposely disguised their routes and sources of trade wealth to confuse competitors, no doubt the Romans had reason to minimize the riches that flowed from Dacia for the same reason. The program of wild spending that ensued in beautifying Rome, and the swift effort and determined plan to colonize Dacia, offer ample evidence that the Romans had again found a remarkable "Prize of Victory."

Dacia was settled systematically and became thoroughly Romanized. Among the ancient cities and monuments to Roman enterprise to be found in Romania today are the ruins of Tropaeum Trajani at Adamlissi between the Danube and modern Constanta on the Black Sea. Towering walls were built in many places to restrain the encroachments of surrounding barbarians. One wall, called the Great Wall of Trajan, ran from Constanta to meet the Danube at Cernavoda. Another wall ran from ancient Mursa (modern Osijek), crossed the Danube and coursed northeastward to the Mures River, symbolic of the superhuman effort made by the Romans to encircle their golden prize in Dacia.*

*The Transylvanian Erzgebirge, or "ore mountains" of present Romania, today contain one of the principal gold-bearing regions of Europe, as they did in antiquity. When one reviews the numerous mining districts that have been worked in modern times, it becomes obvious that Dacia was a lucrative source of gold for the Romans. In an isolated range of hills north of modern Deva and centered about Abrud are the districts of Offenbanya, Bucium and

Trajan's Fabulous Booty

When Trajan returned in triumph to Rome after his conquest of Dacia, in addition to the huge tribute which he was allowed to keep for himself, he distributed a gift of 650 denarii each to 300,000 citizens, equivalent to about 75 million dollars. But that was only the smaller part of the booty. With the remainder, Trajan embarked upon a vast program of public works including a magnificent new forum, the Forum Traianum, one of the architectural wonders of the world.

An outstanding feature of the forum was Trajan's column. It was erected in A.D. 114 to commemorate the conquest of Dacia. Today it may be seen standing 97 feet high, 12 feet in diameter, undiminished in grandeur. More than 2500 figures superbly carved in marble ascend in a continuous spiral with impressive majesty to the top. These dramatic reliefs depict scenes of battle, burning villages, soldiers parading spoils of war and chained prisoners, Dacian princes drinking poison from goblets, costumes of the soldiers and native dress of the barbarians. It is one of the most amazing and authentic records of military conquests ever created. The column and its decorative format have been imitated endlessly throughout the world to commemorate various heroes and historical events.

Atop the column stood a heroic bronze statue of Trajan holding a globe in his hand, symbolic of nearly 400 years of Roman supremacy of the world. At the age of 64 Trajan died on the coast of Cilicia, in A.D. 117. His ashes were brought to Rome and deposited in a golden urn at the base of the great marble monument. It so happened that this rite also marked the Roman Empire's last raid upon the treasure chest of a foreign land.

Emperor Hadrian

Hadrian, Trajan's nephew and successor, was

Vulcoiu Corabia. At nearby Verespatak, now known as Rosia Montana, evidence of considerable Roman mining can be seen.

Near Brad, there are more districts, such as Karacs, Ruda-Barza, and Muszari, which are rich in silver as well as gold. About 12 miles southwest of Petroseni is the important district of Sacaramb (Nagyag), famed for its gold-bearing telluride ores found in veins traversing the base of an ancient volcano. Little remains of the famous and heavily fortified Dacian capital of Sarmizegetusa, although its site has been identified south of Deva near Hunedoara. The gold deposits, so profusely scattered over a wide area surrounding Sarmizegetusa, now stand in mute testimony to the wealth in gold and silver that was reaped by the Romans in this region.

perhaps Rome's most capable emperor. During his many journeys throughout the empire, Hadrian became enamored with the cultural heritage of ancient Athens. Returning to Rome, Hadrian resolved to make the empire's capital the grandest city ever known. He restored the Pantheon, first built in 27 B.C. to honor Roman gods. By using sections of cast concrete, an invention of the Romans, one monolithic mass was created forming a huge circular dome 143 feet in diameter and exactly the same height. The dome was covered with bronze, brilliantly plated with gold. Hadrian's great bronze doors still remain, but have been shorn of the gold that once covered them. Today the Pantheon stands as the best preserved building of the ancient world.

Both Hadrian and his uncle Trajan were born in the same little Spanish town of Italica near Seville. Both men were honored with everlasting memorials in Rome. In A.D. 138 Hadrian died at the age of 62, and was entombed in the magnificent mausoleum which he had built for himself beside the Tiber River. Hadrian's Tomb, now called Castel Sant' Angelo, can be reached over Hadrian's bridge, the Pons Aelius, a statue-lined approach of graceful dignity.

Under Hadrian the Pax Romana flowered to the fullest. After Hadrian came gentle, modest, able Antoninus, titled *Pius* by the Roman senate. His reign was also prosperous and peaceful. After Pius came Marcus Aurelius, an industrious and devoted ruler who wrote his *Meditations* and concepts of morality while encamped with his army during campaigns against Germanic invaders along the Danube.

Edward Gibbon, the noted English historian, in his 'The Decline and Fall of The Roman Empire' stated, "the period covering the reigns of Trajan, Hadrian, Antoninus and Aurelius, was the most happy and prosperous the human race ever enjoyed in the history of the world." Considerable credit can be given to such provinces as Spain, Britain, Noricum and Dacia, whose metallic resources flowed in a seemingly inexhaustible stream to bolster and sustain the economic wealth, splendor and power of the Roman Empire.

The Flowering of Gaul

Protected from barbarian depredations under the Pax Romana, Gaul also became a fruitful province. But Gaul's principal bonanzas were found in her green fields of grain, cereals, livestock, and wine producing vineyards. The Gallic frontier also attracted Syrian and Sidonian artisans who, after first migrating to Italy, went on into Gaul where they introduced their superior craftsmanship and founded prosperous industries producing enamelware and glassware.

As the Romans opened Gaul to civilized influences, more than 15,000 miles of roads were built connecting such cities as Lutetia (Paris), Aurelianum (Orleans), Lugdunum (Lyons) an important iron and glass center, Lemovices (Limoges) famed for its porcelain wares, and Burdigata (Bordeaux) the noted wine capital. Aqueducts, stately public edifices and amphitheaters were erected at such places as Pont du Gard, Nimes, Arles and elsewhere. They may be seen today, testifying to the greatness of the Roman Empire. The Romanization of Gaul marked a notable milestone in the spread of civilization throughout western Europe, as Gaul became the cornerstone upon which eventually was erected the nation of France.

Rich Radiant Rome

For over 400 years the Romans were the sole possessors of all the profitable metallic ore deposits of their time, the richness and extent of which have seldom been equalled in the history of mankind. Many deposits of Spain, Britain, Raetia, Noricum, Cyprus, Thrace, and Asia Minor were of such magnitude that they have been productive even in modern times. With wealth pouring into the imperial treasury and into the hands of emperors, officials, bankers, merchants and various citizens, never before had such a broad spectrum of a nation's inhabitants enjoyed such prosperity.

The fluency, convenience, and abundance of money as a transacting medium gave people a new sense of exhilaration and power never experienced by so many in former generations of history. No city in the world ever hummed with greater excitement and activity than imperial Rome. Centered about its magnificent marble forums and lavish palaces on the Palatine, Rome was a thriving city of one million people, jammed into 45,000 multi-storied apartment houses and dwellings.

Rome was not only rich and money-mad, it was also a pleasure-bent city. Hundreds of thousands of thrill-seekers huddled in the marble faced Colosseum, the Flavian Amphitheater, and the Circus Maximus with its marble seats for 150,000 people. All howled with delight at the chariot races and gladiatorial contests. Roman festivals were carried on endlessly by the emperors who used their vast wealth to entertain and gain the support of the public, or as a palliative to the poor and unemployed.

The middle class and the rich formed a large segment of Roman society. They eagerly sought the bazaars that lined Rome's busy streets, seeking exotic articles and valuable objects of art imported from Greece, Egypt and Mesopotamia. Villas of the wealthy were very pretentious and virtually museums loaded with sculptures, paintings and classical art. Grecian columns, so popular among the Romans, and floors were often of imported polychrome marble, onyx, alabaster, or granite. Bath fixtures were sometimes of silver, and occasionally of gold, as senators, merchants, and bankers sought ways to outdo each other in lavish living.

Jewels for The Rich

The collection of jewelry became a notable fetish of the rich. Articles were imported from the East or were made by expert artisans who had migrated to Rome from Syria, Egypt, Greece, and Asia Minor. They used precious stones from India, Arabia, and Africa, making the gem-cutters of Rome known world-wide. From Sidon and Tyre the art of glass blowing came to Rome and spread into the provinces. Thereafter, Roman artisans themselves achieved a degree of perfection in glass working unequaled by any other people. Vases, cups, phials and bowls of magnificent red and blue glass were eagerly collected by Rome's emperors and affluent class, and just as avidly by museums of today.

Great quantities of sculptures and paintings were gathered by the Romans from their subjugated world, and they developed excellent techniques of their own equal in merit to those of Greece. Roman friezes, and especially their portrait busts and heroic figures, were carved with exceptional vitality and realism. Painting was even more popular than sculpturing. Fresco painting was a favorite form of decoration in homes, temples, and public buildings. Murals graced the homes of the wealthy, depicting pastoral scenes and mythological subjects.

As in all civilizations of the past, affluence cultivated leisure and the desire for cultural betterment. For various reasons certain wealthy individuals became sponsors of those possessing literary and artistic talents. Under the stimulating prosperity of Augustus, and the generous support of his rich friend Maecenas, Rome entered her Golden Age of literature.

Giants of Roman Literature

A brief roster of Roman greats and some of their works include Horace and his *Satires* pertaining to the life of Rome and its money-mad citizens; Vergil and his poems, *Eclogues, Georgics* and *The Aeneid. The Annals of The Roman Empire*, from Rome's founding in 750 B.C. to 9 B.C., were written by Titus Livius. Ovid was banished from Rome by Augustus, but his witty, frivolous and unrestrained style, often considered shockingly immoral as in his *Amores* and *Ars amatoria*, had become popular and appealed to the prevailing tastes of Roman society.

Rome's Silver Age of Literature, marked by melodious prose and rhetorical poetry, included the works of Petronius, Martial and Juvenal, who employed polished barbs and candid ridicule to satirize the growing vices of Roman life. Lucius Seneca wrote his *Dialogues* and moral letters and dedicated himself to Stoicism. He tutored young Nero, and when Nero as emperor later condemned his tutor to death, Seneca emulated Socrates. He drank hemlock and calmly opened his veins and slowly bled to death.

Suetonius and Tacitus were historians of that age. The latter wrote his *Historiae* and *Annales*, and criticized the corruption and degeneration of various public officials. Plutarch, author of *Parallel Lives*, was noted for his heroic style, depicting distinguished Greek and Roman figures. Many authors of later days were inspired by the works of Plutarch.

Men of science were few in Rome, and added little to the knowledge handed down by the Greeks and Egyptians. Pliny "The Elder" however, was a remarkable scholar, soldier and inquisitive traveler. His *Historia Naturalis* embraced nearly every subject: gods, men, animals, astronomy, medicine and the mining of metals. Claudius Ptolemy of Alexandria, a great astronomer and geographer of Hadrian's time, was the last of talented scientists of the ancient world. Although his *Ptolemaic System* was erroneous, based on the theory that the sun, stars and planets revolved around the earth, it was the standard belief for centuries. The Polish astronomer, Copernicus, in 1530 would correct this concept by assigning the earth and the planets their true orbits about the sun.

Rome's Decay and Downfall

With the passing of Marcus Aurelius in 180 A.D. at Vindobona (Vienna) 200 years of Pax Romana came to an end. This high tide of Roman intellectual and artistic achievement, world domination and provincial prosperity, spanning the reigns of Trajan, Hadrian, Antoninus and Aurelius, was also a period immersed in opulence and glitter. It was in that debilitating climate that the germs of Rome's decay and downfall were planted.

After Aurelius came his son Commodus, whose reign was one of unrestrained immorality and sadistic cruelty. Excessive waste of public funds resulted in debasement of Roman currency by 25 percent. At the age of 31, Commodus was strangled to death by one of his favorite wrestlers. Septimus Severus next became emperor by employing bribery and a bold march on Rome. His campaigns of war over a period of 12 years were so costly that the currency was devalued an additional 25 percent. His advice to Caracalla, his son, was, "Make your soldiers rich, disregard anything else."

Caracalla endeavored to quieten the barbarian chieftains by paying them heavy tributes, and spent extravagant sums on public works, resulting in further debasement of the currency. His incredibly luxurious baths were completed by Alexander Severus, a wise and able ruler. But Severus, too, was slain by his infuriated soldiers while seeking to buy off hostile German tribes. For the next 50 years, as the army alone aspired to select Rome's leaders, 20 emperors paraded through a chaotic era of anarchy. Silver coinage again suffered devaluation, this time by 90 percent. Copper coins were simply washed with a coating of silver. Inflation staggered the nation. The finances of the empire collapsed.

Diocletian, who became emperor in 284, saw himself as an oriental sun-god, and dressed accordingly in robes embroidered with pearls and precious stones. With a relentless hand he restored a degree of political order and established a sound gold currency. But his efforts to check soaring prices by fixing ceilings on products and wages failed completely. By using absolute power, however, Diocletian did end 50 years of civil strife. He was not entirely to blame for an empire that was tottering on the verge of economic ruin, besieged on many of its frontiers by irrepressible barbarians. As Cassius Dio said, "Our history now plunges from a kingdom of gold to one of iron and rust."

A Ruinous Trade Imbalance

Another weakness that enfeebled Rome was its inadequate home industry. Western Europe was an abundant source of raw materials, but it was mainly the East and Middle East that supplied Rome's demand for finished articles. The incomparable craftsmen of Sidon, Tyre, Antioch, Alexandria, Rhodes, Miletus, Ephesus and other centers of the Hellenized East were the exporters who filled the wants of affluent Rome.

In return, the chief export from Rome was money, possessed by rich citizens who felt no compulsion to keep their funds at home. India alone, valuing her store of silver, took 550 million sesterces per year in coin or bullion from Rome, according to Pliny. China, who also desired silver, drained over 100 million sesterces per year in payments for silks which had become highly prized in Rome.

This imbalance in trade contributed greatly to Rome's ultimate ruin. Paying for lavish quantities of imports, in amounts that exceeded exports, with a currency that had been depreciated since the Punic Wars and further debased by such emperors as Nero, Aurelius, Commodus, Caracalla and Severus, Rome's currency was becoming unacceptable. The Empire's trading capital, the basis of its economic life, was being destroyed.

Rome's Depleted Resources

According to Suetonius, Emperor Vitellius even replaced the gold and silver that was stored in the temples with alloys of zinc, silver, copper, and lead. By 218, Emperor Elagabalus, who loved oriental splendor and spent as much as 3,000,000 sesterces on a single banquet, made the denarius a coin wholly of copper. It was repudiated by eastern traders, a disastrous blow to the long held commercial supremacy of Rome.

With Rome thus facing economic disintegration, nothing could have added greater distress than the withering of her metallic supplies. Germanic hordes everywhere were rising in constant revolt. They began to overrun provinces of the Empire, pillaging Gaul, Spain, Macedonia, Cyprus and Asia Minor, long the storehouses of Rome's invaluable mineral deposits. Sorely in need of precious metals to reinforce her failing currency, and to maintain her industries and trade, Rome's river of riches dried up. Her economy and political stability were strangulated through the want of the very same metallic resources that had stimulated her rise to power. The impoverished, overtaxed and spiritually bankrupt colossus that once was the Roman Empire was ready to fall.

Seeds of Destruction

Historians have dwelt considerably upon the decay of Rome, its depravity, and the vulgar indulgences of its pleasure-mad emperors and citizenry. Whether this view of Roman life was exaggerated by contemporary writers, perhaps appealing to public clamor for sensational exposes, is hard to determine. There is ample evidence, however, of the unbelievable excesses in sensuality, incest, and barbarous, maniac cruelties of such emperors as Nero, Caligua, Commodus, and the inhuman populace. Obviously, the unrestrained saturnalia of the ruling class encouraged disrespect for law, and hastened deterioration of ideals and principles.

Rome's contemporary writers often ridiculed the growing effeminacy and laziness of the male population. Rome's code of rigorous, dedicated and hardy stoicism that had enabled her to acquire leadership of the world, gave way to enervation, political apathy and even anarchy. Overwhelming affluence had induced indolence, moral laxity, and indifference to national well-being. All of these enfeebling circumstances, added to the shattering effect of Rome's economic woes, contributed to the collapse of the Roman Empire. It was no foreign foe that conquered Rome. It was decay from within. Crumbling at its foundations, Rome became easy prey for hardier peoples who were about to take their turn in the fields of conquest.

In the forests and steppes beyond the Empire's frontiers, barbarian Germanic tribes had long eyed Roman culture and opulence. Recognizing Rome's growing weakness, in 410 the Visigoths under Alaric swept into Italy and sacked Rome, while the Vandals, Suevi and Alani tribes took over Gaul and Spain. In 455 the Vandals, too, invaded Italy and captured the magnificent capital of the Roman Empire, sacking it so ruthlessly that the term vandalism ever after became a synonym for wanton destruction. Submerged under a tide of barbarism, Rome's domination of the world came to an end. Thereafter, Europe entered a period of turmoil and terror often called the Dark Ages. It would be over 700 years before civilization would resume its forward march.

Rome's Legacy to Mankind

Shining stones of the earth had aided Rome's rise to wealth and power, and had also led to her decline and downfall. Nevertheless, it can be said that these riches also germinated Rome's priceless legacy to mankind. They provided the lure, and the support, for Rome's many expeditions in search of her "Prizes of Victory." Rome's conquests may have been ruthless, but under her wise and usually tolerant administration, centuries of peace and prosperity came to provinces that otherwise would have been overrun by barbarian hordes.

To those distant realms, seeing the first rays of civilization, Rome transmitted the cultural heritage of ancient Egypt, Babylon, Asia Minor and Greece. Without Rome's unprecedented expansion across seas made safe from piracy and lands made accessible over her astounding network of roads, ancient culture and technology might never have reached the western world, or at least would have been delayed indefinitely.

Rome's gifts to mankind were countless. The art of Roman statecraft and government, regardless of their imperfections, had never been equalled. Rome's system of law and basic concepts of justice, shaped by such men as Caesar, Hadrian and Justinian, gave the western world its fundamental rules of social order. Latin, the language of Rome, and its natural provincial alterations, became the mother tongue of Italy, France, Spain, Portugal, Romania, and Latin America. Latin today forms the terminology of law and science.

Affirming Hellenic principles of beauty and form, Roman architecture and engineering genius are reflected everywhere today throughout the world. Using a new form of building material, colossal casts of concrete, the Romans erected magnificent public structures, aqueducts and bridges, and perpetuated the arch and great vaulted domes which have been copied in churches and capitols of every land. Roman arches of triumph, and the handsome facades of Roman temples, have become the archetype of countless public buildings throughout Europe and America.

The memory of Rome's imperial grandeur has been outshone only by its intellectual achievements. The writings of its gifted orators, philosophers, poets, historians and political theorists, such as Cicero, Caesar, Livy, Tacitus, Virgil, Horace, Justinian, Lucretius, Seneca, and Plutarch have been an unending source of inspiration and stimulation for all mankind.

Rome's Role in Christianity

Rome played an outstanding role in the spread and survival of Christianity. Unknowingly, the first step was in Palestine when the Romans, under Titus, destroyed Jerusalem and completely dispersed and nearly obliterated the practice of Judaism during the great Diaspora. This left the Christians free, while engaged in their efforts to reform Judaism, to disseminate their faith throughout the Middle East without serious interference. Later, after the terrible era of persecution had passed, under Constantine, the first Christian emperor, Christianity became the Roman state religion in 313. Thereafter, protected by imperial power, the Church grew strong, until, during the Middle Ages it exerted an important influence in shaping the course of European history.

Mighty Rome, a victim of self-indulgence and other human frailties, was eclipsed by centuries of barbarian depredations during the Dark Ages, while the Church survived to preserve the Latin classics and the legacies of antiquity. The ancient Roman Empire faded from the face of the earth, but its glorious heritage would live on. During the Renaissance, as we shall see, the brilliance of Rome's achievements would blaze forth anew to awaken and inspire mankind with her classical past, enriching all generations to come. Rome's intellectual prestige and her great wealth in art once again would become preeminent in the world. Even today Rome is the center of one of the most enduring religions. Thus, for over 2500 years, longer than any such span in man's history, Rome has maintained some form of supremacy. It is little wonder that Rome is known throughout the world as The Eternal City.

Chapter 9

PRELUDE TO THE EMPIRES OF EUROPE

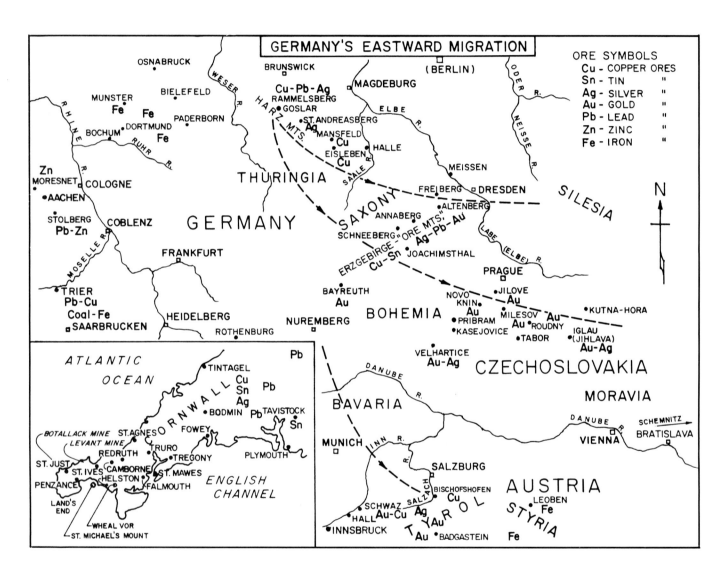

Plate 87 *Rothenberg, Germany*, is typical of the medieval towns that became walled cities during the barbarian invasions. p. 94

Plate 88 *Charlemagne the Great*, after the "Dark Ages," revived mining and established a stable currency. p. 94

Plate 89 *The Rammelsberg mine, discovered in 938 near Goslar, Germany*, started an eastward rush of pioneers. p. 94

Plate 90 *Rammelsberg's copper, lead and silver ores* have supplied Europe with metals for 1,000 years. p. 94

Plate 91 *Jewels of the Orient* aroused in Holy Land Crusaders desires that awakened Europe's industry and commerce. p. 94

Plate 92 *The famed emerald and diamond dagger of the Topaki Museum* is a sample of Oriental splendor. p. 94

The Barbarian Invasions

During the days of the Roman Empire, the Germanic tribes east of the Rhine and north of the Danube had remained beyond Rome's control, constantly posing a threat to the security of her frontiers. Among these Teutonic peoples were such groups as the Goths, Saxons, Angli, Alamanni, Vandals, and Burgundians. In the early centuries of the Christian era, these tribes had been caught up in a maelstrom of migrations, seeking new lands, plunder, and perhaps escape from over-population, or aggression.

The West Germans, who had come from the Scandinavian region about 1000 B.C., included the Franks. Less nomadic than their kindred folk, the Franks took root along the lower and middle Rhine. After the Romans invaded their land and conquered Gaul, these Teutonic Franks, forbears of the French, became loyal subjects of the Roman Empire, and ardent converts to the Roman Church. Therefore, their speech was influenced by the Latin liturgy.

When Rome was captured and sacked in 410 by the Visigoths and again in 455 by the Vandals, the Roman Empire disintegrated, forcing the proud legions of Rome to withdraw from their provinces in order to defend Italy. Within the vacuum thus created, hordes of restless Germanic tribes began to ravage the land. In Gaul, only the flickering vestiges of Christianity withstood the onslaught.

Burning and pillaging marked the paths of the barbarians. The once thriving provincial towns of Gaul shrank miserably in size and became small, jittery walled fortresses. (Today, one may see their remains in such picturesque towns as Rothenburg, Germany, and Carcassonne, southern France.) Villages clustered around a monastery or a manor. Lords of the manors guaranteed protection to the harassed peasants, in return for which the peasants pledged their lords everlasting servitude. In order to obtain security, the peasants bartered their freedom, and became. serfs bound to the lords for life. Thus, a new form of existence came into being, called Feudalism and Serfdom.

The Dark Ages

Markets and trade involved only the needs of the manor or monastery. Unused roads became deserted; enterprise and commerce lay prostrate everywhere in the strife-torn land. With trade at a standstill in these Dark Ages there was little need of metals for crafts or currency. The mining of metals ceased almost entirely, except for iron which was needed in weapons of defense and to till the fields. The skilled mining and engineering methods once used by the Romans were soon forgotten. Shafts and adits became overgrown with trees and shrubbery, ignored by the villagers whose only concern was cultivating the fields for their daily bread.

In 486 Clovis, the first Merovingian ruler, united the Salian Franks of the lower Rhine with the Ripuarian Franks of the Middle Rhine (Strasburg) and later made Paris his capital. The first organized state in Central Europe was beginning to take shape. After Clovis' death, quarrels between his four sons resulted in division of the Frankish lands: Neustria, west of the Meuse River, and Austrasia to the east. Under the influence of Romanized Gaul the Franks in Neustria had acquired a transformed Latinized speech, the French language of today, while the tribes in the lowlands of Austrasia had retained their low German dialect. This divergence of speech became a divisive force and a serious omen for the future.

In the period of the Merovingian rulers there was little metallic currency in use. Enough Roman gold had been left in the land to enable the aristocracy to import some articles of luxury from Byzantium and the Middle East. As the accumulated stocks and hoards of Roman coins were depleted, Europe became starved for the precious metals needed to maintain a base for her purchases, and to arouse industries and commerce from the stagnation that had engulfed the land.

After endless feuds and divisions of territories between the descendants of Clovis, Charles Martel became ruler and again reunited Neustria and Austrasia. Martel's most dramatic exploit was his defeat of the Moslem invaders from Spain in 732, ending the dire threat of Arab domination of western Europe. Through Martel a new dynasty, the Carolingians, came to power. It was Martel's grandson, Charlemagne The Great, who attained an immortal place in history, and initiated Europe's emergence from the Dark Ages.

Charlemagne The Great

Charlemagne inherited not only Neustria and Austrasia, but also the fierce pagan Saxons on his northeastern border. In 785, after 14 years of fighting Saxon revolts, during which 4500 Saxons were put to the sword in one day, Charlemagne brought the land under his control. A few years later he subdued the Avars in what is now Hungary, and annexed Bavaria. On the borders of Spain and Italy, and mineral-rich Bohemia and Thuringia he established marches, or frontier forts, which became important outposts for colonization and Germanization. A new day, marking the dawn of the pioneer spirit, had come to western Europe.

On Christmas day in the year 800, Charlemagne was crowned Carolus Augustus, Emperor of the Romans, in Rome by Pope Leo III. Thus, in unifying lands which later became France and Germany, and in laying the foundation of the far-flung Holy Roman Empire, Charlemagne became the first and most powerful sovereign in Western Europe. His strength protected the papacy, and thus stimulated Christianity, which evolved as a very important force of unification throughout most of Western Europe.

Charlemagne's wars of expansion were also ardent crusades of religion. Magnificent churches, monasteries, and Bishoprics began to rise across the land. During this period occurred a turning point in history. In the libraries of the many monasteries, monks began copying and preserving for posterity priceless works of Latin literature. While disseminating the Christian faith, they were perpetuating the scientific and artistic legacies of antiquity. This intellectual revival is known as the Carolingian Renaissance.

A spirit of enterprise had arisen, awakening an interest in the use of metals. Goldsmiths and other metalworkers began to show great skill. Beautiful gold disc brooches made of bronze overlaid with gold and decorated with gems and glass pastes were created. Individualized Frankish designs began to show lessening influences of Byzantine and Roman artisans. In addition to the precious metals, lead came into strong demand for roofing the increased number of cathedrals being built everywhere.

The Mines of Charlemagne

During Merovingian times life had centered in Gaul, but, as Charlemagne came to power, the focus of expansion moved east of the Rhine, to the Weser River in Saxony and beyond to the Elbe, and into Bohemia, Moravia, and Slovakia, which we now know as Czechoslovakia, one of the great metalliferous provinces of the world. Charlemagne's campaigns were claimed to have been religious and preventive wars, but the quick settlement of the lands and the commercial ventures that followed indicate that the natural wealth of the regions was a strong inducement to conquest. These eastern and purely Germanic parts of Charlemagne's realm supplied him not only with men for his armed forces, but also with highly important metal resources.

Using captive Saxons, in the year 770, Charlemagne began working the rich silver and gold bearing lead deposits of Schemnitz (Bankska Stiavnica) and Kremnitz in the Hungarian Erzgebirge (located about 80 miles northeast of Bratislava in modern Czechoslovakia). In 786 he granted mining concessions and the right of coinage to his two sons. The mines yielded important quantities of silver, which enabled Charlemagne to introduce a new silver denier bearing a cross and his name on the coin. Silver then replaced gold in the coinage system of the Carolingians, and for centuries thereafter formed the principal currency of Western Europe.

Of greatest significance was the fact that the mines of Schemnitz and Kremnitz signalled the awakening of metal mining and the revival of industry from the torpor into which they had fallen during the barbarian upheavals. With the production of precious metals came renewed prosperity, stimulating the cultural renaissance that at last brought Europe out of the Dark Ages.

Feudalism

Charlemagne's achievement was chiefly the product of his own dominant and enterprising personality. His empire fell apart when his sons and their heirs parceled it out to relatives, friends and lords in order to gain their individual allegiance, or to pay for favors received. As the number of these landed fiefs increased, in the absence of a stable, centralized authority, the system of Feudalism became the medium of providing protection to members of each lord's domain.

These great landed estates grew enormously important in the form of powerful duchies. In France they became known as Frisia, Normandy, Francia, Burgundy, Aquitaine, Brittany, Lorraine, and Gascony. In Germany they became Saxony, Franconia, Swabia, Brunswick, Bavaria, Bohemia, Austria, Silesia, and Carinthia. For centuries these duchies vied with each other for leadership of Europe. West of the Rhine, while Hugh Capet and his Capetian descendants struggled to establish the Kingdom of France, with Paris as its capital, feudal states east of the Rhine were shaping Germany and the Holy Roman Empire. It was here, east of the Rhine, that Europe's newest and most exciting frontiers of metallic wealth and opportunity were to be found.

The Pioneers of Germany

In 919 a new royal house, the Ottonians, forced the dukes of Germany to recognize its supreme authority over the land. As had Charlemagne, Otto the Great stimulated the expansion of German frontiers toward the east, probing lands of high economic promise. Reviving Charlemagne's policy of creating outposts, or marches, Otto extended his borders by building fortress stockades and manning them with soldiers to protect the settlers. Colonists were encouraged to develop towns around these fortified centers, and to explore the virgin lands. Unlike America's momentous westward migration of the 19th century, Europe was going to find its glowing rainbows of promise toward the east.

During this period of the 10th century, Central Europe was sorely in need of silver to serve as a base for an expanding currency, and of copper, lead, and tin which were in urgent demand to supply and encourage the metal industries. As with fortune hunters of the past, there were also many among the Germans who were engrossed in the search for nature's riches. But where and how could these stony ores be found on this untrod eastern frontier?

Occasionally mineral deposits have been revealed by the whims of nature. A sudden flood may lay bare a vein of ore, or a forest fire may expose the outcrop of an ore body. Even animals have played their parts in discovery. Attracted to bright objects, squirrels have exhumed from their burrows shining pieces of metallic ore, or gemstones. The number of stray burros who by chance have led prospectors to riches is legion.

In Germany at a most auspicious time, according to tradition, it was a horse who discovered a world famous ore deposit, and made one of Otto's new frontier posts in Saxony the center of a frenzied mining boom. About 938 a German noble was riding upon the once thickly forested hill that rises 1200 feet above the present town of Goslar in the Harz Mountains of Saxony.

Intent on hunting, the nobleman dismounted and tied the reins of his horse, named Ramelus, to a tree. While waiting for his master the horse impatiently pawed the earth with his iron hoofs. When the hunter returned he saw in the hollow scooped out by the horse a gleaming, silvery exposure of ore. That glistening patch of sulphides, concealed beneath a thin covering of pine needles, was the tiny exposure of a great silver-lead and copper lode. Miners came and dug deeper, following the lode downward between walls of bedded slate. With each descending foot the lode grew wider, until its great size stood revealed, varying from 10 to 100 feet in width. Today, the mine is known the world over as Rammelsberg, named after the horse, Ramelus.

Beacon To Adventure

Rammelsberg soon became the most important source of copper, lead and silver in Central Europe. It became also an invaluable experimental and training school in developing the techniques of mining, geology and prospecting. It proved of immense aid to other hopeful treasure hunters who eagerly sought new discoveries in ever widening circles. At Mansfeld in the south-eastern Harz, an immense deposit of copper in folded shales was opened in 1150.

For 300 years following its discovery, the Rammelsberg mine and the city of Goslar enjoyed great prosperity. Production was frequently interrupted, however, by feudal wars such as the struggle for the imperial throne between Philip, Duke of Swabia, and Otto, Duke of Saxony. Otto captured Goslar and reaped a huge amount of bullion from the mines. Thereafter, in 1201, Otto's imperial title was validated by the Pope. Emperor Frederick II also gained considerable wealth from Rammelsberg, and became a noted patron of literature and science. In 1235 he assigned sovereign rights to the mine to the Duke of Brunswick.

Having been worked from the time of Otto the Great, Rammeslberg has provided valuable economic aid to Germany for 1,000 years. Today, the great mine is still producing, and celebrating its 1000th anniversary. The town of Goslar nearby is a medieval gem. Its streets are lined with picturesque examples of Gothic and Renaissance architecture. Still standing are several towers of the town's medieval system of defense.

Rammelsberg's electrifying revelation concerning the presence of metallic wealth in Central Europe was to Germany in 938 what the historic discovery of gold in California was to the young United States in 1848. Hordes of prospectors and miners, followed by farmers and merchants, hurried eastward into Saxony to become settlers and developers of the land. First came the Franks from Franconia, but they were soon outnumbered by the Germans. The Harz became the rallying ground and the springboard for wave after wave of fortune seekers pushing into Germany's eastern frontiers. Their discoveries would come at a very opportune moment in European history, for Christendom's great Crusades to the Holy Land were soon to galvanize Western Europe with demands for new ways of life.

The Crusades Arouse Europe

After the First Crusade in 1096, for 200 years Christendom waged 'holy wars' to recapture Jerusalem from the Moslems. The impact of the Crusades upon the pattern of European life was tremendous. Westerners were amazed at the ordinary delights, as well as the luxuries, which were accepted as commonplace among the Easterners. Europeans marveled at the condiments in use for improving the taste of food, such as sugar, pepper, cinnamon and various spices, and such signs of opulence as Persian rugs, brocades, silks, perfumes, mirrors of glass instead of bronze, the thrilling variety of glassware and metalware, and the abundance of gem stones, pearls and ivory. The Crusaders also studied well the industrial techniques employed by artisans of the Middle East.

After several generations of Crusades, a decided taste and demand developed for these amenities of life and the exotic wares of the cultured East. Unable as yet to establish their own industries for producing a sufficient quantity of these material blessings of civilization, Western Europe turned hungrily to the Middle East for imports. Venice, Genoa, Pisa, Marseilles and Barcelona were among the first seaports to feel the benefits of this trade influx.

After centuries of hibernation Western Europe was stirring with ambition whetted by desire. Rammelsberg's discovery and the lessons of the Crusades had aroused Germany's long dormant industrial spirit. New towns began to sprout across the land, alive with trade fairs and awakening commerce. Money changers were busy converting Venetian ducats, the Saxon denieri and the angevins of Normandy for Byzantine solidi and the Arab dinar. Eastern coins for the purchase of western goods were plentiful, but there was a serious shortage of western money to pay for the luxurious imports of the East. Money changers often had to resort to the old system of barter. Increasing amounts of western money were being drained eastward, not only for eastern goods, but also to maintain the costly Crusades and military expeditions to the Holy Land.

Release from Serfdom

In order to defray the heavy expenses of their crusades, feudal lords were forced to sacrifice portions of their domains, which soon blossomed into townsites. To supply the growing demand for workers in the settlements, an increasing number of the lord's subjects were released from serfdom. Still more serfs were encouraged to earn their freedom by exploring regal territories for metallic riches.

Since Roman times sovereigns had retained the sole mining rights to wastelands containing precious metals. Following the reign of Barbarossa, emperors relinquished their regalian mining rights to territorial dukes, counts, bishops, and even independent towns, who in turn could invest certain vassals or groups with similar privileges.

Since these lords, lay and ecclesiastical, were always pressed for revenue, they gladly threw open their lands, especially to the Germans who were particularly fascinated with the romance of prospecting. In order to develop the mineral wealth of regal domains, would-be miners and colonists were gladly released from feudal subservience. A serf with a spirit of adventure could thus shoulder his pack and head for the frontier and enjoy the heady, wide-open spaces of freedom, which might also reward him with riches.

If fortune smiled, the poorest villein could become his own master merely by staking his claim and registering its boundaries, an act known as "bounding," one of man's earliest privileges. After digging a pit to expose his discovery, and erecting piles of stones to define the claim boundaries, the prospector applied to a representative of the over-lord for a concession to explore and mine his find, subject to a tribute, or royalty, to be paid to the royal land owner.

During Grecian and Roman times, mines were generally worked either by the state or by certain classes of citizens who employed slave labor. The medieval miner, however, became a free man and was highly respected. Serfdom vanished into the past for those who turned to expanding the frontier by colonizing and mining. Conquering natural obstacles, amid verdant valleys and craggy mountains, lent a romantic glow to prospecting and mining, and instilled a disciplined sense of hardihood and resourcefulness in a breed that was destined to open many of the world's frontiers to his fellowmen. During the 12th century an acute need for the services of these fortune hunters was already developing in Western Europe.

Dwindling Resources

During the Middle Ages the main coinage system of Western Europe was based upon silver. An important source of supply in Germany was the Harz region, including Rammelsberg. The Royal Mint of England derived its silver from mines first worked by the Romans in Somerset and Derbyshire. In Frankish territory, some silver was produced from mines of the Auvergne, Cevennes, Limosin, and Alsace regions, while some gold came from the placers of the Tarn, Aveyron,

and Garonne Rivers, and the Ardech in Languedoc. But the supply of precious metals on the continent was dwindling due to increased technical problems encountered in mining the deeper ores, and in part to depletion of older ore deposits.

Existent metal reserves were becoming seriously inadequate for the burgeoning needs of an awakening Europe. To provide the materials to build growing cities, to raise a vast number of magnificent cathedrals, to expand new industries and stimulate commerce, and to create an ample, reliable currency, nothing at this moment in Europe's history was more crucial than a new discovery of substantial metallic resources.

The finding of Rammelsberg and other deposits of the Harz region had fired the adventuresome spirit of Germany's prospectors, which would open the door to new worlds. It is a well recognized fact that the lure of prospecting ran high among Germany's pioneers, and that the gleam of precious metals was a decisive stimulant to German expansion toward the east. Somewhere along the lonely frontier farther east, perhaps Fortune would beam again upon a new generation of bonanza seekers.

Silver Mountains of Bohemia

Centuries ago, about 200 miles southeast of Rammelsberg a range of forested mountains and rolling foothills known today as the "Ore Mountains," or Erzgebirge of Bohemia, lay in peaceful, untouched solitude near the headwaters of the Elbe River. During the year 1170 salt was the only mineral being produced in this region. That year some traders from Halle located on the River Saale were enroute to Meissen with wagons loaded with salt. On previous occasions they had often transported copper and silver ores from Goslar, and therefore were familiar with the ore's appearance.

Carefully they threaded their way along the muddy, bumpy road, for its ruts had been worn deeply by recent torrents. Suddenly, the alert drivers noticed a vein of galena, a bright silver-lead ore, gleaming in the eroded wheel tracks. Excitedly, they jumped from the wagons, tore at the shining vein with picks and shovels, and loaded chunks of the ore into their wagons to be taken back to Goslar for testing. The samples proved richer than the average Rammelsberg ore. The news spread swiftly. Soon, there were waves of hopeful prospectors rushing toward a new far eastern frontier, in Bohemia.

It is easy to picture the jubilant scenes of discovery that occurred in these historic Ore Mountains 800 years ago. Prospectors who had been only recently released from serfdom were exhilarated by their newly found liberty as they trekked the wild, trackless mountain slopes for shining stones of wealth. They were experiencing, as have all explorers of the wilderness, that the ecstasy of pure, unrestrained freedom is never so all-encompassing and impressive as when one stands alone surrounded by lofty, craggy peaks, with an infinite sky above to see, the clean scent of earth to breathe, and no sound to hear but the call of the whippoorwill. To these enchantments of nature add the intoxicating lure of seeking earth's hidden treasures; that is the manna which beckons the prospector over the horizon to fulfill his dreams.

Famous Mines of Bohemia

About 30 miles south of Meissen, explorers of the 12th century entered the pineclad Erzgebirge which trends southwesterly for a distance of over 100 miles. In the present Zinnwald and Altenberg districts they came upon hills of granite seamed with veins containing the black tin mineral cassiterite, associated with minerals of molybdenum and tungsten. On the westerly slope of the Ore Mountains near Annaberg prospectors found veins rich in silver, which also contained bismuth and cobalt. A few miles farther west, at Schneeberg, more ore deposits were found; they yielded silver, copper and nickel.

In the Erzgebirge's eastern foothills, one of the world's most noted bonanzas lay waiting for its lucky discoverer. Descending the slopes of a wooded valley, explorers gazed in amazement at the rich seams of native silver, and patches of black silver sulphides, argentite and pyrargyrite, associated with minerals of bismuth and cobalt. These were the telltale signs of the great bonanza that lay in the depths below, at a place called Joachimsthal, now known as Jachymov, Czechoslovakia.

The Ore Mountains of Bohemia became famous over the world for their varied and prodigious wealth in metals. It was from the silver *thalers* minted in Joachimsthal that America later derived the name "dollar" for one of its silver coins. In modern times rich ores of uranium were found in the mines. In 1898 Joachimsthal furnished the uranium ore which Marie and Pierre Curie used to isolate and discover the elements polonium and radium.

Germany's momentous eastward migration had indeed unearthed a large and invaluable treasure of silver, tin, copper and other useful ores. This remarkable region has played an important role in man's progress, including the ascendancy of Western Europe's budding empires, for over 3500 years. As early as 1600 B.C. it was in this general area that the Unetice culture of the Danubian Bronze Age found the ingredients of bronze, copper and tin, in such convenient association.

Gold Rush of The Middle Ages

After the discovery of the Bohemian Erzgebirge's ore deposits, the lure of riches to be found along the far eastern frontier grew stronger. German pioneers, intent on mining, farming and settling, pushed farther southeastward into Bohemia, into lands held by the Slavs and Magyars. The greatest migration came under the reigns of Wenceslas I of Bohemia, and his son Ottoker II (1253-1278). The Gold Rush of the Middle Ages burst open another treasure vault southwest of Prague, in what is now Czechoslovakia. There, prospectors first found glittering gold in the streams, and then in the veins of the granite hills, spread over an area 100 miles long and 40 miles wide.

From Jilove 20 miles southwest of modern Prague, the gold mining belt continues 80 miles to include such districts as Novo Knin, Milesov, Kasejovice and Velhartice. About 40 miles southeast of Prague are the rich gold and silver mines of Mt. Roudny, and many more near Tabor. About 40 miles east of Tabor German prospectors discovered the famed silver mines of Iglau (modern Jihlava) in the Bohemian Moravian highlands. Iglau was one of the first mining towns in history to be granted a charter (1249), which developed into one of the first practical codes of mining law. Following the opening of its celebrated silver, copper and tin mines, Bohemia became the wealthiest of medieval countries.

Prospectors Spur Migration

Always farther eastward went the epical German migratory movement, penetrating the Hungarian Erzgebirge in the southern Carpathians. The mines of Schemnitz and Kremnitz north of Budapest, once worked by Charlemagne, were revived and produced considerable gold, silver and copper. The Saxon miners who worked them were acclaimed far and wide for their knowledge and proficiency. Their fame spread so far that the merchants of Venice induced them to lend their skills in the development of mines in Serbia. Ragusa, now known as Dubrovnik, on the Adriatic coast of modern Yugoslavia, became the outlet for operations carried on in the hinterland by the Saxons.

The quest for riches also led explorers southward into the Alpine region where scattered districts had produced wealth as early as the 10th century. Mountains of the Tyrol always had been a lure to medieval prospectors. Lush, verdant, deeply cut valleys, echoing to the music of streams cascading from snowy Alpine peaks, made this one of the most beautiful and romantic regions in the world to seek nature's treasures.

Near Hall and Schwaz, in the valley of the Inn River, 17 miles east of modern Innsbruck, lead, silver, and copper mines were among the most productive in Europe. At Gastein, near the modern resort of Badgastein, quartz veins yielded much gold in the Middle Ages, and were reopened after the first World War. East of Gastein near Oberndorf and Schellgaden, and westward at Prettau, Hippach and Zell, more districts produced gold, making the Alpine region an important contributor to the wealth of Western Europe.

Revival of Trade

During the 12th and 13th centuries, a period that marked the discovery of Central Europe's extensive mineral wealth, including Bohemia's, Europe witnessed the most brilliant cultural era of the Middle Ages. People emerged from the shackles of servile bondage. Frontier posts rose to the status of burgs. Business expanded in and about the towns, restoring old routes of commerce. Metal industries thrived. Traders became merchants and bankers, a new class of entrepreneurs known as 'burgers' in Germany, 'bourgeois' in France and 'burgesses' in England. It was this class, spearheaded by the adventuresome prospectors seeking metallic wealth, who supplied the incentive and led Europe out of the dormancy of the Dark Ages.

An outstanding development, and one of far reaching consequence, that became identified with this period was the growth and preservation of a common religious faith. Among the hodgepodge of hereditary princes who ruled their feudal domains unbeholden even to kings, one unifying force alone commanded the allegiance of peasants and lords alike.

That force was Christianity. It had emerged as a solitary state religion in Europe; therefore it was considered universal, or *catholica*. Memorializing this religious fervor with the lavish use of stone, bronze, gold and silver, a fantastic wave of church building swept over the land. Stimulated also by the benign influence of the newly found metallic riches of Saxony and Bohemia, medieval metalsmiths, sculptors, painters, and mosaicists perpetuated one of man's most inspired architectural achievements in adorning their Gothic cathedrals.

"Bibles in Stone"

Stately church design had been introduced in Western Europe about the year 800 when Charlemagne built his palace and chapel at Aachen, adopting the Romanesque style. Huge, high domes supported by massive walls, which contained a few small windows, were typical of the basilicas that Romans had used to glorify their cities and pagan gods. Following Charlemagne's example, during the 11th century over 1500 Romanesque type churches had been built in France alone.

Using new concepts of design, in 1137, Suger, the brilliant abbot, restored the abbey of St. Denis near Paris, which had been founded by a Merovingian king in 626. Slender, ribbed columns were used to form supports for lofty pointed arches, eliminating the rounded Roman vaults. Thick, windowless walls were replaced with thinner exteriors braced by graceful "flying buttresses." Magnificent stained glass windows, a miracle of medieval art, filled these new exterior walls and flooded the interiors with multihued light.

The hallmark of Gothic design was the profusion of ornamental carvings in stone and sculptures in bronze. Tall, majestic spires and bell-towers, visible from all directions of the countryside, rose above imposing portals embellished with literally thousands of animated statues of Biblical figures and sculptured religious scenes, carved pediments and lacy arches. Outstanding features of the Gothic cathedrals were their ponderous bronze doors, elaborately sculptured with themes of Biblical times, and their impressive altars of bronze richly decorated with gold and silver. Much of the precious metals, and the copper and tin ores used by the bronzesmiths, came from the mines of the Bohemian Erzgebirge.

By the mid-13th century, over 500 Gothic cathedrals had risen above the fields of France. Among them were such noted edifices as Notre

Dame of Paris, Chartres, Reims, Amiens, Rouen, Bourges, and Tours, while in Germany the cathedrals of Cologne, Ulm and others testify to the creativity of Medieval man. To the classical minded Romans, the intricately carved and decorated steeples, buttresses, arches and portals of the French and German cathedrals appeared "barbarian." Hence they applied the epithet "Gothic," after the barbarian Goths, as a term of derision for western Europe's medieval architecture.

Metals for Culture and Commerce

While various cities and bishops strived to build the tallest and grandest cathedrals, the copper and tin resources of Germany furnished the bronze materials for the marvelous church bells of this epical period. Countless bronze bells pealed their peaceful messages across the countryside. Less benevolent were the guns and cannon first made of bronze from techniques learned in bell-casting, for they thundered omens of death and destruction. On the battlefield of Crecy in northern France, in one of the earliest uses of bronze cannon and gunpowder, during the Hundred Years War the English won their first victory over the French in 1346.

The metal deposits of western Europe, exploited since the time of Charlemagne, had contributed greatly to raising Europe to new heights of achievement. They gave impetus to a remarkable eastward migration, an epic of the German people, which led to colonization and development of the land. The metals that were produced created a dependable currency, and revived European industry and commerce, which transformed frontier posts and medieval villages into great cities of culture and commerce.

These same bonanzas furnished the materials and the financial means to enrich the numerous monasteries which for centuries were the guardians of classical Greek and Roman cultures, and were prime contributors to the building of Europe's magnificent cathedrals which became the inspiration and directing force of medieval unity. In short, the earth-bound wealth of Central Europe, found by "the miner who digs for his metals and thereby hurts no man," lent its timely and energizing support to the preservation of ancient legacies and the establishment of European civilization.

Mining Goads Inventors

While wresting with the forces of nature in the mining of metals, medieval men were forced to draw upon their ingenuity and inventive powers. After the outcrops of virgin deposits had been easily mined, the deeper ores were extracted with more difficulty. Not only new methods for raising water from the workings were needed, but deeper shafts and longer adits penetrating the hillsides were required to reach the ore zones. As mining and metallurgical problems grew more complex, inventiveness and greater capital investment became a pressing necessity.

Difficulty encountered in deeper mining was only one of Europe's mounting problems. The Black Death, perhaps a bubonic plague, in 1357 reduced the population by one-third. Recurrent wars and political strife between European princes, as well as nations, seriously disrupted the production of metals. Mines and smelters were attacked by rival forces and left in ruins. After enjoying 200 years of flush production and resultant prosperity, the mining industry entered a depression caused by obsolete mining methods and Europe's many woes. The mining of metals ceased; only the ironmaking districts, maintained by needs of war, were active.

Europe quickly felt a grave shortage of precious metals, especially silver for coinage. Again, as in the past, some rulers endeavored to remedy the situation by reducing the silver content of the coins. It became obvious that economic recovery and the revival of industry depended a great deal upon the restoration of mining operations. Then, as political conditions gradually became more stabilized, medieval miners found themselves challenged to overcome the technical dilemmas which had previously plagued the industry.

Medieval Water Power

Goaded by necessity, men were forced to turn their minds toward invention. It was the profusion of streams tumbling down the mountain slopes of Central Europe that gave medieval men the idea of developing machines operated by water power. Borrowing the principles of a water mill formerly used by the Chinese, Moors, and Romans for grinding corn, the Germans put water to work to run machinery for pumping water out of the mines, for crushing the ores, for operating blast furnace bellows, and for running forging hammers. This led to utilizing similar methods in the cloth, leather, and lumber industries.

Where water was unavailable, horses were

hitched to large wooden wheels placed horizontally in underground chambers 50 feet in diameter, and driven in a circular path to operate the main shaft of the pumps. At Schemintz in the Carpathians, 96 horses, working 8 at a time in short intervals, operated wheels placed on three separate levels. Using several of such lifting levels, water could be raised over 600 feet. Gentle, inclined adits formed twisting ramps down which the horses were led to the pumping levels.

As miners delved deeper in their operations, another enigma confronted them. The ore grew more complex in composition. Their silica content made them harder to mine. Being more refractory they were more resistant to smelting. Since silver, lead, copper and other metals were often intimately intermixed in the form of sulphides, the ore minerals were also more difficult to separate.

Not only did expensive mining machinery become necessary, but laboratories also had to be established to conduct costly metallurgical experiments. Therefore, this was a period when the mining and treatment of earth's metals assumed a new form of industrial enterprise, demanding heavy capital expenditures. Until now, prospectors and miners, or groups of associated miners, had been able to work their near-surface ores with little capital.

Advent of Capitalism

In order to work the deeper veins they sold 'parts' or shares to local merchants, monasteries, or town governments. Often, the miners borrowed money from traders and bankers. Now and then they fell into debt. Creditors then took over the mines, chose experts to manage the enterprise, and then employed the miners as workers. Thus came into being the era of bankers, capitalists and wage earners, stimulated by inventions and new industrial techniques.

Mines were also operated by various lords who owned the regalian rights. They were always at wits end for money to finance the colossal festivities celebrating their coronations, which were attended by thousands of courtiers, officials and visiting royalty. An endless succession of marriage dowries, extravagant court life, and the maintenance of huge palaces induced further financial straits. These lords had little heart or ability for managing the costly mining administrations within their realms. Instead, the duchies of **Brunswick, Saxony, Bohemia,** and **Austria,** which possessed the greatest metallic wealth, turned to the rich merchants and money lenders on many critical occasions.

The large silver output of the Germans during the Middle Ages provided an ample base of currency which enabled German financiers to become leaders of the financial world. Flourishing mine and smelter industries proved a rich and expanding field for investment. The fortunes of many banking families were bolstered by their interests in mines spread across the land.

Members of the Fugger and Schusselfelder families first loaned money and then gained control of copper smelters at Eisleben, Martin Luther's home town. The Welsers, a wealthy mercantile family of Augsburg, lent large sums to Charles V and acquired interests in the silver mines of Schneeberg. And, as the Medici family was the all-powerful banking concern of Italy, so were the Fuggers the greatest merchant princes of Germany.

The Powerful Fuggers

The Fugger financial dynasty was founded by Johannes Fugger, a weaver in Augsburg, and enlarged by his sons and grandson Jacob, who dealt in oriental silks and spices. However, it was the mining loans and ventures in the Tyrol, Carinthia, Austria, and Spain that provided the Fuggers with their greatest wealth. The Fuggers played a very influential role in European politics, national economy and even religion. They not only lent money to monarchs, they also loaned funds to the Pope, and zealously supported the Roman Catholic Church. Possibly this delayed Martin Luther's Reformation movement, which ultimately swept over Germany.

To Maximilian I, King of Germany and Emperor of The Holy Roman Empire, Jacob Fugger loaned such huge sums of money that Maximilian mortgaged the County of Kirchberg and the lordship of Weissenhorn to the banker. Maximilian I was the colorful and dynamic founder of the fabulous Habsburg dynasty of Austria, and the progenitor of dukes, archdukes, and kings of Bohemia, Hungary, and Spain.

Dedicated to perpetuation of the Habsburg line, Maximilian began early in his reign to borrow money from the Fuggers to pay the costs of the numerous elaborate weddings and the huge dowries of his many offspring. Through an amazing complex of marriages, the Habsburgs dominated the political, religious, and matrimonial affairs of the multinational royal houses of Europe for over six hundred years. The silver and copper mines in the Tyrol and Hungary, owned by the Habsburgs, time and again provided the security for Maximilian's loans.

But for the help of Fugger financial assistance, and additional aid from the Welsers, it is doubtful if Charles V, grandson of Maximilian, could have been elected Emperor of The Holy Roman Empire in 1519. It was common practice for some of the seven prince-electors, who included the lords of Bohemia, Hungary, Saxony, Brandenburg, and three arch-bishops to cast their votes for the highest bidder.

Mineral Wealth and History

The election of Charles signaled a decisive test of strength between France and Germany, pitting King Francis I against the house of Habsburg. Surrounded by the formidable domain of the Habsburgs, the Holy Roman Empire on the east, Netherland on the north, and Spain on the south, the French king was prepared to spend as much as 500,000 ducats, or roughly one million dollars, to swing the vote of each elector.

Already heavily burdened with debt and torn with doubt, the Habsburgs turned to the powerful Fuggers and Welsers for funds to pay the bribery demands of the electors, who were shrewdly offering their votes to the highest bidder. Money, estates, even royal children were thrown onto the bargaining scales. All Europe was aghast at the frantic game being played in Frankfurt where the election was taking place. A few partial factions even began to concentrate troops.

The weight of the money and the political influence of the Fuggers, plus the loyalty of the German people to the memory of their beloved Maximilian, finally tipped the election and made Charles V of Spain Emperor of the Holy Roman Empire. The crown had cost Charles over a million gulden, a debt from which he never fully recovered.

The Fuggers also gained control of and leased mines in Spain, including the famed Almaden mercury mines first worked by the Romans. Raymund and Anton Fugger lent large sums to Philip II of Spain, and to Edward VI and Henry VIII of England. In 1530 Raymund and Anton Fugger became Swabian Counts and were given the rights of princes, including the privilege to coin gold and silver. The Fuggers were loyal subjects of the Austrian crown. More than all the other nobility of the realm, it was the Fuggers and the wealth which they won from the mines of Germany, Austria and Spain that sustained the powerful history making Habsburg dynasty.

Mining Booms of The 15th Century

Silver had played a vital role in medieval commerce and industry. When metallurgical techniques were devised to extract silver from complex sulphide ores of copper, the production of copper also increased. The Rammelsberg mines were reopened in 1453 and entered their centuries of greatest prosperity. In the southeastern Harz, the silver-lead deposits of St. Andreasberg were opened in 1520 and remained rich producers for 300 years. As many new discoveries came to light, and older districts were revived with new mining methods, during the years 1450-1550 the greatest mining boom of the Middle Ages swept over Europe.

At Clauthsal-Zellerfeld, 32 miles southwest of Brunswick, deposits of lead, copper, silver and zinc were opened, and the city became a government minting center. From the mines of Hall and Schwaz along the Inn River, and from Annaberg, Schneeberg, Joachimsthal and Kutna Hora, streams of silver poured into the economy of Germany. From such mines as Altenberg, Zinnwald and Obergraupen over one million tons of tin were produced, rivaling the output of the great Cornwall region of England, which was now again coming into production.

Discoveries of enormous deposits of calamine, an ore of zinc, at Moresnet near Charlemagne's old capital, Aachen, brought the long neglected manufacture of brass, an alloy of copper and zinc, back into prominence. This also stimulated the demand for copper. Important metal manufacturing centers blossomed forth in Central Europe. Antwerp became known for its lead wares, and Luneberg for its copper products. Aachen and Nuremberg also grew prosperous with their metal crafts.

Cologne on the Rhine River became one of the richest cities in Europe, not only because of its commerce and textiles, but also for its famed metalwares. Cologne's bells of peace, its swords and helmets of war, and its copper-beating crafts grew world renowned under the guidance of Frederick of St. Pantaleon, master metalworker of the age. West of the Rhine, Huy and especially Dinant were famed for their copper and brass wares, known as "Dindaneries."

The booming metallurgical and mining industries provided a mighty stimulant to the industrial growth of Central Europe. Germany's great wealth in silver, copper, lead, tin, and zinc and its brass and other metalworking plants became the marvel of all Europe. German mining and metallurgical practices were considered unmatched anywhere in the world, with the possible exception of Cornwall, England. The stream of technical knowledge, developed in Central Europe, began to spread to France, England, Scandinavia and Spain, as all Europe awoke to the blessings of its natural resources.

Cornwall's World-wide Renown

Contemporary with the mining and industrial boom of the late 15th century, the legendary land of the Cassiterides, now known as Cornwall, England, also entered its era of flush production. Famed as a source of tin for the Greeks, Romans, and possibly the seafaring Phoenicians, and still producing today, Cornwall has yielded its riches for over 3000 years.

For several centuries after the Romans withdrew from Britain in 410 mining lay dormant. No further word is heard about Cornish tin until the year 600 when it was recorded, during the life of the patriarch of Alexandria, that a boat was sent to Britain and returned loaded with tin. To spice the tale, the chronicler added that during the journey the tin turned miraculously into silver.

Activity was accelerated in 1066 with the appearance of William the Conqueror, whose brother Robert Mortain was made Earl of Cornwall. Thereafter, Devonshire and Cornwall became Britain's source of tin, much of which went to London's Craft of Pewterers for the fashioning of their famed pewter dinnerware, mugs and utensils. Great quantities were used also in making brass cannon, church bells and in plating copper articles.

Richard Coeur de Lion, King of England, had reason to thank the tinners of Cornwall for their contribution to his safe return from the Third Crusade. En route home he was captured near Vienna by his bitter foe, Duke Leopold of Austria, and held for a huge ransom in the duke's castle high above the Danube at Durnstein. (Its craggy ruins are still there.) Excessive taxes were levied against the people, and tributes were gathered from Cornwall and Britain's silver-lead regions, enabling Richard to return to England in March, 1194.

Cornwall's Magna Carta

Cornwall's first charter governing the stannaries, as the tin producing districts were called, was granted by Richard's successor, King John Lackland, in 1201. It defined the rules for digging of tin, for smelting, for obtaining fuel from neighboring woods, and for the royalties to be paid. To the miners this first charter was as important as the Magna Carta which King John was forced to sign at Runnymede in 1215, for the tinners were thus released from feudal serfdom, as were the miners of Germany by similar decrees.

In 1337 tin production reached a high point, coming from the placer tin deposits in the streams that laced Cornwall's countryside. During the ages of placer mining, opinions were rife as to how the dark grains of cassiterite had found their way into the streambeds. Ultimately, the tinners traced the cassiterite to veins, or lodes, locked firmly in or near huge masses of pink granite, which forms much of the western end of the Cornwall Peninsula. By 1450, Cornishmen were digging pits, adits and open trenches to expose the tin bearing veins. Lodes were discovered also in sea cliffs in which tides and floods had exposed them to view.

During the 17th century underground mining predominated over "streaming." Then, using hand tools, miners began drilling holes in the hard, tough granite. Filling the holes with gunpowder, they were able to fracture the rock, an improvement over the slow, ancient method of fire setting. Explosives had been used in the Hungarian Erzgebirge in 1627, when Caspar Weindle introduced the method at Schemnitz.

Mining Launches The Steam Age

As mining had been the mother of invention in Germany, in creating machines to harness wind and water power, so did the need to rid mines of water in England produce the world's first practical steam engine. It was the Englishman, Thomas Newcomen, who perfected the first atmospheric steam engine, which he began to produce in considerable quantities in 1711 for pumping water from the tin mines of Cornwall and Devonshire, from England's coal collieries, and from the silver-lead mines of Somerset and Derbyshire.

James Watt's highly important improvements, devised while repairing a Newcomen engine, led to a wider application of steam power in the following eras, but Watt was not, as widely thought, the inventor of the steam engine. It was Thomas Newcomen, inspired by the necessity of keeping water from England's treasure chest of metals and coal. From such a compulsion, nourished by a nation's mineral wealth, was born one of man's most beneficent inventions, which introduced to the world the Age of Steam.

The Mines of Cornwall

By 1862, 340 mines with hundreds of shafts and thousands of miles of underground workings supported a population of 50,000 in Cornwall. In that century, Cornish men took from their granite-ribbed mines metals worth over 200 million sterling, a prodigious figure in those days of hand drilled openings in the hardest and toughest of rocks. No wonder the "Cousin-Jacks," as Cornishmen were affectionately called, came to be known as the world's finest hard rock miners.

The Penstruthal and Tresavean lodes near Gwennap, within a distance of 3500 feet, yielded approximately $20,000,000 worth of tin and copper. The Levant mine near St. Ives was driven over 700 feet from shore beneath the sea. Through fractures in the rock, seepages of water added to the difficulty of mining. Another great mine whose inclined shaft extended beneath the sea was the Botallack near St. Just, almost at Land's End. Some say that miners could hear huge boulders rolling above on the ocean floor, but Cornishmen were too wise to mine that close to Neptune's domain and tempt the God of the Sea to invade their workings.

Across the Bay of Penzance is the world famous Wheal Vor (Wheal meaning mine), perhaps the richest single producer in Cornwall. After being idle nearly 100 years, the owners managed to reopen it in 1814, but went bankrupt trying to make it profitable. Trustees of the estate bought up the property, and in 1820, at a depth of 900 feet, miners encountered the richest tin lode ever found in Cornwall. The most productive district, however, was later worked between Redruth and Camborne. The three miles between these towns is believed to have given up more metallic wealth than any area of similar extent in all of the Old World.

Deep in Mother Earth

Between 1850 and 1860, Cornwall reached its floodtide of prosperity, leading the world in copper and tin production. Mines such as the Tresavean, Penstruthal and Fowey Consolidated were yielding mainly copper. Then, an alarming decrease of copper ore in the deeper levels dealt the mines a serious blow. But the god of fortune held a surprise in store for Cornwall. Below a depth of 1,000 feet, the thinning copper ores gave way to new and richer deposits of tin. Great tin mines came into production, including the famed Dolcoath, Carn Brea, the Levant, Wheal Kitty, Tincroft, Botallack, and the South Crofty, which continued to work steadily for over 100 years. Many are still producing today.

An indescribable affinity and mutual understanding seems to bind men of the mining breed. Perhaps it is the closeness that comes from being enfolded deep within Mother Earth and being the first to view her long stored untouched treasures. In this world of utter darkness, the blackest of blackness if one's lamp is accidentally extinguished, there is a haunting fascination. Almost unreal are the working conditions: often the air is steaming hot, and at times pungent with the odor of blasting fumes, and water may drip from above or run underfoot. Except in main haulageways there is nothing to light one's way but a small miner's lamp that casts eerie, distorted shadows upon the grimy walls. Echoing through the workings, drifts, and stopes are the sounds of ringing, chattering steel clawing its way through the rock. At certain times are heard the muffled blast of a dynamite charge, followed by a swoosh of air. Occasionally the crunch of restless rocks relieve their stresses. It is no wonder that miners develop an alertness and unified spirit of fellowship found in few other professions.

Cornwall's Legacy

Cornishmen are known over the world not only for their expertise in mining; their colorful personalities, special creeds, and close brotherhood have also won them the respect and admiration of their fellowmen. Despite the drudgery of their tasks and the somberness of their underground world, Cornishmen are known for their hardy, blithesome spirits, and for their jovial, courteous, and friendly dispositions.

They are inveterate practical jokers; they can be keenly but humorously sarcastic, but are extremely charitable and courteous toward one another and to strangers. Especially noted in Cornish tradition are the mine "Captains," the equivalent of a foreman or superintendent. Trained since boyhood, they possess the utmost of mining skill and have a canny understanding of ore deposits, traits inherited from generations. Witty, wily, and wise in the handling of men, Cornish "Captains" form a unique and outstanding class in the mining world.

We shall see Cornishmen again in these pages as they transmit their invaluable legacies to the New World, where they will form the vanguard in unearthing America's fabulous storehouses of metallic wealth. Together with their Saxon counterparts, the Cornishmen will form the backbone of America's mining and metallurgical industrial growth. Wrote a traveler not long ago, "Wherever a hole is sunk into the ground today, no matter in what corner of the globe, you will be sure to find a Cornishman at the bottom of it, searching for metal."

The Renaissance

Under the aegis of mining and industrial booms of the 14th, 15th and 16th centuries, and the stimulus of capitalism, Europe experienced an era of thriving economy and abundant prosperity, attended by vigorous intellectual and artistic achievements. This period, marking Europe's emergence from medieval stagnation to the awakening of modern thought, is known as the Renaissance.

The European Renaissance was first a decidedly Italian phenomenon, which later spread to the rest of Western Europe. The seeds sprouted when late medieval societies of increasing wealth, leisure and freedom, consumed with yearnings to study and revive the classical cultures of Greece and Rome, aspired to greater excellence, higher learning, and human betterment.

Since Italy was the possessor of the most revered and enduring landmarks of ancient brilliance, it was mainly in Florence, Rome, Venice and Milan, and a score of smaller cities such as Siena, Parma, Rimini and Mantua, that the Renaissance received its impetus. Of these cities, Florence became the cradle and the leader in the movement. Its strategic location at the hub of trade routes from Italy's coastal ports to Central Europe via Alpine passes, made Florence a flourishing and prosperous city.

Renaissance Economy

The diversity of Florentine economy is shown by the 21 guilds, which included wool traders, cloth manufacturers, silk importers, winedealers, furriers, ironworkers, and silversmiths. Control of the city rested in the hands of the bankers and rich merchants. As the Fuggers and Welsers had become politically and culturally influential in Germany, so did the Perussi, Bardi, and Medici banking families play a prominent role in Florence, Italy.

The Medici dynasty was founded in 1397 by Giovanni de Medici, a wool dealer, and included such noted figures as Cosimo, Piero, Lorenzo The Magnificent (1478-1492), Catherine Medici and several dukes, queens, cardinals and popes. Medici wealth stemmed from trade in wool, textiles, spices, jewelry and silver plate. They controlled alum mines near Volterra, which provided the chemical required in the dyeing of woolen cloth. Loans and banking, however, provided the basis of Medici wealth and power.

Thriving industries and expanding trade made men in Florence, Venice, Genoa and Pisa, and in Germany, Burgundy and France exceedingly rich, enjoying levels of self-indulgence and elegance which had once been reserved only to princes and kings. Eager to emulate the classical past, while engaging in benevolent activities, merchant princes spread sponsorships by employing talented artists and craftsmen to decorate their palaces, and vied with one another in building grandiose and generously endowed churches.

Sumptuous estates and villas were filled with treasures of classical art, and adorned with newly inspired works of contemporary painters and sculptors. Devoted to chivalric philanthropies, and often self-eulogy, bankers and merchants zealously encouraged the development of humanism, the revival of learning, and the advancement of literature, art, and architecture.

Immortals of The Renaissance

Florence became the fountainhead of creative urges, represented by such writers as Petrarch (called the Father of Humanism), Dante and Boccaccio, and such painters and sculptors as Giotto, Masaccio, Botticelli, Leonardo da Vinci, Donatello, Ghiberti, Cellini and Michelangelo, and the architect Brunelleschi. Other contributors to the immortal legacies of the Renaissance were: the painters Raphael, Rosselli, Pintoricchio, and Michelangelo while in Rome; Titian, Georgione, Tintoretto, and Veronese in Venice; El Greco and Velasquez in Spain; Durer, Holbein, Rubens, and Rembrandt in Germany and The Netherlands. In England, such humanists as Erasmus, a Flemish scholar, Linacre, Colet and Thomas More provided the intellectual stimulation that greatly influenced the political thinking of the western world.

The element necessary for the transformation of these intellectual and artistic urges into monumental works of literature, philosophy, and art was patronage, which meant money. Without the financial support of the merchant princes, and the incalculable patronage of the popes, who had the enormous revenues of the Church at their disposal, the Renaissance period could hardly have developed the latent genius of those times. It is significant that after the death of Lorenzo The Magnificent, Florence's greatest benefactor, the Medicis were driven into exile and their palace was sacked, bringing to an end the patronage of this remarkable dynasty, and with it, the Golden Age of Florence.

An Era of Mineral Wealth

It was not only the Revival of Learning, which was inspired and stimulated by the Latin classics and ancient Greece, that brought about the European Renaissance. Preceding the intellectual revival, during the Middle Ages there had been a regeneration of industries and trade throughout Europe. A prerequisite to this economic surge was the discovery of extensive mineral deposits, which motivated the exploration, settlement and development of large areas of the continent, and furnished the metals that were required to establish basic industries, vitalize commerce, and stabilize coinage.

Humanists and artisans living in the burgeoning trade centers became the beneficiaries of this newly created prosperity and leisure. Indeed, the Renaissance was a rich man's era, as evidenced by the countless extravagantly adorned palaces and churches now seen across the land. One wonders whether man would have risen to such eminence without first having the timely and invigorating aid of Europe's economic revival, in which its vast metallic resources played a fundamental role. The question arises, in the absence of widespread wealth during the Renaissance, how many of the cultural legacies and splendid edifices would mankind be enjoying today?

The most outstanding and providential heritage of the Renaissance was the unleashing of the human spirit. New ideas and new freedoms led not only to the rediscovery of man, they inspired the discovery of new worlds. The Renaissance had nurtured well man's desire for progress and his inborn yearning for enterprise, preparing him for his most venturesome era, the great Age of Discovery.

The Age of Discovery

For centuries, following the Crusades, Western Europe had been bewitched by the luxuries and riches of the East. People had been stirred also by Marco Polo's tales of the wealth he had beheld in Persia, India, and China, and of the houses roofed with gold that he had seen on the island of Cipangu (Japan). Spectators had seen merchant ships in the ports of Venice, Pisa, Genoa, Barcelona, and Marseille, loaded with exotic wares of the Orient. There was no doubt that Asia, the "Indies," was a land of fabulous treasure. But the trade routes overland and by sea were long, costly and dangerous. Inventive minds, born of the Renaissance, began to dream of a better route.

Portuguese explorers, inspired by Prince Henry the "Navigator," were the first to begin probing their way southward around Africa. Diaz reached the Cape of Good Hope in 1488, and ten years later Vasco da Gama circled the Cape and landed in India. But even this southern route had its disadvantages. Perhaps a better way could be found; instead of sailing eastward, possibly India could be reached by sailing westward.

Many men of science knew the world was round, and not flat. Such men of antiquity as Aristarchus, Eratosthenes, Aristotle, Strabo, and Ptolemy were aware that the earth was spherical, and during the Renaissance, many who were familiar with the classics held the same opinion. But this knowledge seemed to be of little practical significance to most men. There was one important exception: a man named Christopher Columbus was obsessed with the idea of doing something about it.

Christopher Columbus

Columbus, born in Genoa and son of a weaver, was not a scholarly philosopher, nor a learned scientist, he was simply an able, highly experienced seaman and navigator, a trustworthy trader and a skilled map maker and geographer. He was also nearly penniless. He was a man of calm physical courage, possessing a singular purpose and boundless confidence in his ultimate success. Lacking one of those wealthy patrons such as had so readily sponsored geniuses of the art and literary world, Columbus found little backing for his dream of probing beyond the visible horizon.

Unsuccessful in his efforts to enlist the aid of King John II of Portugal, Columbus went to Spain. There, he endured seven long, aggravating, heartbreaking years endeavoring to overcome the disbeliefs of the committee of scientists and personal counselors of the Spanish sovereigns, Isabella and Ferdinand. The committee finally advised the king and queen that the project "was impossible and only worthy of rejection, as any educated person, however little learning he might have, would well know."

When all hope of assistance appeared lost, it was Queen Isabella who revived the enterprise at the last moment and sanctioned the expedition. Her faith in Columbus always had been strong. To the Queen, Columbus had recounted repeatedly Marco Polo's descriptions of the tremendous wealth to be found in the Indies, China (Cathay), and Cipangu. Earnestly and convincingly, Columbus vowed that his expedition would make their Highnesses the richest sovereigns in the world, with a fortune greater than all the combined treasuries of Europe. So, it was treasure again that formed the lure leading to the discovery of new worlds.

Admiral of The Ocean Sea

Under a contract with the king and queen, Columbus was appointed Governor-General over all lands he might discover; he was to retain one-tenth of all precious metals, gemstones, spices and other products resulting from his discovery, and henceforth he was to bear the noble title of Don Cristobal Colon, Admiral of The Ocean Sea.

At Palos, located on the Rio Tinto, Columbus obtained his three ships, the Niña, Pinta and Santa Maria, and many of his crew. One may still see the venerable old church of St. George where Columbus and his 90 competent sailors attended mass prior to sailing. Near the church is the same well of sweet water from which the water casks of the ships were filled.

On August 3, 1492, the Niña, the Pinta and the Santa Maria, with their sails bearing the cross of Christendom, moved down the Rio Tinto past the monastery of La Rabida, which had harbored Columbus on his first arrival in Spain. Slowly the ships entered the estuary of the Rio Saltes, and then entered the trackless void of the great Atlantic. One by one the little ships vanished into the mysterious unknown.

After 68 days of haunting uncertainty, overcome with fear and distrust, the crew came close to mutiny. Then, branches appeared in the water, and hopes ran high that land was near. During the early hours of October 12, 1492, in the pale light of a nearly full moon, a lookout saw a faint line on the horizon, a white cliff of coral gleaming in the moonlight. "Tierra, Tierra!" he shouted. Then all joined in the cry, "It is land, it is land." It was not the mainland, but an island some 375 miles southwest of Florida.

A New World

After waiting for morning's light, the caravels turned south and rounded a point of land on the island's protected, leeward side. Cautiously the ships passed through a break in the outer reef, white with crashing waves. Slowly they entered a shallow bay, now called "Long Bay." There, the sails were furled and the anchors dropped. Columbus and captains Martin Pinzon of the Pinta, and Vicente Pinzon of the Niña, dressed in their finest, then went ashore carrying the royal standard of Spain. Kneeling upon the ground, and embracing it with tears of thankfulness for their salvation, they named the island San Salvador, and claimed the land for Spain.

This same historic spot, still remote from habitation, is virtually unchanged. It is located about five miles south of the tiny village of Cockburn town, San Salvador's only port. A lone 15 foot high concrete cross, dazzling white in the sun, now marks Columbus' landing site. Near the cross, waves of the clear blue sea lap upon the very same protruding ledges of coral limestone that induced Columbus to note in his log that "they would make excellent flagstone for building." Out toward the sea, white crests of foam reveal the same two reefs through which Columbus took his ships that fate-laden October day in 1492, opening a new chapter in the history of mankind.

And that is where, for now, we shall leave Christopher Columbus, Admiral of The Ocean Sea, and discoverer of a New World. We have ended our long, long journey through the Old World; we have visited the Stone Age villages of France and The Fertile Crescent; we have seen the first civilizations rising in the valley of the Euphrates, Egypt and Asia Minor, and in Crete, Mycenae and Greece; we have watched the growing might and the disintegration of the Roman Empire; we have peered into the darkness of the Middle Ages, and witnessed the return of enlightenment and inspiration during the Renaissance.

Now, with Columbus, we have come ashore touching a continent heretofore totally unknown to European man, a New World. Here, later, we shall pick up the trail of the Admiral of The Ocean Sea and the horde of explorers and Conquistadores who will follow him. Then we shall behold one historic discovery after another, as pioneers reveal the secrets of new lands, new riches, and a parade of bonanzas greater than the world has ever known. And, as we shall see, they too will have their inevitable effects upon the course of history.

Chapter 10

LURES OF THE NEW WORLD

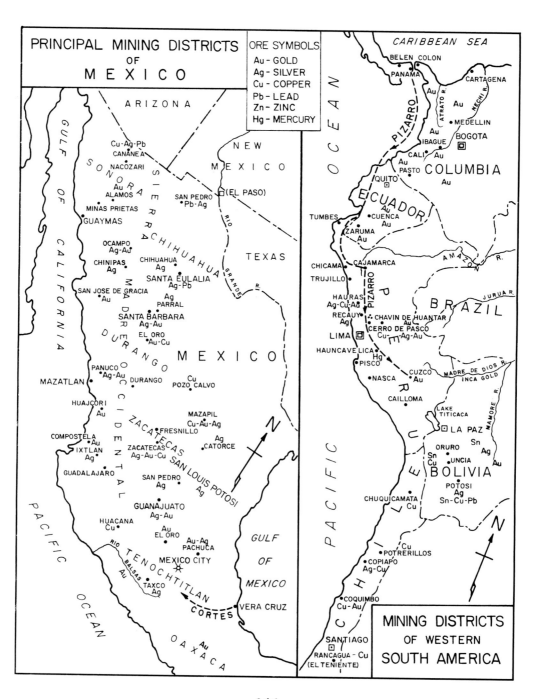

PRINCIPAL MINING DISTRICTS
OF
MEXICO

ORE SYMBOLS
Au - GOLD
Ag - SILVER
Cu - COPPER
Pb - LEAD
Zn - ZINC
Hg - MERCURY

MINING DISTRICTS
OF WESTERN
SOUTH AMERICA

A Pristine Land

On that memorable day, October 12, 1492, when Christopher Columbus raised the Royal Standard of Spain upon the coral beach of a little island, known to the natives as Guanahani, he also awakened a primordial continent that had slumbered in anonymity since the dawn of creation. For thousands of years civilizations had come and gone, while half the earth, the Western Hemisphere, insofar as the Old World was concerned, had remained an unsuspected wilderness.

Others before Columbus had seen this untouched land, but for various reasons they had failed to establish a foothold. Eric the Red and his Vikings had touched the coast of Greenland about 980, and twenty years later Leif Erickson had been driven onto the North American shore, which he named Vineland. About 1006, a party under Thorfinn Karlsefni apparently tried to establish a colony on the New England Coast. The remains of a Norse settlement recently unearthed near the village of L'Anse au Meadow, on the tip of Newfoundland, offers more definite evidence. Carbon-14 tests of a crude iron smelter reveal that the Norse sea rovers reached American shores 500 years before Columbus landed upon San Salvador Island.

There was a notable difference, however, in the motivations which incited the actions of the Vikings and those of the Spaniards. In a land covered with forests and seemingly barren of metals, the Norsemen found little evidence of metallic wealth, nor were they exposed to the lure of gold; otherwise, America might have become a Norwegian domain. Columbus and his followers, on the other hand, were driven by the urge to find the glittering riches of the Indies and Cipangu. It was the lure that laid bare a New World.

That auspicious quest, begun by a man with a dream, led to the most astounding treasure hunts known to man. The excitement generated by Columbus' discoveries was the spark that lit the flame. Overwhelming momentum was added to the quest after the arrival of the Conquistadores, who gathered a golden harvest exceeding their wildest dreams, for the Spaniards, unlike the Norsemen, had stumbled upon one of the most incredible storehouses of mineral treasure the world had ever seen. It was this wealth that spurred the Spaniards on, until they had opened a continent to new races and new civilizations. But the first steps of this trek, taken by Columbus, were faltering and disappointing.

Columbus Seeks Cipangu

When Columbus first greeted the natives who crowded about him on Guanahani's coral sands, he was vexed and chagrined by their appearance. Not only were they naked and bereft of any sign of golden possessions, they had never heard of Cipangu or Cathay. Thinking he had reached India, Columbus referred to the natives as "Indians." Ever since that day America's earliest inhabitants have been known as Indians.

Endeavoring to direct the Spaniards in their bewildered search for the mainland, the Indians uttered the word "Colba." At once Columbus felt certain it was the native word for Cipangu. Eagerly he took aboard Indian guides to show him the way to Cipangu, whose houses he believed were roofed with gold. When the Spanish appetite for gold became apparent to the Indian guides, they delighted in inventing mischievous tales which not only lured Columbus to "Colba," which was Cuba, but to one island after another throughout the Caribbean.

As the ships creaked lazily through waters that changed magically from azure blue to emerald green, the Spaniards looked spellbound at flying fishes skimming over the sea, and the lush, verdant land that lined the shores. It was a strange, chimerical world, wholly new to these intruders from Europe.

Ashore, the treasure hunters were entranced with the profusion of fruits and flowers, the brightly plumed jungle birds singing gay, unfamiliar songs. If these lands were as bright with gold as the skies were blue, they exclaimed, this indeed must be the long sought terrestrial paradise. But there was no Grand Khan, no golden cities, no spices, pearls or gold; all the dismayed Spaniards found were villages of mud huts, and natives smoking rolls of dried leaves, tobacco, the Indian's first and dubious contribution to European life.

The First Settlement

The unhappy shipwreck of Columbus' flagship, the Santa Maria, in the inky blackness of Christmas eve, 1492, on a coral reef off the northwestern tip of an island now known as Haiti, led to the founding of La Navidad, a crude fort built of timbers salvaged from the wreck. Born of necessity, this was the first European settlement in the New World.

After a long, futile search, fate had deposited the Spaniards upon the only Caribbean island sufficiently rich in gold to light the torch that would lead a parade of Conquistadores on their historic treks for treasure. The heavy bracelets and necklaces of gold worn by native women who came with curiosity to greet the strange white men was the guidepost to riches which the bug-eyed Spaniards had long been seeking. Members of Columbus' crew hurried to the nearby Rio Yaque del Norte, and there they found grains of gold gleaming in the river sands.

While Columbus was hurrying back to Spain with the joyful news of his discovery, the founders of La Navidad, hoping to find hoarded gold, ransacked the nearby Indian villages and ravaged the women. The incensed natives attacked the fort, massacred all of its defenders and burned it to the ground; then, they found and killed the Spaniards who were panning gold in the nearby river. When Columbus returned on his second voyage, a new settlement called Isabella was established on the coast east of La Navidad. It had been heard that gold was more plentiful in the highlands above Isabella, a land which the Indians called "Cibao." It was a magical word, for the Spaniards promptly took "Cibao" to mean Cipangu.

Gold in Hispaniola

Columbus immediately organized an expedition and marched into the hills where he established a fort named Santo Tomas, near the present village of Janico in the Cordillera Central of modern Haiti. Columbus was so enthusiastic over the island's rare beauty, reminiscent of Spain, that he named it La Isla Española, which became known as Hispaniola, Spain's first possession in the New World.

A fair harvest of gold was wrung from the long accumulated hoards of the Indians by looting the villages of the Cibao region, and by enforcing a yearly tribute of four hawks bells filled with gold dust from every male over 14 years of age. The penalty for nonpayment was death. When the Indians finally rebelled and refused to comply, the Spaniards rounded up 1500 natives who were shipped in chains to Spain. This marked the beginning, in the New World, of the inhuman allotment of Indian slaves to favored hildalgos, soldiers, and conquerors. Thereafter were taken the first steps in the long campaign of Spanish conquest, brutality, and plunder.

After the gold of Cibao became exhausted, in 1496 the capital of New Spain was established on the opposite or southern side of the island, and named Santo Domingo. Located at the mouth of the Ozama River, it provided a good harbor, fertile fields, and some unworked gold-bearing streams nearby. Santo Domingo then became the first permanent white settlement in the New World, and the springboard for future Spanish explorations of western, central and southern America.

The First Regulations

While Columbus was preparing his first return to Hispaniola, the Spanish sovereigns asked the Admiral to offer recommendations for colonizing the land. A plan was drawn up to control civil affairs, and to carry out the crown's sincere desire for conversion of the Indians. But the chief emphasis concerned regulations for the gathering of gold; prospectors were to be licensed and limited to settlers, and all discoveries were to be subject to a royalty payment to the crown. Thus, the search for gold was of primary importance, and became a special inducement for the settlement of New Spain.

From 1492 to 1503, in remarkable feats of seamanship, dead reckoning, courage, and perseverance, Columbus sailed four times to the New World. In 1498, on his third voyage he kept more to the south. After sighting three pinnacles, which he named Trinidad, he entered and landed upon the shore of the Gulf of Paria. Unknowingly he became the first European to touch the mainland of South America. It was the northeastern coast of Venezuela. He noticed natives wearing ornaments of gold alloyed with copper. Near the Peninsula de Araya he saw women wearing necklaces of pearls, but with supplies spoiling in the holds of his ship, he was forced to go on to Santo Domingo. Alonzo Ojeda, in 1499, would discover the famous pearl fisheries of nearby Margarita Island, from which Spain later reaped great wealth. Columbus unhappily seemed fated to always miss the greatest riches in the lands he discovered.

On his return to Santo Domingo, Columbus was outrageously placed in chains by the new commandant, brutal, arrogant Bobadilla, and sent to Spain to answer the perjured charges of his jealous detractors, who had long derided Columbus' six years of unsuccessful search for the riches of Asia. It was only one of several cruel indignities suffered by the Admiral of the Ocean Sea during his long quest. But by 1502, at the age of 51, Columbus regained the confidence of the Spanish sovereigns and sailed from Seville on his fourth and most crucial voyage.

First Signs of Treasure

Still seeking a passage to Asia through the labyrinth of Caribbean islands Columbus touched the coast of Honduras near modern Trujillo where he found the Jicaque Indians, the most advanced culture yet seen. Most surprising were their hatchets and bells made of copper, and the crucibles in which they melted the metals. The highlands of Honduras were rich in placer gold, and veins containing silver, gold and copper. Columbus was making the first contact on the American continent with a people versed in the melting and casting of precious metals, a culture that would soon be attracting the fortune-seeking Conquistadores.

At this point in his journey, the Admiral made a critical decision. If he had chosen to follow the mainland farther westward to Yucatan and beyond to the coast of Mexico, he would have found evidence of the fabulous wealth of the Aztecs. Instead, Columbus turned eastward and southward, explored the coasts of Costa Rica and Panama, and missed the greatest prize of all, the riches of Mexico.

Convinced by Indian tales that he was following the isthmus of a great continent separating two vast oceans, and shorn of his hope of finding a passage to Asia, Columbus devoted himself to hunting for gold. Entering the Rio Belen, some 30 miles west of the present Panama Canal, Columbus found a region called Veragua, where the Guaymi Indians had long obtained placer gold.

The Gold of Veragua

Using their knives for tools, the Spaniards collected exciting amounts of the yellow metal, and promptly endeavored to establish a settlement named Santa Maria de Belen. But since their ships had become dangerously worm-eaten, which threatened to leave them stranded, the party was compelled to abandon Belen and sail to Hispaniola to make repairs.

En route to Santo Domingo, Columbus was forced to run his two sinking ships aground in what is now St. Ann's Bay, Jamaica. Side by side the ships were shored up to keep them erect, and cabins were built on the decks to serve as shelter. There, during a year of despair and failing health, surrounded by a distraught, mutinous crew, Columbus lived amid the wreckage of his hopes, a frustrating and ignoble end to the daring dreams of the Admiral of the Ocean Sea. In June, 1540, loyal Diego Mendez, with 10 Indians, paddled across 350 miles of ocean to Santo Domingo, and returned with a rescue ship which took the ailing Admiral back to Spain.

With funds gained from the gold-diggings of Veragua and Hispaniola, Columbus lived comfortably in Seville. He sought constantly, but in vain, to force King Ferdinand to disburse the share of royalties which the Admiral had been guaranteed under his original contract with the sovereigns. In 1506, after he had painfully followed the court to Valladolid, his health faded rapidly. On May 20, at the age of 55, Columbus died. His simple funeral was unattended by any member of the royal court. Only Columbus' sons Diego and Ferdinand, his brother and a few devoted shipmates formed the little band assembled to honor the man who had brought so much fame and wealth to Spain.

Trail's End For Columbus

Today, one may see an elaborate stone sarcophagus in the Cathedral at Seville, Spain, containing the remains of Columbus. A venerable, rusty-hued stone church in Santo Domingo, the Primate Cathedral of America, claims the same distinction. Standing in the lofty arched entrance of the church, there is a high, white, delicately carved marble altar enfolding three black iron coffers. The people of Santo Domingo say this is the last resting place of Christopher Columbus, his son Diego, and his brother Bartholomew.

Ironically, the name "America" stems not from its discoverer, Columbus, but from an Italian navigator named Amerigo Vespucci. In 1499 and 1505 Vespucci is believed to have explored the coast of Venezuela and the Darien region with Alonzo Ojeda. Accounts of his voyages were published in 1507 by Vespucci's admirer, Martin Waldseemuller, a German cartographer, who labelled his maps "America" named after Amerigo. The true significance of Columbus' feats did not dawn upon Europeans until the name for the New World had become well established.

Columbus never knew that he had discovered a vast new continent. To the last he believed he had reached some part of Asia. But countries, cities, rivers and countless monuments now bear his name throughout the world. When Christopher Columbus sailed westward as Admiral of the Ocean Sea, he inspired others to challenge far away seas and set in motion man's great Age of Discovery. In daring the Unknown, his exploits wrought significant changes in European life, and widely influenced the very course of civilization.

The First Americans

During his 4th and last voyage in 1502, after touching the coast of Honduras, Columbus had turned southward and found the gold placers of Veragua, a rich domain later granted his heirs under the title Duke of Veragua. But had he sailed the same distance northward and westward he probably would have encountered evidence of Montezuma's golden wealth. Instead, it was to be left to Cortes, 17 years later, to conquer the Aztecs of Mexico and seize their fabulous treasure. Who were the Aztecs? The routes by which many early peoples, including the Aztecs, migrated to the Western Hemisphere and became America's first inhabitants are well known.

For a half million years or more, Stone Age peoples had roamed over the Old World, while the Western Hemisphere apparently had remained without a trace of human life. Isolated by two great oceans and the polar ice caps, the earliest humanoids had been unable to wander from their points of origin into the Americas. When water was withdrawn from the seas in the form of ice during a glacial age, a land bridge appeared in the Bering Strait connecting Asia and North America. Then the forebears of the American Indians, following the hunt and their means of survival, entered the Western Hemisphere, turned southward along the ice-free valleys and dispersed to all corners of North, Central and South America.

Imperishable stone artifacts and carbon-14 dating have revealed 12,000 year old spearpoints at Folsom and Clovis, New Mexico, and 20,000 year old implements in a Sandia Mountain cave not far away. Similar evidence has been found in the Plains States, in the Valley of the Mississippi and around the Great Lakes, where early Americans made spearheads of native copper. The most culturally advanced peoples, including the Mayas, Incas, Toltecs, and Aztecs found their way into Mexico, Central and South America.

Prehistoric Mexico

By 1500 B.C., in the Valley of Mexico near modern Mexico City, the villagers of Tlatilco and Cuilcuilco were tilling fields of maize, beans, and squash with wooden plows, and were hunting deer, wild pigs, and water fowl with flint and obsidian spearpoints. The use of metals then was unknown. Around 600 B.C., Cuilcuilco was engulfed by lava flows of the nearby volcano, Xitle. The whole valley of Mexico, ringed with towering volcanoes and covered with ancient lavas, has had a turbulent volcanic past, setting the stage for the violent human events that were to follow. Cuilcuilco's buried ruins may be seen today on the outskirts of Mexico City.

About A.D. 300, when barbarian hordes were devastating Europe, a religious center arose at Teotihuacan, 40 miles northeast of modern Mexico City. Later, around A.D. 900, from out of the northwest came the earliest of the Nahuatlan tribes, the Toltecs, who founded their capital nearby at Tula. Soon thereafter, the Toltecs seized Teotihuacan and built a vast complex of temples, including a 216 foot high Pyramid of The Sun facing a broad avenue lined with palaces of the high priests. To their chief deity they built a shrine decorated with huge stone serpent heads;

the god's name was Quetzalcoatl. Teotihuacan symbolized ancient Mexico's classical age.

Quetzalcoatl

Quetzalcoatl was the Toltec god of the wind and air, inventor of the arts and crafts, and sponsor of the good life and peace. He introduced a calendar and apparently the art of metalworking, for thenceforth a profuse use of gold and silver for trade and adornment came into use. Fortunately, nature had endowed the land abundantly with these metals. Legend says that Quetzalcoatl was a white man with blond hair, blue eyes, and a beard. His emblem was the plumed serpent, derived from the brilliantly feathered Quetzal bird and the serpent, Coatl.

When Quetzalcoatl endeavored to outlaw the barbarous Toltec custom of human sacrifice, Tezcatlipoca, the Toltec god of war, managed to overthrow and banish Quetzalcoatl from the realm. The peaceful god went to Cholula (east of Mexico City) where he created the greatest of all Nahuatlan religious centers, perpetuating throughout all Nahua history the name Quetzalcoatl.

As unrest again came to the land, Quetzalcoatl went to Yucatan and made Chicen Itza his capital. Among the Mayas he became known as *Kukulcan*. After years of peace and prosperity among the Mayas, who developed one of ancient America's greatest civilizations, Kukulcan departed and sailed away eastward, promising that one day he would return across the eastern sea, scour ancient Mexico of its evils, and establish everlasting peace.

The Aztecs

The Valley of Mexico, meanwhile, was being invaded by kindred Nahua-speaking peoples. The fiercest of these were known as Aztecs. They settled and built their capital, Tenochtitlan, on a small island along the shore of Lake Texcoco, about 1325. The site is now known as Mexico City. In less than a century the Aztecs had conquered all the neighboring tribes of Mexico and incorporated the culture of the Toltecs, including the heroic legends of Quetzalcoatl, with that of their own. Their ruling passion, however, was their war god Huitsilopochtli, whose insatiable thirst for human blood necessitated continual warfare in order to obtain living captives for their sacrificial altars.

To the top of the great Teocalli pyramid in Tenochtitlan, and in other Aztec cities of the realm, prisoners were led to be spread upon the altar stone where their pulsating hearts were cut from their breasts. Their bodies were then cast down the blood drenched steps to warriors dancing below in homage to the sun and war god, and to serve the cannibalistic ceremonies of the populace. When the Great Teocalli was dedicated in 1486, 20,000 were sacrificed during the four day festival.

The Aztecs became amazingly proficient in the melting, soldering and casting of precious metals, using the cire-perdue wax process, an art inherited from the Toltecs. They had also begun to work copper by hammering. With the abundant supply of gold and silver which fate had conveniently provided in nearby regions, such a hoard of metallic riches was accumulated by the Aztecs that their name became synonymous with prodigious treasure. Only the ruling chiefs and priesthoods, however, possessed this wealth. It was used solely for personal adornment and in the decoration of the temples; the people were not permitted to acquire it; therefore gold had no monetary value.

Montezuma's Rich Realm

In 1502, Montezuma II became Emperor, and powerful, wealthy Tenochtitlan, teeming with 250,000 people, was the artistic and intellectual center of Mexico. An aqueduct brought fresh water from the mainland; centered in its spacious plaza was the towering teocalli, two smaller pyramids, a warrior's arena, and the Emperor's reviewing stand, all surrounded by a great wall of serpents carved in stone. Facing one side of the plaza was the palace and royal treasury of Montezuma, filled with golden creations rivaling the wealth of the ancient Pharaohs of Egypt.

But signs of doom haunted Montezuma. Lightning had struck a temple and its altar had been destroyed; Lake Texcoco had suddenly risen, sending waters of destruction into the city; a comet came to light the heavens and terrify the people. Soothsayers prophesied that calamity was near, and they were right. Men with sticks which spit fires of death, and ferocious half man, half animal creatures were landing on Mexico's shores. Most startling was the news that these men were of white skins, wearing beards! The apparition of Quetzalcoatl's legendary return to reclaim his empire consumed Montezuma with mingled awe, confusion and fear. Such was the Valley of Mexico when the Spaniards under Cortes landed at Vera Cruz in 1521.

Rumors of a Golden Land

The daring feats of Christopher Columbus, who had dispelled the terrors of unknown seas, brought forth man's great Age of Discovery. Bold adventurers, penniless soldiers and ambitious hidalgos, or nobles, were now flocking to the New World seeking fame and fortune. From Cuba in 1517, Ferandez de Cordoba sailed forth and discovered Yucatan and the Mayas. In May 1518, Velasquez, governor of Cuba, sent his nephew, Juan de Grijalva, on an expedition which reached an island off the coast of Yucatan. Grijalva returned with a glittering harvest of golden vessels, ornaments and armor-like plates of gold, gathered along the Rio Tabasco and beyond from tribes who said that they were subjects of a great and powerful Aztec emperor named Montezuma. The friendly Indian chiefs, or caciques, gladly exchanged their gold for trinkets, beads and colored glass offered by the Spaniards. The news of this easily gathered treasure swept through the islands, heightened by wild rumors of unbelievable wealth.

Hernando Cortes

Velasquez next selected dashing 33 year old Hernando Cortes to organize and lead an armed expedition to subjugate and colonize this golden land of the Aztecs. As an inspiring leader, Cortes had few equals in history. His cordial disposition, wit and good humor, daring disregard of personal danger, his indefatigable endurance and willingness to share in the hardships, won him the respect and affection of his soldiers. Beneath his amiable manner he was cool and calculating, unusually gifted in the art of persuasion, which would extricate him from impossible situations when force and power failed. Cortes was the ideal Captain-General to lead one of the most fearless expeditions in man's history.

There was no secret concerning the prime objective of the venture; it was to barter with the natives for gold, although it was well cloaked with righteousness. Cortes was commanded to treat the Indians with kindness, to carry out their Catholic Majesty's most ardent wish, the conversion of the natives. Serving the cross gave the Spanish cavalier a wonderful, chivalrous feeling, even if he had to force his beliefs with a sword in one hand, while bartering with a Bible in the other.

On February 10, 1519, Cortes sailed with 11 ships carrying 553 soldiers, including cross-bowmen and arquebusiers, 110 sailors, 10 heavy cannon, four small falconets and 16 horses. Such was the diminutive force that set out, with unbelievable audacity, to conquer an empire of fortified cities and millions of inhabitants dedicated to lives of savage warfare.

The fleet crossed the Yucatan channel to the island of Cozumel, where the Castilians paused and forced some of the natives to accept Christianity, after tumbling their idols from atop the Mayan pyramids. Anchoring in the Rio Tabasco, where Grijalva had reaped a friendly golden harvest, the Spaniards were forced to fight. Their victory was rewarded with some gold and a gift of 20 female slaves, including one who would play an important role in the conquest.

Sold into slavery by a jealous step-mother, the girl had been the daughter of a rich and powerful Mexican cacique, therefore she spoke Aztec with eloquence. Attractive, intelligent and ambitious, she quickly learned to speak Castilian, fell in love with the dashing commander, became his invaluable interpreter, secretary, and finally his devoted mistress. The Spaniards honored her with the name, Dona Marina, and since the Aztecs called Cortes, "Malinche", the same name was applied to his constant companion.

Gifts From Montezuma

It was April 21, 1519 when Cortes landed his forces and mounted his guns upon the sandy hillocks where the city of Vera Cruz, Mexico, now stands. Friendly Indians came to greet them led by an Aztec chief named Teuhtlile who presented gifts of fine cottons, magnificent featherwork, and articles of gold. Meanwhile, Indian artists were busy making colored paintings portraying the Spaniards, their dress, ships, guns, and horses, acquiring information to be dispatched to Montezuma. When Teuhtlile admired a soldier's shining helmet, Cortes offered it to the chief, saying, "the Spaniards are troubled with a disease of the heart, for which gold is a remedy," adding that he hoped that Montezuma would return the helmet filled with grains of gold, that it might be compared in quality with their own.

In Tenochtitlan Montezuma received the news, amply illustrated, of the bearded white men with thunderous, fire-spitting weapons and strange four-legged beasts landing upon his shores. The presaged return of the legendary white God Quetzalcoatl surely seemed at hand. A proud, able, and fearless warrior himself, Montezuma nevertheless received the news with superstitious fear and consternation.

Aware of the stranger's love of gold, Montezuma decided to send propitiatory offerings to the Spaniards, hoping that they would be satisfied and leave his land. At the same time, his ambassadors would forbid the army to approach the Mexican capital. In shelters erected in the Spanish camp, while clouds of incense filled the air, upon delicately woven mats slaves poured forth an array of shields, helmets and plates of pure gold. There were collars, bracelets and sandals of gold, fans and robes of brightly-hued feathers interlaced with gold, silver, pearls, and precious stones, and exquisite reproductions of birds and animals fashioned of gold and silver.

The Spanish helmet, which had been sent to Montezuma, was returned filled to the brim with grains of gold; but the most magnificent articles were two circular plates as large as carriage wheels, one of solid gold and one of silver, richly embossed with plant and animal designs. The wheel of gold alone weighed 3800 ounces, worth about $135,000; but its value in metal was far surpassed by the incomparable beauty of the craftsmanship. Despite the warnings of Montezuma's ambassadors, this dazzling display of opulence only sharpened the Spaniards' appetite and determination to proceed at once to the emperor's capital, Tenochtitlan.

The March to Tenochtitlan

Today, one may easily trace Cortes' route of conquest from Vera Cruz to Tenochtitlan, and sense the same aura of mystery that was encountered by the Conquistadores who first viewed it, for many of the landmarks are surprisingly unchanged. Crossing the subtropical coastal plain, one comes first to Cempoalla, once a Totonac city of 20,000, which was then suffering under the Aztec yoke of oppression. There, in one bold move characteristic of Cortes, the Spaniards overturned the city's idols and tumbled them down the gore-covered steps of the sacrificial pyramid, and thus convinced the awe-struck Cempoallans of Spanish invincibility. The Totonacs then gladly joined the Castilians in their campaign against the Aztecs, Cortes' first stroke of good fortune.

Leaving part of his army on the coast to garrison the base, with his allies, Cortes and 400 soldiers set forth on their long march to Tenochtitlan, August 16, 1519. They traveled westward through the Tierra Calienta lowlands covered with aromatic shrubs, cochineal plants, cacao and palm trees. Southward they could see their first Mexican volcano, 18,700 foot high snow-crested Orizaba. Nearing Jalapa the air turned cool and clear; shady oaks dotted the landscape. Climbing gradually, the road now passes beside the 14,000 foot high extinct volcano, Cofre de Perote, but the Spaniards had to thread the mountain's rocky gorges. Thenceforth the route ascends to Mexico's 7000 foot high interior plateau, dotted with Organ Pipe cacti, graceful mescal plants and the white plumed Yucca, called Spanish dagger.

About 18 miles east of the venerable city of Tlascala another towering volcano, named Malinche after Cortes' mistress Dona Marina, looked down upon its smaller volcanic offspring, a rocky eminence called the "hill of Tzompach." Tlascala, once a strong and valiant republic, had long maintained its independence against the Aztecs. Nor would it tolerate aggression from the strange foe who was endeavoring to cross its domain.

The Battle of Tzompach

Tlascalan chiefs, wearing armor made of thin gold and silver plates, and headdresses of brilliant feathers sprinkled with gold and precious stones, led a sea of defiant warriors whose painted bodies were clad only in loin cloths. Some were covered with tunics of colorful featherwork, a special art of all Anahuac tribes, and wore helmet-like animal heads made of wood or leather. All were armed with bows and arrows, slings, two-handed swords, and long javelins set with razor-sharp flakes of obsidian. For protection the warriors carried shields of wood or leather, and wore vests of quilted cotton. As hideous war cries and shrill whistles filled the air, an avalanche of Tlascalans threw themselves fearlessly upon the strange man-beasts, horses they had never seen before, and dared the cool fire of crossbowmen and arquebusiers.

As the tide of battle went against the Spaniards, they managed to reach the little "hill of Tzompach." There, on its rocky crest, for three weeks they repulsed wave after wave of Tlascalan attacks. Finally, the Tlascalans called the battle off, and invited the Spaniards into their city. Convinced that the Castilians were capable of conquering their old enemy, the Aztecs, they now became staunch allies of Cortes, and later were important contributors to his success in Mexico.

Today, in Tlascala one may visit the old Church of San Francisco, built in 1521 to replace the city's frightful teocalli. Within the church is the font where the four chiefs of Tlascala were baptised, the first Mexican converts to Christianity. Below the "hill of Tzompach" a myriad of mescal plants, under Mexico's bright sun, etch their sharp shadows on the field where thousands of arrows once covered the strife-torn soil. Sleepy-eyed donkeys, loaded with bulging burdens of firewood, plod across the scene. Only the braying of a distant burro breaks the peaceful silence.

Massacre at Cholula

On went Cortes and his Indian allies to Cholula, the holy city of Anahuac, containing 150,000 people loyal to Montezuma and 400 temple towers surrounding Quetzalcoatl's colossal Pyramid of Cholula. An attempt to ambush the Spaniards within the city was quelled by Cortes, as 6000 Cholulans were slain mostly by Tlascalans. It was one more warning to Montezuma that Quetzalcoatl's promise of rebirth was near, to be delivered by the "white gods," the Conquistadores.

Today, upon the great mound which marks the ruin of the Pyramid of Cholula stands the church of Nuestra Señora de los Remedios. Below, in the city and nearby countryside there are now about 365 smaller churches, built during the Spanish colonial period upon each pagan temple site.

From Cholula, one may follow Cortes' route across the plateau as it ascends a pass between two snow-capped volcanoes, 17,888 foot high Popocatepetl, "the mountain that smokes," and 16,200 foot high Iztaccihuatl, "the sleeping lady." Together they form a brooding gateway to the Valley of Mexico. A plain stone monument bearing a weather-beaten bronze plaque in the center of the 12,000 foot high pass now marks the spot where Cortes and his army camped before descending to Tenochtitlan. Popo was then belching smoke and cinders, an ominous warning to the Conquistadores.

Tenochtitlan—Venice of the Aztecs

As the little Castilian army emerged from the mountain pass, they saw in the valley below white walled cities, green fields, and the gleaming blue lakes of Xochimilco and Texcoco. The center of this diadem of flowers, orchards, and lakes was the far-famed "Venice of the Aztecs"

gracing the shore of Lake Texcoco. Its huge teocalli pierced the blue sky, surrounded by palaces and homes of stone and plaster. Nothing such as this had ever been seen before in the New World. How could such a superior civilization, with its fearless armies and numerous allies, be subjugated by 400 Spanish cavaliers? If there were any inclined to falter, the thought of the treasure to be gained quickly sharpened their will to march on to Tenochtitlan.

Cortes boldly led his well groomed army onto a great stone causeway, which was wide enough for 10 horsemen riding abreast. At the battlemented gateway Cortes met Montezuma. The emperor's royal palanquin, borne on the shoulders of Aztec nobles, blazed with gold. Over the litter nobles held a canopy of gorgeous featherwork, sprinkled with jewels and fringed with silver.

With impressive dignity and courtesy, the 40 year old Emperor welcomed Cortes to Tenochtitlan. Cortes responded with profound expressions of respect. Thereupon, Montezuma delegated his brother, Cuitlahuac, to conduct the visitors to their quarters, the palace of the emperor's father, Axayactl. The palace was large enough to house Cortes' entire army. Unknown to the Spaniards, it also contained a secret chamber where an immense hoard of gold and jewels, Montezuma's inheritance, was stored.

Across the square stood the emperor's newer palace, huge and rambling. Crystal clear waters from Chapultepec played in numerous courtyard fountains; ceilings of the spacious rooms were of ingeniously carved fragrant woods; walls were covered with brightly colored cotton fabrics and wild animal skins; draperies were made of brilliant featherwork; mats of palm leaf covered the floors; and bowls of incense diffused their odors throughout the apartments.

Montezuma's Treasure

While searching for a place in Axayactl's palace to set up a Christian chapel, the Spaniards discovered the secret chamber holding Montezuma's own private treasure and that of his father. It was an incredible accumulation of riches, far greater than all the presents formerly offered by the emperor. It consisted of great quantities of gold and silver ornaments, precious stones, jewelry, gold and silver bars, and piles of rich ore. As tempting as this prize was, its secret had to be kept—for the time being.

Due to the continued presence of the armed

Spaniards, and their detested allies, the Tlascalans, the natives of Tenochtitlan began to seethe with unrest. With 400,000 rebellious Aztecs and numerous drawbridges menacing his position, Cortes decided to seize Montezuma and hold him as a hostage. When the emperor had been made a prisoner, Cortes sent his men to the top of the teocalli where they destroyed the images of the Aztec gods and cast them down the steps.

More humiliation awaited the Aztecs. Added to the degradation of their emperor and their gods, a cacique was brought before the teocalli in chains, accused of murdering a Spaniard, and burned alive in the plaza. Then, after Montezuma was forced to pledge his allegiance to the Spanish king, Cortes had the emperor send collectors throughout the land gathering tribute, adding greatly to the treasure already stored in Axaycatl's palace.

A clamor now arose among the Spaniards for sharing of the spoil, for which these cavaliers claimed they had left their homes, endured hardships, famine, and repeated peril to their lives. After deducting one-fifth for the Spanish crown, and one-fifth for the Captain-General, every man's share was set aside. The value of the treasure, considering the delicate and priceless examples of the goldsmith's art, was incalculable. But Cortes and his men, utterly insensitive to artistry, melted the entire mass and reduced it to solid gold bars, valued then at over seven million dollars.

The gold that had been received by Cortes from Montezuma on the beach at Vera Cruz had already been shipped to Spain, where its magnificence aroused great excitement. But when the crown's share of the amazing hoard in Axaycatl's palace was dispatched to Spain, it was captured at sea by French corsairs, and therefore the treasure went not to Charles V of Spain, but to Francis I of France.

Fury of The Aztecs

Although Cortes' forces in the palace had been reinforced by 900 men recently brought to Mexico by Panfilo de Narvaez, the position of the Castilians grew increasingly precarious. By late spring, smoldering discontent in the Aztec capital was ready to burst into violence. On June 25, 1520, waves of Aztec warriors stormed the Spanish garrison. Montezuma appeared before the angry mob milling about the palace and implored them to seek peace. A volley of stones from the crowd brought the deposed Emperor to his knees, seriously wounded. Three days later Montezuma died. The Aztecs chose Montezuma's brother, Cuitlahua, to replace the emperor. Deprived of Montezuma's friendship, Cortes decided that escape to his allies in Tlascala offered their only salvation.

A few moments after midnight on July 1, 1520, the men loaded themselves greedily with all the gold they could carry, and in a cold, drizzling rain the column moved stealthily onto the giant causeway that led to Tacuba (Tlocopan). Suddenly the dark waters beside the causeway came alive with shouting warriors in a sea of canoes. With the fury of a tempest, thousands of Aztecs fell upon the Spaniards. During the early night the Aztecs already had destroyed the many bridges along the causeway. At these watery gaps the Spanish column piled up in a mass of wreckage. In the wild hand to hand uproar, soldiers weighted down with gold cast their useless and fatal loads into the water.

Cortes and his cavaliers dashed to and fro endeavoring to help their struggling comrades, but many were killed, and many were captured to die on the altar stones of the hideous teocalli. When the battered column at last reached Popotla, Cortes sat beneath a giant cypress tree (it is still there) and wept, as he surveyed the bleeding remnants of his army. 450 Spaniards and 4,000 Tlascalans had lost their lives during that night, known in Spanish history, as La Noche Triste "the sad and melancholy night."

Conquest of Tenochtitlan

Cortes later returned, and with the invaluable aid of his Tlascalan friends, finally conquered Tenochtitlan. Thirteen brigantines were built and piece by piece transported by 20,000 Tlascalan porters over a mountain pass 70 miles to Lake Texcoco, where they were assembled and launched. After a furious assault by water and by land, and a terrible siege, the brave 25 year old defender of Tenochtitlan, Cuauhtemoc, who had become emperor upon Cuitlahua's death, was forced to surrender the city.

Cortes promised Cuauhtemoc immunity, and honors befitting the Emperor's station. But some of Cortes' officers insisted that the defeated monarch be tortured by fire, in order to wrench from him the secret burial places of more Aztec treasure. When the barbarous plan failed to budge Cuauhtemoc, Cortes relented and released the suffering emperor. The Aztec domination of Mexico thus came to an end on August 13, 1521. This date also marked the rise of another power in the New World. It would become known as New Spain, and it would develop into a realm of astonishing riches.

Upon the ruins of Tenochtitlan, the Spaniards built Mexico City. But it took Aztec slaves four years to clear the rubble, fill the canals and remove all traces of the city they had so proudly created. Where the Great Teocalli once stood, in 1524 the Spaniards erected the first Christian church in Mexico, using for its foundation stone images and serpentheads taken from the teocalli. In 1573, the huge cathedral that now faces the Plaza, or Zocalo, was begun, but it was not completed until 1667.

Sunset for Cortes

As for Cortes, a year after the fall of Tenochtitlan, Charles V appointed him Governor and Captain general of New Spain. But in 1527, after 20 months absence from Mexico, while seeking more gold in Honduras, Cortes lost his leadership. Charles V appointed an Audiencia to govern New Spain. Endeavoring to regain his rights, Cortes returned to Spain. He was received by the court with honors, but denied the governorship; instead he was given a huge grant of land, including 25 towns, and the title Marquis of the Valley of Oaxaca. In 1530 Cortes returned to Mexico to enjoy his new realm and his palatial estate at Cuernavaca.

In 1540 Cortes again returned to Spain, and for three years sought in vain to have his former position restored. Near Seville he was taken ill, and on December 2, 1547, in his 63rd year Cortes died. His body was first laid to rest in a family vault near Seville, but in 1562 his remains were moved by his son Don Martin to the monastery of St. Francis at Texcoco near Mexico City. In 1794, with great military and religious pomp his body was moved again to the Hospital of Jesus of Nazareth, which Cortes had founded and endowed in Mexico City.

In 1823, a mob of Mexican patriots, celebrating their independence from Spain and their detestation of all things Spanish, were preparing to seize the crystal coffin, which had been bound with bars and plates of silver, but friends of the Cortes family removed the relics to an unknown place of safety. To this day, one may travel the length and breadth of the land and never encounter a monument raised in honor of Hernando Cortes, conqueror of Mexico.

The Bonanzas of Mexico

At Taxco, 100 miles south of Mexico City, Cortes had initiated the first attempt to locate the sources of Aztec wealth. Writing to Charles V, Cortes described his efforts to obtain tin, required in making bronze cannon, at the village of "Tacho." There was no tin at Taxco, but it did become a famed silver producer, perhaps the first mining town on the American continent. South of Taxco, a source of Aztec gold was found later in the sands of the Rio Balsas.

After the Conquest, among the thousands who arrived from Spain, there were many interested in prospecting for metals. As ancient Spain had once been the promised land for the Phoenicians and Romans, Mexico would now become the world's greatest untapped treasure vault. Trained in Spain in the art of prospecting, men spread out in ever widening circles searching for deposits of metallic riches in Mexico. Fifty miles west of Mexico City, the El Oro, Esperanza, and Dos Estrellas mines eventually became the second largest gold producing district in the Americas.

In 1534, sixty miles northeast of Mexico City, Spanish prospectors discovered rich silver veins in the hills surrounding Pachuca, which developed into one of the greatest precious metal districts in the world. At nearby Real Del Monte, the Spaniards worked the "colorado" or red outcrops of veins containing cerargyrite, or horn silver. The Trinidad mine alone yielded 40 million pesos* in silver within 10 years. When Bartholomew de Medina invented his celebrated Patio Process for efficiently treating the silver ores, he revolutionized the silver mining industry world-wide. Crushed ore was churned in large patios by driving mules through a mixture of ore, salt, and mercury, collecting the silver by amalgamation. The process enabled the Del Monte mines to produce fabulously for years.

The fulfillment of dreams found in the various sagas of mining is exemplified by Romero de Terreros, a nobleman who invested his entire fortune of $60,000 and all he could borrow, determined to acquire the Real Del Monte mine in 1739. He had barely begun to explore the workings when his miners broke into a bonanza which yielded 15 million pesos. With such wealth he was able to present the King of Spain with costly gifts, including two battleships and a loan of over

*The peso, or Mexican dollar, contained about an ounce of silver, then roughly equivalent in value to the American dollar.

one million dollars, for which Terreros was named Count of Regla.

Fabulous Guanajuato

As exultant prospectors continued the search northward, they found a great belt of silver, gold, lead, and zinc deposits reaching into the State of Queretaro. Beyond Queretaro, an explorer found one of the greatest of all silver and gold bonanzas, Guanajuato, destined to produce more than one billion pesos in wealth. In 1550, a Spanish prospector came upon the surface exposure of one of the largest and richest veins of silver ore ever discovered. Extracting ore from the mountainside, nine years elapsed before he realized the extent of his find. When the Mellado mine nearby opened a similar deposit, the course of the great La Veta Madre, or Mother Vein, became evident. Before long other mines, the Tepeyac, the Sirena and others were laying open the immense silver wealth of Guanajuato.

By 1700, with a population of 16,000, Guanajuato had become a world famous mining center. One bonanza after another poured wealth into the coffers of the Spanish crown, and into the laps of such as Jose de Sardaneta who became Marquis de Rayas, and Francisco Mathias, owner of the Cata and Secho mines who became Marquis de San Clemente. Antonio Obregon, who discovered the fabulous Valenciana, which alone produced over 800 million pesos worth of silver, was made Count of Valenciana and Spain's wealthiest subject.

Zacatecas and Chihuahua

There seemed no end to Mexico's mineral treasures, and the avid Spanish explorers who were pushing New Spain's frontiers outward were sure to find them. In 1546, an expedition under Cristobal de Onate and Diego de Ibarra subdued the Zacatecas, and saw for the first time the virgin outcrops of silver veins which were to make Zacatecas one of the richest states in Mexico. The city of Zacatecas and its environs, which now stand upon a honeycomb of ancient mines, produced about 730 million pesos in silver, gold, and copper from 1548 to 1832.

In 1539, the Spaniards founded San Felipe el Real Royal, now known as the city of Chihuahua, capital of the State of Chihuahua, a region of incredible metallic riches. Its wealth was first revealed in 1547 when outcrops gleaming with gold and silver were discovered in a region now known as Santa Barbara, 120 miles south of Chihuahua City. In an unparalleled display of generosity, nature next revealed the rich silver and gold deposits of nearby Parral, whose great Veta Colorado (red vein) made the Parral district world renowned. In 1580, due to the uninterrupted stream of gold and silver flowing from this region to Spain, Santa Barbara became the seat of government for the vast territory of Nueva Vizcaya, comprising what are now the Mexican states of Chihuahua, Coahuila, and Sonora, and the North American states of Texas, New Mexico, Arizona, and California. Such was its importance, entirely due to metallic riches, 50 years before the Pilgrims landed at Plymouth.

Throughout the land wherever a new bonanza came to light, memorial churches were built by the rich, elated mine owners, sometimes aided by the congregations, in gratitude to their tutelary saints. Many such mining churches, "flamboyant" with baroque, Churrigueresque exteriors, and altars filled with precious relics of solid gold and silver taken from the mines, also graced the city of Santa Barbara. A favorite Indian church, La Virgen del Rayo, was built with funds supplied by an Indian miner, who brought a gold ingot every Saturday to finance the work. To this day, no one knows where the taciturn miner obtained his gold.

Mexico's Incredible Wealth

The mineral laden Sierra Madre Occidental range, coursing northwest from Chihuahua into Sonora, which now adjoins Arizona, was also a happy hunting ground for treasure seekers. In Sonora, in 1739, they discovered the famed Magdalena district, and east of Hermosillo, the mines of Alamos gave up over 50 million dollars in silver and gold. Near the Arizona border, in Sonora, the Cananea and Nacozari mines, became one of the great copper districts of the world.

Nearly every state in Mexico was a storehouse of astonishing mineral wealth. In the State of Oaxaca, the realm of Cortes, the Conqueror gathered gold from deposits which had furnished the metal for the unrivaled artisans of the Zapotecs, Mistecs and Aztecs. These pre-Columbian peoples had first founded the village of Ahuizotl on the Atoyac River, now the city of Oaxaca, because of the prolific gold and silver deposits which occurred within a radius of 50 miles of the settlement.

These are but a few of the many bonanzas comprising Mexico's incredible wealth of metallic treasure, one of the most extensive and varied on the face of the earth, found and exploited by the Spanish Conquistadores and their followers. Columbus, the daring trailblazer, opened the floodgates to this New World; Cortes, man of the hour, with heavy hand placed the seal of ownership upon the land, and venturesome fortune hunters laid bare its long hidden resources. As if these glittering riches alone were not enough to raise Spain to the height of European power, another Conquistador was on his way to Peru to seize the golden hoard of the Incas, and to unlock the immense mineral wealth of South America. His name was Francisco Pizarro.

The Early Peruvians

Pizarro knew little, and cared less, about Peru's early history, or how the Incas acquired the gold that now was luring their conquerors. The Incas had become the only real empire builders of prehistoric America, but only after a long period of South American Indian evolution. Early farming sites in Peru have been found near Pisco in the Paracas Peninsula, dated about 4,000 B.C., also at Acon 20 miles north of Lima, and at Huaca Prieta near the mouth of the Chicama River, dated about 2500 B.C.

Between 1000 and 500 B.C., such famous centers as Chavin de Huantar in the northern highlands began their primitive hammering of gold which they found in the nearby streams. Near the beginning of the Christian era, newcomers appeared and built stone fortresses, irrigation canals, roads and religious centers. They excelled in weaving and pottery making, and showed great skill in working precious metals and copper. Actually, the Peruvians, using open mold as well as cire-perdue methods, made ingenious castings of the precious metals a thousand years before the people of Mexico became equally adept.

With added culture and wealth came increasing militarism, repeating the behavior of the ages. In northern Peru, helmeted warriors living in the Moche and Viru Valleys, known as the Mochica, launched campaigns of conquest with savage cruelty. The Mochicas then fell before a newer power, the Chimu, who occupied the nearby coastal region and the Chicama Valley near modern Trujillo, where the ruins of their mud-brick capital now cover several square miles.

By A.D. 700, the Chimu were melting, casting, and soldering large quantities of precious metals in many forms, and they were beginning to make bronze. Their expert metallurgical techniques spread to Ecuador in the north and crept to Nasco in the south, and to the great ceremonial center of Tiahuanaco on the southeast end of Lake Titicaca. Under Tiahuanaco influence, for the first time Peru was brought under the domination of a single culture, and an increasing use of precious metals in Peru became widespread.

The Incas

In the highlands northwest of Lake Titicaca where the Inca tribe had settled about A.D. 1200, the well governed little city state of Cuzco managed to avoid Tiahuanaco domination. When the Chanca, another highland tribe, tried to subdue the Incas about 1438, their great king Pachacati led them to their first taste of victory and spoils of war, opening the door to Inca expansion. Topa Inca, later extended Inca rule as far north as Quito in Ecuador, and conquered the people of Cajamarca, as well as the Chimu from whom he gathered an immense booty in golden treasure. In addition he captured craftsmen well versed in the working of metals. After Topa Inca's death in 1493, Huaya Capac succeeded him and conquered northern Ecuador.

From the Chimu, the Incas also acquired the art of producing woven articles, exquisitely colored cloaks, ponchos and other textiles, using the wool of the llama, alpaca, and vicuna. Their weaving techniques have remained unmatched even by modern artisans. The Incas were also spectacular builders and engineers, constructing over 3,000 miles of empire roads and hundreds of suspension bridges over deep Andean canyons. Their great fortress of Sacsahuaman near Cuzco, and their mountain stronghold of Machu Picchu, reveal their masterful craftsmanship in stone; blocks weighing as much as 150 tons were so tightly fitted that a knife blade seldom could be forced between them.

Mineral-rich Inca Land

Although most Inca chieftains used spears and axes of copper, and occasionally of gold or silver, bronze was making its appearance. The homeland of the Incas, near the border of Bolivia, was extremely rich in ores of copper and tin, the ingredients of bronze. Like the early bronze makers of the old world, the Incas no doubt benefited by the fortunate association of tin and copper in the local ores.

Gold and silver were also especially abundant

PLATE 93. The Manger in Bethlehem, goal of the Crusaders, is marked with their crosses.

PLATE 94. Crusaders built a fort at Byblos. Many knights disposed of lands to finance their journeys.

PLATE 95. Lords of such castles as Nuremberg encouraged their serfs to prospect royal lands for metals.

PLATE 96. At Joachimsthal, Czechoslovakia, discovery of a great mining region in 1170 brought prosperity.

PLATE 97. Emblems of medieval guilds represented serfs who had found freedom through mining and industry.

PLATE 98. This magnificent silver mug was made by master artisans to honor the miners of their times.

in the streambeds and countless outcrops containing native metal, but as with the Toltecs and Aztecs, the accumulation of precious metals was permitted only for the aristocracy and the priesthood, and for the adornment of temples and tombs of departed royalty. In addition to the mass production of gold and silver by the Incas themselves, immense booty taken from the Chimu and other subjugated tribes of the empire filled the treasure vaults, temples and tombs of the Inca kings with such gleaming opulence, that sooner or later it was bound to attract envious, predatory eyes. As the world well knows, it was Francisco Pizarro and his Spanish Conquistadores who came to rob the Incas of their long accumulated wealth, shortly after Cortes stripped Mexico of its riches.

Balboa Discovers The Pacific—and Gold

Vasco Nuñez de Balboa, seeking surcease from his debts, joined a party of gold seekers in 1510, sailed to the Isthmus and founded the town of Santa Maria de la Antigua on the narrow Gulf of Darien. After quarrels had divided the leaders, Balboa found himself in charge of the region. During one of his raids into the adjacent country collecting ornaments of gold, a friendly young cacique named Comogre scornfully scattered the metal being weighed and exclaimed, "If this is what you prize more than life, I can tell you of a land where people eat and drink out of vessels of gold." The excited Spaniards were told that this land was six days journey to the southward. This was the first guidepost pointing to Peru.

Leading 190 men, including Francisco Pizarro, Balboa crossed the 60 mile wide mountainous Isthmus, climbed the divide, and upon September 25, 1513, became the first European to gaze upon the Pacific Ocean, which he named the South Sea. King Ferdinand appointed Balboa Adelanto of the South Sea and governor of Castilla del Oro, Golden Castile, as the Isthmus was then called. But the bold explorer himself fell victim to the intrigues that often wracked these colonial appointees. Pedro de Avila, better known as Pedrarias, appeared to falsely accuse and replace Balboa. Pedrarias caused Pizarro to arrest his former comrade, Balboa, who was imprisoned and later executed at nearby Acla in 1517. Thus, it was not Balboa, the gallant cavalier, but Pizarro, a greedy, uncouth and brutal character, who became the conqueror of Peru.

The Splendor of "Piru"

In 1519, benefiting by Balboa's original suggestion, Pedrarias moved the headquarters for exploring Pacific shores from Darien to Panama, whose ancient site is east of the present city. It was not until 1522 that an organized expedition under Pascual de Andagoya sailed southward a short distance along the west coast of the mainland. Pascual returned with exciting rumors of a vast continent south of the Isthmus, which natives repeatedly referred to as "Piru", where a mighty civilization lived in golden splendor. It was at this time also that news of Cortes' discovery of Aztec gold was firing fortune seekers with increased zeal. There were three men in particular, consumed with the lure of treasure, who decided to enter into a partnership to seek the wealth of Peru: Francisco Pizarro, Diego Almagro, and Fernando de Luque.

Pizarro, an illegitimate foundling, unable to read or write, was hard, crafty and cruel. After sailing with Columbus, at the age of 50 he turned to the New World as his only hope for a better life. But this black-bearded, unsmiling illiterate was to become one of the most feared and renowned conquerors of history. Diego de Almagro was Pizarro's best friend, also a foundling and illiterate, but an ambitious, gallant soldier. Fernando de Luque, a priest, through wise investments had grown rich in the New World and was eager to acquire more. Luque was to finance the enterprise while his partners risked the dangers of the wilderness.

Pizarro Seeks Inca Gold

In November 1524, Pizarro set forth with 80 men in a small vessel, crossed the Gulf of St. Michael and steered south for the land of "Piru." Groping along the unknown coast, stopping here and there in the jungle, months were spent searching the tangled undergrowth. Harassed by storms, heat and hunger, the battered explorers were nearly overwhelmed with discouragement. Beyond Punta Quemada they found their first crude villages, ornaments of gold, and savages who fiercely resisted the Spaniards. In spite of his armor, Pizarro was wounded seven times.

Meanwhile, Bartholomew Ruiz, an experienced seafarer, set forth to probe the coastline farther south. After passing San Mateo Bay he found a decidedly superior culture, as friendly villages appeared along the shore. When huge balsa rafts came alongside the caravel, the Spaniards were astonished at the fine woolen cloths, and especially the splendid articles of gold and silver worn by the natives. They said they were from Tumbes, a city farther south, and added that gold and silver was almost as common as wood in the great palaces of their monarch, the Inca of Peru. At once, Tumbes became the lodestar of Spanish hopes.

With this happy news, Ruiz hurried back to inform Pizarro, who was struggling in the steaming jungle. Ruiz's glowing accounts so rejuvenated the famished, dejected men that all were now determined to proceed quickly to Tumbes. En route, the party anchored off the port of Atacames when they saw that it was a town of 2,000 houses, whose inhabitants wore elaborate ornaments of gold and precious stones. These included emeralds that came from the region of Quito, now in Ecuador, northern limits of the Inca empire.

However, 10,000 warriors displayed such hostility that all thought of subduing the city was abandoned. While Pizarro entrenched his party on the small island of Gallo, Ruiz sailed for Panama to obtain reinforcements. But the new governor, skeptical Pedro de los Rios, sent Ruiz back with two ships and orders to return with every sick and disenchanted Spaniard.

Pizarro's Line of Destiny

Pizarro spurned the order. Drawing a line in the sand from east to west, he turned to his men, and said, "On the south lies Peru and untold riches; on the north lies Panama, ease and poverty. For my part, I go south. Who will follow me?" Of his party, thirteen cavaliers chose to dedicate their lives and fortunes to the enterprise. It was this moment that decided the fate of Pizarro and the Incas of Peru, and opened the door to the Spanish conquest of South America.

Then, the little band embarked on Ruiz's ship and sailed for Tumbes, gateway to the Inca realm. When they anchored in the bay and visited the city, they saw thousands of white stone and plaster houses and many temples, gleaming in the sun. Rising beyond the narrow strip of coastline above Tumbes rose the magnificent heights of the northern Andes. The Spaniards were amazed at the degree of culture evidenced by the city, but the massive walls and the large garrison which protected it, eliminated all thought of conquest for the time being.

Here they had seen, however, the first signs of Inca wealth. They saw temples blazing with plates of precious metals, and artisans creating magnificent reproductions of animals and birds in pure gold and silver. When an Inca noble, who happened to be at Tumbes, described the even greater marvels of his own capital high in the Andes, and the power of the Inca ruler, Pizarro knew that his fondest dreams could now be realized. Discreetly, he bade the native chiefs a friendly farewell, promising to return and repay them for their favors and hospitality. Unknown to these kindly people, they had looked upon their conqueror.

Knights of The Golden Sword

Despite the booty displayed on his return to Panama, it became necessary for Pizarro to go to Spain to get support for a new expedition. In July 1529, a contract with the crown reserved to Pizarro the rights of discovery and conquest of Peru, or New Castile as it was called, and named him Governor of Spain's newest province. His thirteen brave companions of the Island of Gallo were created hidalgos and named "Knights of the Golden Sword." In January 1530, accompanied by his three brothers, Hernando, Juan, and Gonzalo, Pizarro set sail in three ships from the mouth of the Guadalquivir, Spain, for Panama. One year later, with 183 men, 27 horses, and a few men of the church, including Vicente de Valverde, Pizarro set forth from Panama and headed southward on his conquest of Peru.

Pizarro had intended to go directly to Tumbes, but contrary winds forced him to land farther north on the shore of San Mateo Bay, and there to begin his invasion overland. Passing through the province of Coaque, whose streams were rich in placer gold, the Spaniards preferred to reap their harvest an easier way, by looting the villages of large quantities of gold and silver, and the emeralds for which the region was noted. All the treasure was piled in a heap, and after deducting a fifth for the crown, the remainder was distributed among the officers and men. When the booty, worth 20,000 castellanos, was sent back to Panama, it quickly induced 30 more adventurers to join Pizarro when he reached a place which he named Puerto Viejo. The newcomers were led by a brave and able cavalier named Sebastian de Balalcazar, who was to make his mark in Peruvian history.

Civil War in The Andes

As the party moved on toward the east, parallel-

PLATE 99. Upon their mines in the Tyrol, Austria, the Habsburgs borrowed money to perpetuate their
dynasty.

PLATE 100. In Frankfurt's Coronation Hall merchants displayed wares during the mining boom of the 15th
century.

PLATE 101. The mines of Cornwall yielded tin in ancient
times and trained America's first breed of miners.

PLATE 102. The tin ore, cassiterite, first came from placers.
Later, in deep mines Cornishmen learned their
trade.

PLATE 103. In Florence, Italy, the Renaissance was born,
nourished by prosperity and riches won from the
earth.

PLATE 104. Cosimo the Elder, of the Medici banking family,
greatly stimulated the Renaissance.

PLATE 105. Here on the Island of San Salvador, Christopher Columbus discovered a New World in 1492.

PLATE 106. The pagan splendor of the Aztec capital, Tenochtitlan, amazed the Spaniards who captured the city in 1521.

PLATE 107. The staggering hoard of Aztec jewelry, marvelously created, spurred further conquests.

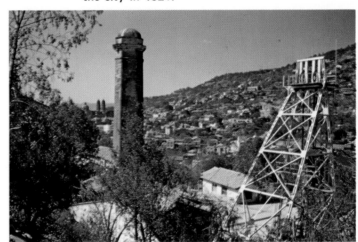

PLATE 108. Seeking sources of Aztec wealth, the Spaniards first found the silver mines of Taxco.

PLATE 109. The Rayas mine of Guanajuato was discovered in 1550. The district became a world famed silver producer.

PLATE 110. Owners of the Valenciana and Rayas mines became Spanish noblemen because of their gifts to the crown.

ing their route towered the northern reaches of the Andes, including the broad summit of 20,560 foot high Chimborazo, and a restless giant, the snowcrested volcano, 19,350 foot high Cotopaxi, which is not far from Quito in what is now Ecuador. Finally reaching the Gulf of Guayaquil, as it is now called, Pizarro set up camp on Puna Island facing Tumbes. At this point two vessels arrived with 100 welcome volunteers including the dashing swordsman and cavalier, Hernando de Soto. When the Spaniards crossed over to Tumbes, they were dismayed to see the famed city deserted and leveled to the ground. It was here that Pizarro learned of the civil war that had recently disrupted the Inca empire, leaving devastation in its wake.

When the recent Inca ruler, Huayna Capac, died in his new kingdom of Quito in 1525 he left his realm divided, contrary to custom, to his elder son and rightful heir, Huascar, and to his younger and favorite son, Atahualpa. Quito was bequeathed to Atahualpa and Cuzco went to Huascar. Contention between the two sons had become acute in the spring of 1532, a few months before Pizarro's arrival. Atahualpa, at the head of his army, met Huascar at Cajamarco and drove his half-brother back to the Peruvian capital, Cuzco. Huascar was later captured and imprisoned in the fortress of Xauxa, leaving the ambitious war-like Atahualpa alone to assume the scarlet diadem of the Inca realm. His victory, however, would become his undoing, for it was to be the fate of the ruling Inca to meet a humiliating death at the hands of Pizarro.

The March To Conquest

In May 1532, Pizarro's forces left Tumbes, continuing their long march southward. In the valley of the Tangarala, the Spaniards established a base known as San Miguel de Piura, on the Piura River, the first European settlement in Peru. Leaving 50 soldiers to protect his base, Pizarro continued southward with 177 men across the dry, dusty, furnace-like Sechura desert to Motupe, and reached the coast again at Lambayeque. Then he turned eastward to finally enter the mountainous labyrinth of the Inca empire. Somewhere ahead, within 12 days journey, was Atahualpa, ruler of the Incas, and his powerful army of 50,000 warriors, bastioned by the forbidding Cordilleras of the Andes and a webwork of angry streams rushing through deep, defiant canyons. There in that craggy fastness,

Atahualpa had to be dealt with or Pizarro's dream would be over. With only 110 foot soldiers and 67 cavalrymen, Pizarro's determination to hazard a confrontation was inconceivably daring, matching the audacity of Cortes, from whom Pizarro often derived his inspiration.

Embassies now appeared bringing invitations from Atahualpa to visit his headquarters at Cajamarca, located beyond the Cordillera. As Montezuma had been, Atahualpa was disturbed over the appearance of the white men. The myth of Quetzalcoatl and his white-skinned followers was alive also among the Peruvians, but their white god bore the name of Viracocha. Pizarro, as did Cortes, was quick to profit by the superstitious terror and partisan strife, then existing in the area he was invading.

The Sublime Andes

Eager but wary, Pizarro resumed his march and in three days reached the base of the mountain range beyond which lay Cajamarca. Before them rose the gigantic wall of the Andes, cleft by shaggy, rocky passes, so narrow and twisting that a handful of men could easily defend themselves. Looking down in haughty grandeur were the isolated snow capped peaks of one of the highest, most wildly chaotic, and sublime mountain vistas in the world. Near the crest of the Cordillera, the Spaniards marched past the open pits from which the Incas gathered some of their gold. And as they went on through the dangerous defiles, the men dreamed of the golden prize ahead, unmindful of the evil omens flying high above, the giant condors, vultures of the Andes, following the army's wake instinctively seeking scenes of blood and carnage.

After descending the eastern side of the sierra, the verdant valley of Cajamarca came into view. Copiously irrigated by canals and aqueducts, and hemmed in by the Cordilleras of the Andes, the valley was a carpet of variegated greenery. White stone and plaster buildings of the city and thousands of tents of Atahualpa's army on the outskirts, glittered in the sun, a spectacle which startled the Spaniards with this evidence of high Inca culture and military might. Moving cautiously into the city, the Spaniards found it silent and deserted; the population had fled to the mountains. The little army then brazenly set up their quarters in Atahualpa's palace, on November 15, 1532.

Pizarro Lures Atahualpa

De Soto was dispatched to convey greetings to

Atahualpa and appraise the situation. His report that the Inca's forces were being arrayed for battle confirmed Pizarro's belief that his army was in imminent peril. Borrowing from Cortes' classic seizure of Montezuma to allay resistance in Tenochtitlan, Pizarro invited Atahualpa to return to his palace in the city, and the unsuspecting Inca accepted. The meeting took place in Cajamarca's main plaza which was surrounded by low stone structures, including the palace. Pizarro meanwhile had hidden his soldiers and his artillery in the buildings.

After deploying his own forces along routes by which the Spaniards might escape, Atahualpa and his royal procession entered Cajamarca in blazing splendor. His palanquin was decorated with brilliant plumes and shining sheets of gold and silver; his throne was of massive gold, and a collar of emeralds encircled his neck. When the Inca and 600 unarmed members of his retinue entered the plaza, they found it empty and still; nowhere were the Spanish troops to be seen.

A lone figure emerged from Pizarro's stronghold. It was Fray de Valverde, with a Bible in one hand and a crucifix in the other. Coming face to face with Atahualpa, the Dominican friar began by expounding the tenets of Christianity to the startled and bewildered monarch; then the friar described the division of the world by the Pope and a treaty which had awarded Peru to Emperor Charles V. When Atahualpa was given the ultimatum to accept Christianity and acknowledge the Spanish ruler as his sovereign, the Inca at first was stupified, then incensed. His eyes flashed fire and his voice was filled with menace as he replied, "I will be no man's tributary." Grabbing the Bible, the Inca threw it to the ground. Outraged by such sacrilege, Valverde hastened to Pizarro, exclaiming, "We are wasting our time with this heathen; the Indians are surrounding the plaza, strike now, I absolve you."

Massacre at Cajamarca

Then came the prearranged signal; Pizarro waved a white scarf, shots rang out, and the Conquistadores leaped from their hiding places shouting their old battle cry, "Santiago and at them!" The Peruvians fell by the hundreds under the fire of cannon, arquebusiers, and the charges of the cavalrymen, while 5000 Indians outside the plaza milled in horror, unable to penetrate the Castilian's wall of fire. Pizarro rushed to Atahualpa's side, extricated him from the melee,

and dragged him to safety within the palace.

The massacre continued unabated until every Peruvian in the plaza was dead or had fled in consternation. The number slain was reported over 2,000. Atahualpa's general, Ruminagui, believing that all resistance was hopeless, ordered his thousands to retreat. The Inca's once proud army did not cease its flight until it reached Quito 700 miles to the north. The Knights of the Golden Sword, and Viacocha were unconquerable. The Peruvian people, accustomed to centuries of conquerors and passive obedience, accepted their new masters in silent resignation.

Atahualpa's Ransom

Observing that the Spaniards' religious zeal was exceeded only by their love of gold, as had Montezuma, Atahualpa the prisoner endeavored to buy his freedom with Inca treasure. He told Pizarro that he would cover the floor of his guarded room, which was 22 feet long by 17 feet wide, as high as he could reach with ornaments of gold, and an adjoining room twice full with silver, if he were allowed two months to collect the treasure.

Even though he was stunned by the incredibility of such a feat, Pizarro agreed to abide by Atahualpa's offer. Messengers were sent out at once over the network of Inca roads from Quito to Cuzco. The pile of gold grew higher and higher as the two months went by. Then came an offer from Huascar in prison at Cuzco to nearly double Atahualpa's bribe, if the Spaniards would set him free. A few days later, upon Atahualpa's orders, the Inca's half-brother, Huascar, was assassinated.

Litters heavy with gold, borne by Indian porters, came from all parts of the empire. To Cuzco, Pizarro sent his brother, Hernando and a group of cavalrymen to appraise the capital and hasten the flow of treasure. On the way, the iron shoes of the horses were worn through, and since no iron was available in the country, they were shod with silver and copper.

At Cuzco, Hernando was amazed by the wealth of the Inca capital. In the great Temple of the Sun, the Castilians beheld the long line of royal mummies, each seated in a golden chair with robes covered with ornaments of gold and jewels. The interior of the temple was literally covered with plates of gold. The Spaniards removed over 700 of such plates, each the size of a chest cover, and sent them on to Cajamarca. Indians were forced to strip the temple of its gold and silver decorations, all except the cornice

PLATE 111. Mines at Pachuca invented the Patio Process for treating silver ores, benefiting the industry for centuries.

PLATE 112. The supreme artistry and awesome hoard of Inca goldwork led Pizarro to conquer Peru in 1533.

PLATE 113. Gold doubloons and other coins were minted and vastly increased the monetary power of Spain.

PLATE 115. 16 of Spain's famed Pillar Dollars, called "Pieces of Eight" were worth one gold doubloon.

PLATE 114. Most of the Mexican and Peruvian jewelry, of incalculable value, was melted and cast into bars.

PLATE 116. The Saugus Ironworks, birthplace of the American iron industry, near Boston.

PLATE 117. Sterling Furnace, first foundry in New York state, made iron for the Revolutionary War.

PLATE 118. Eads Bridge at St. Louis was the first steel truss built across a river. Needs for iron greatly increased.

PLATE 119. Iron pits on the Mesabi Range supplied much of America's growing demands for iron ores.

PLATE 120. The Mather No. 7 shaft stands near the site where the Marquette Range was discovered in 1845.

PLATE 121. Sarah Jordan's boarding house in New Jersey was the first home to be lit with electricity.

of pure gold which encircled the edifice; it was so firmly set that it could not be removed.

Priceless Artistry

By July, 1533, the ransom of gold and silver filled the rooms to agreed levels. The delicacy of the workmanship gave the articles a haunting beauty. They consisted of gold goblets, jugs, trays, vases of every shape and size, utensils, tiles and plates from the royal palaces, temples, and public edifices. Among the most beautiful, which included magnificent reproductions of animals and plants, were golden ears of corn, sheathed in leaves of silver and tassels of gold. It was decided to send a quantity of these priceless examples of Indian artistry to the Emperor, and reduce the remainder to ingots, a more transportable form. Indian goldsmiths, undoing centuries of inspired Inca craftsmanship, were forced to melt and recast the mountain of gold and silver. Estimates of the value of the bullion alone range from 3½ to 15 million dollars, but the artistry revealed by the objects made the treasure valuable beyond measure.

One-fifth was set aside for the Emperor; Hernando Pizarro, De Soto, and Almagro each received wealth equivalent to from 40,000 to 80,000 pesos, while the cavalrymen were each awarded 8,800 pesos, and each infantryman received 4,000 pesos. Francisco Pizarro took 57,000 pesos and Atahualpa's gold service plate worth about $200,000. No military adventurers in history had ever reaped such a fortune in ready, convertible form.

Atahualpa's Betrayal

Atahualpa had kept his promise, but the perfidious Spaniards had decided that as leader of the Incas he must now be destroyed. The monarch was charged with conspiring to incite a revolution, despite his guarded seclusion, and of having ordered the death of his brother, Huascar. A sham tribunal sentenced Atahualpa to be burned alive. On August 29, 1533, having been ignominiously shorn of his empire and his wealth, Atahualpa was led in chains and bound to a stake in the plaza. As the fagots were about to be kindled, Fray Valverde prevailed upon the shaken but brave monarch to accept baptism and conversion. For becoming a Christian, the last of the Incas escaped death by fire and won the privilege of having a noose placed around his neck and dying of strangulation.

The Silver Road to Cuzco

In September 1533, Pizarro took the great Inca Road across the high Andean plateaus heading for Cuzco, passing a succession of mineral deposits whose richness, had they known of them, would have amazed the Spaniards beyond belief. In addition to Atahualpa's treasure, at El Punre and in the Hualgaye district near Cajamarca, there were rich veins of silver, gold, and copper. But these Conquistadores were not miners; they were predators and despoilers.

Entering the beautiful valley corridor of the Huaylas River, the Spaniards were awed by the majesty of the scene. To the west was the Cordillera Negra, which contained the silver districts of Yungay and Recuay. To the east rose the over-powering snow-whitened wall of the Sierra Blanca, crowned by mighty Nevado Huascaran, elevation 22,205 feet, highest in Peru. As the Conquistadores continued southward they passed ore deposits that would become known as the districts of Hauri, Tulla and Chavin, some of which no doubt supplied the Chavin de Huantar culture 3,000 years ago.

Entering the present departments of Pasco and Junin, the army trod over one of the world's richest storehouses of silver, lead, and copper. The Spaniards would have been awestruck had they known that where the city of Cerro de Pasco now stands, the low hills that they were passing contained nearly a billion dollars worth of metals. In 1630, a great mass of oxidized ore, known as *pacos*, was discovered which produced within a century over 550 million dollars worth of silver. Below these surface ores, rich copper deposits containing silver and gold were found, which are being worked on a huge scale even today, making the Cerro de Pasco district one of the largest metal producers in the world.

Past Lago de Junin and through Tarma marched the fortune-seeking Spaniards, oblivious to the famed silver and copper deposits of the Morococha district on the east side of the Andes. Today, from Ticlio near the Andean divide, a branch railroad line runs nine miles to Morococha, attaining an elevation of 15,806 feet, highest railroad in the world. Nearby, another silver district lies below the 17,000 foot summit of Cerro Casapalca.

The Plunder of Cuzco

On November 15, 1533, following his pitiless betrayal of Atahualpa, Pizarro marched boldly into Cuzco. The streets were lined with natives, awed by the glittering pageant of white men in shining armor marching to the sound of blaring trumpets and clattering hoofs of the cavalry. The Spaniards were impressed with the size and beauty of the city's edifices and the well laid out streets. But they lost no time in plundering the dwellings, the palaces and religious buildings.

After the city was sacked completely, the whole mass of treasure was melted and cast into ingots, and after the crown was allotted its share, the remainder was divided among the captains and the soldiers. No reliable figure has been named for the treasure's value; some say it far exceeded the ransom of Atahualpa. One thing is sure; no adventurers in history had ever fallen into such glittering wealth. A few sought to gain more by gambling among themselves; some were able to return to Spain to live regally, but many, grown accustomed to dangerous adventure, later died by violence or in poverty. Their riches, however, became an irresistible beacon which stimulated others to seek fame and fortune in the New World.

The Curse of Cuzco

Cuzco's easy wealth soon became a curse and the seed of discord in Peru; the Conquistadores began to war among themselves. Meanwhile, in the valley of the Rimac, six miles from the sea, Pizarro absorbed himself with the dream of building his capital, bestowing upon it the name Ciudad de los Reyes, City of the Kings, January 6, 1535. It would be known as Lima, Peru. Charles V named Pizarro Marquis de los Atavillos, and granted him the rights of discovery in northern Peru, under the name of New Castile. Pizarro's partner, Almagro, was granted southern Peru, or New Toledo, and zealous Father Valverde was made Bishop of Cuzco. But where were the exact limits of Pizarro's and Almagro's realms? In that uncertainty lay the sources of conflict between these two erstwhile partners.

The blood that flowed in the fratricidal strife which followed, now came mainly from Spanish veins. Quarreling over the ownership of Cuzco, while Pizarro pursued his dream of building Lima, 600 of Almagro's followers and 800 soldiers of Hernando Pizarro dueled to the death on the plain of Los Salinas a few miles from Cuzco. The Peruvians watched gleefully as their former enemies, all loyal subjects of Spain and once brothers-in-arms, charged and disemboweled each other with flashing lances.

Almagro was defeated and was forced to surrender. Brought before Hernando Pizarro, Almagro pleaded for mercy. Sentenced to die, a rope was placed around his neck, and like Atahualpa, the Marquis' former partner and ally was garroted to death. Diego Almagro, the executed man's half-breed son, seized the torch of retribution, determined to avenge his father's death, and organized a conspiracy against Francisco Pizarro, now the sole master of Peru.

At the age of 64, tired of warfare, the Marquis in his sumptuous palace in Lima administered the affairs of the province through trusted lieutenants. One Sunday in June, 1541, while dining with about 20 loyal friends, a band of Almagro's followers burst into the palace, shouting "Death to the tyrant." All but five of Pizarro's guests fled from the scene, leaving the Marquis to the mercy of his enemies. Calmly, Pizarro went to his room, strapped on his armor, took up his sword, and returned to join the five faithful cavaliers who were attempting to stem the tide. One by one they fell.

Soon the Marquis, pressed on all sides, was fighting alone. Parrying the thrusts with the skill of a master, erect and defiant, he finally weakened. A blade found its mark; then Pizarro fell and died alone in a pool of his own blood. A faithful servant and his wife gathered up the body, wrapped it in a white cotton cloth and took it to the cathedral, founded by Pizarro himself, where a grave was stealthily and hastily dug in an obscure corner of the yard. In the light of a few feeble candles furnished by the humble domestics, a short service committed the conqueror of Peru, once a man of great wealth and power, to the lowly dust of the earth.

A few years later, after order was restored in the country, Pizarro's remains were placed in an ornate coffin and buried in the cathedral. In 1607, the relics were moved to the new cathedral where they lie today, in a sarcophagus guarded by a vigilant lion of bronze, symbolic of the tribute now paid to Francisco Pizarro, who so greatly extended the realm, wealth, and power of Spain.

Legacies of Conquest

Beginning with the discovery of America, and during the explorations and treasure hunts of the Conquistadores, Europe was booming with early Renaissance inspiration, productivity and prosperity. But further expansion in Europe was being threatened by a growing shortage of

PLATE 122. Discovery of the Cliff mine in northern Michigan in 1846 answered America's cry for copper.

PLATE 123. Michigan's famed 'Copper Country' became the largest producer of pure, native copper in the world.

PLATE 124. Sperr Hall, now replaced by modern buildings of Michigan Technological University, was a research center for the Copper Country.

PLATE 125. Inured to the deepest mines, like the Quincy, and the hardest rock, Cornishmen later spread their skills all over America.

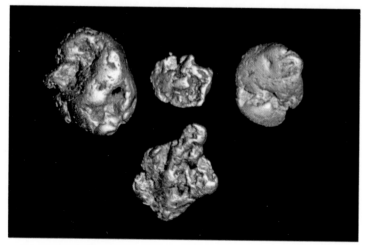

PLATE 126. Golden nuggets, flakes and dust, found in California's streams, started the greatest migration in history.

PLATE 127. James Marshall points to the spot on the American River at Coloma where he discovered gold in 1848.

PLATE 128. On scales of the Wells Fargo Express Office in Columbia was weighed 80 millions in placer gold.

PLATE 129. A white quartz outcrop of California's great Mother Lode was discovered in 1850.

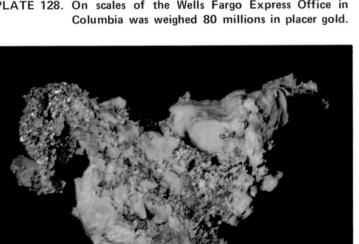

PLATE 130. The gold in quartz then had to be crushed, milled and smelted.

PLATE 131. The great Empire Mine at Grass Valley produced for 100 years, and contained 200 miles of workings.

PLATE 132. Virginia City, Nevada, seen from the Combination shaft, was famed for its silver-rich Comstock Lode.

PLATE 133. Residence of James Fair in Virginia City. Fair, Flood, Mackay and O'Brien were known as the Bonanza kings.

precious metals, not only as a base for currency, but also for art and industry.

The search for lands abounding in gold and the shortest route to reach them were the primary aims of Columbus as well as the Portuguese kings. Religious zeal to convert the Indians veiled the stronger urge to find new metallic wealth, particularly gold. Whatever were the purposes, fate chose a most propitious time in the history of men to disclose the riches of the New World which were to come to the aid to the Old World.

The first trickle of gold from Hispaniola following Columbus' discovery, according to Alexander Von Humboldt, amounted to $250,000 per annum. By 1550 Europe had received a total of nearly 100 million dollars in gold and silver, doubling its existing supply of monetary metal. With additional riches pouring forth from the mines of Mexico, Peru, Chile, Bolivia and Colombia, by the year 1600 Europe had increased its stock of gold and silver four fold, approximately 600 million dollars, which then had a purchasing power much more than it has today. To the monetary metal, if one adds the quantities of jewelry, emeralds, and pearls, it represents a treasure outshining any of the legendary past. Individual fortunes also were being created at a rapid rate, all of which had its beneficial effect upon art and commerce.

Unfortunately, comparatively little of this supply of gold and silver benefited the Spanish people as a whole, or contributed to the ultimate good of Spain. Much of the precious metal remained inert, hoarded by the rich, or used in adornment of churches and palaces of the royal family and the clergy. The nation's vast amounts of increased coinage went out of the country to buy commodities which Spain had failed to produce at home. Instead of serving the commerce of Spain, it stimulated the industries of her growing enemies, England, France and the Low Countries. Also, with increased stocks of money and accelerated importations came rising prices, hurting some, favoring others.

As European economies surged upward, industries thrived. The fetters of serfdom were further removed from craftsmen, skilled artisans and farmers, while added prosperity came to merchants and bankers, adding in general to the well-being of all Europe. This invigorated Renaissance creativity and inventiveness throughout Europe, and also inaugurated a period in Spain which enjoyed its Golden Age in art, literature, and science.

The New World's Vast Wealth

It is almost beyond the power of imagination to conceive the extent of the riches which Cortes, Pizarro and their followers had stumbled onto in the New World. Mexico's contributions alone in metallic wealth to humanity, especially in silver, have been enormous. From 1521 to 1922, the mines of Mexico yielded 155,000 metric tons of silver, worth approximately three billion dollars, which then amounted to two-thirds of the world's silver production. In recent years Mexico has led all other countries in the mining of silver ores, producing 35% of the world's total tonnage. (In 1968 and 1969 Canada surpassed Mexico slightly.)

For a vision of inestimable wealth, add to the riches of Mexico the billions in gold, silver, tin, copper and lead that have come from South America: from the mines of Cerro de Pasco, Colquijirca, Casapalca, and Morocho of Peru; from the silver and tin deposits of fabulous Potosi, Uncia and Oruro of Bolivia; from the mines of Huantaja, Teniente, Potrerillos and Chuquicamata (the world's largest copper mine) of Chile; from the gold placers of the Nechi, Porce and Atratro rivers of Colombia; from the gold veins of Zaruma and the placers of the Santiago River in Ecuador, and from the gold and diamond fields of Mato Grosso and Minas Gerais of Brazil.

This torrent of mineral treasure, streaming across the Atlantic from America to Seville in pirate-harassed galleons, had a tremendous effect upon the Old World. But its greatest contribution to mankind's advancement was the stimulus given to the discovery, exploration, settlement, and development of the Western Hemisphere, despite the terrible toll in human misery and the despoilation of America's hapless aborigines.

"Fate Leads The Willing"

Evaluations related to man's behavior during the evolution of his civilizations are highways of philosophical thought that have been avoided purposely in these pages. Instead, this book has been concerned primarily with events leading to the development of man's natural resources, and their effects upon the course of history. But the precious few centuries, that have been free of war and strife throughout the six thousand years or more of man's civilized existence, present a point to ponder.

The mysterious workings of destiny are

sometimes difficult to fathom. It does seem ironical that the birth of a new civilization on a virgin, unspoiled continent should have been inaugurated by insatiable greed for gold, inhuman cruelty and wanton depredations. Perhaps this dark chapter in human history cannot be measured in the light of modern principles. In the 15th century, European man was not far removed from the cruel practices of the Dark Ages and the concepts of human rights that prevailed in medieval times.

None but the bold, and certainly not the timid, were qualified to defy the terrors of the ogre enshrouded wilderness then supposed to exist in the New World, or to withstand its primitive, rigorous challenges. Whatever might be the judgement of history, or Providence, it is a fact that these avaricious adventurers did open to civilization an area almost doubling the size of the known world, which eventually added immeasurably to mankind's spiritual and material well-being.

These Spanish conquistadores made the New World a flaming beacon of unbridled opportunity and individual freedom. Attracted to these shores would come millions of Europe's oppressed and disadvantaged peoples, some seeking simply freedom to worship in their own way, others to enjoy the heady elixir of free, unspoiled lands and untouched riches.

It was a bizarre spectacle that startled the Old World with the New World's presence. But it made such a vivid, memorable impression upon European consciousness, the world was never to be the same thereafter. A whole new epoch in human relationships and endeavors was to mark the beginning of modern history, nourished by the miracles of a new land, called America.

PLATE 134. The Colorado Rockies near Ouray. Prospectors began revealing Colorado's wealth in 1858.

PLATE 135. The mines of Telluride included the rich Smuggler-Union, Liberty Bell and others.

PLATE 136. Leadville, Colorado, was discovered in 1860. From Carbonate hill stemmed the Guggenheim fortunes.

PLATE 137. H. A. Tabor's Matchless mine produced millions but he and his wife died in poverty.

PLATE 138. Cripple Creek was discovered in 1890 by a cowboy. The Elkton mine was one of the rich gold producers.

PLATE 139. Butte, Montana is called the "Richest Hill on Earth." First a silver camp, it became a great copper district.

Chapter 11

AMERICA--MIRACLE OF THE WILDERNESS

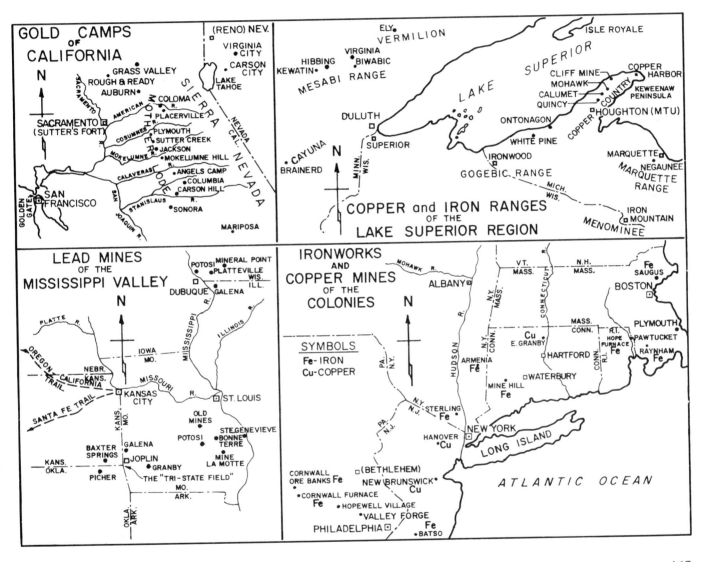

Plate 116 *The Saugus Ironworks*, birthplace of the American iron industry, near Boston.   p. 167

Plate 117 *Sterling Furnace*, first foundry *in New York State*, made iron for the Revolutionary War.   p. 167

Plate 118 *Eads Bridge at St. Louis* was the first steel truss built across a river. Needs for iron greatly increased.   p. 167

Plate 119 *Iron pits on the Mesabi Range* supplied much of America's growing demands for iron ores.   p. 167

Plate 120 *The Mather No. 7 shaft* stands near the site where the Marquette Range was discovered in 1845.   p. 167

Plate 121 *Sarah Jordan's boarding house* in New Jersey was the first home to be lit with electricity.   p. 167

Golden Cities of Cibola

After Cortes and Pizarro had wrung fantastic booty from the Aztecs and Incas of Mexico and Peru, any wild rumor of riches was enough to send adventurers scurrying into unknown frontiers. In 1528, the Narvaez expedition sought gold in Florida and was later shipwrecked on the Gulf of Mexico. Four lone survivors, including Cabeza de Vaca, wandered westward six years across Texas and Arizona. During periods of captivity among Indian tribes, they heard descriptions of great cities having streets and roofs of gold. Finally, the disheveled castaways reached Mexico City where they repeated their fanciful tales to Viceroy Mendoza.

Mendoza was wise enough to send a priest, Fray Marcos de Niza a zealous missionary, northward to what was thought might be the fabled Golden Cities of Cibola. After Fray Marcos, a born optimist and dramatist, had gazed warily from a safe vantage point upon the shining walls of an unknown city, he hurried back to Mendoza with the joyful news; he had indeed seen the Golden Cities of Cibola. Mendoza then appointed bold, handsome and popular 25 year old Francisco Coronado to lead an expedition and seize the legendary wealth.

In one of man's most amazing examples of travail, perseverance and gullibility, after searching for nearly two years across the present states of Arizona, Texas, New Mexico and as far east as Kansas, Coronado and his men found only a parched land lacking any sign of riches. When the crestfallen Spaniards looked upon the long sought object of their dreams in July, 1540, Cibola turned out to be only a Zuni Indian pueblo, glowing in the golden rays of the setting sun. Its crumbled ruins may be seen today, about 40 miles south of Gallup, New Mexico, now entirely forgotten. It was this historic quest for gold by Coronado, however, that broke the trail for a long parade of Spanish explorers and missionaries who colonized and eventually made the Southwest an important part of New Spain.

The Spanish Galleons

While Spanish padres, plodding afoot in the wilderness, established missions, that later grew into cities, from the Rio Grande to the Pacific Coast, Spain's galleons, creaking with their loads of New World treasure, sailed along the Spanish Main across the Atlantic to the booming ports of Seville and Barcelona. With this seemingly inexhaustible wealth, Spain became the dominant power in Europe. And with her widespread colonies in the New World, the possession, religious control and future of North America rested firmly and solely in the hands of Spain.

Meanwhile, the wily, Machiavellian queen of England, Elizabeth I, while feigning to keep the peace with her rival Philip, the Catholic king of Spain, secretly encouraged English privateers to prey upon the rich Spanish settlements and treasure-laden galleons. It was during this undeclared war, sharpened by religious conflicts and voracious appetites for plunder, that England developed the navy and found among her audacious buccaneers the admirals, such as Drake, Hawkins, and Frobisher, which enabled her to challenge Spain's mastery of the seas.

On July 19, 1558 an English fleet sallied forth into the English Channel, met and defeated Spain's Invincible Armada. It was a crucial turning point in history. England came to rule the waves, while Spain faded into eclipse as a world power. With control of the seas, pathways were now open for English colonization of the North Atlantic region.

English Colonization

Religious intolerances and repressions of the monarchial systems drove most European colonists to the Atlantic seacoast of North America. But tales of riches reaped by the Spaniards induced many English, Dutch, Scandinavian, and German migrants to seek precious metals in the New World. Unfortunately, the coastal lands were heavily forested and concealed the presence of many mineral deposits, unlike the nearly bare, rocky terrain of Mexico where outcrops of ores were easier to detect.

Early authorities on English-American potentialities frankly reported the country to be barren of metallic deposits, excepting inferior ores of iron. Even wise, well-informed Benjamin Franklin, endeavoring to support a paper currency, stated that North America possessed no useful ores of the precious metals. Such were the pessimistic predictions concerning a nation that was soon to astound the world with its vast storehouse of mineral treasure.

It was an imperative need for tools, plow-shares, implements and nails that led the early colonists to seek deposits of iron, and to launch the first mining industry. The earliest deposits of iron were known as bog-ore, found in marshy places where iron had been carried in solution; there it had been concentrated by evaporation and chemical reaction with decayed vegetation. These deposits were usually small, but sufficient to meet the needs of early days.

The iron smelters were known as "bloomeries." Charcoal, mixed with limestone flux, reduced the oxide ore to an impure "bloom" of metallic iron and slag. The bloom then had to be hammered, forged or wrought to squeeze out the slag, thus producing "wrought iron" which was used by blacksmiths and other fabricators. Many iron-works became known as Forges, such as Valley Forge and others.

Sinews of Independence

An ironworks built in 1646 at Saugus, north of Boston, now a national landmark, claims to be the birthplace of America's iron industry. First known as Hammersmith, due to difficulties attending a pioneer development, the venture was unprofitable. But it did become an important training school for many ironmasters who were taught European techniques, and later spread their skills throughout New England.

When hard, magnetite iron ores were discovered in Pennsylvania, the famed Coventry Forge was built in 1732, followed in 1743 by Hopewell Village, now a National Historic Site, west of Philadelphia. In 1742, Peter Grubb of Cornwall founded Cornwall Furnace 40 miles west of Hopewell Village. The Cornwall ore banks, as the ore deposit is known today, is still producing from a huge open pit, dug in solid magnetite, under the management of Bethlehem Steel Company. All of these early ironworks made cannon and shot for George Washington's army. The Sterling Iron Works in New York state forged the huge chain that stretched across the Hudson River during the Revolutionary War.

More ironworks were created in New Jersey, at such places as Atsion, Hannover, Batso and Boonton. These and other colonial iron furnaces played vital roles in furnishing the sinews of war which won American independence. By the time George Washington became president, small iron-works were operating in all of the 13 colonies. By 1810, the value of iron products manufactured in the United States had grown to over $10,000,000. But this was but a fraction of the real iron needs that would soon face the nation.

Inventors Create Demands for Iron

When Thomas Newcomen discovered that steam could be put to work pumping water from English coal, tin and silver mines, a great new source of power became available to mankind. After James Watt improved Newcomen's engine in 1769, the use of steam swept rapidly over the world. Heretofore, industries had utilized machines driven by water wheels located on swiftly flowing streams, or had employed tread-mills operated by horses or men. When water power drove the machinery, many of America's weaving mills had been attracted to New England's rivers. Now, with steam available they began to use steam-powered machines.

The use of steam to propel boats attracted American inventors after John Fitch built, in 1786, a vessel which attained a speed of three miles per hour. It was Robert Fulton, however, who made navigation by steam a success. He obtained a Watt engine from England and installed it in a side-wheeler named the Clermont. In August, 1807, belching smoke and cinders, the boat headed up the Hudson River and managed to reach Albany. By 1846, paddle-wheeled steamboats lined wharves as far west as St. Louis, disgorging cotton, cattle and wide-eyed emigrants. Steam powered machines made of iron were making astonishing progress.

In 1830, the first attempt at railway transportation was made when an upright boiler on wheels was built by Peter Cooper, proprietor of an ironworks in Baltimore. Named the Tom Thumb, this one and one-half horsepower contraption became the first locomotive to pull passenger cars on a regular railroad, the Baltimore and Ohio. The engine was proudly matched in a horse race, and when a belt slipped it was ignobly defeated. But a horse never beat a steam engine thereafter. By 1840, there were 2,800 miles of railroads spread over the eastern United States. English tracks, formerly made of woodbeams topped with iron straps, had been replaced by American inventors with rails of solid iron.

The Cry For Machines

As the cry arose for more machines, in 1793 Eli Whitney developed a cotton gin, short for "engine," which separated seeds from cotton 50 times faster than hand sorting. In 1831, young Cyrus McCormick ended thousands of years of reaping by hand scythes, when he invented a horse-drawn mechanical harvester, a wheeled rig geared to a bar with movable shears.

All across the land, engines made of iron were beginning to do the work of man, in the fields, mills and factories. Railroad yards of growing cities were filled with diamond-stacked, woodburning locomotives, hitched to chains of freight and passenger cars. The Industrial Age was bursting upon the scene, ready to ride across the American continent on roads of steel. The baronial ironmasters of colonial times had trained and pioneered a vital industry, but the national supply of iron ores would soon be unable to meet the requirements of the times. Sorely needed now was a dependable source of iron ore sufficient to match a nation growing from ocean to ocean.

Not only were huge reserves required; it was necessary also to find deposits which could be worked economically, in order to provide manufacturers with low-cost material. If the young,

virile United States were to continue an onward course, a fortuitous discovery seemed imperative. In the forested wilderness of Northern Michigan, Wisconsin and Minnesota, the world's most extensive deposits of iron ores were waiting to be found.

One day in 1844, while plodding through an untrod thicket near the south shore of Lake Superior, William A. Burt, a surveyor, noticed the erratic behavior of his compass needle. Knowing that such a variation could be caused by the presence of a body of iron material, Burt and S. T. Carr set out with an Indian chief to search the wilderness.

Crimson Mountains

Suddenly, they came upon a red-hued "mountain of solid iron ore 150 feet high," its crimson color made brighter by the velvety-white bark of the birch trees growing upon its slopes. The discovery date was July 23, 1845; the location: near the present town of Negaunee, Michigan. Today, a huge open pit marks the site where the mountain was leveled and excavated, forming the famed Jackson mine. Colorful walls of red hematite iron ore, beautifully banded with red jasper, outline the ore deposit.

The Jackson mine discovery, not far from Marquette, was followed by more important finds grouped along a narrow area called a Range. After the Marquette Range came the Menominee Range, discovered in 1872, followed by the discovery of the Gogebic Range, which extended from Northern Michigan into Wisconsin. Then came the finding of immense iron deposits north of Duluth in northern Minnesota. Due to the rich red color of the ore and surrounding soil, the area became known as the Vermilion Range.

The greatest Range was the Mesabi, opened in 1892 north of Duluth, around such towns as Hibbing, Virginia, Eveleth, and Biwabik, extending over 80 miles from east to west. Fortunately, the ore occurred in thick horizontal layers seldom over 200 feet beneath the surface. By stripping off the glacial drift, the ore could be mined with giant power shovels in huge open pits at lower costs. The Hull-Rust mine near Hibbing boasts of having the largest open pit in the world.

Iron's Crucial Role in The Civil War

The Civil War greatly increased the demand for iron. It was used in large quantities in weapons, armored ships and numerous factories. Most important was the use of iron in the expansion of the railroad system that played such a crucial role in the transportation of Northern troops. It was the North's industrial supremacy, fed by its iron resources, that enabled the North to win the Civil War.

The Iron ore deposits of this Lake Superior region have been the most productive the world has ever known. Over 70 million tons of iron ore per year, 80 to 90 percent of the United States' total domestic production, have come from this "Iron Country," as the region is often called. Supplies of iron and steel from this bountiful red treasure not only preserved the Union during the Civil War; but these iron deposits were also instrumental in creating the framework of America's unparalleled economic growth.

Countless mills and factories, innumerable cities studded with lofty buildings, a gigantic network of railroad and steamship lines, miraculous bridges and myriads of products used in the home, based upon the use of iron and steel, have made the United States the greatest industrial nation in history. These ruby-red layered pits have also furnished the sinews to wage two world wars in the defense of nations dedicated to the principles of democracy. Had it not been for America's enormous deposits of iron ore, the course of history might today be pursuing an entirely different direction.

Copper Comes of Age

Copper was man's first working metal. Utilized to shape the stones of the Egyptian pyramids over 4500 years ago, and in the bronzes of remotest antiquity, for thousands of years copper had waited to come of age, to perform its greatest service to mankind. Long before the marvels of the Electrical Age, copper was enjoyed chiefly as a luxury metal, used in copper pots and pans, and various decorative forms. Later, copper was employed to sheath the bottoms of wooden vessels in order to retard marine growth.

During American colonial times, after former miners of Cornwall and Saxony managed to find small deposits of copper near their settlements, which today still bear the names of their homeland, the limited needs of the communities were adequately supplied. One of the first finds of copper was at East Grandby north of Hartford, Connecticut, in 1705. The state's governor, Fitz John Winthrop, organized a copper mining company and imported miners and smelter workers from the Harz region of Germany.

The first copper coinage produced in the colonies was minted in this region by John Higley, in 1737. Known as "Higley pennies," they were stamped 'I am good copper—Value me as you will.' Unsuccessful as a mine, it nevertheless gained notoriety as an underground prison. In its old mine "stopes", or caverns, 90 feet beneath the surface, Tories, debtors, and thieves were incarcerated during the Revolutionary War.

A small, rich deposit of native copper was found at Hanover, New Jersey, in 1719. The ore was shipped in barrels to England, the only place where, by law, it could be refined. At that time colonists were not permitted to engage in certain industrial activities. Much of the early American copper production came from deposits near Vershire, Vermont (then known as Ely). Operated by the ever skillful Cornishmen, during the mid-1800's the mines supported a population of 2,000. A crippling strike in 1883 forced closure of the mines.

Copper for The Electrical Age

By 1850, Yankee ingenuity was beginning to bring about a transformation in the living habits of mankind. About to take place was a miraculous new age, the Age of Electricity. In 1838, Samuel Morse, already famous as a portrait painter, had satisfied his scientific urge by inventing the magnetic telegraph. His historic message, 'What hath God wrought,' sent over copper wire from Washington to Baltimore in 1844, introduced instant communication. The singing copper wires of the telegraph linked the cities of the eastern United States, and replaced the flying hoofs of the Pony Express across the plains and mountains all the way to the Pacific coast.

In 1858, Cyrus W. Field began the first of his several heartbreaking attempts to lay a heavily insulated copper cable, reinforced with strands of steel, across the Atlantic floor. In 1866, his dream was fulfilled, and copper wires then united the American continent with Europe in the rapid exchange of communications. Another Yankee inventor, Alexander Graham Bell, filed his patent for the telephone in 1876; by 1890 over one and one-half million telephones were carrying the voices of America over copper wires strung across the land.

Few inventors so revolutionized humanity's mode of living as did the wizard of Menlo Park, Thomas Alva Edison. In 1869, he began taking out the first of over 1,000 patents to be developed during his brilliant career. His patent for the electric light was filed in 1879; then came his designs for electric dynamos, commercial power plants, wiring systems, and the kineto-scope. Homes and city streets came out of the darkness with a new form of lighting in every city of America.

New York's blazing Bowery was a classic example of the new age of invention; stores brightly lit by Edison lights and Edison power stations; street cars and elevated trams driven by electrical motors, and made safe by George Westinghouse's new automatic air brakes; all testi-fied to the rising tide of American enterprise. Yankee wizardry had created a colossal need for copper. No longer could the small copper resources of the eastern coastal states meet the burgeoning demand. As in the development of its iron deposits America again was faced with the problem of finding metal reserves, this time of copper—if its booming economy was to live and thrive.

Keweenaw's Copper Boulders

The remote southern shores of Lake Superior, particularly the Keweenaw Peninsula of what is now known as Northern Michigan, for ages had been rumored to contain copper. Explorers and Jesuit missionaries such as Legarde, Allouez, Marquette and Duluth, as early as 1636 had referred to the presence of native copper boulders in the Lake Superior region. A boulder of pure, "mass" copper weighing over three tons, found on the Ontonagon River of the Keweenaw Peninsula, became a famous landmark for early visitors.

Father Dablon hacked off a piece of pure, native metal which he sent to King Louis XVI in 1665. Over a hundred years later, in 1771, Alexander Henry, an English trader, attempted the first mining operation by digging beneath the boulder, but the ground was found barren. The boulder had been transported to its local position by glaciers from a source unknown.

Masses of native copper, torn and scoured from their Keweenaw outcrops, had been scattered by the great Wisconsin ice sheet far southward over many areas. Crude implements made of this vagrant copper by prehistoric Indians have been found in pre-Columbian burial mounds in Wiscon-sin, Ohio, and the Mississippi Valley.

The Keweenaw was obviously a beacon of promise. But Michigan came close to losing its rich Upper Peninsula. In 1787, according to the Northwest Ordinance, Michigan's southern boundary was to have been a straight line from east to west, and to have included the lower tip of Lake Michigan and the Toledo area. When Congress readjusted the boundary to its present position, Michigan citizens launched the bloodless "Toledo War" to regain the severed area.

After Michigan was admitted to the Union as the 26th state in 1837, as a gesture of conso-lation for relinquishing the Toledo area, the new state was awarded the unexplored, apparently worthless wilderness which is now the Upper Peninsula. Later, it would be found to contain boundless wealth in copper, iron and timber alone.

Fate stepped in again in behalf of Michigan in 1842, when the Chippewa tribe ceded to the state the last remnant of their ancestral holdings, the Keweenaw Peninsula and Isle Royale. Under the treaties of 1807, 1819, and 1821, the Chippewa, Ottawa, Wyandot, and Potawatomi nations already had relinquished most of their lands to the young Territory of Michigan. This last gift to the white man's march of progress was to be worth billions in metallic resources.

Douglass Houghton's Report

A hint of the hidden merits of the Keweenaw country had been revealed in 1830, when 29 year old Douglass Houghton, Michigan's first state geologist, spurred by centuries of rumored riches in the north, undertook to survey the area. His report, issued in 1841, stated that "ores of copper are abundant." Most remarkable was the fact that the copper occurred in the pure metallic state.

In October, 1845, Houghton drowned while attempting to land in a small boat at Eagle River near the tip of the Peninsula, but his sanguine reports, and the opening of the Indian lands to prospectors, started a copper rush to the northern wilderness. Settlements and boom towns sprang up from Copper Harbor and Eagle Harbor near the tip of Keweenaw Point to Ontonagon farther south.

Greenhorns, expecting to find precious metals as well as copper strewn over the ground, soon lost their fervor when they encountered heavy thickets of brush and pine woods concealing all signs of riches. The more persistent and experi-enced began to examine ancient pits which had been dug by prehistoric Indians in search for malleable, native copper for their implements.

And, everywhere the prospectors searched they were greeted with an astonishing discovery: the copper was always found as pure metal, a notable rarity among the world's ore deposits. Excepting for minor amounts of native copper in near-surface zones, copper is usually combined with sulphur and iron, forming the brassy sulphides. The reasons were unknown to the prospectors, but eventually would be understood. It would help to visualize this unusual setting if the circumstances were explained at this point.

Birth of The Keweenaw Peninsula

Approximately a billion years ago, during one of earth's crustal revolutions, a great outpouring of lavas from many volcanic vents built up a series of innumerable flows piled one upon another, reaching a thickness of over 15,000 feet and extending from Keweenaw Point to and beyond the southern and western shore of Lake Superior. This great effusion of molten magma emptied its huge sub-surface reservoir, causing a portion of the earth's crust to collapse, forming a saucer shaped depression which is now occupied by the western arm of Lake Superior.

The eastern rim of the saucer is now the rocky ridge of lavas which forms Keweenaw Peninsula, whose lava beds slope westward toward and under the lake. Steam and gases, escaping from the tops of the viscous lavas as they poured out over the pristine surface, created an upper porous zone of bubbly holes, called amygdules. In certain places, slumping of the cooling mass opened large cracks, or fissures, cutting across the layered lavas.

Later, solutions containing copper, which originated perhaps in the same lava reservoirs, entered and deposited native metal in the amygdaloidal tops and fissures, favoring certain places where chemical composition of the lavas, and porosity, influenced deposition of the metallic copper. Keweenaw's native copper was unalloyed with any other element, except on the immediate surface where a thin coating of green carbonate covered the metal. Occasionally, native silver was found associated with the copper. Such was the treasure that for millions of years had awaited the first influx of fortune hunters.

America's First Mining Boom

It was a young Pittsburg pharmacist, John Hays, hard bitten with the spirit of adventure, who made the 'copper country's' first important dis-covery. He reached Copper Harbor in July, 1843, and after several fruitless attempts near the town, turned his attention to the bald face of a high greenstone lava cliff, where a small outcropping of native copper lay exposed.

At the base of the cliff, Hay's men drove an opening, or adit, into the hill. They were following a fissure vein which cut deeply into the bluff. Within the short distance of 70 feet, miners encountered a solid mass of copper that was so huge it could be mined only by cutting it apart with hammers and chisels. The Cliff mine, as it was named, marked the beginning of the famed copper boom of Northern Michigan, the first extensive copper discovery in America. By 1906 the Cliff deposit became exhausted, but by then its shareholders had received over 2½ million dollars in dividends.

A few miles northeast of the Cliff Mine, in 1854, prospectors inspected ancient Indian pits at the base of the greenstone bluff, which led to the discovery of another great "fissure" copper deposit. This became the Central Mine which produced 52 million pounds of copper, until it closed in 1898. Such fabulously rich masses of pure copper attracted not only eastern miners, but also an influx of Cornishmen who, for generations, had gained experience working the 'hardrock' tin mines of ancient Cornwall, England. These 'Cousin Jacks', as they were affectionately called, were to form the backbone of the great mining industry soon to blossom across the United States.

The Ontonagon Boulder

The huge Ontonagon copper boulder, 65 miles southwest of the Cliff Mine, meanwhile was interesting a Vermont tavern keeper named Sam Knapp. For four years he had traced chunks of 'float' copper and had examined nearly every Indian pit, trying to find the source of the boulder. In 1847, while excavating a likely depression beneath winter snows near the Ontonagon River, Knapp and his companions came upon a huge hoard of stone hammers, mill stones and chunks of native copper turned green with age. Further digging uncovered a mass of copper weighing about six tons.

This was the beginning of a copper bonanza that became the world famous Minesota Mine (the extra 'n' was left out by the original recorder of the claim). In 1856, a mass of native copper 48 feet long, averaging 11 feet in thickness and weighing over 500 tons, was uncovered.

Fifteen months were required to cut and divide the malleable mass into smaller pieces which could be taken to the surface. By 1880, the Minesota had produced 53 million pounds of copper and paid over two million dollars in dividends.

These first mines which encountered bonanzas of mass copper concentrated in fissures cutting across the lava beds, were highly spectacular. But the great mines that made the copper country world renowned were found in the lower grade but more extensive deposits, where the copper occurred in myriads of grains in the amygdaloidal lava tops, coursing the entire length of the peninsula. Even in the amygdaloids, masses of copper weighing several tons were also found.

The Amygdaloid Mines

On a hill south of the present city of Houghton, prospectors found an amygdaloid lode defined along a mile of prehistoric Indian pits. This became the first amygdaloid mine, the Isle Royal, which sunk a shaft in 1852 to explore the find. North of Houghton atop the hill above the twin city of Hancock, in 1856 several shafts were sunk by the Quincy Mining Company, following the downward dip of the lode at an angle of 45 degrees to the west.

Working and paying handsome dividends steadily for over a century, the Quincy became known as the Copper Country's "Old Reliable." Its workings eventually reached a depth of over 9,300 feet along the incline, or close to 6,000 feet vertically beneath the surface. Following the Quincy came a galaxy of mines such as the Atlantic, Baltic, Allouez, Centennial, Osceola, Kearsarge, Wolverine, Mohawk, Ahmeek, Tamarack, Champion and others.

The Michigan Legislature recognized the importance of scientific methods in mining and authorized, in 1861, a mining school at Houghton in the heart of the Keweenaw peninsula. The war of 1861-1865 delayed funding so that the Michigan Mining School (now Michigan Technological University) was finally established by statute in 1885.

The Conglomerate Mines

Perhaps the most famous of the Copper Country's mines was the Calumet and Hecla, discovered by Edwin J. Hulbert in September, 1864. A polished, intelligent young man, educated in Detroit schools and the University of

Michigan, Hulbert found chunks of unusual copper float while surveying a road along the Copper Range. To some people, Hulbert's rocks were considered "freaks" because they in no way resembled the amygdaloidal lavas. Instead, they were reddish in color and consisted of pebbles cemented in a matrix of hardened sand, a water laid formation known as conglomerate. But native copper also splotched these curious rocks.

Wisely using a knowledge of geology which he had acquired while working as a surveyor, Hulbert traced the float to an outcrop of conglomerate rock. Beside it he found a pit filled with Indian baskets, stone hammers and a cache of prehistoric copper metal. The find happened to be on unclaimed government land, which enabled Hulbert to stake the ground and to organize a mining company, joined by Boston friends Horatio Bigelow, J. W. Clark and Quincy Adams. The property was named the Calumet Mining Company, after a ceremonial peace pipe used by North American Indians. Later, additional ground was acquired and called the Hecla. When mining began on this strange, reddish lode in 1866, Calumet and Hecla stock rose from $1 to $75 per share.

Difficulties encountered in milling this new type of rock retarded the company's progress, until Harvard educated Alexander Agassiz, sent by Boston directors, placed the operation on a sound basis. Agassiz gained renown in the mining world for his expert management. By 1882, Calumet and Hecla had produced copper valued at over 70 million dollars. In 1923, the Calumet and Hecla, Osceola, Ahmeek, Allouez and Centennial mines were combined to form the great Calumet and Hecla Consolidated Copper Company.

By 1930 this combination had produced five billion pounds of copper valued at over one billion dollars and had paid 185 millions in dividends, one of the most profitable mining companies on earth. By then, the Copper Country had furnished America with 8 billion pounds of copper and paid shareholders over 340 million in profits.

The Cornishmen

But millions of dollars could not begin to measure one other contribution of the Copper Country to American progress. Its miners, millmen, engineers, and inventors, inured to the hardest rock, the deepest mines, the largest openings, and at times the lowest grade ore (often less than one percent copper) taught the United

States how to mine and mill the widespread ore deposits that later were discovered in the West.

Swedes, Finns, Irish and Scandinavians were numbered among the Copper Country's ethnic groups. But it was the Cornishmen, with their rare skills, quaint speech and traditions, who created the mining lore of America by training and handing down to later generations a heritage which stemmed from the ancient tin mines of Cornwall and the Copper Country. These keen, good-humored people would always be found in the vanguard, bringing to the surface the ores of one bonanza after another throughout the Western Hemisphere, and especially the United States. Together, Cornishmen and the Copper Country laid the foundation of America's great mining industry.

American inventors had indeed launched the Electrical Age, but it was the mines and these people of the Copper Country who met the burgeoning demand for the industry's first requirement, copper. Michigan's famed copper district, and the iron deposits of the Lake Superior region, became indispensable cornerstones of America's industrial growth. Without the timely discovery and development of these two pillars of industry, the economic headway of the United States would have been seriously impeded. But these two districts were but the first of an amazing array of mineral provinces yet to serve America's needs.

Bullets Along the Mississippi

In 1673, Louis Joliet, a fur trader, and Jacques Marquette, a Jesuit missionary, exploring southwestward from the Great Lakes, found and descended the upper reaches of the Mississippi River. But it was Robert de La Salle, in 1682, who set out from Quebec, proceeded westward to Lake Michigan, thence down the Illinois River to the Mississippi, and then followed the great central water route all the way to the Gulf of Mexico. The great basin the river drained became known as Louisiana, named after Louis XIV, the Sun King of France. It also became the domain of the French-Canadian voyageurs who came later, paddling their canoes in search of trade and furs.

Traders, carrying their long cumbersome guns, and the Indians who exchanged their furs for fire arms, depended upon a supply of lead for their bullets. Fate had placed, for their convenience, many outcrops of lead ores throughout the Mississippi Valley. The Franciscan friar and explorer, Louis Hennepin, in 1680, published a map of Louisiana noting lead deposits centered around Dubuque, Mineral Point, and Galena in northwestern Illinois. The Frenchman, Nicolas Perrot, an astute trader, was the first to start lead mining along the Mississippi. As commandant of the Wisconsin territory, Perrot built frontier posts and traded with the Sioux and other tribes. In 1690, Indians led him to lead deposits near present Dubuque, which he worked successfully with Indian labor.

In 1712, Antoine Crozat, a French banker, obtained a 15 year trade monopoly for Louisiana and sent Antoine de La Mothe Cadillac to open mines in the Ozark hills, now in Missouri. The district was believed to contain silver; instead it was a lead deposit, still shown on the map as Mine La Motte, located about 40 miles southwest of present Ste. Genevieve on the Mississippi River. John Law, a Scottish financier and notorious promoter, took over the property in 1717, and launched a vigorous prospecting program in southwest Missouri. Mine La Motte shipped its lead ores down river to New Orleans and thence to France, while rumors of other rich finds caused the company's stock to soar fantastically. But Law's fanciful scheme, known as the Mississippi Bubble, finally burst and ended in bankruptcy.

Miners Create Settlements

Lead mining along the Mississippi Valley from Missouri to Illinois and Wisconsin attained considerable importance. The voyageurs were transients interested only in trapping. Mining, on the other hand, required settlements, roads, and harmonious relations with the Indians. As discoveries were made in widening circles, the lure of metallic wealth attracted bright-eyed prospectors, followed by farmers, millers, and merchants. Lead, for guns along the Mississippi, had started a boom which opened the land to progress.

After the United States acquired the Louisiana Territory in 1807, all lands containing mineral were reserved to the government, but could be leased at a royalty of 10 percent. Then came the usual swarm of fortune seekers who, in addition to acquiring government leases by chicanery or force, also made "treaties" covering lands reserved to the Indians. Strife between red men and white men resulted in ambuscades, massacres, and various depredations, highlighted by the shameful war upon Black Hawk, a Sauk Indian chief.

Henry Dodge, in his prestigious years, was three times governor of the Wisconsin territory, delegate to Congress and United States senator. But he got his start in 1827 by squatting on lead-bearing lands of the Winnebago Indians in the Wisconsin Valley. With a small army, Dodge took possession of hills blessed with abundant lead ores located conveniently close to the surface. Neither the Indians nor the government agent could dispossess him. Securing an Indian treaty, Dodge retained the mines and ownership of 1,000 acres of land, which eventually brought him great wealth and power.

The Great "Tri-State" Lead Field

By 1828 important mining centers had developed in southwestern Wisconsin at Hazel Green, Dodgeville, Platteville, and at Mineral Point where the stone homes of Cornish miners on Shake Rag street can still be seen. Thrifty Cornishmen were soon leasing their own lead-bearing lands, as mining became the first stable industry in the Mississippi Valley. In 1867, great reserves of lead ores were developed near Bonne Terre, Missouri, resulting in the organization of the St. Joseph Lead Company; and another influx of Cornish miners began.

In the far southwestern corner of Missouri, near present Joplin, David Campbell, a prospector, examined an old Indian, or possibly Spanish excavation, and found a rich layer of pure galena, an ore of lead. Nearby, while digging for worms, a Negro boy turned up large chunks of lead ore on Joplin Creek, so close to the surface were the ore deposits of the district. By 1888, Joplin had become a boom town of 8,000 people busily mining zinc as well as lead, laying the foundation for the consolidation of mines by the noted Eagle-Picher Mining Company. The aggregate value of the district's production would later reach over one billion dollars.

Additional discoveries were made across the Missouri line in Kansas and Oklahoma, which became known as the "Tri-State Field." Webb City, Galena, Baxter Springs, Picher, Granby, Aurora, and Joplin became the booming centers of this great region, which mined as much as 24 million tons of ore annually. The discovery and production of lead and zinc in one of the richest metalliferous provinces in the world, the upper Mississippi Valley, was a decisive factor in bringing civilization to the land. Pioneered by the prospector and miner, and by the settlers who followed, America's Manifest Destiny seemed to be beckoning more and more in the direction of the western horizon.

'Manifest Destiny'

Only the dim outlines of the immense, primeval region between the Mississippi River and the Pacific Ocean had been seen by a few explorers and traders, such as Lewis and Clark, Zebulon Pike, William Becknell and a handfull of daring Mountain men. In July, 1845, John O'Sullivan, writing in the United States Magazine, urged the nation to embark on its "Manifest Destiny," to expand American rule across the continent to Pacific shores. Actually, the phrase only echoed the dreams of Thomas Jefferson and his minister to England, James Monroe, one of the negotiators of the Louisiana Purchase. Widespread fear of British expansion gave additional substance to such a doctrine.

But it was not the high sounding phrase "Manifest Destiny" that impelled the trappers to comb the stillness of the mountains, nor the traders to blaze desert trails to Santa Fe, or the hopeful farmers of Oregon and Texas to plow the virgin soil. And it certainly was not the creed of the 15,000 Mormons who migrated to Utah in 1846. Those men, women, and children, many of whom pushed handcarts over 1,400 miles of primitive, death-dealing trails in order to reach their promised land in the barren valley near the Great Salt Lake, were impelled only by the wish to worship in their own way.

All of these stout hearted precursors of American civilization were simply displaying their inborn spirit of self-reliance and willingness to challenge the unknown; the same spirit that had brought their forbears to the untrod shores of the New World. These dispersions from the eastern states prior to 1846 were just a beginning. One of the greatest migrations known to mankind was waiting for the starting gun to signal a sweep westward across the land.

Gold in California!

The ink on the Treaty of Guadalupe Hildalgo, signed February 2, 1848, ending the United States' war with Mexico, was hardly dry when shouts of joy rang through the forest announcing the discovery of gold on the American River in California. In an ironical prank of fate, just nine days earlier on January 24, 1848, James W. Marshall, a carpenter, had found flakes of gold in the tailrace of a sawmill he had been building for John Sutter.

Of the $15,000,000 that the United States paid to Mexico for the territory which now comprises California, Nevada, New Mexico and Utah, the proportion representing the cost of California was small indeed compared with riches the land was soon to yield. Following Marshall's discovery, California's gold laden streams and her famed Mother Lode would ultimately produce gold valued at two billion dollars.

Prior to the treaty, California already had won a measure of independence through the efforts of native-born dons and the "gringo" settlers from eastern states, all of whom resented Mexico's arrogant rule. Under John C. Fremont, the "Path-finder," in June 1846 the Californians had successfully, but briefly, set up an independent republic, the "Bear Flat Revolt." After the treaty, California became a Territory of the United States in 1848.

The "Forty-eighters"

Then came the cry of gold. It reverberated across the nation, echoed in far away Australia, China and all the countries of Europe. Three months after Marshall's discovery, there were 4,000 men tearing up the ground around Sutter's sawmill. As the diggings became too crowded, men rushed to other streams, the Stanislaus, Tuolume and Mokelumne rivers, tumbling forth from the Sierras over a distance of 120 miles from north to south.

There, men found an incredible hoard of gold, untouched and unclaimed. For countless ages, nature had been patiently gathering placer gold in the form of grains, flakes, "dust", and nuggets, captured from the eroded outcrops of a great yet-to-be discovered Mother Lode in the mountains high above. Slowly, the heavy grains of gold had collected along the stream bottoms, or had settled in still water holes, in crevices and on the sand bars, waiting for millions of years for that certain adventurous soul to come along and find them. The gold belonged to anyone who found it; one had only to drive a pick into the ground and stake a claim, usually 30 to 100 feet square, a code handed down by the Old World from the mines of Cornwall and Saxony. As yet, California had no land laws.

Most of the men were young, resilient, and hardy; many were educated; a few were criminals and gamblers, but, with rough codes of conduct, justice was dealt fairly well on the frontier. Spurred on by individual initiative, they practiced private enterprise in its simplest form, a system which would yield a harvest of riches to the young United States greater than any nation had gathered in the history of mankind.

Sudden Wealth—and Free!

Stories of sudden wealth swept like wildfire across the land. Spectacular finds became the lore of the Gold Rush, and goaded others on to more feverish efforts. Two men at Placerville, using gold pans to wash away the lighter rock particles from the heavier grains of metal, obtained $17,000 in gold within one week. One man found a pocket of gold dust that nearly filled his hat. A few men, working together, divided their golden fortune in tin cups. Many men made from $100 to $500 per day; most of them averaged about $25 per day. Many searched in vain, bedeviled by bad luck or poor judgement. They found nothing, but of them there was little news.

Walking up to the edge of a stream, the first greenhorns were startled to find the river sands alive with what seemed golden flakes of gold. They soon learned the meaning of "fools gold." Mica, a mineral constituent of the Sierra granites, had been fed by erosion also into the streams, but much more abundantly than gold. The newcomer grew to know that mica was brassy in color, rather than golden-yellow, that it was lighter in weight and could be split into thin plates and crushed to a powder by a knife, while gold's malleability made it flatten under hammering. Iron pyrites, found later in the rocks of the Mother Lode, was also known as fool's gold. Its brassy pieces, unlike gold, could also be pulverized under pressure. But miners learned to recognize without fail gold's characteristic heaviness (specific gravity) and bright, yellow gleam.

One of the richest camps was Columbia. In one month, 8,000 miners came to pry into the cavernous limestone stratum surrounding the town, where gold grains and nuggets had been trapped in the still-water pot holes. Eighty million dollars in gold soon passed over the scales in the local Wells Fargo Express office. Rip-roaring boom camps aptly named Rough and Ready, Dutch Flat, Mormon Bar, You Bet, Eldorado, Mokelume Hill, Angels Camp, Melones, Sonora, Jamestown, Chinese Camp and others witnessed many exciting, humorous, and even pathetic scenes, after the cry of gold resounded over the world.

Gold Pans and Rockers

As gravity and the action of flowing water had

sorted and concentrated the gold particles in the placer deposits, so did miners employ the same agents in recovering their gold. The shovel and gold pan were the first tools used, and were the easiest to carry in testing and mining. With a 16 inch pan of gold-bearing gravel, the miner repeatedly dipped the pan into the water, while shaking and gently swirling its contents, which gradually washed the lighter pieces of sand and rock over the sides, leaving a string of gold particles in the corner of the pan. Heavy black sand, or magnetite, sometimes gathered in the pan and had to be carefully separated from the gold.

Soon it was found that a wooden box about three feet long with a metal sieve in the bottom, mounted on a rocker, would enable a man to work more ground. Later, longer boxes, called 'long Toms,' were made with cleats, or riffles, set in the bottom to catch the heavy particles of gold. As groups of men banded together to work larger areas or leaner ground, long boxes 12 inches wide and 10 inches deep were put end to end to form sluices of considerable length. Pay dirt was shoveled into the sluices, while running water disintegrated the dirt and collected the gold in the riffles, or upon the fibres of woolen blankets placed in the boxes. Finally, mercury was placed in the riffles, to catch by amalgamation the finer gold "dust" which formerly was lost.

Seemingly an act of Providence, when California sorely needed mercury, or quicksilver, in the production of gold, one of the few important mercury mines in the United States was discovered in 1845, 12 miles south of San Jose. For centuries, Indians had been using the bright red ore of mercury, cinnabar, as a pigment. A Mexican officer, Andreas Castillero, recognized the ore and named his mine the New Almaden, after the ancient Almaden mine in Spain. This rare deposit became vital to the amalgamation process used by the mines, and went on to yield mercury valued at over 80 million dollars.

During the discovery year, 1848, over $10,000,000 in gold was quickly scooped up from California's virgin hoard. The news of this free and easy wealth, basking in Sierra streams, was the siren call that propelled America westward, one of the most portentous events in the nation's history. More than half of the continent would be explored, settled and developed during the most amazing era of expansion ever known. All this was to come about, as a result of finding a treasure house of gold in California.

The Gold Rush of '49

After the 48ers came the hectic influx of 49ers, who were often called the Argonauts in memory of Jason and his seekers of the Golden Fleece. They, too, washed their gold over woolen fibers. In 1849, eager adventurers, young and old, including farmers, doctors, lawyers, merchants, soldiers and sailors followed three principal routes. Those who could afford the easier way took a ship around the Horn, a journey of 18,000 miles, requiring four to eight months. Some sailed to the Isthmus of Panama, followed jungle streams by muleback across the Isthmus to Panama City on the Pacific Coast, and then took ship again to California.

The rough, rutted, unbridged trails westward over the prairie and mountains carried the greatest numbers. The Oregon Trail, which branched southwestward at Soda Springs, Idaho, to form the California Trail was the most heavily traveled. It tested the mettle of the most resolute, but it was the least expensive. Westport, now Kansas City, was the starting place; there, wagon trains of prairie schooners were organized.

In one three week period, 18,000 wagons were floated across the muddy Missouri River at Westport. Thereafter, every creek and river had to be crossed on crude ferries or by floating the wagons. Despite the agonizing toil, desert rainstorms, prairie fires, choking dust, and Indian raids, lusty voices cheerfully filled the air with such refrains as "Oh Susannah" and plodded onward.

The historic trail can easily be followed today up the Platte River to a steep rim overlooking Ash Hollow, into which wagons were lowered on windlass ropes wound around a wheel hub. Then came memorable campsites such as Chimney Rock, Scotts Bluff, Fort Casper, and Independence Rock. By the time Devils Gate was reached, grave markers revealed the toll exacted by accidents and deadly cholera.

Hardships of The Pioneers

The long, gradual climb over historic South Pass, now in southern Wyoming, forced weary immigrants to discard stoves and treasured armchairs to lighten the load. At South Pass, a stone monument now stands where some wagons turned southwestward to Salt Lake City, and then continued on over the Old Spanish Trail to Los Angeles. Some parties met tragedy trying to take short cuts, as did the Bennett-Arcane families while crossing Death Valley.

Many parties kept to the Oregon Trail to Soda Springs or Fort Hall, now in Idaho, then branched southwestward along the small, thirsty rivulet called the Humboldt River. Where Lovelock, Nevada now stands, they reached the dread, never-to-be-forgotten, dried up Humboldt Sink. After enduring 1,500 miles of primitive trail, this 40 miles of glaring, blistering heat, smothering alkali dust, and waterless campgrounds was almost unbearable. Thousands of oxen and cattle perished along the Humboldt trail.

The cool, clear waters and green meadows of the Truckee River, near present Reno, Nevada, offered a campground of heavenly relief. Next came the back-breaking climb over the Sierras. One party, the Donners, misjudged winter's temper and suffered horrible deaths, trapped by deep snows in a pass that now bears their name.

For the more fortunate, Sutter's Fort, now the city of Sacramento, California, marked the welcome end of the long, arduous journey by trail. And for those who came by sea, the harbor entrance to San Francisco justly earned its name, the Golden Gate, for it was indeed ablaze with high hopes and the glitter of California's widely heralded gold.

By 1850, the influx of 48ers and 49ers, mostly Americans, had swelled the population of the gold fields to 100,000. In these two years, they gleaned enough gold to equal three times the amount the United States had paid Mexico for the entire Southwest. While Coronado sought in vain the Golden Cities of Cibola, there was gold in California's streams that far exceeded the Spaniard's dreams, free and open to all. It was this gold, and the enterprising band of American settlers who came to the gold fields, that induced the United States to admit California to the Union as a free state on September 9, 1850.

The Mother Lode

Experienced prospectors knew that the placer gold in the streams had been washed down from some unknown eroded veins in the mountains above, so they began searching for the mother source, the Mother Lode. Near Grass Valley, in 1850, George McKnight came upon a white quartz outcrop streaked with gold. It was so rich that men thought gold might lose its value. This was the first surface exposure of the Mother Lode, which would be found later in the rocks of the Sierra foothills over a distance of 120 miles from north to south. McKnight's discovery became the noted Empire-Star group of mines at

Grass Valley; over a period of 100 years it developed 200 miles of underground workings, and has produced over 120 millions in gold. The Empire shaft followed the lode downward into the earth over 11,000 feet on the incline.

Since the gold now occurred in a matrix of quartz, the rock had to be crushed. First used was the Mexican arrastra, a circular pit or tank containing a heavy, abrasive stone, which was dragged in a circle by a mule to grind the ore. Then came the more efficient stamp mill, consisting of a row of wooden or iron stems, or stamps, with iron bottoms, or shoes. The vertical motion of the stamps, hammering the ore in a mortar-like bedplate, ground the ore to a "pulp." Water, and mercury with its remarkable affinity for gold, mixed with the pulp, served to collect the gold by amalgamation. Gold was later recovered from the amalgam by vaporizing the mercury in iron retorts.

As the golden ribbon of the Mother Lode coursed southward, so did the gold seekers. At Plymouth and Amador City, the Bunker Hill and Keystone mines were discovered. At Sutter Creek, prospectors found the Central-Eureka, and the Lincoln or Union mine, from which Leland Stanford gathered the beginning of his financial empire. To the south, the Argonaut and Kennedy mines at Jackson became famous on the Mother Lode, reaching depths of over a mile. Angels Camp attained fame from its Utica mine, and particularly through Mark Twain's story of the Jumping Frog, which he is said to have first heard in an Angels Camp saloon.

The Riches of Carson Hill

This was also Bret Harte country. His story, "Mrs. Staggs' Husband," and his epic prank concerning the pliocene skull created considerable excitement and dismay among the anthropologists of those days. About mid-point along the Mother Lode is the now somnolent camp of Carson Hill, once the richest mine of all. Below the hill, Mexicans had been getting gold nuggets the size of melon seeds from the Stanislaus River; therefore the camp was named Melones. Later it was named 'Slumgullion,' believed to have been immortalized in Bret Harte's story, "Luck," as Roaring Camp. High above the river loomed a hill that no doubt was one of the sources of the golden melon seeds.

James H. Carson had prospected a ravine beneath the hill and recovered 200 ounces of gold in 10 days, but like some impatient souls he became overly-eager to find a more lucrative field afar, which if he had only known was on the hill above. Two years later a man named Hance climbed the hill and came upon a large, white quartz outcrop, the Mother Lode, bristling with gold. He was able to hack off a chunk of gold weighing 14 pounds. Hance was more than happy to sell his claim to Colonel Alfred Morgan for a minor interest in the future mine.

Soon thereafter, from a trench on the surface twelve feet long, six feet wide and nine feet deep, over $300,000 worth of gold was excavated. The Morgan Mine leaped into world prominence in 1851 when a single mass of gold and quartz was found deeper, shaped like a huge crab, weighing 195 pounds and then worth about $46,000. Carson Hill now bears a huge scar, or glory hole, on its northern side, marking the site of the famed Morgan Mine where over 26 million dollars worth of spectacularly rich gold ore was produced.

Fate's Way

Many of the colorful gold towns of the Mother Lode country have retained their aura of romantic times, thriving again with newly found activities, tourism and tall stories of the past. Sutter's Fort, with its ivy-covered walls, ranch house, workshops and defensive cannon, now stands completely restored near the heart of Sacramento. Here, Sutter ruled in baronial splendor a 50,000 acre Mexican grant, where he had hoped to build his "New Helvetia."

What happened to Captain Sutter, on whose American River property the gold discovery was made? He was pushed aside by the mad rush; men overran and destroyed his land; butchered his cattle, and ruined his dream of a colonial empire. Four years after the discovery he was bankrupt. In vain, for years he sought redress from Congress, while the state of California paid him $250 per month. In 1880, Sutter died brokenhearted in Washington, D.C., after Congress had adjourned without recognition of his long, hard-pressed claims.

As for James Marshall, he half-heartedly prospected other streams, always seeming to choose the wrong place. He became very bitter, and at the age of 74 he died in poverty. His only reward was a belated monument erected above his grave in 1890 on a hill overlooking the village of Coloma, the site of Sutter's sawmill. Marshall's tall, gaunt, bronze figure tops the monument; his outstretched hand points to the place where he electrified the world with his discovery of gold there below on the American River in 1848.

The Rush to Ballarat and Bendigo

Not only did California's gold discovery focus attention upon the Pacific Coast, it also brought Australia into the limelight. Among the 49ers who joined the rush to California was Edward H. Hargraves, an Australian squatter. After noticing that California's gold formations were similar to those he had seen in New South Wales, he returned to Australia and, on February 12, 1851, found placer gold in a tributary of the Macquarie River.

Within a year, thousands of gold seekers, or "fossickers" as they were called, were spreading out over Australia. A rush to Ballarat and Bendigo, west of Melbourne in Victoria, began after men found the rich placers and lodes of the region. In the year 1852, Victoria yielded $45,000,000 in gold, including the famed 200 pound nugget, "Welcome Stranger," worth then about $48,000.

As prospectors scurried over the land, north of Bathurst they found the spectacular Hill End district. Later, in 1872, one mass of quartz weighing 630 pounds yielded $60,000 in gold; in another find nearby, 10 tons of quartz contained 5½ tons of gold, valued at $2,600,000. Then came the noted Broken Hill district in western New South Wales, which yielded lead, silver, and zinc valued at over $800,000,000.

In Western Australia, the districts of Kalgoorlie, Coolgardie, Niagara, Norseman, Yilgarn, Meekatharra and many others leaped into prominence. In Queensland, such districts as Charters Towers, Gympie and Mount Morgan became producers of gold, silver, and copper. Thus, in the land "Down Under," the prospector's pick and shovel built the foundation for the settlement and development of a great land.

California's gold fields, indeed, had played a stimulating role in history. Its most significant effect was to stir all America with a spirit of enterprise and adventure that eventually would draw people from all walks of life into every state west of the Mississippi River. There, a host of prospectors would find the vast and prolific stores of metallic resources that ultimately would form the cornerstones for the prodigious economic growth and power of the United States.

Silver Bonanzas of the Comstock

Many parties traveling the Overland Trail to California, seeking surcease from the blistering Humboldt Sink, branched southward along the Carson River, and then paused to rest at a little spring and clump of cottonwood trees near the present hamlet of Dayton, a few miles east of Carson City, Nevada. Small amounts of gold had been found in a nearby stream, which the few workers named Gold Canyon. By 1851, prospectors had edged their way upstream toward a peak emigrants had named Sun Mountain. Buried at its feet, known to no one, was one of the world's richest silver bonanzas, the Comstock Lode, neatly concealed beneath 20 feet of over-burden, which had been washed down from Sun Mountain's slopes.

Although 50,000 people had passed the mouth of Gold Canyon, they had hurried on with only one desire, to get out of this burning wasteland and on to the golden streams and forested hills of California. The few who stayed cursed not only the barren hills, but they especially damned the "blue stuff" that clogged their gold pans and sluice boxes, for it had to be removed before clean gold could be won. But there were two intelligent and observant brothers, Hosea and Allen Grosch, possessing some knowledge of mining and assaying, who discovered that the "blue stuff" was a silver mineral, known as argentite. Before they could benefit from their discovery, Hosea injured himself while digging, and died of blood poisoning; in 1857, Allen perished of exposure while crossing the storm bound Sierras. Their secret died with them.

The Rainbow Chasers

The discovery of Sun Mountain's hoard would be left to a group of less educated prospectors who had chosen to gather a scant but convivial living in Gold Canyon while ensconced in a camp called Johntown, where kindly Eilley Orrum ran a cozy boarding house and served good food. One of this group was James Fennimore, a young, illiterate Virginian, who, because of his native origin and bibulous capacity for "tarantula juice," had earned the sobriquet of "old Virginny." Early in 1859 he found sparkling grains of gold on a red hill far up Gold Canyon. Virginny, and the John-towners who hurriedly joined him, began working the decomposed outcrop. But they failed to realize that they had touched the southern end of the great lode.

Meanwhile, two other Johntowners, Patrick McLaughlin and Peter O'Riley, were approaching Sun Mountain from the east, prospecting up Spanish Ravine. While deepening a spring at the mountain's base, the Irishmen encountered a heavy layer of blue dirt saturated with spangles of gold. As they prepared to stake their find, "old Pancake" Comstock rode up on a mangy mule, let out a whoop of astonishment, then calmly informed the prospectors that he had located the same ground the previous winter. Comstock had long posed as boss of the diggings, bragging, bully-ing, claiming to know the secrets of the Grosch brothers, of which he was totally ignorant. But he had managed to plaster the area with dubious, unworked claims, which he labelled with gusto, the "Comstock Diggins"—and the name stuck.

Rather than start a feud, the Irishmen made Comstock a partner in the discovery, the first to expose the barely hidden top of the great Com-stock Lode. Here at its northern end it later became the noted Ophir Mine, invoking the name of Solomon's famed mines of Ophir. Celebrating the rich find, while in a mellow mood, old Virginny led a party of friends one moonlight night over Sun Mountain's slopes. Sprinkling some whiskey upon the hillside Virginny solemnly exclaimed, "I baptize this place Virginia Town." It was to become known as Virginia City, one of the most renowned silver camps in the world.

The "Washoe Rush"

The city's fame, however, came only after a Grass Valley assayer found that the pesky "blue stuff" was a rich mineral of silver, combined with gold. His samples ran $3,876 in silver and $900 in gold per ton of ore. The Johntowners had been cursing and throwing away, as worthless, three-quarters of every shovel full. News of the assay spread quickly. Then came the first "Washoe Rush" which swelled in 1860 to 10,000 miners and camp followers.

By 1861, mines and mills were sprouting along the trend of the Comstock Lode, exposing its rich, long hidden treasure. By 1862, the first mining exchange in the United States opened at San Francisco, born of the public's desire to participate in quick and easy wealth. Shares of such mines as the Ophir, the Gould and Curry, the Gold Hill bonanzas, the Yellow Jacket, Kentuck, Crown Point and the Belcher, led the frenzy of stock transactions. In 1863 these mines produced $12,400,000 in silver and gold. In 1872, the yield increased to $135,000,000, as one bonanza after another was uncovered beneath Sun Mountain, which is now known as Mt. Davidson.

The Vicissitudes of Fortune

Compared to a treasure that eventually would produce over 400 million dollars in wealth, its original finders received very little. Boastful Henry Comstock accepted $11,000 for his share of the Ophir, which yielded $17,000,000. A few years later, half demented, he shot himself. Old Virginny, on a spree, died a pauper after a fatal fall from a balky mustang; McLaughlin sold out for $3,500 to young George Hearst, and ended up as a cook on a Montana ranch; O'Riley held on and received $40,000 for his share of the Ophir, but went broke speculating in stocks, and died in an asylum.

Sandy Bowers, a teamster, married Eilley Orrum the boarding house keeper, and by pooling their frontage on the lode they enjoyed a few dizzy years of bliss while reaping over $1,000,000. They built a grand mansion in Washoe Valley, wined and dined their friends in child-like generosity, traveled in Europe, tried in vain to present the Queen of England with a service set fashioned from Comstock silver, then went broke buying antiques during their European journey. Today, Sandy and Eilley lie peacefully side by side on the hillside that overlooks Washoe Valley and their dream castle.

Such were the vicissitudes of Fortuna, who smiled possibly without design upon these first believers in the rainbow. Terence said, "Fortune favors the brave," but Publius warned, "It is more easy to get a favor from Fortune than to keep it." Nevertheless, whether blind or not, Fate seems to have chosen this unquenchably optimistic and adventuresome breed of men, armed with the capability of withstanding hardships and disappointments, to turn the latch-key on many great storehouses of treasure. The men who came later, to exploit, develop, and reap the greater rewards, were of a different class on the Comstock and elsewhere.

Silver Kings of The Comstock

Taking the place of the pioneer discoverers came such men as Flood, Fair, Mackay, O'Brien, Hearst, Sutro, Sharon, and Ralston whose names would highlight the saga of the Comstock, and be echoed in the unfolding of the west. Exploiting the full potential of an important mineral deposit was far different from exposing its outcrop to the light of day. Expensive deep mining methods on the Comstock, and new metallurgical techniques for extracting the silver and gold from the complex sulphide ore, were challenges to be met.

Many of the builders of the free enterprise system, the inventors and the creators of industry, like the mining entrepreneurs of the Comstock, rose from obscurity. John W. Mackay, ultimately founder of the Postal Telegraph Company, was an Irish immigrant boy who, in 1851, at the age of 20, first worked the gold streams of Downieville, California, and then joined the 1859 rush to the "Ophir diggins." Rising from laborer to mine superintendent he shrewdly accepted some of his wages in stock, and acquired an interest in such mines as the Bullion and Kentuck. A bonanza found in the Kentuck provided Mackay with the seed of his fortune.

Young James G. Fair heard the call to Ophir in 1865, where his alertness and experience also earned him a position as superintendent. In 1867 Fair interested Mackay in the undeveloped Hale & Norcross Mine. Together they enlisted the aid of their friends, James C. Flood and William S. O'Brien, saloon proprietors of San Francisco, in acquiring stock and control of the property. Their partnership, purely a verbal agreement, was called "The Firm." Fair and Mackay ran the mines, while Flood and O'Brien handled the stock transactions in San Francisco. When their Hale & Norcross encountered ore, The Firm made its first million dollars, which enabled them to acquire control of the Best & Belcher and the Consolidated Virginia.

Borrowing $1,000 and selling a small gold property in California, George Hearst had raised enough to pay Pat McLoughlin $3,500 for his Ophir interest. Within a few years the mine yielded ore valued at $7,000,000. With his Ophir profits, George Hearst invested further in the Gould & Curry which paid $4,000,000 in dividends from 1862 to 1864, making Hearst and his associates the first of the Comstock millionaires. This marked the beginning of the vast Hearst fortune.

The 'Big Bonanza'

The first six bonanzas of the Comstock had been found near the surface, and by 1870 seemed close to being exhausted. Gloom descended upon the Comstock. Then the Crown Point, managed by John P. Jones, who endured much ridicule for deepening his mine, found a bonanza 1,000 feet beneath the surface, hidden like a raisin in a cake. The finding of deeper ore at the Crown Point, induced Mackay and Fair to explore a 1,300 foot section of the Lode that had been generally considered unfavorable. Their expertly directed explorations gradually revealed one of the richest single bodies of silver and gold ore ever found.

Dan DeQuille, noted editor of the Virginia City Enterprise, aptly named the discovery the Big Bonanza, described in his fascinating book called 'The Big Bonanza.' Said DeQuille, "Walls were a solid mass of black sulphuret (argentite) ore flecked with native silver, while the roof was filled with stephanite, or silver, in the form of glistening crystals." The Big Bonanza, famed around the world, was an incredible mass of rich ore, a $160,000,000 plumb in the Comstock pudding. It paid $78,000,000 in profits, making Mackay, Fair, Flood and O'Brien known everywhere as the Bonanza Kings.

Virginia City became a thriving mecca of 25,000 people, including several millionaires. In the luxurious six story International Hotel, attracted to the glamorous silver center, one might see such actors as Edwin Booth, Otis Skinner, Lotta Crabtree, and Lola Montez, and such national figures as President Grant and the noted mining engineers, Clarence King and John Hays Hammond. Also there were such men as Adolph Sutro, the audacious tunnel builder, William Stewart, Comstock lawyer and U.S. Senator, and of course, Mark Twain, who began his colorful career on the staff of the Territorial Enterprise.

Technology on The Comstock

The great Comstock Lode, while producing over $400,000,000 in silver and gold, became the training ground and research center which established methods for exploiting the mineral wealth that was later discovered throughout the West. In 1860, Philipp Deidesheimer, a young German engineer, devised a system of timbers set in multiple square sets to support the walls of the huge stopes, or caverns, of the Ophir Mine. The square set system later became standard practice in other mines of the West.

The treatment of silver ores was little known in the West prior to the opening of the Comstock. The first ores were milled in arrastras, and then by the old Mexican patio process. But the big bonanzas required more efficient methods. Numerous stamp mills were erected to crush the ore, which was then treated by the new Washoe process. Water, mercury and a little copper sulphate and salt were added to the pulp in the stamp pan, thus expediting amalgamation of the silver and gold. In six hours this method accomplished as much as did the Mexican patio process in four weeks. The art of mining and treating much of America's mineral resources, thus was further improved on the Comstock Lode.

Metals of Destiny

The silver of the Comstock and the gold of California played important roles in the destiny of the United States. San Francisco became a booming gateway to riches and the financial, industrial and cultural center of the West. But the greatest influence of this wealth was exerted upon the outcome of the Civil War. California was admitted to the Union as a free state in 1850; Nevada became a territory in 1861, and a state in 1864. Both states had been settled mainly by Northeasterners; therefore they were supporters of the Union during the Civil War.

Over $180,000,000 in gold and silver from California and Nevada went to the North during the years 1861 to 1864, protecting the North's international credit and providing monetary aid in carrying on the war. If these resources had not been available to the North, or had been utilized by the Confederacy, the United States might not exist as such today. As the silver of Laurium once saved the Greeks and their classical civilization, so did the silver of the Comstock and the gold of California help preserve the unity of the United States of America.

Chapter 12

DAWN OF THE GOLDEN WEST

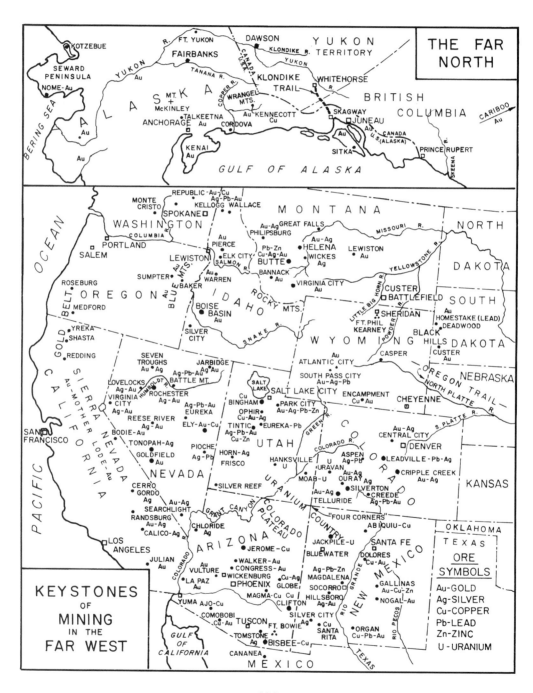

THE FAR NORTH

KEYSTONES
OF
MINING
IN THE
FAR WEST

ORE
SYMBOLS

Au-GOLD
Ag-SILVER
Cu-COPPER
Pb-LEAD
Zn-ZINC
U-URANIUM

The discoveries of California's gold and Nevada's silver were the trumpet calls that aroused the same pioneer spirit which earlier generations of Americans had shown when they explored and settled the region between the Allegheny Mountains and the Mississippi River. With the ring of gold and silver echoing across the land, the whole nation dreamed of prodigious riches hidden in the little known Far West. Now, every corner of this unexplored wilderness would be combed by prospectors plodding afoot behind their burros, ranging from hot, sandy deserts to cool, forested mountains. These men would be the first to witness the dawning of the Golden West.

They would unearth stores of mineral wealth that would transform American Territories into States of the Union, having, as their capitals, cities that once were primitive campsites. Farmers and merchants would come to settle and develop the land, and soon the West would bloom and incubate a treasure of lusty folklore that would fascinate the world. Inasmuch as their deeds are recent history, unobscured by time as are the events of antiquity, henceforth we shall witness the individual experiences and vicissitudes of fortune that actually created the legendary west.

Colorado's First Camps

Pike's Peak had guided the explorer Zebulon Pike in 1806 and again became the beacon for the argonauts of the 1850's. In 1858, some Kansans found a little gold on Cherry Creek and named their settlement Denver, in honor of the Kansas Territorial governor. The news caused thousands of gold seekers, in Conestoga wagons emblazoned with "Pike's Peak or Bust," to rush westward on the rutted trail. Within six months one-third of the wagons were homeward bound. Scrawled across the pledge were the words, "Busted, by gosh."

Tom Golden was one of the few who kept on searching. On Clear Creek, 15 miles west of Denver, where Golden and the Colorado School of Mines now stands, Tom made a rich strike. Then in January, 1859, George Jackson and an Indian named Black Hawk found gold a few miles farther upstream, which became the camps of Jackson Bar, Idaho Springs, and Black Hawk. The following May, John Gregory made his great strike which became famous as Central City. Horace Greeley, who visited the diggings, reported that 4,000 men were crowded into Gregory Gulch living in tents or under pine boughs, with 500 more arriving daily. The rosy, exciting picture painted by Greeley, editor of the New York Tribune, left no doubt as to the virgin wealth of the Rockies.

Robust new camps appeared in widening circles, named Tarryall, Hamilton, Buckskin Joe, Fairplay, and Breckenridge in the western Rockies. At the entrance to Ute Pass, a town named El Dorado sprang up, later called Colorado City, now known as Colorado Springs. These were lands once officially set aside for the Utes, Arapahoe, and Cheyenne Indians, but "Manifest Destiny" was now on the march.

As each new digging became overcrowded, the late-coming "59er's" left Colorado City, followed Ute Pass leading into South Park and the hinterland and searched along the upper Arkansas River, until at 10,000 feet they reached a valley overlooked by snowy Mt. Elbert, Colorado's loftiest peak, and Mt. Massive, both over 14,400 feet high. Then it was a still and lonesome valley; today it is the famed city of Leadville.

Riches in The Rockies

In April, 1860, Abe Lee was the first to fire a pistol, telling his companions that a gleaming string of gold grains taken from a hole dug beneath the snow lined his pan. The ravine was named "California Gulch," anticipating another California Eldorado. Among the first in the rush that followed was H. A. W. Tabor and his wife, Augusta; it was a rare sight to see a lady in such surroundings. By midsummer, the Tabors had erected a log building and were operating a store and post office, while 10,000 miners swarmed over the hills and plastered every foot of the creek bed with their claims. The maze of tents and log huts was named Oro City.

By 1870, after giving up $5,000,000 in gold, Oro City and California Gulch became practically deserted. All during those placer days, the miners cursed the heavy, black and rusty mineral that clogged their pans and sluices, as had the early Comstockers, unaware of the real treasure hidden in the rock beneath the gulch. It was Alvinus B. Wood of Ann Arbor, Michigan, having some knowledge of geology and metallurgy, and his partner William Stevens, an experienced miner, who traced some float, or pieces of rock, to an outcrop. After being assayed it was found that the dirty brown material was carbonate of lead containing 20 to 40 ounces of silver per ton.

Fortunes of Fryer Hill

"Carbonate" mining swept over the hill from California Gulch to the area above present Leadville. Iron Hill, Carbonate Hill and Fryer Hill became studded with the headframes of such mines as the Carbonate, Morning Star, Shamrock, Big Chief, the A. Y. and Minnie Lee and many others. Both Fryer Hill and H. A. W. Tabor leaped into the limelight in May, 1878. Two lazy prospectors named Rische and Hook, after wheedling a grub-stake from Tabor, chose a shady but unpromising place to dig on Fryer Hill. Barely below the surface, their picks dug into a fabulous silver-lead deposit that became the Little Pittsburg Mine.

Six months later Hook sold out to Rische and Tabor for $98,000, and a year later Rische sold his interest to J. B. Chaffee and David H. Moffat for $293,000. In September, 1879, Tabor sold his share to Chaffee and Moffat for $1,000,000. The grubstake had cost Tabor $34. Soon thereafter, a wily character named "Chicken Bill," adept in "salting" mines (a method used to enrich barren

walls by impregnating them with grains of high grade mineral) sought Tabor as his next victim. Flush with his first million, Tabor bought the chrysolite claim on Fryer Hill for a small but unknown sum. At the shallow depth of 20 feet, miners struck an ore body from which Tabor soon extracted $1,500,000. A year later, Tabor sold the property to a New York company for an additional $1,500,000.

Midas of Leadville

Higher on the hill was the Matchless Mine. Warmed by Lady Luck's favors and desiring a mine of his own, Tabor paid $117,000 to three promoters who gladly sold the Matchless since it showed little sign of value. Experts dubbed this venture, "Tabor's mistake." In September, 1880, as the Matchless workings were being deepened, fortune smiled again; the miners uncovered carbonate ore and the Matchless became the richest mine on the hill. Tabor's wealth began to increase by $80,000 to $100,000 net profit per month. Within a few years, at the age of 47, H. A. W. Tabor had amassed a fortune of $9,000,000—an impressive figure in those days.

In 1873 Tabor was elected Lieutenant Governor of Colorado, and later, for a brief period, served as senator. He generously shared his wealth, built opera houses in Leadville and Denver and erected an imposing mansion. Due to lavish living and bad investments on a wide scale, Tabor lost both his wife, Augusta, and his fortune. In 1883 he married a Mrs. Doe, known as Baby Doe, and by 1895 he was destitute. A few years later Tabor died, admonishing his wife to "hang on to the Matchless."

For 36 years, reduced to extreme poverty, Baby Doe lived in a small tool shack close by the long silent Matchless shaft, steadfastly fulfilling her trust. There she was found one winter day by concerned neighbors, huddled beneath a pile of old newspapers, dead. But her lonely vigil had been in vain; the exhausted Matchless is now only a forlorn historic site, partially restored by Leadville citizens, a testimonial to sudden success and folly on America's raw western frontier.

Beneficent Wealth

Far different is the saga of the Guggenheims. Among the capitalists who awoke early to the possibilities of Leadville was shrewd and inquisitive Meyer Guggenheim. Originally a poor immigrant from Switzerland in 1864, Meyer saved the money he had made as a tailor and dealer in laces in Philadelphia. In 1884 he acquired an interest in the A. Y. and Minnie Lee mines in Leadville as a result of a $5,000 loan he had made to the mine owners.

Investigation led Meyer to feel that smelting ores already mined was the better part of the industry; therefore, with his son, Benjamin, he built a smelter at Pueblo to treat the ores of Leadville and other districts. Thereafter, with his seven sons, Meyer Guggenheim & Sons Corporation built or acquired one smelter after another in Mexico, Idaho, Montana, Utah, Kansas and other states. Later, they gained control of the huge American Smelting and Refining Company.

With Daniel, the eldest son, and Isaac, Murray, Solomon, Benjamin, Simon and William, the Guggenheims extended their interests to include gold mines in Alaska, tin mines in Bolivia, nitrate deposits in Chile and rubber plantations in Africa. Then came their notable philanthropic foundations, schools and fellowships, to promote "the well-being of mankind." The carbonate stones of Leadville's Minnie Lee mines, indeed, were a blessing to humanity when they nurtured the enterprising and benevolent Guggenheim dynasty. Many more philanthropies would stem from earth's bountiful wealth.

Miners Pioneer Self-Government

Following Leadville's boom, as rumors of other rich discoveries reverberated through the Rockies, wild rushes occurred in many places. In 1873, the high and remote San Juan region, which had been assigned by treaty five years earlier to the Ute Indians, was thrown open to prospecting and settlement. Rich gold and silver strikes were soon made at Silverton and nearby Cunningham Gulch and Eureka. A few miles to the west, over the snow-crested Continental Divide, gold in the unusual form of telluride compounds was found in the Smuggler, Liberty Bell and Tomboy mines. The district went on to produce $120,000,000 in gold; and the city of Telluride, sitting in a verdant bowl-shaped valley beneath the towering peaks of the Divide, made its mark in mining history.

As pioneers grew anxious for self-government, in 1859 the Miners' and People's Courts were established first at Gregory Gulch, which became the pattern for government in other districts. Thus, throughout the wild, and as yet untamed west, it was the miner who first introduced the principles of law and democracy to the land.

By 1861, less than 25,000 people were scattered across this western part of the Kansas Territory, but as a result of their demands the new Territory of Colorado came into being. Stimulated by the influx of settlers and the booming gold and silver districts of Black Hawk, Gergory Gulch, Leadville, Silverton, and Telluride, the population increased greatly, numbering 200,000. Colorado was coming of age; on August 1, 1876, 100 years after the Declaration of Independence, the territory was admitted to the Union as the 38th State. Its constitution still reflects the ideals of the state's founders, the Miners' and People's Courts.

The Persistent Prospector

After becoming a state, Colorado continued to astonish the world with new finds of mineral wealth. There were many, but the most renowned was Cripple Creek, located on a 10,500 foot high plateau along the southern shoulder of Pike's Peak, about 40 miles west of Colorado Springs. The place apparently received its name from the small creek that meandered across the plateau, in which cows were often caught in the mire and crippled. There in the cow pasture, a fun-loving, part-time cowboy and prospector named Bob Womack unceasingly searched for gold. But Bob's perennial sprees and rambling boasts, together with the region's bad reputation, earned by several salted mine hoaxes, elicited only scorn and ridicule from local miners.

In 1890, Bob's pick and shovel uncovered a vein of unusual gray-purplish material. When he had it assayed in Colorado Springs everyone was amazed; it ran $200 per ton in gold. This ore, too, contained the rather rare telluride compounds of gold, calaverite, and sylvanite. Expert mining men now hurried to the cow pasture, with Bob jubilantly in the lead. When the experts confirmed the strike, prospectors streamed into Cripple Creek, staking claims and tearing up the hills and vales, as Bob Womack looked upon the scene overjoyed at the vindications of his prophesies. Bob already had staked his claim, the El Paso.

The Golden Volcano

It was then that the nature and shape of the ore occurrence came to light. A thin covering of grassy soil concealed the core of an eroded, multi-million year old Tertiary volcano which occupied the three mile wide area of the Cripple

Creek plateau. Eons ago the crater collapsed, allowing gold bearing solutions to rise later toward the surface along crevices in the broken breccia, and along the contact of the volcano's walls with the adjoining Pike's Peak granite. Veins and irregular bodies of ore were thus formed, to be found later outcropping on the plateau.

Men were first puzzled by the absence of discernable free gold in the rock. It should be borne in mind that in most commercial grades of ore, gold is so finely divided as to be invisible to the eye. Because of its scarcity gold is valued by the ounce ($35). A few ounces of gold sprinkled through a ton of rock makes fairly good gold ore. By comparison, in an ore of copper, the metal is much more evident and abundant, and valued by the pound. A copper ore would have to contain many pounds of copper to equal the value of a one-ounce-per-ton gold ore. At Cripple Creek the presence of gold was masked by not only its fineness, but also by its unusual composition in the form of tellurides.

Unlike the unmistakable yellowish gleam of native gold, the telluride minerals are silvery-yellow to brassy in color, and might be mistaken for pyrite, or "fool's gold." However, calaverite's platy, lath-shaped crystals distinguish it from the cube-shaped crystals of pyrite. But Ed de La Vergne and the other experts who inspected Bob Womack's cow pasture, recognized the tellurides and the possibilities of the district.

The Educated Prospector

It was Winfield Scott Stratton, a carpenter turned prospector, who made the discovery that put Cripple Creek in the world spotlight. For 17 long, discouraging years Stratton had roamed among the Colorado Rockies, of which 51 peaks are over 14,000 feet high. Tired of failure, at the age of 43 he decided to learn the elements of geology, mineralogy and metallurgy; he went to the School of Mines at Golden which had opened in 1874. There, he learned to test ores with a blow-pipe whose high temperature flame, when applied to a piece of telluride ore, will produce droplets of pure gold.

Armed with better methods of prospecting Stratton returned to Cripple Creek in 1891, milled about the diggings with other prospectors and finally selected a rust-stained outcrop on Battle Mountain where the present town of Victory now stands. He had chosen a favorable place, the contact of the volcano walls and adjoining granite, where mineralizing solutions

had circulated. He took samples of the outcrop and had them assayed in Colorado Springs. They ran $380 per ton in gold, a very rich ore. Stratton's fortunes now became as good as they had been notoriously bad.

From 1891 to 1898, the Independence netted Stratton $2,400,000, making him Cripple Creek's first millionaire. When a rich vein was found adjoining the Independence on an overlooked claim fraction named the Portland, Stratton arranged to consolidate the two mines. In 1899, he sold his interests to an English company for $10,000,000, after which the Independence and Portland mines went on to yield an additional $90,000,000 in gold.

The Lessons of Cripple Creek

During boom times such mines as the Elkton, Ajax, Gold Coin, Strong, Golden Cycle, Vindicator, and Mary MacKinney made millionaires of former doctors, lawyers, and merchants, whose ornate homes in Colorado Springs graced "millionaires row." The most spectacular find was the "Cresson Vug" in the Cresson mine, a cavern 40 feet high and 20 feet wide, lined with sparkling crystals of calaverite and sylvanite. 1,400 sacks of crystals, scraped from the walls, sold for $375,000. In four weeks the cavern yielded gold worth $1,200,000. The mine's total output came to over $50,000,000.

Fate's method of dealing the cards of fortune are unfathomable. Behind pure luck often stands dogged persistence. Most of the discoveries of metallic wealth have resulted from good judgement and the application of science. Stratton stands as a testimonial to the sagacious, well-informed prospector. After his success, this once obscure carpenter, shy and touchy, lived in Colorado Springs and busied himself with philanthropies: for example the Myron Stratton Home, named after his father, for poor and dependent children, and for the aged. On the campus of the Colorado School of mines now stands Stratton Hall, his contribution to science.

As for Bob Womack, despite his glowing prophesies, Bob sold his interest in the El Paso, the discovery claim, for $5,000 and quickly dissipated the sum. His greatest pride came from being pointed out as the district's discoverer, as he strolled along the bustling streets of Cripple Creek. He had seen the city grow to a population of 30,000, numbering among its inhabitants many nationally prominent figures. Ultimately, his old cow pasture would yield gold exceeding 400 million dollars in value, and become known as one of the great gold districts of the world.

Pay Dirt in Montana

America's ageless mineral deposits, unknown and untouched through all the pageantry of Old World civilizations, at last were being revealed one after another. Again, as throughout history, it was the indefatigable prospector who made the initial discoveries. John White and William Eads made the first notable gold strike in Montana on the Beaverhead River in July 1862, as gold fever spread to the Northwest. A tent-shack town named Bannack, after the local Indian tribe, was soon swarming with miners and producing $4,000,000 in placer gold. In May 1864, influenced by Bannack's boom, Congress created the Territory of Montana, and President Lincoln named Sydney Edgerton its governor. Bannack became the territorial capital.

In the spring of 1863, Bill Fairweather, Henry Edgar and six young companions, after fighting off the Crow Indians, found a little stream farther east lined with alders and well laden with gold. The news spread swiftly; within 90 days there were 10,000 miners jammed into the gulch over a distance of 10 miles, reveling in a rich harvest of gold. $10,000,000 was recovered that first year. By 1868, over $30,000,000 in gold had been sluiced from the gravels of Alder Gulch, and Virginia City, Montana became a rich, wild, and wicked town of 15,000 inhabitants.

Coarse gold, nuggets, flakes, and dust from miner's pokes were scattered freely over the bars and gambling tables. Stage coaches and traveling miners were waylaid with startling regularity by a gang organized by none other than the respected sheriff of Bannack, Henry Plummer. The West's first group of Vigilantes was formed, and finally Plummer's vicious record of 102 murders was disclosed. Plummer and his henchmen were promptly hanged on Boothill at the edge of town, ending the road agent's rule of the district. Such was justice then on the frontier.

Last Chance Gulch

In 1864, prospectors hurrying to Alder Gulch stopped and found some placer gold in a little creek which they called their "last chance." The creekside trail along Last Chance Gulch, over which mule and ox teams brought supplies to their tent town, today is the Main Street of Helena, Montana. Gold placers and lodes were found in every direction about Helena, in the Scratchgravel Hills, in Confederate Gulch; and at Montana Bar miners recovered as much as $1,000 per pan. Up to 1876, the gold that came from placers alone amounted to $150,000,000 in value.

Lode mining was carried on in districts not far from Helena, such as Elkhorn, Philipsburg, Rimini, and Marysville, adding more millions to Montana's golden riches. Because of this wealth and resulting expansion of activity, Helena was made the territorial capital of Montana in 1875. Meanwhile, a mountain honeycombed with silver, gold, and copper had been found some 65 miles south of Helena, which would become known as "the richest hill on earth." Under the beneficent influence of these vast resources, Montana was taken into the Union, as the 41st State, in 1889.

'The Richest Hill on Earth'

Of the discoveries in Montana one was to overshadow all others, although its immensity would be revealed slowly. Gold was discovered on Silver Bow Creek in 1864, and the camp flourished until it had produced about $1,500,000. By 1867 the placers had petered out and the district was nearly abandoned. William L. Farlin then began to prospect the rock outcrops above the creek, sending his ore by ox team, by river, and by rail to New Jersey. The freighting cost proved prohibitive, so he sent the next shipment to Utah. His faith and persistence were rewarded with the news that the ore was worth $400 per ton, not in gold, but in silver.

When the word spread that the black quartz outcrops of Butte, as the camp then came to be called, were rich in silver, the old gold camp entered a silver boom. From every direction came eager claim stakers to swarm over the mountain side. Up to the end of the Seventies, the boom cycle in Butte had gone from gold to one of the famed silver camps of the world. The excitement brought new faces to Butte; among them were two young men known as W. A. Clark and Marcus Daly, who would stage a bitter dramatic feud for control of Butte's billions in mineral treasure.

Feud of The Copper Kings

Thirty-three year old Clark came to Butte in 1872, having already made his first stake at Alder Gulch. He was shrewd, cautious, and supremely ambitious. After carefully inspecting Butte, he armed himself with a knowledge of geology and mineralogy by attending the Columbia School of Mines in New York City. Returning to Butte in 1873 he examined the ores exposed in the few shallow shafts, and soon had acquired options from several hard pressed mine owners. The booming camp's silver output was already rivaling the Comstock Lode.

In 1876, the Walker Brothers, leading bankers of Salt Lake City, sent 35 year old Marcus Daly to investigate the rising activity at Butte, and especially to examine the Alice mine. Daly was the very antithesis of Clark. Emigrating from Ireland at 15, Daly had landed in America with nothing but his "Irish smile," but his alertness and the experience he had gained in the silver mines and mills of the Comstock had won the confidence of the Walker Brothers. Snatching the Alice from under Clark's nose, Daly bought the mine atop Butte hill for the Walkers and retained an interest for himself.

While Daly was making the Alice a successful silver producer he was inspecting other mines to which his friendly ways gained him easy access. His 15 years of practical mining experience and discriminating analysis of geological conditions, had made him more than an equal to Clark in discerning the camp's potentialities. After working the Alice to a depth of 200 feet, and seeing further evidence in other mines, Daly became inspired with the vision that Butte's veins in depth would turn from silver to rich copper. One of the mines that particularly excited him was the Anaconda—a name to become world famous. The mine was owned by Michael Hickey, a former Union soldier, who had never forgotten Horace Greeley's editorial declaration that McClellan's Army would surround Lee's forces "like a giant anaconda," the powerful reptile of the South American tropics. The word now symbolizes the producer of vast mineral wealth.

Daly urged the Walkers to buy the Anaconda, but the experts who were sent advised unwisely against the purchase. Daly then sold his interest in the Alice for $30,000 and bought control of the Anaconda and the Neversweat mine nearby. Lacking sufficient capital to adequately develop the Anaconda, Daly quickly found three men familiar with his ability, who provided ample funds. They were J. B. Haggin, Lloyd Tevis and George Hearst.

Birth of The Anaconda

Daly was right. At a depth of 300 feet, silver values in the Anaconda declined. As men of lesser vision grew panicky, Daly shrewdly closed down the Anaconda and acquired more mines at bargain prices. He then reopened the mine, sank a new shaft and upon the 300 foot level discovered a five foot vein of solid chalcocite, a rich copper ore. Thus Butte entered its third boom, from gold, to silver, to copper, and Marcus Daly became head of one of the world's most powerful copper producers.

Meantime, W. A. Clark had acquired a number of rich silver mines. He had an insatiable desire to accumulate a vast fortune, but preferred to dominate the custom smelting field, as well as banking, railroads and newspapers. He published the 'Butte Miner,' while his rival controlled the 'Anaconda Standard.' Clark's consuming desire was to become politically powerful. Amid charges of bribery and unstinted violence, Clark was elected United States senator, only to lose the position after an investigation labelled the election fraudulent. Elected again, Clark was able to walk down the senate aisle, vindicated. Both Clark and Daly spent huge sums in this relentless war of the Copper Kings.

Clark aspired to become a financial giant and did so. No one ever questioned the wise and honest management of his empire's resources. He went on to acquire the sole ownership of other rich properties, and became noted for his philanthropies and donations to art museums and universities. William Andrews Clark was both a product and shaper of the great western frontier, a pioneer prospector, miner, banker, railroad builder, and national benefactor.

Marcus Daly's dream was to induce nature to yield the colossal treasure buried within the mountain overlooking Butte. It was Daly who created the mighty, world-wide enterprise that is today the Anaconda Mining Company; it was Daly who brought to light "The Richest Hill on Earth," producer of over three billions of dollars in mineral wealth. Such were the metallic resources that were found and developed by bold and resourceful men during the dawn of the fabulous Golden West.

Mormon Country

In 1847, when Brigham Young, leader of the Mormons, stood at the mouth of Emigrant Canyon and looked out over an untrod sagebrush desert to the lifeless Great Salt Lake, he said, "This is the Place." Then came the hardiest, most determined group of pioneers ever to cross the country, many of whom pushed handcarts over 1,400 miles of plains and mountains. Seeking a place to worship in their own way, they chose this utterly forsaken land, believing they would be free of intrusion. But unknowingly, they had taken up a station directly in the path of empire. By 1849, feverish followers of the Gold Rush were descending upon the newly born settlement of Salt Lake City, on their way to California.

Desiring agricultural self-sufficiency and geographical isolation, Young forbade prospecting for precious metals in their Provisional State of Deseret. The search for coal and iron, and lead for bullets, was encouraged; but "gold," said Young, "is for paving the streets of hell." Despite Mormon restrictions, many prolific deposits of mineral riches would be discovered in years to come. Later, in 1850, Deseret became the Territory of Utah.

Bingham Canyon

An inkling of Utah's resources was first revealed in 1862. Colonel Patrick E. Connor, violently anti-Mormon, actively encouraged his soldiers to prospect for metals. Thomas Bingham, while running cattle, found pieces of ore in a canyon a few miles south of Salt Lake City. The place was named Bingham Canyon, but the first notable discovery there was made by an apostate Mormon, George Ogelvie, who took his samples to Connor. The ore was rich in lead, silver, and gold. In 1863, the discovery was named the West Jordan, the first mining claim staked in Utah.

It was the discovery of gold placers in 1864, by a party of miners returning from Montana, that began Bingham Canyon's prolific career. By 1870, $2,000,000 in gold had been gleaned from the creek, and the town called Bingham Canyon started to thrive, squeezed into the bottom of a steep V-shaped ravine which was barely wide enough for a narrow, twisting roadway. In the hillsides above the placers, veins carrying rich silver-lead ores were discovered in 1873, and such mines as the Jordan, Galena, Yosemite, Brooklyn, and Highland Boy began production.

Originally started as a gold and silver mine of dubious value, the Highland Boy, promoted by Samuel Newhouse and managed by Thomas Weir, suddenly encountered rich sulphide ore assaying 15 percent copper, and made its first shipment in 1896. This introduced copper as an important new source of wealth in Bingham Canyon and led to the thriving Highland Boy and other claims

being acquired by the Utah Consolidated Mining Company in 1899, controlled by the Standard Oil Company of New York and John D. Rockefeller.

A Mountain of Copper

Bingham Canyon won its greatest claim to fame after an observant miner found that a whole mountain in the upper reaches of the canyon was a colossal body of low grade copper ore. In 1887, Enos A. Wall, a highly regarded and experienced miner, came to Bingham Canyon and was attracted to the reddish coloration, marked with streaks of blue and green, on the hill above the road. Wall examined the ground and found that the mountainside was minutely but uniformly impregnated with copper minerals. An opening, or adit, 90 feet long had been driven into the hill; but, because the rock assayed only 2.4 percent copper (48 pounds per ton of rock), too poor in those days for exploitation, the property had been abandoned.

Wall quietly acquired 200 acres on the copper-laden mountain and spent $20,000 in exploratory work. Wiseacres ridiculed Wall's attempts to develop such a low-grade property, but Wall was not a promoter, instead he was a serious miner imbued with the dream of inventing a process for extracting the enormous supply of low-grade copper commercially. After Wall had endured many discouragements, an old friend, Captain Joseph De Lemar finally paid $375,000 toward development of the property.

Mining's Technological Revolution

Lemar brought two young mining engineers, Robert C. Gemmel and Daniel C. Jackling, to sample the property and test the ore. Their report was to change the methods and history of mining all over the world. Jackling proposed an unheard of system of large-scale surface mining in open pits, where huge mechanical shovels could be used to load trains of ore cars which would take the ore to be ground and milled in immense tonnages. He reported the presence of 12,385 tons of 2 percent proven ore and 25,000,000 tons of probable ore, until then an unheard of figure.

With the assistance of Spencer Penrose and the Guggenheims, the Utah Copper Company was formed in 1903, and the erection of a mill and smelter began. Wall received $385,000 for 55 percent of his stock, became a director of the company, and lived to see a ten year period in which the mine yielded 67,000,000 tons of 1.4% copper ore.

By the end of 1929, exploratory drilling had increased the ore reserves from the original 12,000 tons to the incredible total of 640,000,000 tons. By 1930 the giant Utah Copper Company had mined ores of copper, gold, and silver valued at $839,700,000, and had paid $200,000,000 in dividends and $60,000,000 in taxes. The property is now a division of the Kennecott Copper Corporation, and will soon have produced two billion dollars worth of metals. Wall's former mountain is now an enormous hole, one of the largest open pit mines in the world. With the development of these ingenious methods to mine and mill huge low-grade ore bodies, a momentous new era dawned in man's attempts to win from the earth its long stored treasures of metals.

Great open pits throughout the world began yielding ores that formerly had no commercial value. Those in the United States included mines at Santa Rita, New Mexico; Miami and Morenci, Arizona; and Ely and Weed Heights, Nevada. The latter was named after the Anaconda Copper Company's eminent president, Dr. Clyde E. Weed, a graduate of the Michigan College of Mines (now the Michigan Technological University.)

Utah's Mineral Wealth

Elsewhere in Utah, prospectors found important districts other than Bingham Canyon. In 1869, Colonel Connor's soldier-prospectors discovered rich silver-lead ores in the Park City district, 22 miles southeast of Salt Lake City. Since 1870, $390,000,000 in silver, lead and zinc have been produced in such mines as the Silver King Coalition and Park Utah Consolidated. George Hearst, who seldom missed a mining boom, also held interests in the Park City district.

Sixty miles south of Salt Lake City, prospectors discovered the Tintic district, named after a Ute chieftain whose favorite campsite was later occupied by the Centennial-Eureka mine, which produced $15,000,000 in silver, lead, and gold. A single carload of ore from this mine netted close to $200,000. Beautiful specimens of its ores were displayed at the Vienna Exposition in 1873. The district eventually produced silver, gold, lead, zinc, and copper valued at over $380,000,000.

Hundreds of other districts contributed to Utah's growing wealth: the mines of Ophir, where Marcus Daly and W. A. Clark won early fortunes, Alta, Mercur and the famed Horn Silver mine at Frisco, between Beaver and Milford. There, silver chloride resembling in texture and color the horn of an animal was so soft and rich it could be whittled with a knife. From Utah's innumerable mines, came a multi-billion dollar treasure, in a land which the Mormons had hoped would be limited to the peaceful development of agriculture.

From Gold Pan to Statehood

"There is a tide in the affairs of men ... which, when taken at the flood, leads on to fortune" wrote Shakespeare. Such a floodtide did occur in America in the years 1848 to 1890; it marked an auspicious turning point for a country less than a century old, barely an infant among nations. Gold and silver created the states of California and Nevada in 1850 and 1864; Colorado's gold, silver, and lead kindled statehood in 1876; rich gold, lead, and silver discoveries in the Boise Basin, Owyhee Mountains, Coeur d'Alene, and Bunker Hill region brought Idaho into the Union in 1899, while the prolific placers and copper deposits of Montana prompted statehood in 1890. The gold pan and miner's pick had energized a bright, new frontier, which thereafter became a magnet for a great westward migration.

The march toward America's Manifest Destiny became undeniable after this crescendo of mineral discoveries, even though the process was slowed temporarily by the Civil War. After the war ended, many soldiers of both the blue and the gray, side by side, sought new lives in the west. Many became full or part-time prospectors and accounted for several more important mineral discoveries. Another aftermath of the war: federal armies were released from eastern duty and turned their attention to the Indian tribes who were resisting invasions by settlers and railroads.

In 1869, at Promontory Point, Utah, rails of the Central Pacific and the Union Pacific were joined to unite the west and east coasts of the nation. The Northern Pacific, Southern Pacific, and the Atchison, Topeka and Santa Fe soon followed, aided by government grants of land and money. For every mile of track the railroads received free a 400 foot right-of-way and 12,800 acres in alternate sections of public land within a 20 mile strip parallel to the railroad.

Gold Foments Indian Warfare

When the Indians found themselves evicted from railroad property by incursions of gold seekers, as well as by settlers under the Homestead Act of

1862, the long period of Indian warfare began. Reservations were established in exchange for huge land concessions within the hunting domains of the tribes, with the promise of protection and inalienable permanency. But often the march of progress altered the nation's treaty obligations, with an ultimate loss to the Indians.

The next big gold strike was to come in a land the Indians called "Dakota," meaning "allied," or "many in one," containing several tribes of the Sioux. Under the treaty of Traverse des Sioux in 1851, the Indians ceded to the United States all lands east of the Big Sioux River, leaving to the Indians most of present South Dakota; but in 1859 the Sioux tacitly agreed to permit settlers to enter lands as far west as the Missouri River. When President Buchanan signed a bill creating the Dakota Territory in 1861, there were less than 2,500 white inhabitants in that region.

In 1865 the Sioux were asked to sign a treaty to permit travel on the Bozeman Trail, running from the Platte and Powder rivers to Three Forks on the upper Missouri, to be used by miners going to the gold fields of Montana. Red Cloud, the great Oglala Sioux warrior, foreseeing the ruin of the last of his buffalo ranges, refused to sign. After federal troops built forts along the trail, 1865 became known as the 'Bloody Year on the Plains.' The Sioux, under Red Cloud and their Cheyenne allies, closed the trail and for two years besieged Fort Phil Kearney at the foot of the Big Horn Mountains in what is now Wyoming. No Indian chief had so restrained the U.S. Army before.

Invasion of The Hunting Grounds

In 1868, a Peace Commission was sent west. Under the Fort Laramie Treaty white men were forbidden to go into the Powder River country. All the land between the Big Horn Mountains on the west, the Platte River on the south, and the Missouri River on the east and north, was reserved to the Dakotas, Kiowa and Sioux Indians as a permanent hunting ground. The treaty could be altered only with the consent of three-fourths of the braves affected. Just as it had been the matter of access to the gold fields of Montana and Colorado, which had stirred the bitterness between Indians and whites in 1865, it would be gold again that would set in motion the final battles of Indian warfare.

In the late summer of 1874, General George A. Custer led an expedition westward with orders to establish a route to the Black Hills, a huge,

mysterious land of dark, pine-clad mountains, rising like an island above the Dakota plains. The Sioux word for these mountains was Pahasapa, Black Hills, which they regarded with awe and apprehension—and for good reason, for in these hills lay the metal that would destroy forever the hunting grounds of the Plains Indians.

On August 2, 1874, two prospectors, Horatio Ross and William McKay, camping with the Custer party, found placer gold on French Creek near the present town of Custer, South Dakota. The news filtered eastward and brought 28 gold seekers, who were promptly arrested for violating the treaty which had reserved these lands for the Sioux, Dakota, and Kiowa tribes. In the summer of 1875, Professor Walter P. Jenney and Henry Newton were sent to make a scientific examination of the Black Hills. They reported the presence of considerable gold in the streams of the district.

Gold Seekers and the Sioux

In the fall of 1875, the Sioux were summoned to meet at Red Cloud's agency to approve a government proposal permitting the white men to extract all precious metals from the Black Hills, after which they would abandon the territory to the Indians. When Indian resistance convinced the military that such a plan was impossible, all further efforts to restrain the whites were discontinued. Gold seekers poured into the area, and in 1875-6, thousands of men were roaming through the craggy, forested hills, testing the virgin streams under the watchful eyes of the Sioux. Many prospectors were silently and swiftly done away with.

North of Custer, in a lonely, rugged gulch between the present cities of Deadwood and Lead, in October 1875, John Pearson panned a rich find of placer gold. Within one year thousands of eager miners rushed into Deadwood Gulch. Lacking an organized government, since they were actually squatters on Indian land, the rough justice which blossomed in Deadwood Gulch became the basis for many florid pages in frontier history, involving such names as Calamity Jane, Wild Bill Hickock and his killer, Jack McCall.

Late in 1876, General George Crook was dispatched to subdue Indian uprisings, and at Slim Buttes his forces fought a determined band led by Crazy Horse. The battle was a stalemate, but Crook's men tramped over the graves of their fallen brothers to conceal their losses. Then

Crook's expedition went on to the Black Hills to protect the joyful miners of Deadwood Gulch and surrounding area.

Crazy Horse and Sitting Bull

As Indian rights were rapidly being eroded, such great chiefs as Crazy Horse and Sitting Bull were making their last stands. On the Little Big Horn in Montana, the massacre of Lieutenant Colonel George A. Custer and 250 men of the elite Seventh Cavalry on June 25, 1876, shocked the nation and galvanized the military into at last organizing a program to end Indian domination of the plains. In February 1877, President Grant approved a treaty in which the Sioux, Cheyennes, and Ogallalas relinquished their claims on the Black Hills, in return for various concessions. Thereafter the Black Hills was declared to be public territory.

Deadwood Gulch soon became a roaring camp of 25,000 hilarious, busy gold seekers. The fame of Black Hills gold and the wide-open, boisterous town of Deadwood reverberated throughout the nation. After the late winter snows had melted in 1876, Fred and Moses Manuel left Deadwood Gulch, crossed the divide to Gold Run Creek, found an abandoned lode claim called the Golden Terra, and then became attracted by numerous pieces of rich quartz float nearby. In expert fashion, Moses traced the float to the bottom of a small ravine. There, rushing water from melting snows had exposed a white quartz vein, gleaming with gold. The next day, on April 9, 1876, with Hank Harney's help, Moses staked out what he called the Homestake lode where the town of Lead now stands.

The Great Homestake Mine

With a crude "arrastra," the Mexican term for a stone crushing mill, the Manuels recovered $5,000 in gold that winter, and in the spring they sold the Golden Terra for $35,000, but they hung onto the Homestake claim. When a young man named George Hearst arrived with his pockets well lined with Comstock wealth, the Manuels asked $70,000 which Hearst promptly agreed to pay. George Hearst and his partners, James B. Haggin and Lloyd Tevis, organized the Homestake Mining Company in November, 1877. Within two years, from an open cut, the company mined ore that was low grade but on such a large scale that it yielded $920,000 in gold. Although the ore ran only $4.00 to $8.00 per ton in gold, utilizing supe-

rior technology it has produced over one billion dollars in gold since 1879, making the Homestake the most productive gold mine in the western hemisphere. In 1972 the mine was still producing at the rate of $20,000,000 per year. Thus, the Ophir mine on the Comstock lode and the Homestake became the cornerstones of the vast Hearst financial empire, which went on to have widespread influences in America.

Following discovery of gold in the Black Hills came the great boom period of the Dakotas. After the gold seekers came the settlers, and then the railroads, such as the Northwestern and the Milwaukee lines. In November 1889, North and South Dakota were admitted to the Union as "Sister States." Manifest Destiny, spurred by the gleam of gold, was heading swiftly across the ancient homelands of the Western Indians.

The Hot, Hostile Southwest

The conquest and settlement of the Southwest had much in common with the central plains and northwest regions, insofar as overcoming the hostility of the Indians was concerned. But the land itself was vastly different. Unlike the grassy plains and forested mountains of the central and northern West, the domain of the Apaches and Comanches was hot, desolate, and waterless. Prospecting was arduous and agonizing; travel was dangerous and harrowing.

Indian opposition in the Southwest was also more ferocious, stemming from earlier causes. Beginning with Coronado's brutal subjugation of the Zuni and Tiguex Indian villages of New Mexico, in 1540, during his fruitless search for the fabled Golden Cities of Cibola, the first seeds of undying hatred for white men were sown centuries prior to unrest on the plains. But even more fateful was the rage which filled the hearts of the Southwest Indians when, in 1838, the Mexican states of Chihuahua and Sonora set bounties of 100 pesos on every Indian warrior's scalp, 50 for the scalp of a squaw and 25 for that of a child.

Regardless of which side started this frightful duel, warfare between the Mexicans and Indians had risen to an unquenchable heat when the Americans, who were quickly classified as similar enemies, began to arrive. White prospectors, searching for rumored wealth and lost mines of the early Spanish explorers, and for virgin, undiscovered mineral deposits, soon came face to face with the braves of such chiefs as Cochise and Mangas Coloradas.

Spanish Prospectors

The Spaniards, of course, had been the first to search Arizona and New Mexico for minerals, spreading outward from the prolific mining camps of northern Mexico. Following the Rio Grande into present New Mexico, in 1582 Antonio de Espejo, a wealthy merchant from the Santa Barbara mining district of Chihuahua, led the first prospecting expedition into the Southwest. Espejo's exciting reports induced Don Juan de Oñate, a rich mine owner of Zacatecas, Mexico, in 1598 to establish San Juan, the first capital in the Southwest. In 1609, Santa Fe was founded nearby and became the permanent capital of New Mexico. Thus, 300 years before gold was discovered in California, the Spaniards launched their great colonization and missionary movement in the Southwest, impelled by the attraction of metallic wealth.

In 1736, at a place called Arizonac in northern Sonora, Mexico, prospectors found large masses of native silver, which were promptly claimed by Captain Juan Bautista de Anza in behalf of King Philip V of Spain. But the find started a rush of prospectors northward into what is now the state of Arizona, named after the site of the rich discovery, Arizonac.

In 1848, after paying $15,000,000, the United States acquired the Mexican Cession under the Treaty of Guadalupe Hidalgo, which ended the Mexican War. The area comprised the present states of California, Nevada, Arizona, Utah and the western parts of New Mexico and Colorado, generally known as the Southwest. An additional strip south of the Gila River in Arizona was bought from Mexico, the Gadsden Purchase, for $10,000,000 in 1854.

Stout Hearts and Fast Guns

Despite the desolate terrain and the terrifying reputation of the Indians, who were not consulted in the territorial exchange, an influx of miners and ranchers began to filter into the country. The sparse population included a liberal mixture of escaped convicts and refugees from vigilante committees, eastern states, and Mexico. This lawless element and the belligerent Indians made the Southwest a region where stout hearts and fast guns wove a saga of the frontier, which now occupies a special niche in the world of literature and entertainment.

Legends of fabulous lost mines, first worked by Spaniards and Jesuit padres, and a few known gold, silver and copper deposits, made Arizona the promised land for the early bonanza hunters. Well known was the rich copper outcrop near Santa Rita, New Mexico. Indians had long utilized its green and blue minerals for pigments. In 1804, masses of native copper, because of their purity had been carried on pack mules 1200 miles to Mexico City to be used for coinage. Generations later, the Indian diggings would become a great open pit, after its immense low-grade copper ore body was mined and milled by methods first developed in Bingham Canyon, Utah.

In 1854, Colonel Charles D. Poston started mining surface ores of oxidized and native copper at Ajo in the Papago Indian country. The ore was rich enough to be hauled by oxcarts across the desert to the Colorado River at Yuma; thence it was barged down the river and carried by ships across the ocean to a smelter at Swansea, South Wales. Years later, beneath the surface ore a huge low-grade copper deposit covering 55 acres would be found. It was to become the noted New Cornelia open pit mine of the Calumet & Arizona Mining Company.

Apaches, Bandits and Gold

In 1858, six United States army officers found silver-lead deposits, formerly worked by the Jesuits and Mexicans, in the Patagonia district. A few years later, Pauline Weaver, a rugged, distinguished frontiersman, despite his given name, found gold in a dry, cactus-covered gulch above the Colorado River, a few miles north of Ehrenberg, at a place later named La Paz. Similar placers yielded rich returns in gold on the Gila River, 10 miles east of Yuma, and along Weaver Creek south of modern Prescott, which led later to discovery of the noted Octave, Congress, and Crown King lode mines.

In 1863, a rich gold mine was discovered by Henry Wickenburg 12 miles southwest of the present town of Wickenburg. Named the Vulture mine, after the birds often seen circling above the victims of desert tragedy, Wickenburg's lode was found outcropping boldly on a saguaro studded hillside, liberally sprinkled with gold. The mine's bunkhouses were made of rock showing specks of free gold. The town of Wickenburg became noted for its violent history. In 15 years over 400 whites were slain by Indians, and by highwaymen who regularly seized the Wells-Fargo boxes containing gold bullion.

As the importance of the region's metallic

wealth, found in these and other mines, became obvious Arizona was made a Territory in February, 1863. But the Civil War forced the recall of Federal troops stationed in the area and deprived the early Arizona mining camps of badly needed protection. Then, Indian raids and banditry wrought havoc upon the Southwest. Communications were disrupted, and the dare-devil Pony Express riders were murdered on the trail, the most dangerous stretch being Apache Pass.

Betrayal of Cochise

It was here, in 1860, that occurred the betrayal of Cochise, which launched the Apache chief on his blind vendetta against all whites. For years, dedicated to peace, Cochise had forbidden his Chiricahua warriors to molest the Americans. When a young, inexperienced army lieutenant invited Cochise to his quarters in Apache Pass and accused the chief of cattle stealing, a struggle ensued. Infuriated, Cochise slit the tent and escaped. Six of Cochise's warriors, including his brother, were captured and brutally slain. Thereafter, for 12 long, bloody years, the Apache chief made life miserable for every white man, while his tribe lived in an impregnable stronghold amid the granite crags of the Dragoon Mountains.

In 1862, Fort Bowie was built at the crest of Apache Pass to protect the immigrant trail and a nearby Butterfield Stage station. In July, 1862, eleven companies of infantry at the fort were attacked by Apaches led by Cochise and his friend, Mangas Coloradas, chief of the Mimbre Apaches. From every rock on the rugged hillside came volleys of Apache musket fire. Only the shells of the Union howitzers forced the Apaches to retreat.

In the years that followed, many soldiers, prospectors, express riders, and immigrants died on the dangerous trail. But Cochise was never beaten. Through the intercession of an Indian agent named Tom Jeffords, blood-brother of Cochise, wise old General O. O. Howard was taken to the stronghold and persuaded Cochise to end his revolt. Today, Fort Bowie's adobe walls lie strewn upon the ground, abandoned. But Apache Pass, far from modern roads, is completely unchanged. Scattered among the yuccas and bristling cacti on the steep hillsides are the same granite boulders that sheltered the roaring guns of the Apaches. All is now peaceful and deathly quiet.

Prospecting Apacheland

After the Civil War, despite the harshness of the land and continuing danger from the Indians, prospectors and soldiers persisted in their search for precious metals. In 1871, it was the soldiers who found the copper stained mountain in the Clifton-Morenci district, which today is one of the great mines of the Phelps Dodge Corporation. Soldiers also found the fabulously rich Silver King mine in the shadows of the red, craggy walls of Superstition Mountain. Spectacular crystals of native silver, and much wire silver, formed the ore. Miners attracted to the district found the Silver Queen mine, which ultimately became the famed Magma Copper Company at Superior, Arizona.

It was rich, rugged Tombstone, Arizona, that marked some of the most boisterous pages of western history. Early in the summer's heat of 1877, a prospector named Ed Schieffelin, about to set out from Fort Huachuca in search of a bonanza, was told by soldiers, "All you'll find is your tombstone." But with his burro at his heels, Schieffelin went forth and followed the greasewood covered valley of the San Pedro River, practically in the tracks of Coronado who trod the same soil in 1540. He, too, was looking for gold. Due east, Schieffelin could see the granite ramparts of the Dragoon Mountains, Cochise's recent stronghold, but for the lone prospector the lure of bonanza was stronger than the fear of Apaches.

Ascending a low, limestone peak, Schieffelin spied a good looking outcrop, stained bluish with minerals of silver. With ironic humor, he staked a claim and named it the Tombstone. After being joined by his brother Alfred, and an assayer friend Richard Gird, the men staked more claims. "You're a lucky cuss" said brother Alfred to Ed; therefore one claim was called the Lucky Cuss. It became one of the richest mines in the camp, which today is still known as Tombstone. Other claims were named the Tough Nut, the Goodenough, and the Contention.

Sinful, Silvery Tombstone

Prospectors, gamblers, outlaws, promoters and nationally known marshals of the law flocked to Tombstone, giving melodramatic substance to scores of books on the wild, wild West. In 1879, the Schieffelin brothers received $1,000,000 for their interest in the Tough Nut, and later, Gird received an equal share. Still young and flushed with wealth, Ed Schieffelin went first to New York, then to Chicago, Washington and other cities to enjoy the glamor of civilized places. As it did to most men of his type, city life seemed artificial and illusory.

The call of the wilderness could not be suppressed. Rearmed with his old prospecting outfit, Schieffelin went to Oregon to prospect for gold in the clear, forested streams. There, one day he was found in a lonely cabin, where he had chosen to die in peace and solitude. After his remains were returned to Tombstone, a tower of stones was erected over his grave, during the grandest funeral in the camp's torrid history.

Tombstone went on to produce $80,000,000 in silver, and a cavalcade of characters such as Wyatt Earp, Doc Holliday, the Clantons, the McLowerys, and Curly Bill. In an unending stream of books, magazines and television plays, Tombstone has been made a landmark of frontier life, portrayed with deplorable distortion. It was the miner's pick and the settler's plow, not the blazing guns, that opened and won the Golden West.

Bisbee's Copper Queen

Twenty-five miles south of Tombstone, in what is now Mule Canyon, far greater benefits to mankind were achieved at a place called Bisbee, one of the world's great copper districts. Jack Dunn, an army scout, made the discovery while chasing renegade Apaches in 1877. George Warren, a bibulous prospector, staked the claim for Dunn, but failed to include Dunn's name in the location notice and neglected to do the assessment work. Two Civil War veterans, George Eddlemay and Marcus Herring, relocated the claims and named one of them the "Copper Queen" because its limestone surface was streaked with blue and green carbonates of copper.

But it was James Douglas, chemist and metallurgist, who made the Bisbee mines a success and the name "Copper Queen" known around the world. In 1881, Dr. Douglas was sent by Phelps, Dodge & Company, a highly successful mercantile firm in New York, to investigate the rumored richness of an open cut in Mule Canyon, a cut which had revealed an amazing treasure of copper ore. William Martin and John Ballard, two railroad contractors of little mining experience, had purchased the property and had exposed the first bonanza of the Copper Queen. Many beautiful blue azurite and green malachite specimens of Copper Queen ore now rest in noted mineral museums.

Unable to obtain the Copper Queen, Douglas acquired an option on the adjoining Atlanta claim, and started underground exploration. After he had spent $70,000 without success, his principals in New York advised abandoning the property. Douglas proposed spending an additional $15,000 in a final effort. Work was resumed. Guided by Douglas' technical knowledge, within a few days miners suddenly burst into a body of fabulously rich copper carbonate ore.

Meanwhile, the Copper Queen appeared to be nearing depletion. Martin and Ballard were glad to accept Douglas' plan to consolidate the two claims. Through the wise efforts of Dr. Douglas, a number of other claims were secured; then the Copper Queen Consolidated Copper Company became one of America's great producers. It is now a division of the Phelps Dodge Mining Company. Dr. James Douglas became one of the most highly respected men in the mining world.

Mines and Characters

There was one claim, the Irish Mag, which the Copper Queen Company had been unable to procure, due to the uncertainty of its title. Its owner, an Irishman named James Daley, was a fugitive from justice. Daley's long suffering common-law wife was finally awarded title to the property by the United States Supreme Court. James Hoatson of the Michigan Copper country, while visiting Bisbee, realized the Irish Mag's potential, hurried back to Calumet, raised $500,000, organized the Calumet and Arizona Mining Company, and acquired the claim, which turned out to be one of the richest in the district.

One other parcel, consisting of 108 acres, had been held onto by Lem Shattuck. In the early days of 1882, 15 year old Lem had been a hard working ranch hand near Bisbee. Saving his money, he invested and prospered in a lumber company, a saloon, and a small bank in the rear of a jewelry store. Gradually, he picked up a few outlying mining claims. A friend, Maurice Denn, owned another group nearby. Together, they sunk a shaft 350 feet. Fortunately, they encountered a large body of high grade ore. The Shattuck-Denn Mining Company became a prolific producer, and later expanded its operations elsewhere in the West.

Bisbee was named after a San Francisco judge named Dewitt Bisbee, who arranged the first purchase of the Copper Queen for Martin and Ballard. The mining district was named after George Warren who, despite his laxity in validating Dunn's discovery, managed to obtain a one-ninth interest in the "Queen."

PLATE 140. Butte miners have sent to the surface over 3 billions of dollars worth of mineral wealth.

PLATE 141. Copper is precipitated from mine water on vast amounts of scrap iron and tin cans in reclamation tanks.

PLATE 142. The Silver King mine in Park City is one of many rich metal deposits found in Utah.

PLATE 143. Mining engineers devised methods to make a mountain, now an open pit, yield billions in wealth from low grade ores at Bingham Canyon, Utah.

PLATE 144. Anaconda's mine at Weed Heights is an example of man's ability to win metals from very low grade deposits.

PLATE 145. A monument at Weed Heights honors Anaconda's president Clyde E. Weed, a 1911 graduate of Michigan College of Mines, now the Michigan Technological University.

But one Fourth of July in uproarious Bisbee, in a festive and drunken mood, Warren wagered that he could outrun a horse over a 100 yard course. He lost the race and his share of the Copper Queen, which ultimately was worth millions. Jack Dunn, whom Warren had defrauded by excluding Dunn's name in the discovery notice, was able to recover $3,000. Most of the district's wealth went to those who sagaciously and scientifically explored it and financed its full development.

Arizona—The Copper State

In 1931, the Phelps Dodge Mining Company bought the Calumet & Arizona, bringing its holdings to 9,000 highly productive acres. After other great mining districts were found and developed in the state, for 55 years Arizona was able to lead the nation in the output of copper. Total metal production throughout the state reached a value of twelve and one-half billion dollars, including copper, lead, silver and gold, an important contribution to the state's industrial and social well-being. Of this sum, approximately three billions in wealth came from the Warren mining district, centered about Bisbee—a region that was totally unknown, a wild frontier in Apacheland, less than 100 years old.

Riches Along The Verde

In 1582, Antonio de Espejo, Arizona's first prospector, stood upon the edge of a lofty plateau and looked down upon a luxuriant valley, verdant with Indian fields of maize and threaded by a green tinted stream, later called the Verde River. Beneath his feet the ground was colored brightly with green and blue carbonates of copper. But since the property was too remote from his homeland in Mexico, it had to remain unexploited. Nearly 300 years later, Alfred Sieber, a noted Indian scout, staked a claim here and named it the Verde. This region was about 30 miles east of present Prescott, Arizona.

Later, other men, including M. A. Ruffner, John and Angus McKinnon, who were rancher-prospectors, staked more claims. After trying to work the isolated property, they were happy to sell it for $500 cash and a note for $15,000 to F. A. Tritle, territorial governor of Arizona. In need of further financing, Tritle enlisted the aid of eastern capitalists, represented by attorney Eugene Jerome, member of a distinguished New York family that included one who was to be the mother of a man known as Winston Churchill.

The name Jerome was given to the picturesque camp that clung precariously on the steep mountainside high above the Verde Valley, and during the first year the United Verde Copper Company produced ore valued at $1,000,000. But the excessive cost of hauling the smelted copper 60 miles to a railroad at Ash Fork, and the depletion of the rich surface ores, forced the suspension of operations.

Knowledgeable W. A. Clark

In 1887, Dr. James Douglas endeavored to secure the property for Phelps-Dodge, but the seller's antics in raising the price caused Douglas to abandon the venture. Meanwhile, wise and alert W. A. Clark, of Butte fame, noticed exhibits of United Verde ore at the 1885 New Orleans Exposition. Having educated himself in geology and metallurgy, Clark recognized that the rich oxidized outcrop, and the presence of gold and silver in the assays, were indications of an important mineral deposit existing at greater depth. Soon thereafter, Clark managed to acquire 99 percent of the company's stock, and thus became the sole owner of the mine.

Possessing the financial means and the expert guidance of his mine manager, J. L. Giroux, Clark deepened the mine. Below the shallow workings an enormous mass of glistening copper sulphide ore was discovered. A railroad was built along the precipitous mountainside, a huge smelter was erected, and Jerome became one of the busiest and most colorful mining towns in America. Quite unsung, the United Verde ore deposit went on to yield copper, gold and silver ore valued at $410,000,000, making W. A. Clark the possessor of "the richest, individually owned copper mine in the world."

Geologic "Offspring"

The Verde Valley, however, was to surrender yet another bonanza of copper. The huge brassy mass of sulphide ore which composed the United Verde deposit had a geological "offspring." After the orebody had been formed in its host rock aeons ago, it had been covered by many layers of limestone and lava. Then, in the more recent geologic past, a few million years ago, convulsions of the earth caused a break, or fault, which gradually split and dropped a segment of the United Verde orebody downward and eastward about 1600 feet.

Meanwhile, a long period of erosion along the

fault escarpment had exposed the upper segment and had oxidized its brassy ores to green and blue carbonates of copper. Such was its position when later seen by Espejo and eventually mined by W. A. Clark. But the downhill or eastern segment still retained its uneroded 700 foot capping of limestone and lava. Beneath this cloak, nature seemed to be challenging man to find this faulted, invisible orebody.

The suspicion that the ground below the celebrated United Verde mine might contain an ore deposit was entertained by several alert men. In 1889, the United Verde Extension Gold, Silver and Copper Mining Company was organized, and a year later, J. J. Fisher sunk the Little Daisy shaft through 300 feet of limestone and lava without finding ore. Later, the shaft was deepened to 865 feet and a few patches of very rich ore were found; however $500,000 had been expended and no mine had been discovered.

Scientific Explorations

In 1908, James Douglas Jr. optioned the property and first offered it to Phelps-Dodge who rejected it. Douglas then raised the sum of $225,000 among friends, including a number of engineers, whose confidence rested in the promoters of the venture. A new shaft, the Edith, was sunk to a depth of 1,200 feet; drifts and crosscuts were driven in a wide search westward, eastward, and southward for the elusive orebody.

By September 1914, the $225,000 had been expended, making a total of $750,000 already spent searching for a theoretical offspring of the United Verde orebody. But James Douglas' faith and the reasoning of his consulting geologists warranted the decision to spend $50,000 more. With renewed efforts, the drift on the 1200 foot level was extended a few feet farther. And then it happened: that rare, seldom equalled moment of exultation when miners burst into an opening resplendent with one of earth's long concealed treasures.

The "U.V.X." ore deposit (as it was called) was one of the marvels of the mining world. By a process of weathering, copper in the original sulphide orebody had been leached, reconcentrated and enriched, forming nearly solid black chalcocite ore averaging 23 percent copper, sometimes as high as 45 percent. The United Verde ore, always in the form of brassy, primary sulphides, ran from 3 to 7 percent. The first shipment of less than two carloads of ore from the U.V.X. brought $75,000. From the first orebody discov-

ered in the mine, $600,000 in copper was recovered the first year.

Although not as large as its husky parent, the United Verde, the total yield in copper, gold, and silver from the U.V.X. was valued at $75,000,000. Because the ore was so rich, a very high ratio of profit resulted, amounting to $50,000,000. Mining men who came from all parts of the country to inspect the mine were amazed by the incredible richness of the black chalcocite bonanza, and the scientific skill and efficiency employed in discovering and developing it.

Boom Days in The Sagebrush

The mines described in the preceding pages are but a few of the thousands, too numerous to list, that were found throughout the western United States. Some of these were stumbled onto through sheer luck, largely due to their surface exposures being open to the sky, undisturbed for ages. But the majority of important mine developments came from the application of training and science.

It may have been a lucky occasion when an uneducated, inveterate prospector named Jim Butler, while rounding up his burro, was wise enough to chip off a piece of silver-rich rock. For this marked the beginning of the great Tonopah boom in Nevada, in 1900. During its several decades of boutiful production, Tonopah yielded $153,000,000 in silver and gold, mostly silver.

It was expert, perceptive and experienced prospecting, however, that led fortune hunters from Tonopah, in 1902, 25 miles southward to a barren, treeless and waterless country that harbored the rich veins of Goldfield, Nevada. Such men as Billy Marsh, Harry Stimler, Al Myers, Bob Hart and Charles Taylor, working on a grub-stake, found and staked famous gold veins later known as the Jumbo, Mohawk, Combination, January, Laguna, Florence and Red Top, whose content of gold proved fantastic.

Most of the early prospectors reaped fair rewards. Preferring quick money, Marsh sold his interest for $1,000; Stimler held on for a while and received $25,000. Al Myers, one of the wiser and more experienced prospectors, received $400,000 for his interest in the properties he staked, while C. D. Taylor, who located the Jumbo claim, netted $1,250,000 for his efforts. But as usual, such tycoons of finance as Charles M. Schawb, Bernard Baruch, W. A. Clark, John W. Brock, J. P. Loftus, August Heinze, and the

PLATE 146. The Santa Rita open pit in New Mexico also exemplifies technology's success in behalf of mankind.

PLATE 147. The Homestake mine in South Dakota was opened in 1876. It was then in disputed lands of the Sioux.

PLATE 148. Young George Hearst and partners organized the Homestake Mining Company in 1877. With remarkable efficiency it has produced over one billion in gold from very low grade ore. It is still yielding $20,000,000 in gold per year, the most productive gold mine in America.

PLATE 149. Invading Apacheland alone in 1877, on the distant hill Ed Schieffelin discovered the Lucky Cuss mine.

PLATE 150. Schieffelin named the town that arose, Tombstone. It grew famous in western lore and silver production.

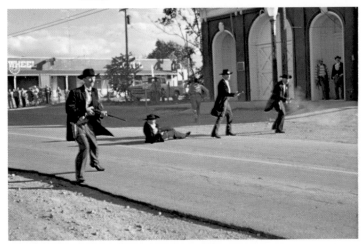

PLATE 151. The fight at the O.K. Corral is enacted for tourists. It was the miner, not the gunman, who won the West.

PLATE 152. A glory hole on the right is where the famed Copper Queen mine in nearby Bisbee was discovered.

PLATE 153. As Sacramento Hill in the center of Bisbee was dug away, it became present day Lavender Pit.

PLATE 154. The Warren Mining District, which includes Bisbee and scores of mines, is renowned worldwide.

Nevada bankers, George Wingfield and George S. Nixon, investing capital to build the mine plants and mills, gathered the greater fortunes.

The Golden Cornucopia

The ore was astonishingly rich in free, visible gold and the tellurides of gold. One 47 ton carload of ore from the Hayes-Monette lease in the Mohawk mine, after freight and smelter charges, netted the lessees $574,958. Its fame traveled around the earth. Within 106 days, the four men who were working under a one year lease, took over $5,000,000 from the Mohawk mine. Such unprecedented richness in gold ore made Goldfield a blazing beacon to miners throughout the country.

High-grading (stolen gold) became the mine owners' greatest problem. The ore was so rich that one miner could seize a piece of rock seamed and splotched with gold in an unguarded moment, and purloin from $200 to $1000 in one working shift. Miners even paid shift bosses secretly for the privilege of working underground. Over 60 fences, in the guise of assayers, bought stolen gold.

High-graders took many millions in gold from the mines. The Mohawk's loss alone amounted to $2,000,000. Goldfield's known mine production was over $90,000,000. Added to the millions produced by the Comstock, Tonopah, and other districts such as Austin, Rochester, Midas, Hamilton, Eureka and Ely, as had Utah and Arizona, Nevada took its place as an important contributor to the nation's wealth.

Gaudy, Glittering Goldfield

Goldfield, a city of 20,000, was the living embodiment of a boom-town in its gaudiest, most glittering form. While rumbling freight wagons and strutting horses, hitched to buckboards, threaded the seething streets, a multitude of prospectors and miners in hobnailed boots, and eastern promoters in broad-brimmed hats affecting western style, jammed the planked sidewalks. Flushed with gold fever, they reveled in the many raucous saloons, and filled the city's lush, new, red-brick 4-story Goldfield Hotel.

In the hotel's spacious lobby, replete with flowered carpets and red velvet drapes, financiers ogled gleaming specimens of gold ore handed to them for appraisal by the proud mine owners. Over the moist, smoke shrouded mahogany bar off the lobby, promoters bandied millions, while the clicking of roulette wheels and the jingling of

gold and silver coins sang their siren songs. It was heady stuff for a young boy (this author) who, while accompanying his father, witnessed these scenes of boom-fever in its most sensational form. It was typical of the incredible era which marked the discovery and development of America's vast metallic resources. In less than a century, American mining men had uncovered stores of earth's riches on a scale greater than mankind had ever seen, which provided a stimulant of far reaching consequences in the subsequent growth and prosperity of the United States.

Sourdoughs Open The North

Attention had been drawn toward the north as early as 1858, when the San Francisco mint reported that gold was being received from the Fraser River country of western Canada. A rush followed and such places as Yale, Boston Bar, and Thompson Creek gave up their long hoarded stores of placer gold. Reaching Quesnel, some prospectors turned eastward into the Cariboo country. There, while miners ridiculed their efforts, Bill Barker and three friends dug a hole in an unlikely spot on Williams Creek.

The little hole yielded $600,000 in gold, found strewn along the bedrock of the creek, and Barkerville became the center of the famed Cariboo district, which ultimately produced $45,000,000 in gold. Building of the Cariboo Road then opened the northern wilderness and brought about the construction of the first trans-Canada railroad. Then, the former British Crown Colony, controlled by the Hudson's Bay Company, became the province of British Columbia. The Cariboo discovery also focused attention upon the Far North.

"Seward's Folly"

In 1867, when Secretary of State Seward paid Russia $7,200,000 for what is now Alaska, the purchase was labelled "Seward's Folly." Alaska, an Indian word meaning the "great country," was to repay this investment a thousand fold.

The first mining in Alaska began in 1877 at Silver Bay on Baronof Island near Sitka, the old Russian capital. In 1880, gold was discovered on the mainland at the mouth of a small creek near present Juneau by Josephy Juneau and Richard Harris. Following the creek into the mountains, prospectors found gold-bearing quartz veins in what is now Silver Basin. A rush resulted in establishing the town of Juneau on the edge of Gastineau Channel, surrounded by towering mountains and glacier fields.

In April, 1881, while prospecting the eastern slope of Silver Basin, John Olds saw so much gold-bearing float, gleaming between patches of melting snow, he thought he was dreaming. Olds had indeed found a bonanza, the Perseverance and Groundhog lodes which became the famed Alaska-Juneau mine, producer of $34,500,000 in gold.

A year later, in 1882, John Treadwell began to work a gold-bearing outcrop and to operate a mill across the channel on Douglas Island. The property developed into the renowned Treadwell mine, with the financial assistance of D. O. Mills, and went on to produce $64,100,000 in gold. Suddenly, in 1917, sea water from the Gastineau Channel broke into the workings and drowned the mine beyond recovery. In 1959, born of gold and sustained by mining operations, the city of Juneau became the capital of Alaska.

Rush to The Klondike

During a lull in gold fever, in 1897, the steamship Excelsior quietly docked at San Francisco and disgorged miners carrying sacks of gold dust valued at $500,000; three days later the Portland brought a cargo of miners and $1,000,000 in gold to the port of Seattle. That started the famous rush to the Klondike. Within a few months, 35,000 gold-seekers, called 'sourdoughs' because of their habit of carrying sour dough as a leaven in making bread, were heading for the Yukon Territory of Canada.

In 1896, George Carmack, accompanied by his Indian wife Kate and her two brothers, Skookum Jim and Tagish Charlie, had discovered rich pay dirt on a tributary of the Yukon River, which the Indians called Thronduik, transformed later to Klondike. As the news spread, a booming camp named Dawson, after George M. Dawson, Director of the Canadian Geological Survey, sprang up at the junction of the Yukon and Klondike rivers.

The stampede to the Klondike was one of the most frenzied in mining history. Those who could afford the less arduous way took steamers from San Francisco northward into the Bering Sea to St. Michaels, and then up the long Yukon River to Dawson, a distance of 4,000 miles. Others went by ship to Skagway a few miles north of Juneau, and then climbed the steep, often snow-bound Chilkoot Pass with everything they owned packed upon their backs. Many left Skagway and

ascended White Pass over the storied Trail of '98, which took them to the town of White Horse on the upper Yukon. So intense was the excitement that in the dead of winter, 1897, over 30,000 bewhiskered, determined gold-hunters braved blizzards and temperatures of 40 degrees below zero to reach the fabulously rich creeks of the Klondike. Many perished along the way.

Dawson on The Yukon

At the head of navigation on the Yukon, White Horse arose out of the wilderness, offering steamer service downstream to Dawson. When the Yukon froze in winter, dog teams and overland stages on sleighs made their difficult way through 330 miles of primeval timberlands in sub-zero weather to Dawson. Log-built road-houses, heated by roaring wood fires, were welcome havens along the road. Many of them are still there.

By the spring of 1898, 30,000 excited gold-seekers were milling about Dawson's noisy streets. Cheechakos, or greenhorns, looked wide-eyed upon pokes bulging with gold dust that miners brought into Dawson banks, or spread lavishly across the bars and gambling tables of the town. Jack London and Robert Service sang the praises of Dawson and the Far North in vivid terms, while the frozen ground beneath the creeks named Bonanza, Eldorado, Hunker and other tributaries of the Klondike River poured forth their streams of gold. The $10,000,000, produced the first year, swelled in 1901 to over $200,000,000, entirely in placer gold.

After the hectic boom had reached its zenith, big dredges, run by a few men, came to glean from the bedrock of the creeks the gold that miner's pans and sluice boxes had been unable to catch. As Dawson now dreams of its boisterous and colorful past, its once ornate buildings stand awry, settling slowly into the eternal permafrost, while summer tourists pour over their guide books describing the glamorous personages and glittering days of the Yukon and of Dawson on the Klondike.

Golden Sands of Nome

Closely in Dawson's wake came the rush to Nome. There, to their surprise, in June, 1899, sourdoughs discovered grains of gold on an innocent looking beach washed by the icy waters of the Bering Strait. Later, they also found gold back on the moss-covered plain where higher and parallel beaches, created in ages past, lay con-

PLATE 155. A desert in springtime bloom greeted the discoverer of the Vulture mine near Wickenburg, Arizona.

PLATE 156. Superstition Mountain's Lost Dutchman mine still lures believers in the countless legends of lost treasure.

PLATE 157. In 1582 blue-green ores of copper were first seen in Arizona by the Spaniard, Espejo. Beneath the surface was a huge body of sulphide ore.

PLATE 158. In 1886 W. A. Clark bought the property, the richest individually owned copper mine in the world, the United Verde at Jerome.

PLATE 159. Tonopah's rich Mizpah and Belmont mines were opened in 1900, starting booms anew on Nevada's desert.

PLATE 160. In 1902 fabulously rich Goldfield was discovered. One 40 ton car of ore netted $547,000. Only the waste dumps remain today.

PLATE 161. In the Cariboo country, in 1858, prospectors found a 45 million dollar gold district, which focused attention on the Far North.

PLATE 162. The Alaska-Juneau mine contributed to Alaska's statehood. Juneau became the capital.

PLATE 163. These old paddlewheelers once plied the Yukon River during the 1898 stampede to the Klondike.

PLATE 164. Dredges now work Klondike streams for gold the miners could not recover with gold pans.

PLATE 165. Carnotite was the only available uranium ore in the United States when the atomic bomb ended World War II.

PLATE 166. In mine tailings on the Colorado Plateau only 800 tons of uranium oxide existed in 1940 to meet America's vital needs.

cealed by arctic tundra. Working with goldpans and rockers, miners gathered as much as $200 per day. By 1900, Nome had become a city of 30,000. As other districts discovered on the Seward Peninsula added their production to that of Nome, a total yield of $100,000,000 was recovered from Alaska's soil, justifying Seward's wise purchase.

Kennecott's Beginning

One of nature's most thoroughly concealed treasures was found in the glacier covered Wrangell Mountains of Alaska. Gold-hungry sourdoughs had passed it, unaware of its presence, on their way from Valdez and Cordova to the Klondike. In 1906, at the foot of a rugged, snow-covered peak high above timberline, nearly concealed by a glacier, prospectors found one of the richest outcrops of copper glance (chalcocite) ever seen.

The discovery warranted the building of a 196 mile railroad from tidewater at Cordova along the Copper-Chitna River to the Wrangel Mountains, an epic of railroad building that formed the background of the Rex Beach novel, 'The Iron Trail.' After a mill to treat the ore was built near the lower edge of the glacier, miners "rode the buckets" on the tramline between the railroad terminus and the mine camp above, often in cold as low as 50 degrees below zero.

This extraordinary mineral deposit, known as the Jumbo mine, produced $200,000,000 in copper and gold, and later became the nucleus of the giant Kennecott Copper Corporation. This amount, added to the $600,000,000 in gold that came from the placers alone, transformed "Seward's Folly" into a symbol of "Seward's Bounty" and made Alaska the 49th state, the most promising and fascinating frontier in America.

The Eerie Stone—Uranium

For nearly 200 years since its Declaration of Independence the United States had been building a nation rich in natural and human resources, while rival warlords in Europe prepared for armed conflict. Then, in 1914, came the First World War in which American men and materials contributed to ultimate victory. On December 7, 1941, Japan's 'infamous' attack on Pearl Harbor plunged the United States into the Second World War. Eventually faced with the herculean task of invading the mainland of Japan at the cost of millions of American and Japanese lives, after

excruciating soul-searching, American leaders chose the alternative to end the war, the atomic bomb.

Again it was an eerie stone of the earth that controlled the fate of mankind, for within its tiny atoms there was more authority than in the hands of all the world's potentates combined. This stone, called uranium, was not an unknown mineral, but its awesome power of destruction only recently had been discovered after many years of scientific research.

The mineral's radioactive qualities were first noticed in 1896 by Henry Becquerel who observed that a photographic plate was blackened by uranium salts even when not in contact with the emulsion. It remained for Marie and Pierre Curie, in 1898, using the silver-uranium ores of Joachimsthal, to isolate the radioactive substances and name them radium, thorium, and polonium.

For a number of years thereafter, ores containing uranium were valuable only for their very small percentage of radium, which had to be extracted at great cost. Then, the ores came chiefly from Czechoslovakia, the Belgian Congo, the Northwest Territory of Canada, and a few isolated places on the Colorado Plateau. After extracting the radium, the yellow residue, uranium oxide, was used mainly as a coloring agent in the ceramic industry.

Time Clock and Lethal Power

In 1902, the English scientists Rutherford, Soddy and Ramsey investigated the disintegration processes of uranium and its unstable, radioactive daughter product, radium. After total decay, radium ends in the stable element, lead. Of great interest was the fact that this transition occurs at a fixed rate and with such precision that, by measuring the residual lead, a method evolved for determining the age of the earth and the rocks composing it.

Uranium's half life, or the period required to deplete half of its radioactivity, is five billion years. By measuring the residual lead derived from primary uranium contained in an igneous rock, a geological "clock" is provided for determining the age of rocks. Other elements, through radioactive decay, such as the rubidium-strontium and potassium-argon "clocks" are also used.

But it was uranium's products of decay and the instability of its atoms, which made it possible to split them and thereby release a devastating amount of energy, that became the immediate goal of these experiments. A pervasive fear that Germany was working on an atomic weapon drove the scientists, and President F. D. Roosevelt and his advisers, to hasten efforts to develop an atomic bomb. Conferences between Niels Bohr of Cophenhagen, Albert Einstein, Enrico Fermi and others in January 1939, laid the groundwork for the steps required to produce an explosive chain reaction.

Ordinary uranium, or U-238, so called because of its atomic weight, was discarded in favor of its isotope U-235, or plutonium, the more fissionable ingredient for an atomic bomb. In December, 1942, the first self-sustaining chain reaction pile was put in operation at the University of Chicago. It was a pilot experiment for the controlled release of atomic energy and the manufacture of plutonium.

Birth of The Atomic Age

Huge plutonium plants were built near Knoxville, Tennessee, and on the Columbia River north of Pasco, Washington. An enormous number of problems had to be surmounted before plutonium could be produced in quantity. For the final stages of creating an atomic bomb, a giant laboratory was established in March, 1943, near Los Alamos, New Mexico, 30 miles northwest of Santa Fe. It was under the direction of a brilliant group of scientists, headed by J. Robert Oppenheimer and military experts.

At last the bomb was ready to be assembled and tested. With great exactness, two predetermined masses of plutonium of critical size were made and transported to the explosion site, the sun-baked sands of the Alamogordo Air Base, some 40 miles from a town aptly named Truth Or Consequences. A mechanism, such as a gun, was devised to shoot one mass into the other, instantly letting loose the holocaust. In the pre-dawn of July, 16, 1945, with a blinding flash and a tremendous roar, the Atomic Age burst upon the world.

America's Woeful Scarcity of Uranium

In the throes of war, the United States found itself in urgent need of an immediate and dependable supply of uranium ore. But the nation was woefully weak in possessing known reserves of this material. At a few prospect holes in the sagebrush wastes of Paradox Valley, and nearby Uravan, in southwestern Colorado, a yellowish ore had been mined for its small gold content in 1881.

In 1898, after the Smithsonian Institution found that the ore contained uranium, several tons were shipped to the School of Mines in Paris, and delivered to Madame Curie for her experiments in extracting radium. This bright yellow hydrous oxide of uranium and vanadium was named carnotite, after M. Carnot, France's Inspector General of Mines. Its only value was in the small amount of radium present in the ore.

In 1912, the United States exported 1,200 tons of carnotite from this area to France; the shipment yielded only nine grams of radium. As radium's therapeutic potentialities in the medical field were realized, from 1911 to 1923 the United States became the first major producer of uranium ore and its refined product, radium. Meanwhile, very rich uranium deposits of pitchblende had been discovered at Katanga in the Belgian Congo. By 1923, Katanga dominated the market, causing almost complete collapse of the uranium industry in America.

In the United States, some carnotite and associated roscoelite ores continued to be mined in the Uravan district for their vanadium content, when it was discovered that vanadium was useful in hardening steel. Except for small amounts used as a coloring agent in ceramics, the uranium was valueless and therefore discarded, slowly accumulating in the tailings or waste piles. When the need for uranium oxide arose in the test atomic bomb project, only 800 tons were available in the mill tailings of Colorado. This was a pitifully small reserve of uranium, and the few small mines of the Paradox Basin represented the only known supply in the United States.

The Prospector's Crucial Role

The enormous amount of uranium oxide required to support an atomic program precluded any slow or gradual development of uranium reserves, such as had accompanied the finding of iron, copper, lead and precious metals in previous generations. The need for uranium ore was immediate and fraught with awesome consequences. Since it was believed that Germany was also working on an atomic bomb, it was a fateful hour for America.

Immediately after the war the United States turned to its people and the free enterprise system to maintain its supremacy in the atomic field. America's past had demonstrated how the individual prospector and the incentives which sustained him had played a vital role in the development of natural resources. The advantages of small economical units in early explorations had proved in-

PLATE 167. As in the past, America depended upon venturesome prospectors and the free enterprise system to find the resources required.

PLATE 168. The Colorado Plateau became the center of the search; the wildest, most fascinating region in the West.

PLATE 169. Every desolate canyon and cliff was probed with geiger counters, technology's newest prospecting device.

PLATE 170. Claims were staked in remotest places. Some found riches. Lacking knowledge, many found nothing.

PLATE 171. Flying with a geiger counter beside New Mexico mesas in 1951, Anaconda's Jack Knaebel found an uranium outcrop.

PLATE 172. Beneath the stripped-off surface, the Jackpile mine became America's largest uranium producer.

PLATE 173. Laguna Indians, on whose reservation the mine was found, were trained by The Anaconda Company to run all equipment.

PLATE 174. The Uranium Rush began in 1952 after Charles Steen, a geologist, found his Mi Vida mine near Moab, Utah.

PLATE 175. Steen's ore was the first found in the United States containing uraninite, often called pitchblende.

PLATE 176. Steen's property, easily mined near the surface, made him a millionaire and a highly publicized figure.

PLATE 177. A depleted iron mine on the Mesabi Range warns America of its serious and growing mineral shortages.

PLATE 178. Embargoes and bitter competition over earth's mineral resources may alter world economies and lifestyles.

valuable, reinforced later by the nation's larger corporations with their ready capital and industrial facilities. Thus equipped, the United States was ready to conduct the most portentous treasure hunt in the history of mankind.

The Gold Rush of 1849 was pale in comparison to the uranium stampede which eventually swept over the western United States. Because of uranium's radioactivity, new modern electronic prospecting tools, the geiger counter and the scintillator, made near-experts of everyone. Many found, however, that a knowledge of geology could eliminate useless searching and was an important aid to success. A geiger counter, clicking off the rate of intercepted radioactive rays and a dial which measured their intensity, gave prospectors certain clues as to the region's possibilities, and in some instances led directly to valuable ore deposits.

The Uranium Rush Begins

The uranium rush really started in 1949 when a husky Navajo, named Paddy Martinez, found a piece of yellow carnotite at the foot of Haystack Butte near Thoreau, New Mexico. Since Paddy's find was on land owned by the Santa Fe Railroad, their chief geologist Tom Evans was soon in the field evaluating the discovery, which led to the development of the Haystack Butte uranium mines. To save Paddy from ruinous exploitation, for finding a piece of uranium rock he was put on the Santa Fe payroll for life at $200 per month.

Later, Tom Evans was told how the Navajos had shunned nearby Poison Canyon because sheep who grazed there always perished. Suspecting that the soil might have been contaminated by selenium, often a companion element of uranium, Tom had the area tested and found that a little poisonous pod-covered bush called Rattle Weed, or Astragulus Pattersonia, had been selecting selenium from the soil. Tom's hunch that uranium might be found also in Poison Canyon proved true.

The Anaconda Company was called in by the Santa Fe to build a mill to process the Haystack and Poison Canyon ore. Jack Knaebel was in charge of the operation. An excellent flyer and wise to science's newest prospecting device, the airborne scintillometer, a hundred times more sensitive than a geiger counter, Knaebel launched a systematic search for other possible mines in the Haystack area. In his own plane he cruised remote, unexplored valleys, brushing canyon walls

of the many mesas in ever widening circles. How different from the old-time, plodding prospector with his gold pan and burro, was this winged explorer with his electronic instrument, seeking earth's strangest substance, uranium.

The Winged Electronic Explorer

One morning in November, 1951, while flying down a barren valley close to the face of a red-walled mesa, the airborne observer picked up the hottest radiation signal thus far encountered. It came from a tiny outcrop barely exposed on the edge of the mesa. Men sent to check the spot dug deeper into the mesa wall and revealed a bed of yellowish uranium ore.

Thereafter, a methodical program of diamond and rotary drilling probed through the mesa top and found the largest body of uranium ore ever discovered. Except for the tiny exposure detected by the scintillometer, the ore lay like a blanket entirely hidden under the mesa, buried from 100 to 500 feet beneath the surface. By removing, or "stripping" the mesa top, thus exposing the ore blanket which was from 5 to 50 feet thick, Anaconda was able to mine the deposit in a huge open pit with giant power shovels, dump trucks and conveyor belts.

Since the mine was located on the Laguna Indian Reservation, in addition to receiving substantial royalties, the Laguna Indians were employed exclusively by Anaconda and carefully taught to run every type of complicated equipment. The Jackpile mine named after its discoverer, Jack Knaebel, became the largest uranium mine in the world. Development of the mine had become the pet project of Anaconda's president, Dr. Clyde E. Weed.

Mysteries of The Colorado Plateau

The spotlight of the uranium search was turned next upon the region around Moab, Utah, and the "Four Corners Country" where the states of Colorado, Utah, Arizona and New Mexico form an area clustered about a common corner. Generally known as the Colorado Plateau, it is one of the strangest, yet fantastically captivating regions in North America. It is also the wildest, most remote wasteland in the United States, almost entirely ignored during the search for precious metals in former years.

Its era of earth history is as fascinating as the human drama that would be enacted in modern times. Many million of years ago, during Triassic,

Jurassic and Cretaceous periods of geologic time, the region was occupied by a pristine sea in which successive layers of brilliant red sandstones and shales were deposited, eventually attaining a thickness of thousands of feet. Much later, gradual up-warping of the earth's crust pushed the seabeds above the waters to form areas of land. Upon this surface, over a period ranging from 50 million to 125 million years ago, the dinosaurs roamed. Brontosaurus and others fed upon lush, tropical vegetation, while Tyrannosaurus Rex preyed upon his fellow reptiles.

As the land surface arched farther upward, erosion and the waters of the retreating seas carved spectacular spires and temples, such as are seen in Monument Valley, Arizona. Huge natural bridges and arches of stone, and vast valleys filled with goblin-like figures appeared in Utah's many wonderlands. Even the bones of the dinosaurs, exhumed by erosion, can now be seen in Dinosaur National Monument, Utah, and in northeastern Arizona a forest of petrified trees, colorfully tinted in hues of the rocks which once enclosed them, can be seen scattered over the present surface.

Venturesome Geologist

It was this weird but enchanting country that lured Charles Steen, a man of restless, adventuresome spirit, armed fortunately with an education in geology obtained at the Texas School of Mines. In 1948, while working in Houston, Steen read in the Engineering and Mining Journal about uranium possibilities on the Colorado Plateau and learned that the Atomic Energy Commission Operations Office had been opened at Grand Junction, Colorado, to assist prospectors in the Plateau region.

This forbidden, red-hued desert plateau was almost wholly unexplored, but most of it was public land. To stake a claim of 20 acres, one had only to pay a registration fee of one dollar, after setting up a discovery monument built of rocks and staking the corners. Thereafter, to keep the title valid, $100 in labor each year was required. If the claim proved worthy, after $500 had been expended, a "patent" or fee title to the land could be obtained. For a penniless prospector, such as Steen, opportunity beckoned with open arms.

Steen and his willing wife, Minnie Lee, with their meager savings bought a housetrailer and a jeep, and moved to Dove Creek, Colorado. Efforts there, followed by futile attempts near Yellow Cat, Utah, soon depleted their funds, but in June, 1952, they moved on to Cisco, Utah. While living there in a tarpaper shack, Minnie Lee contracted pneumonia, but kindly neighbors helped to meet the needs of the impoverished couple and their hungry children.

Hearing rumors of prospecting activity 40 miles southeast of Moab, Steen hurried to the district. All of the favored rim rock areas of the valley had been staked, but Steen's reasoning convinced him that the best uranium beds dipped under the valley floor. Needing funds to stake his claims, he obtained help from his mother, Mrs. Rosalie Shumaker and from Douglass Hoot, a machinist friend from Houston; together they staked 16 claims in Big Indian Valley.

From Failure to Success

In June 1952, using a secondhand diamond core drill, Steen drilled a hole to a depth of 193 feet. In vain he examined the cores brought to the surface for the tell-tale streaks of yellow carnotite, the only type of uranium ore then known on the Plateau. Thoroughly discouraged because the cores were black and not yellow, Steen stopped drilling and returned to Cisco.

A gas station owner in Cisco was testing a few odd rocks for his son with a geiger counter. Casually he applied the counter to Steen's apparently worthless black core; back came the furious clicking of intense radiation from a high grade uranium mineral. Until then, no one had suspected the existence of the rich, black oxide of uranium, often called pitchblende. The core drill had encountered the ore on July 6, 1952, at a depth of only 70 feet, and had continued in ore for 14 feet.

Thus was discovered Charles Steen's now famous Mi Vida Mine, which in Spanish means My Life. By 1956, dump trucks could be seen racing into a large haulage adit to reach openings 15 feet high where miners were extracting the first uranium ore containing a high percentage of uraninite to be mined on the Colorado Plateau. As Steen quickly became a millionaire, other companies found uranium deposits adjoining Steen's property along a belt three miles long. A value of over $100,000,000 has been estimated for the deposits of the Big Indian district, unearthed by a destitute young man possessing determination and knowledge.

Steen's discovery, as was Jack Knaebel's, resulted from the application of science. But it was Steen's rags to riches story, glamorized

PLATE 179. A new breed of pioneers in American universities and industries is probing new frontiers.

PLATE 180. Michigan Technological University is one of many fine institutions inspiring and teaching men and women to serve the needs of society.

PLATE 181. The wizardry that placed men on the moon opened the path for exploring and solving the problems besetting humanity; for the ultimate aim of technology is to make this a better world in which to live.

widely by newspapers and magazines, unlike the orderly, unheralded Jackpile development, that seized the public imagination and sent a stampede of prospectors armed with geiger counters, even six-shooters, into every nook and cranny of the Colorado Plateau, and thence all over the West.

Every red-walled mesa and their unscalable cliffs, every desolate canyon and dry creekbed were searched by men using every imaginable mode of transportation, which in the end came down to footwork, as a new breed of American pioneers sought the elusive hiding place of a new form of treasure, uranium. The few who found fortunes were heralded across the land, but the many who searched in vain remained unsung.

Irresistible Adventure

Another name that excited the world of uranium hunters was Vernon Pick. He had lost his small electrical business in a fire in Minnesota. Like Steen, Pick had read about the uranium rush to the Colorado Plateau. With $13,000 in insurance salvaged from the fire, he bought a truck and housetrailer and headed for Grand Junction, Colorado, then the Atomic Energy Commission headquarters and crossroads of the uranium world. There, an official suggested the region westward around Hanksville, Utah, as a good place to begin a search, and Pick had the good sense to follow the advice.

Early in November, 1951, he arrived at Hanksville, just about the jumping off place to oblivion. The town, a store and gas station, lay in a sea of mauve colored badlands, a stark, treeless and lonely land. About 300 miles westward was Capitol Reef National Monument, a land of rainbow colored cliffs, natural bridges and pinnacles of towering red sandstones and shales. On the north was Wayne Wonderland and Cathedral Valley, eroded and carved into fantastic figures of red rocks, a scene of spellbinding majesty.

But to Vernon Pick it was a land of utter desolation and mystery, a vast panorama of brooding mesas and rugged, dry washes as far as the eye could see. For seven long, torturous months he scrutinized every canyon wall, searched every bone-dry creekbed, draining his strength and his enthusiasm. First it was exhilarating, then it became a battle of faith and endurance.

The Undefeated Spirit

In a final effort, Pick managed to reach the upper tributaries, Salvation Creek and Stinking Creek, of the Dirty Devil River. With a heavy pack and a scintillation counter, he endlessly crossed and recrossed the treacherous stream, a maze of precipitous gorges and quicksand. Four days he spent in the stifling heat; crazy with thirst, he drank heavily from the arsenic poisoned waters and fell seriously ill.

Finally, while resting half delirious in the shade of a large boulder, Pick noticed his scintillation counter registering violently. The rock had fallen from the mesa above. Renewed with excited energy, he clambered up the slope to a dark layer in the mesa wall, and there he found an outcrop of rich uranium ore. He staked the ground and named it the Delta; later, he returned to work the mine from which he gained a fortune. In October, 1954, Pick sold the Delta to Floyd Odlum of the Atlas Corporation for $9,000,000, and then retired to California, built a research laboratory and proceeded to live an enjoyable, useful life.

Geiger Counter Stampede

The accounts of Steen's and Pick's fabulous finds, broadcast by newspapers and magazines, sent uranium-seekers scurrying all over the land. Many thought the geiger counter led infallibly down the road to riches, and expended labor and money in fruitless searches. Mines such as Steen's, Pick's and a few others were exceptional because they were high-grade ore bodies near the surface, which could be worked without sizable outside financial aid. But, more often, the resources of a large corporation were required to open up and develop a mine such as Anaconda's Jackpile.

But the hunt for uranium rushed on, reached into Wyoming where important deposits were found in Crook County and near Riverton in Fremont County. In the state of Washington, uranium ores were discovered in Stevens County north of Spokane. In south-central Oregon, mines produced uranium ores near Lakeview. Then, uranium was found associated with the minerals of other ores, as in the famed Sunshine mine in Idaho, America's largest silver producer.

The most important region, however, was the "Four Corners Country" of the Colorado Plateau where 60 percent of America's total uranium reserves were developed. In a strange quirk of fate, much of this critical treasure was found on the reservations of the Laguna, Ute, Hopi and Navajo Indians. From lands once deemed nearly worthless came a rare substance vital to the very survival of a nation who seemed to have nearly forgotten these first Americans. But at last, through substantial royalties, employment and other benefits, the red tinted beds of an ancient sea are pouring forth long overdue blessings to a proud and patient people.

Via The Free-enterprise System

Today, the United States has a great many billions of dollars invested in mines and facilities for producing fissionable material, in which uranium is the principal source. From 15 mines in 1946, the producers of uranium ore increased in 1960 to 1,000 mines which yielded a total of over 7,000,000 tons of ore valued at $160,000,000. By 1972, America's estimated reserves of commercial uranium ores rose to 97 million tons, having 274,000 tons of recoverable U_3O_8.

Uranium now comes also from the gold fields of the Witwatersrand, South Africa, and from the famed Shinkolobwe mine of the Belgian Congo; from the Blind River district of Ontario and other parts of Canada; and from Australia, Czechoslovakia and Russia. But the United States quickly became the world leader in the production of uranium. Its leadership in this crucial material can be credited to the dramatic revival of the nation's pioneer spirit, individualism and system of free enterprise.

It was the same spirit of adventure and initiative that had uncovered and developed the wealth of the copper and iron deposits of northern Michigan, Wisconsin and Minnesota, and the prolific lead regions of the Mississippi River Valley, the gold districts of California and the Black Hills of South Dakota, the silver of Nevada, and the great copper deposits of Arizona, Montana and Utah, all of which added immeasurably to the well-being and eminence of the United States.

Keystones of Civilization

In the preceding pages we witnessed a long parade of earth's riches, playing important roles in history: Copper, brightening the dawn of civilization in Sumer and Babylonia; copper and gold, nourishing the greatness of Egypt; iron, girding the ruthless armies of the Hittites and Assyrians; bronze, made of copper and tin, energizing the commerce and ascendancy of Crete and Mycenae; and Laurium's silver, sustaining the brilliant civilization of Greece.

We saw the metal resources of Spain bolstering the might of Carthage and Rome; silver, gold, copper, lead and tin, stimulating the colonization of Western Europe; and Aztec and Inca gold, luring Spanish conquerors toward discovery of Mexico and Peru. But those were happenings of the distant past.

More recent times have afforded us a closer, more intimate inspection of history in the making; how the timely and fortuitous revealment of America's immense copper and iron deposits of the Great Lakes region formed the foundation of the nation's unparalleled industrial and social development; and how the great westward migration and expansion of the United States, known to every American schoolboy, was set in motion and fed by the amazing discoveries of mineral riches throughout the colorful West.

Earth's Gifts to America

What effect did America's stupendous stores of natural resources have upon the nation's rise to greatness? Would this nation have achieved the supreme peak of eminence it now enjoys, had it not been favored with plentiful bounties of the earth? How did the discovery of these riches promote the development of the United States and influence the American way of life?

Historians have pointed out unanimously that it was America's westward march from the Atlantic to the Pacific that established the pattern of national spirit, ideals, folklore and thought, the very warp and woof of a nation that was carved out of the wilderness. Widespread colonization, achieved within a nation's own borders, was unique in history.

The British, French, Dutch and Portuguese busied themselves establishing colonies in all corners of the world in order to procure materials needed at home. But the United States was able to satisfy its industrial needs and its desire for colonial expansion entirely within its own borders. It was a continent that offered one frontier after another, first west of the Allegheny Mountains and then west of the Mississippi. As lands were opened to settlement, territories became states, which in themselves brought out the utmost in self-reliance during the process of colonization.

America's Pioneer Spirit

In the beginning, resources of vital portent were discovered; then mines, mills, and smelters were erected, stony lands and thickets cleared, fields were sown, social order was established, young democracies flowered, and primitive towns became great cities of industry. Next, Yankee ingenuity inspired a crescendo of inventions that ultimately made the United States the greatest technological nation on earth. The catalyst that hastened industrialization and transformed primeval lands into marvels of accomplishment was the amazing variety of metallic ore deposits found on every frontier. There in America's wilds lay the richest free gift to man any civilization had ever known.

The call of treasure, always a lure to humankind, attracted prospectors and miners who made the first moves to tame the wilderness. Over their trails came the settlers, city-builders and the railroads that opened the floodgates to hordes of hopeful emigrants from all over the world. To these peasants, artisans, and professional people, inured to European repressions and inequalities, tales of free land, opportunities, and rewards won through personal effort were powerful magnets drawing them to America. In 1848, the year gold was discovered in California, the population of the United States was 23 million; in 1860 it rose to 31 million. Then, from 1860 to 1890, 14 million immigrants came to infuse their yearning for freedom into the heart of a growing nation.

America's Industrial Revolution

Meanwhile, the United States was growing hungry for manufactured goods. Prior to 1805, a shortage of capital had seriously impaired industrial growth. England, where the Industrial Revolution had been born, had monopolized world commerce. Many Americans preferred foreign investments and trade. But following the discovery and rapidly increased production of California gold, capital invested in American industry rose from $553,200,000 in 1850 to $1,009,000,000 in 1860.

After 1860, the Civil War propelled the United States into a full scale Industrial Revolution of its own. The boom started while filling the needs of the Union army and continued after the war, as industries mechanized and expanded in order to keep abreast of population growth and immigration. Decreasing imports resulting from European wars during the 1870's, together with an increased demand in the United States for

manufactured goods, brought about an enormous expansion of American industry. The need for mineral resources of its own became an important issue in America.

At this stage in the nation's growth, it was the immense treasury of metallic ore deposits that stepped into the breach, and with hardly a missed step, supplied the requirements of capital and industry. After the mines of Nevada, Colorado, Montana, Idaho, Utah, and New Mexico began to feed the fires of the nation's metal furnaces, the economy of the United States made great progress.

The Frontiers of Freedom

American manufacturers enjoyed the advantage of living in a country generously endowed with raw materials conveniently available for industrial expansion. They were also fortunate in having a government which willingly released its mineral lands for development under the free enterprise system. Not only was industry blessed with an abundant supply of materials and favored by an expanding market, America's union of states was a vast free-trade area bound together with a network of railroads and highways privileged to cross unhampered frontiers.

There is no justification for disparaging the materialism that spearheaded the early pioneer movements, for there always was an altruistic force behind every endeavor. It was the appeal to man's instinct and yearning for freedom; free, unfettered places; free resources, whether earth's metals or its fertile fields; freedom for inventive minds to seek just rewards; freedom to achieve individualism and economic and social equality.

The very vastness of the West and its many resources stimulated the desire and the will to face and conquer problems of magnitude, to make the wilderness blossom, and to establish places in which to live under the fundamental principles of democracy. Many of the pioneers who trekked westward, and left a legacy of incalculable value to America, were not primarily philosophers, writers, painters, or sculptors such as those who endowed the classical past. These men were simply doers: prospectors, miners, farmers, builders, inventors and workers. But they succeeded in creating one of the most soul-stirring chapters in the entire history of the human race.

EPILOGUE

Man on The Threshold

Never in the history of mankind have mineral resources of the earth been so essential to human existence as they are today, nor has proof of their influence upon man's progress and destiny ever been so obvious. During the civilizations of antiquity, populations and needs for natural resources were infinitesimal compared to the ravenous requirements of modern times.

During the past century the United States, considered the world leader in technology and industrial expansion, and over 60 other nations have greatly accelerated their economies, resulting in a tremendously increased consumption of the mineral wealth of the globe. Facing this gargantuan demand for raw materials, man now beholds the spectre of this little planet he calls Earth being depleted of its irreplaceable resources at an alarming rate.

Thus, today, mankind stands upon the threshold of a future which challenges the utmost ingenuity in solving the problems of worldwide material shortages, ballooning energy demands, and threats to global ecology due to uncontrolled pollution.

At present, the greatest public concern is the so-called "energy crisis." Energy, indeed, is the prime force that sustains modern civilization. Without it the wheels of industry, serving endless human needs, would come to a standstill. Aside from power derived from water and wind in earlier times, such fossil fuels as oil, gas and coal have provided the chief sources of energy. In recent decades petroleum has become the world's most important natural resource. Upon petroleum depends much of the peace and progress of mankind today.

Petroleum's Power

In the United States approximately 90% of petroleum products are used for heat and power. 55% of the total petroleum consumed serves as fuel to transport an endless stream of people and commodities across the land. There was a time when America's supply of oil met all of its conceivable needs.

It was E. L. Drake's discovery of oil at Titusville, Pennsylvania, in 1859 that gave to civilization the marvelously versatile substance used for lighting, heating, lubrication, and finally the motive power, gasoline, that set the world on a pandemonium of wheels. For nearly 100 years the United States was the world's largest producer, user and exporter of petroleum. But, by 1958, with the discoveries of oil elsewhere, America was providing only 37% of the world's production, and was importing 18% to meet its own growing demands.

Today, with only 6% of the world's population, America consumes one-third of the total output of energy, much of which comes from petroleum. With its own reserves reaching an all-time low, this once self-sufficient discoverer of oil now has to import over 25% to meet its voracious appetite for oil products. By 1985, it is estimated, this figure will reach 60 percent. The greater part of this oil will come from the Middle East countries of Saudi Arabia, Kuwait, Qatar, Iraq and Iran, and from Libya, and Algeria in Africa.

The Arab states of the Middle East and northern Africa now possess 70% of the free world's proven oil reserves. Goaded by fervent nationalism and controlled by militant, unstable governments, some of these Arab states are using their fabulous oil resources as an instrument of irresistible economic power.

The United States, Europe and Japan on the one hand, and Russia and the communist clique on the other, are arrayed in formidable opposition, vying for the favors of these once impoverished Arab countries. Dangerous political maneuvers between these factions pose a serious threat to world peace.

With oil revenues pouring in at a rate of 3 billion dollars in 1971, and perhaps reaching a total of 100 billion dollars in the 1980's, some anti-Israel Arab nations are dedicated to aiding Palestinian and anti-western activities. Other oil-rich countries such as Saudi Arabia and Iran plan to spend their billions in creating new industries, modern communication facilities and roads for the betterment of national health, education and standards of living.

As these final lines are written, recent embargoes imposed upon the United States, Japan and Europe have been lifted, but may be renewed unless greater support is shown for Arab aims. With their highly industrialized economies, those countries are largely dependent upon Arab oil. Thus, this recent development of one of Earth's most vital resources, petroleum, is having an influence upon human affairs greater than the most powerful army.

If proof is desired concerning the authority which a natural resource can exert upon international politics and human destiny, the Middle East oil situation of today should be convincing evidence. And, how significant is the paradox that these once undeveloped Arab states have inherited nature's priceless gift, found beneath their sun-baked, desolate lands, at the very time when the world has attained the highest peak of industrialization in history.

America's Mineral Shortage

It is not petroleum alone that is of critical concern to the world and the United States. This nation, which once possessed one of the greatest storehouses of mineral riches in the world, is becoming dependent upon other countries for raw industrial materials vitally required to maintain American economy and well-being.

In varying degrees many other major industrial powers, including West Germany, Japan and Soviet Russia, short of certain natural resources, are facing the same problems, forcing them to look toward retarded but mineral-rich lands. As for the United States, with only 6% of the globe's population it consumes over 27% of the world's total mineral production. The question has been asked, "Will the U.S. high level of living and disproportionate use of earth's minerals, drawn from resources of undeveloped countries, deprive those people of their own economic future?"

Many nations are studying their "resource dependency" and preparing to compete in world markets for their mineral needs. The United States government has conducted several comprehensive appraisals of the physical resources that control the nation's social and economic future. In the U.S. Geological Survey Professional Paper 820, titled "United States Mineral Resources" (1973), and the Bureau of Mines Bulletin 650, "Mineral Facts and Problems" (1970), scores of prestigious geologists and technologists, involving several thousand man-years of experience, have thoroughly evaluated America's mineral requirements.

Their reports are prefaced with such remarks as, "The real extent of our dependence upon mineral resources places in jeopardy not merely affluence but also world civilization. In the last 30 years the United States has consumed more minerals than has the entire world during all the past ages. A technological revolution has taken place which has proliferated newly developed industries and consumer demands. In the past 20 years the U.S. has shifted from mineral self-sufficiency and is now more dependent upon world mineral markets, particularly petroleum, iron, aluminum and copper." Following are a few of the critical minerals now in the limelight:

The Critical List

IRON is the principal metal indispensable to modern living, found in every segment of our civilization. Prior to World War II the United States was the leader in iron ore resources and iron production. It was surpassed in 1958 by the Soviet Union, whose current production is now almost double that of the United States. Today, America imports about 30% of the iron ore it requires.

ALUMINUM, next to iron, is the most utilized metal and the most strategic commodity essential to our mode of life and military defense. 87% of alumina and aluminum ores are imported, chiefly from Jamaica, Surinam and Australia.

COPPER is one of the mainstays of the civilized world, supporting the highly developed electrical, construction and transportation industries of the world. Although the United States has long been the largest copper producer on earth, exploding community growth and industrialization during the period 1973-2000 will require increasing imports of this vital commodity.

ZINC is the 4th ranking metal in world trade and production. The United States consumes more than three times the amount of its annual production. Zinc is essential to a wide range of industries that provide our daily necessities, including construction, household appliances, automobiles, electrical apparatus and transportation. Despite being totally self-sufficient prior to 1937, the U.S. now imports about 25% of its zinc supplies, mainly from Canada, Australia, Mexico and Peru.

The U.S. production of LEAD, the 5th most important metal in our industrial economy, is estimated to be adequate for our national needs to at least the year 2000—only 26 years away.

The United States consumes 30% of the TIN produced in the free world and imports nearly 100% of its needs, chiefly from Malaysia (63%), Thailand (30%), Bolivia and Brazil. With virtually no workable domestic deposits, the United States is also almost completely dependent upon foreign sources for MANGANESE, mostly from Brazil, Republic of South Africa, Zaire, Congo and Ghana. Manganese is indispensable to the manufacture of steel.

Nearly 100% of NICKEL, 65% of COBALT, 45% of CHROMIUM and 25% of our TUNGSTEN supplies are now imported from such foreign lands as Canada, Australia, Morocco, Zambia, Peru, South Korea and the Soviet Union. These minerals, important to the economy and security of the United States, constitute super alloys used in the steel, electrical, aircraft, spacecraft, nuclear and medical industries.

85% of our ANTIMONY, used in automobile batteries, plumbing fixtures, anti-friction bearings, solder and other items is imported chiefly from South Africa, Mexico and Bolivia. Formerly self-sufficient in MERCURY, the United States now imports 60% of its supplies, largely from Spain, the U.S.S.R. and Peru. Mercury has innumerable uses, including electrical equipment, catalysts, plastics, paints, instruments and agriculture.

The U.S. consumption of nonmonetary GOLD is 3 to 4 times its annual production. The Republic of South Africa produces two-thirds of the world's gold. Soviet Russia produces much of the remainder. An imbalance of over 100 million ounces exists between the world production and consumption of SILVER, a major industrial metal. Photography alone consumes more than three times the United States' annual production of silver.

50% of our SHEET MICA, a strategically important mineral used in electrical apparatus, vacuum tubes, capacitors and other products is now imported from India, Brazil and Malagasy Republic (Madagascar). For PLATINUM the United States is almost entirely dependent upon foreign sources such as the Republic of South Africa, the Soviet Union, Canada and Colombia. Platinum's electrical conductivity and resistance to corrosion and heat make it an essential mineral in our modern age. Numerous other minerals such as BISMUTH, FLUORINE, TITANIUM, VANADIUM and others are in short supply.

Uranium's Mighty Atom

URANIUM. Since energy is the prime force that sustains civilization, fossil fuels, nuclear energy, solar power from the sun, geothermal heat from the earth, and the oceans and winds are among the sources being vigorously considered. However, it is nuclear energy, using such fuels as uranium or thorium, that is now in the center of the world stage. Silvery white, readily fissionable uranium is the most established mineral available to solve mankind's energy dilemma.

Plutonium and other radioactive wastes produced by nuclear-powered electrical plants, and radon gas present in uranium mines and tailings, present environmental hazards that have aroused resistance to this source of energy. However, nuclear plants do not pollute the atmosphere as do oil, gas and coal fueled generators. Most scientists feel that proper safeguards can be established to make nuclear power the cleanest and most lasting source of energy.

The might stored in uranium's tiny atoms can light our cities and hamlets, serve our burgeoning industries, extract hitherto unreachable oil and mineral deposits, obtain fresh water from the oceans and make parched lands produce more food for hungry millions. Beneficial advancements in science, medicine and human welfare can also be attained, but while man seeks ways to utilize this stone's many blessings, leading powers of the world push on in a race to develop and employ uranium's lethal ability to destroy everything in its path. Man now stands breathlessly on the threshold of the future, beholding Utopia on the one hand and oblivion on the other. Thus, uranium reserves available to various nations have now become a dominant factor in human destiny.

Although defense requirements during World War II led America to develop the first uranium ore deposits, the present total combined reserves of Canada, the Republic of South Africa, Sweden, Soviet Russia, France and others have now surpassed the known reserves of the United States.

The identified, recoverable uranium resources in the United States at present are estimated to be sufficient until 1980. Beyond that date, depending upon the expansion of an atomic energy program, related environmental problems and developments in nuclear technology, enormous additional uranium reserves will be required. If the United States is to avoid a potentially crucial domestic shortage and is not to become reliant upon questionable or unreliable foreign sources, a massive exploration and development project will have to be launched to increase our uranium resources.

An outstanding, even ominous feature in the list of strategic minerals noted above is the global character of the sources from which the United States must secure the supplies necessary to maintain a viable and prosperous economy. Many Americans do not fully realize the degree with which U.S. foreign policy must be directed toward world markets, many of which are in formerly obscure and undeveloped countries. And, to exacerbate the seriousness of earth's dwindling supply of materials, according to scientists "technological progress and innovation will continue to be the main factors influencing the demand for all resources in the year 2000 and beyond."

Challenge to Technology

But, it is through this very same field of technology that man will meet the challenges of his times, as he always has in ages past. "Technology must devise systems for expanding available supplies through utilization of lower grade, sub-marginal ores, for increased production and treatment efficiency, for implementing new techniques in exploration and discovery of additional reserves, for developing substitutes and for extending supply sources through recycling and maximizing recovery of by-products."

Most certainly, the remedy for the world's ills, whether they concern an energy crisis, a pollution dilemma, or the depletion of earth's natural resources, lies in the advancement and fullest application of the science of technology. There, indeed, man faces his future.

His insatiable curiosity and his inventive genius, the very fountainhead of his cultural and economic progress, as it always has, should lead him toward utilizing wholly new concepts and methods, newly developed materials through increased research and greater cooperation with his fellowmen in dealing with the problems that confront him.

Recently we have had miraculous and convincing proof of what thoroughly organized, dedicated, concerted effort can accomplish toward attaining previously undreamed of goals. Through the most unprecedented application of technology the world has ever known, men have at last reached and explored the moon. This triumph over the impossible has become a timely lesson which has incalculable, far-reaching significance for all mankind.

Explorers on The Moon

On July 16, 1969, a huge Saturn V launch vehicle rose from Florida on a blazing plume of flame—destination, the moon. Mounted atop the rocket was Apollo 11, a cone-shaped spacecraft carrying Neil A. Armstrong, Michael Collins and Edwin A. Aldrin Jr. On July 20, after a flawless 240,000 mile journey through space, a spider-legged lunar module, called Eagle, made a precarious descent to the lunar surface. Braking itself on a tale of fire, the little space bug, encased in shining sheets of gold foil, unhesitatingly plunged toward the stark, crater-pocked surface. Only 60 seconds of braking fuel remained as the manned spacecraft was maneuvered to avoid crashing in a boulder-filled crater below. With 20 harrowing seconds left, Eagle's groping legs touched the face of the moon. Contact lights beamed. The engine stopped.

Then, through the dark void came Armstrong's calm voice announcing to Mission Control of the Manned Spacecraft Center in Houston, and a breathless world, "Tranquillity Base here. The Eagle has landed." Six hours later Armstrong descended Eagle's ladder, slowly poised one foot above the mystical surface, then stepped down, saying, "That's one small step for man, one giant leap for mankind."

That historic event brought to an end thousands of years of inscrutable uncertainty concerning earth's satellite. Launched by herculean efforts in science and technology and the most daring exploration ever attempted, man at last stood upon the moon ready to draw aside its veil of secrecy.

For countless ages peoples of the earth had looked with awe upon the moon's radiant face. Poets had long extolled its romantic beauty. Others, filled with superstitions, feared its strange, occult power. Wiser men were inspired to carefully observe it and widen their horizons of knowledge. Because the moon was studied in ancient times with an exactitude greater than any other physical science, this Goddess of The Heavens has been a lodestone of learning through the ceaseless course of time.

As early as the 2nd century B.C., Hipparchus had observed the eccentricity of the moon's orbit. Little more was learned until 1530 when Copernicus refuted Ptolemy's ancient theory and correctly assigned the planets their proper orbits about the sun. Then, such men as Tycho Brahe, Kepler and others further refined the laws of planetary motion. Huge lunar craters now memorialize their names.

It was Galileo, inventor of the telescope in 1609, who first observed the topographical features of the moon, the craters and the vast dark areas called maria or seas, bordered by lighter colored highlands and mountains. After Galileo had focused attention on the heavens, Newton's law of universal gravitation followed, influenced considerably by the comparison of free falling bodies on earth with the known motion of the moon. Thus, for over 2000 years the moon has led mankind onto trails of discovery, revealing laws that govern its existence.

The extraordinary feat of pin-pointing a landing a quarter of a million miles away was not the only miracle of technology displayed; with intense anticipation the whole world watched on television, another creation of science, and witnessed men actually treading upon the weird lunar surface. It was the first time in history that entire populations were privileged to journey with explorers to a frontier of man's farthest reach and participate in a great moment of discovery.

"Moon Stones" and Theories

Transcending the immensely important scientific experiments to be performed on the moon, priority was given to collecting samples of the lunar surface. After the amazingly successful splashdown in the Pacific of the returning voyagers with their priceless treasure from the moon, perhaps no men were ever more excited than the scientists who gathered in the Space Center Lunar Receiving Laboratory in Houston. They were awaiting the arrival of two boxes filled two-thirds with lunar soil, called regolith, and some 33 rocks from the size of a pea to 5 inches in diameter. These stones were about to prove or disprove pet theories long held concerning the origin of the moon, as well as the entire solar system.

For years scientists have held opposing views as to whether it was a "cold" or "hot" moon. Some believed that a concentration of cosmic gas and dust had coalesced to form a cold, rigid sphere which was later captured by earth. Others felt that dynamic tidal forces, energized by the momentum of the earth's rotation, had ejected into orbit a huge portion of the earth's mantle during its early plastic stage to form the moon.

The double-planet theory conceives the moon to have been formed by the coalescence of a ring of planetesimals circling the earth, similar to Saturn's rings. One thing is certain, early in the moon's history it was bombarded intensely by meteors, and aggregates circling the earth, which disrupted the lunar crust allowing lavas to exude and form the dark, sea-like lowlands called maria.

Certain terrestrial geologists, considered "hot-mooners," held that volcanism had played a major role in the moon's evolution, and that lava flows and plutonic formations would be found on the moon. They agreed that bombardment of the moon by meteors and micrometeors had highly altered the original moonscape by dispersing impact dust and debris over the lunar surface. Since the moon lacks an atmosphere, meteoric material falling in a nearly perfect vacuum would not be consumed by friction as it is on earth.

Revealing Luna's Secrets

Such was the status of man's endless and varied speculations over the secrets of earth's satellite as scores of prestigious scientists from the United States, Canada, Germany, Switzerland, England, Australia and Japan gathered to view the most remarkable treasure chest ever opened by man.

Crowded into a glassed enclosed room of the Lunar Receiving Laboratory, flushed with excitement and anticipation, were chemists, and geochemists, physicists and geophysicists, geologists, selenologists, seismologists, biologists and exobiologists, micropaleontologists and planetologists.

An intensely systematic investigation procedure was devised for this momentous occasion. First, 26 scientists having varied interests formed the Preliminary Examination Team. Clustered about a viewing porthole they watched a technician, wearing spacesuit gloves in order to avoid earthly contamination of the specimens, as he gingerly displayed the rocks on a pedestal in a vacuum chamber. Said a NASA official, Dr. King, "This is the greatest moment in scientific history."

Straining for a closer look, some saw rocks covered with black, powder-like dust. Then, someone noticed a sparkling crystal; another observed grains of minerals that obviously had crystallized in a molten, igneous rock. Some detected tiny, bubble-like holes or vesicles, a sure indication that gases had once escaped from fluid lavas. The "hot-mooners" were overjoyed by this confirmation of volcanic activity, which contradicted the theory of a cold moon. Evidently, basaltic lava flows covered the landing site on the Sea of Tranquillity.

After the preliminary examination came a grand program of exhaustive tests. Bits of lunar dust, rocks and core samples were parcelled out to 142 scientists called the Principal Investigators. Detailed analyses were made to determine the elements, rare earths and minerals comprising the samples. The effects of millions of years of solar winds and cosmic rays upon the lunar surface were measured; radioactive elements were tested in order to determine the age of the moon.

And then, early in January, 1970, to a conference in the National Space Hall of Fame in Houston came an august body of 700 scientists: chemists, physicists, astronomers, geologists, selenologists, NASA executives, engineers and astronauts to announce and debate the results of their findings. Luna, the silvery moon-goddess, would no longer be a shrine of total, unfathomable mystery.

Materials of the Moon

The lunar samples were found to consist of three distinctive types of materials: *crystalline igneous rocks* containing gas cavities, petrologically comparable to the basaltic lavas which occur widespread on earth; *microbreccias*, accumulations of lunar debris scattered by volcanism and meteoric impacts, containing angular fragments apparently ejected from distant portions of the moon's original crust; lunar fines, labelled *lunar regolith*, rather than soil, revealing a continuous bombardment by meteorites, solar winds and cosmic rays. A feature of the regolith was the abundance and variety of glassy spherules which appear to be droplets that quickly cooled after being ejected as a fine, molten spray from meteoric impacts.

Lunar geochemistry tests revealed that elements present in the Apollo samples correspond with many known to be dispersed in terrestrial rocks, with significant exceptions. Since many terrestrial igneous rocks contain certain amounts of combined hydrogen and oxygen, or water molecules, one of the most anticipated questions was whether hydrogen was present in lunar rocks. For this would provide future moon visitors with the essential ingredients of water, namely hydrogen and oxygen. Although oxygen occurs in great abundance on the moon in rock forming minerals, hydrogen was found to be virtually absent.

Analyses also showed the Apollo samples to be surprisingly low in such elements as gold, silver, copper, lead, molybdenum, tungsten, cobalt, antimony, mercury and others which were labelled siderophile and chalcophile elements. Either the materials which formed the moon were lacking in these elements, or these more volatile elements were vaporized and removed during certain high-temperature events in the moon's evolution. It should be remembered that these samples come from only a minuscule portion of the moon's surface.

An unexpected find was the high percentage of titanium in the form of ilmenite occurring in lunar basalts. The content was almost equivalent to an ore of titanium on earth. It is a high-temperature, light-weight metal used in rocket construction, important steel alloys and paints. Olivine, a clear, light green mineral, which can be seen scattered profusely in Hawaiian lavas, was also abundant in lunar basalts.

Meteors Bombard The Moon

The long continual bombardment of the moon by meteoric material was confirmed by the presence of considerable metallic iron and nickel. Metallic iron occurs rarely on earth, but both iron and nickel are common constituents of meteoric material found widespread in lunar regolith. It is amazing how slowly this regolith accumulated. On earth the lowest rate of sedimentation in the deepest seas is about 3000 millimeters per million years. But on the moon, the indicated increment of meteoric "dust" is only *one* millimeter per million years. How incredibly slow are the processes changing the face of the moon!

Perhaps it was unkind to probe a lady's age, but scientists found that Luna's birth goes back well beyond 4 billion years. Using the lead-uranium and rubidium-strontium radiometric age dating methods, the rocks forming the mare at the Apollo 11 site were found to have solidified 3.7 billion years ago. Fragments in the micro-breccias, thrown from the highlands by meteoric impact, indicate those regions are the oldest on the moon, about 4.6 billion years. This is also about the time the earth and the solar system are thought to have been formed.

Despite her age Luna's face is remarkably well preserved. On the other hand, earth's countenance has been changed greatly by the huge tectonic wrinkles that have raised lofty mountain chains of igneous, sedimentary, and metamorphic rocks, and by millions of square miles of limestone, shale, and sandstone layers that have concealed her older formations.

The enormous amount of volcanic activity which so profusely pock-marked the moon's surface took place during the first billion years of lunar history. Since then, excepting for the scars left by meteors and the effusion of lavas from younger volcanoes, Luna's face has remained frozen in time, unchanged to this day—a living museum of the cosmic past.

The Wizardry of Technology

Other Apollo missions followed the initial landing of 1969. Apollo 15 went to an entirely different part of the moon. With the aid of unbelievable wizardy in electronics, computers and telemetry, on July 30, 1971, David Scott and James Irwin landed their lunar module, Falcon, within 1200 feet of a predetermined site between the base of the 14,000 foot high Apennine Mountains and a strange canyon called Hadley Rille whose origin is still unsolved.

As though the stupendous achievement of executing a perfect flight through 240,000 miles of space were not enough, the world was treated to another feat of American technology: from the ghostly lunar surface television broadcasts were beamed in live color, accompanied by the instantaneous voices of the astronauts during their three six-hour exploratory excursions aboard a battery powered, four-wheeled lunar rover.

Thrilled by the discovery of a boulder he thought might be anorthosite, Scott dubbed it "the Genesis Rock." On earth anorthosite, a soda-lime feldspar, is found in regions of very old rocks, such as the Adirondacks, the Lake Superior region, Minnesota, Norway, Labrador and in the mineral-rich Pre-Cambrian Shield of Canada, one of the earth's oldest formations.

Color television views of the sunlit walls of Hadley Rille clearly revealed the horizontally

bedded character of the formation, apparently a plateau built of successive layers of lava flows, impact debris or breccias. Scott's "genesis rock" probably had been ejected from the highlands above. These higher regions, thought to be older than the dark, basalt-flooded maria below, form the lighter colored portions of the moon's face we see from earth.

Apollo 17—1972

On April 20, 1972, Apollo 16 became the first to visit the highlands, landing on the rugged, rock-strewn Cayley Plains of the Descartes region. There, on Stone Mountain, samples of anorthosite were obtained. Apollo 17's spaceship America reached the moon in December 1972. It released the lunar module Challenger which dropped precisely into the Taurus-Littrow region, a lava-flooded valley surrounded by an overwhelming panorama of towering, brightly sunlit, hump-shaped mountains called massifs. Disappointing was the lack of outcrops of plutonic rocks such as granite, which forms much of the continents on earth. Again, most of the samples collected consisted of breccias and regolith material.

Scientists have now confirmed the fact that the moon is much like the earth in its igneous origin, and that it is not a dead, cold, inert body as some believed. The moon also contains the same elements prevalent on earth and the solar system, but in different proportions. The more volatile elements, many of the metals used in our present economy on earth, thus far appear to be lacking on the moon.

However, much is yet to be learned about the moon and there are many of its areas yet to be explored. One condition will greatly aid the lunar prospector: the moon's surface is utterly bare. No foliage, forests, rivers, or seas conceal indications of any mineral deposits that might exist. Using remote sensing devices and new techniques, astronauts flying above the moon's surface will be able to discern areas which justify detailed examination.

Although traces of such gases as neon, argon, and helium have been detected on the moon, an atmosphere is almost entirely absent thereby creating a nearly perfect vacuum. In the absence of an atmosphere, primary minerals on the moon have not been "weathered," oxidized or altered. Prospectors are not apt to find the bright blue and green carbonates of copper, nor the reddish hues of altered minerals of iron, such as occur on earth. Lack of oxidation has given the moonscape a drab gray to light tan appearance.

Laboratory of the Future

The importance of the moon as a possible source of mineral wealth, at present, is greatly overshadowed by its value as a platform for innumerable scientific investigations. A large part of the astronaut's activities while on the moon consisted of setting up complex sensors, miniature laboratories, which radio to earth data on solar winds, cosmic rays, the moon's magnetic field, internal heat, ions emanating from the moon, the sun and space, moonquakes, and meteorite impacts. Laser pulses bounced back to earth measure the drift of the earth's continents and the distance to the moon with an accuracy of six inches.

Colonies of scientists and technologists will be the first and most important groups on the moon. While astronomers peer through the black, clear, airless lunar heavens examining the great galaxy that contains our solar system, and the infinite reaches of space, many secrets applicable to man's future will be discovered.

Meteorological observations will lead to accurate predictions of terrestrial weather; experiments in biology and applied sciences which require a nearly perfect vacuum will be carried on in this formerly unavailable laboratory; problems in medicine, chemistry, physics, and astronomy will be solved in the moon's unique environment. A whole new vista of scientific potentialities will be revealed to all mankind.

Few people seem to realize the numerous benefits derived from the Apollo missions, as well as the unmanned automatic orbital satellites that already are contributing immensely to the welfare of mankind. To support manned spaceflights the National Aeronautics and Space Administration, known as NASA, developed new techniques which have tremendously advanced the science of technology.

Apollo's Priceless Gifts

Improvements in earthbound medical practices include computer devices that enhance X-rays, switches operated by sight for patients unable to move their extremities, wireless monitoring in intensive care cardiac units, artificial heart controllers, instruments that detect neurological disorders, and water-bath support systems which, comparable to lunar gravity simulators are now used in helping the handicapped to practice the use of artifical limbs.

In cancer treatments, new uses in radiation therapy, and miniature radiation-dosimeter probes were developed. Automatic blood pressure measuring instruments during exercise, metabolic analyzers to measure oxygen consumption and carbon dioxide production by patients in intensive care all came from the need of monitoring astronauts during their space flights and walks on the moon. The list of medical benefits goes on and on.

The proficient, unbelievable accuracy of NASA's telemetric systems in directing spacecraft to precise landing points on the cratered lunar surface, and within seconds of the overall computed time; in providing instant two-way voice communications with the astronauts, and in sending commands from earth that operated instruments and equipment on the moon all led to the perfection of the numerous orbital satellites now coming into growing use.

Today, these satellites, worlds unto themselves, provide instant transmission of global events, and of educational programs which organize, broadcast and disseminate knowledge to the world's populations. By various forms of remote sensing and color photography they are accurately mapping the earth, investigating hydrologic problems involving rivers, lakes and oceans; determining the sources and causes of pollution; studying geologic structures and possible new mineral resources; and evaluating the spread and prevention of plant, forest, and crop diseases.

Nearly 2000 NASA inventions have become available to the medical, communication, housing, industrial and food segments of American life. High-temperature, hard, resistant kitchenware, high-energy batteries, vital new metals originally designed for rocket engines, insulating materials with a heat loss of less than one degree per year, digital clocks with previously unattained accuracy, heat reflecting fabrics used by the astronauts, fuel cells and new wiring systems useful to the housing industry—all these and many more are dividends already derived from America's space achievements.

Workshops in Space

One of the most portentous programs relates to SKYLAB, the forerunner of many space station workshops that will most assuredly provide mankind with a myriad of experiments and operations that can be obtained only beyond earth's atmosphere, in a zero gravity and vacuum environment.

In addition to having numerous sensors that

will explore and inventory earth's various natural and cultural resources, these space-worlds will be used to make, cast, and weld exotic metals and alloys under vacuum conditions. Crystals, free from flaws and mechanical stresses, can be made which will immensely benefit computers, electronic equipment, and color television. New and ultrapure biological materials will be created in medicines and vaccines. Specialized glasses free from defects, made possible by levitating liquids and cooling them without physical contact with containers because of weightlessness, will greatly improve the performance of optical instruments.

Already, hundreds of manufacturing organizations have become interested in utilizing the processes that apply to their particular industrial activities. Many of these concepts surpass the limits of the most far-out science-fiction ideas imagined today. In fact, because of earth's sensitive and overcharged biosphere, some scientists foresee clusters of orbital workshops in space, within 100 years, engaging in various manufacturing activities which at present are harmful to terrestrial ecology.

The view is held that greatly expanded populations, and an anticipated increase in consumption levels during the next century by a factor of 40, perhaps 100, will require mankind to confine certain critical industries to space, if the environment so unique and precious to this planet is to be preserved. Since energy is the mainstay of civilization, this transference applies particularly to nuclear power plants being assigned to the abyss of space where its infinitely absorbent capacity, and near-vacuum without air or sound, eliminates all threats to terrestrial ecology.

Prospectors in Space

It is even conjectured that man ultimately will have to seek his minerals and other raw materials elsewhere in the solar system where the elements composing the universe, in places, combine to form the physical resources essential to civilization. Earth's supplies of materials obviously cannot last forever, a fact already evidenced by the spectre of countless oil and mineral deposits now standing exhausted or nearing depletion.

During the many millennia of the past, man's unending quest for mineral riches in far away places energized the spread of one civilization after another across the globe. Then, came the development of racial and national consciousness, followed by conflicts of interests, international jealousies and strife.

But, as nations of the world face the alternative of scarcity and want versus dependence upon one another for energy and resources, for the first time in man's existence tolerant, unselfish, willing cooperation will become the ruling power. Hopefully, this will result in a regeneration of the human race, in which worldwide peace and understanding will not only be desirable but utterly and basically indispensable.

Will prospectors of the future blaze trails into the far reaches of space, widening their knowledge and capabilities as they have in ages past? Can man's ingenious capacity for overcoming the emergencies of his age meet this, thus far the greatest of his challenges? Will future generations witness fantastic spacecraft and shuttle-ships bound for the moon, Mars or the satellites of Jupiter, seeking the same stones that always have beckoned adventurers beyond the farthest horizon? Wrote Thoreau, "Man's capacities have never been measured." Anything conceivable is possible.

A Lever To Move The World

"Give me a lever long enough and a fulcrum strong enough and single-handed I can move the world." These were the words of the Greek mathematician and inventor, Archimedes, 2200 years ago.

With the launching of the Lunar Exploration Program, and the many unmanned automatic satellites orbiting the earth and probing the exciting realms of outer space, the United States at last has found the lever and the fulcrum: science, technology, and united human effort, the tool to "move the world"—and, to determine man's destiny.

How fortunate it is for every living thing on earth that man's inquisitive nature still remains unquenchable and unabated, for it was this human trait that launched him upon the most consequential adventure in all the ages of history. Without that trait the process of human betterment would stagnate and die.

Stimulated by the challenge of sending the first missions to explore the moon, never in man's history have such miraculous peaks of technology and national will been attained. However, the most valuable lesson learned stems from the supreme accomplishment of organizing and carrying out the program itself. Thus was demonstrated the means, so sorely needed, for solving the enormous ecological, social and economic problems of the world.

The Apollo program constituted the greatest concentration of scientific activity toward a common goal known to man. An astonishing workforce of over 400,000 people, including hordes of humblest toilers, thousands of contractors, scientists and giant corporations, all dedicated to one united thought, pooled their skills, knowledge and resources to reach and explore the moon. And, that they did—with unimaginable success. In demonstrating what can be done through technology, human will and unanimity, perhaps mankind can be inspired to similar endeavors toward solving the modern ills of the world.

The Goal of Technology

By multiplying the Apollo program but a few times, efforts can be organized in the same efficient, dedicated manner to reach cherished new goals: to rid life on earth of pestilence and disease; to purge the earth's air and waters of pollution; to make the earth's soil and rocks produce abundance and prosperity for all, and thus dispel the ogre of want, discord, and covetousness that have wracked so many periods of history.

In daring to adventure into space the United States responded to the inborn instincts of a long parade of pioneer forbears, and took the first giant step toward the next and most promising frontier, realizing that the ultimate aim and responsibility of science and technology is to fulfill human aspirations and make this a better world in which to live. With most of earth's frontiers conquered perhaps man will now move on to newer and more glorious horizons—and, ultimately discover himself.

The miracles of science, unity of purpose and the innate spirit of adventure that enabled American astronauts in six lunar landings to gather and bring home 840 pounds of precious stones from the moon, let us hope, will eventually make this beautiful blue-skied, fleecy-clouded, green-clad, sea-girded paradise we call Earth, a bountiful and fraternal homeland for all humanity.

CHRONOLOGY

STONE AGES

B.C.   **Chapter 1 — STONE AGE TREASURE**

1½ Million   Australopithecus (Southern Apes)
1 Million   Zinjanthropus (Tanganyika) Leakey
500,000   PALEOLITHIC begins: Pithecanthropus (Java)
                    Sinanthropus (Peking)
300,000   In France: Abbevillian—Chellean (2nd interglacial)
                    Heidelberg Man, Homo Erectus
80,000   NEANDERTHAL (4th and last interglacial stage)
35,000   CRO-MAGNONS—Aurignacian, Solutrean, Magdalenian
10,000   NEOLITHIC begins

                    Chapter 2 — THE CRADLE OF CIVILIZATION — MESOPOTAMIA

                    Agriculture Begins. First Communities form.
7,500   Caves of Carmel, Jarmo, Jericho, Hacilar, Hassuna
5,500   Iran, Susa, and Sialk. Copper in use.
5,000   Annealing, hammering METALS
4,500   First settlers in Sumer, Ubaid, Eridu, Ur
                    Melting and casting of METALS
4,000   THE GREAT FLOOD (Epic of Gilgamesh)
3,800   New cities of Sumer, Uruk (Biblical Erech, now Warka)
                    PROFUSE USE OF METALS
3,500   DAWN OF METALLURGY—King Enmerker, 1st Dynasty-Sumer
3,000   BRONZE IN USE—Introducing THE BRONZE AGE
2,500   Royal Cemetery of Ur
2,100   GOLDEN AGE OF UR—King Ur-Nammu

                    Chapter 3 — EGYPT

                    Pre-5,000 B.C. High art in flint
4,000   Hammered copper appears
3,500   METALS at Gerza, from Mesopotamia
3,300   MENES from Heirakonopolis founds MEMPHIS—First Dynasty
3,000   Copper Mined in the SINAI—Semerket (1st D.)
                    Snefru (4th D.) Ramses III (20th D.)—(2,000 years)
2,900   Saqqara Pyramid (King Zoser). Egypt begins to use stone.
2,800   Copper carves stones for the Pyramids at Gizeh
1,700   Under control of the Hyksos
1,510   Thutmose I. HATSHEPSUT'S SHIPS TO PUNT (1490)
1,479   THUTMOSE III conquers Palestine (18th Dynasty)
1,370   Amenhotep IV (Ikhnaton) and Nefertiti build Armarna.
1,350   TUTANKHAMEN
1,250   RAMSES II—Karnak, Luxor
1,200   RAMSES III—Exodus of the Israelites, Copper trail to Sinai

Chapter 4 — THE BRONZE AGE BOOM

3,000	Bronzes in Luristan, Egypt and Crete
3,000	Stone Age TROY (Hissarlik, Troy I)
2,350	Sargon I (Earlier Kish of The Semites, 4,400 B.C.)
2,200	Bronze Age TROY. Gold treasure, Troy 2
2,100	Ur's Golden Age
2,100	Hittite Kingdom at Hattusas
1,900	HAMMURABI, First Babylonian Empire
1,800	The Hittites destroy Babylon
1,700	The Rise of ASSYRIA—Trade in Anatolia
1,276	Shalmaneser rules Assyria

Chapter 5 — CIVILIZATION SPREADS TO EUROPE

3,000	Bronze Age reaches CRETE, Knossos
2,000	Phonetic writing in Knossos
1,700	Knossos destroyed
1,600	Brilliant Knossos revival, to 1400
1,400	Knossos leveled by explosion of Thera
1,300	ACHEANS enter Greece
1,200	The Rise of MYCENAE—CYPRUS Copper
1,180	Acheans under Agamemnon destroy Troy
2,400-2,000	THE BRONZE AGE REACHES EUROPE
	Tiber, Arno, Po Rivers in ITALY. Los Millares, SPAIN. Cintra, Estoril PORTUGAL
1,500	Bell Beaker Folk in BRITAIN—Stonehenge
1,600	Bronzesmiths on The Danube—Unetice Culture

Chapter 6 — DAWN OF THE IRON AGE

1,450	Discovery of ironmaking. The Chalybes and Hittites
1,385	The Hittite Empire under King Suppilluliumas
1,200	The Exodus, Israelites return to Canaan
1,150	With Iron the Philistines invade and conquer Canaan
1,013-973	King David rules Israel
1,000-625	The metalworkers and traders of Phoenicia
1,100	The Phoenicians founded Cadiz, Spain
973-935	The rule of SOLOMON. Copper of the Sinai. Gold of Sheba.
853	ASSYRIAN CONQUERORS—Shalmaneser III, Tiglath-Pileser III, Sargon II, Ashurbanipal II (880)
(814)	Phoenicians establish CARTHAGE.
586	NEBUCHADNEZZAR destroys Jerusalem.

Chapter 7 — THE GREEK CIVILIZATION

1,000	The Dorian Invasion. Sparta established
to 750	The great expansion and colonization of the Greeks
560	Croesus of Lydia—Invention of COINAGE
541	Peisistratus, Tyrant of Athens. Rise of Commerce
546	CYRUS OF PERSIA seizes Lydia, Croesus.
490	Cyrus attacks Attica, Battle of Marathon
480	BATTLE OF SALAMIS. A fleet financed with LAURIUM SILVER
447	The Parthenon and THE GOLDEN AGE OF GREECE

371	Thebes leads the Greeks
336	ALEXANDER THE GREAT, succeeds King Philip
331	Alexander plunders Susa
323	Alexander dies in Babylon, begins THE HELLENISTIC AGE

Chapter 8 — THE ROMAN WORLD

800	Arrival of The Etruscans.
734	The Corinthian Greeks found Syracuse
524	The Greeks defeat the Etruscans at Cumae
509	Tarquin The Proud, Etruscan king defeated. ROMAN REPUBLIC established on the Tiber
272	Romans invade Magna Graecia, capture Tarentum and Rhegium
264-201	Rome attacks Carthage. FIRST & SECOND PUNIC WARS
208	Scipio seizes the silver of Castulo, Spain
168	Paullus defeats Macedon
149	Rome destroys Carthage
146	Rome destroys Corinth. GREECE BECOMES A ROMAN PROVINCE. ROME EXPLOITS THE WEALTH OF SPAIN (200 B.C.-400 A.D.)
69	CAESAR APPOINTED QUAESTOR IN SPAIN
61	Caesar returns to Spain as Propraetor
60	First Triumvirate: Caesar, Pompey, Crassus. Gaul assigned to Caesar.
58	Caesar defeats Ariovistus (near Rouffac)
56	Caesar defeats The Veneti
55	Caesar Invades Britain
47	Caesar retakes Parthia (Veni, Vidi, Vici)
44	CAESAR ASSASSINATED—20 years of civil war follow.
27	Octavian becomes Emperor AUGUSTUS

A.D.

14	Augustus succeeded by Tiberias, Caligula (murdered)
43	Claudius begins CONQUEST OF BRITAIN.
54	Rules of Nero (54), Vespasian (75), Titus (79) (Jerusalem)
101	TRAJAN CONQUERS DACIA. Vast mineral wealth.
117	HADRIAN creates glory of Rome. Rebuilds Pantheon, builds Tivoli, Castel Sant' Angelo.
161	MARCUS AURELIUS (after Antoninus Pius). PAX ROMANA ENDS.
180	Commodus, Septimus Severus, (COINS DEVALUED). Caracalla, and Alexander Severus (222) DEVALUE COINAGE.
284	Diocletian basks in oriental splendor. Rome's history goes "FROM GOLD TO IRON AND RUST."
410	VISIGOTHS SACK ROME. VANDALS COME IN 455

Chapter 9 — PRELUDE TO THE EMPIRES OF EUROPE

450	Beginning of THE DARK AGES
486	Clovis unites Neustria (West) and Austrasia (East)
732	Martel Repels The Moslems
770	Charlemagne revives mining: Schemnitz & Kremnitz, Czech.
800	CHARLEMAGNE THE GREAT. Crowned in Rome, Emperor of the Romans.
919	Ottonians stimulate eastward migration.
938	RAMMELSBERG MINES DISCOVERED (Goslar, Germany)
1096	First Crusade to The Holy Lands. New desires, new needs.
1170	ERZGEBIRGE OF BOHEMIA (Ore Mountains) discovered. Zinnwald, Altenberg, Joachimsthal. The rush to mineral wealth.

1249	Charter of Iglau (Jihlava) near Prague, Czechoslovakia.
10th to 12th Centuries	THE GOTHIC CATHEDRALS—needs for metals.
1519	CHARLES V, King of Spain, Holy Roman Emperor.
1530	THE FUGGER BANKERS, lenders, Swabian Counts
1550	GREAT MINING BOOM OF THE MIDDLE AGES.
1215	MAGNA CARTA signed in ENGLAND.
1337	Tin Mining increases in CORNWALL
14th, 15th, 16th Centuries	THE RENAISSANCE IN EUROPE
1478	Lorenzo the Magnificent
1498	Vasco da Gama rounds Cape of Good Hope to India

Chapter 10 — LURES OF THE NEW WORLD

1492	COLUMBUS DISCOVERS AMERICA
1494	America's First Gold Mines: Santo Tomas, Haiti
1498	Columbus sees golden jewels on Gulf of Paria.
1502	Columbus' 4th and last voyage. Finds gold of Veragua.
1506	Death of Columbus at Valladolid, Spain.
1521	CORTES CONQUERS TENOCHTITLAN (Aztecs) MEXICO.
1534	MEXICO'S WEALTH UNFOLDS. Silver Mines of Pachuca.
1546	The great Zacatecas district discovered, also Chihuahua.
1550	The silver of Guanajuato discovered.
1513	BALBOA sights the Pacific Ocean
1524	PIZARRO'S first effort to find the wealth of "Piru".
1533	PIZZARO SEIZES ATAHUALPA'S TREASURE OF GOLD, AND CONQUERS PERU. Dies in Lima, 1541. Inca wealth preceded by the cultures of Chavin de Huantar (1000-500 B.C.), the Mochicas and Chimu, who were master metalworkers.

Chapter 11 — AMERICA—MIRACLE OF THE WILDERNESS

1540	Coronado explores the Southwest, seeking the Golden Cities of Cibola. Grand Canyon of Arizona discovered.
1588	England defeats the Spanish Armada, opening America to English colonization.
1607	Jamestown founded by the English.
1620	The Pilgrims establish the Plymouth Colony
1646	First ironworks at Saugus, Mass. Birthplace of American iron industry.
1732	Coventry Forge, Hopewell Village use newly discovered magnetite ores. Ironworks in all 13 colonies.
1769	James Watt improves Thomas Newcomen's steam engine, built to pump water from English mines. *Opens the Age of Steam.*
1786	James Fitch uses steam engine to propel boats.
1830	Peter Cooper's steam locomotive pulls first railroad train.
1831	Cyrus McCormick invents harvester. Rapid increase in machines made of iron. Need of low cost iron becomes urgent.
1845	Marquette iron range discovered, opening vast iron ore deposits of the Lake Superior region.
1841	Douglass Houghton, Michigan State Geologist, reports "ores of copper abundant" in Keweenaw Peninsula, N. Mich.
1845	Cliff Mine starts production. RUSH TO THE COPPER COUNTRY
1852	Isle Royale starts amygdaloid mining.

1845	Lead mining opens Mississippi Valley to settlement.
1845	John O'Sullivan, in United States Magazine, urges America embark upon its MANIFEST DESTINY
1848	GOLD DISCOVERED IN CALIFORNIA. Becomes a state in 1850.
1859	Silver of the COMSTOCK LODE DISCOVERED. Nevada becomes a state in 1864. Gold and silver influence the Civil War.
1860	Leadville, Colorado discovered. Colorado, a state in 1876.
1864	BUTTE, MONTANA—first a silver district. Montana becomes a territory in 1875. Butte known as "richest hill on earth"
1864	Gold, then copper in BINGHAM CANYON, UTAH. Statehood, 1896.
1867	Seward buys ALASKA.
1868	Peace treaty grants permanent rights to the Sioux.
1874	Gold Discovered in the BLACK HILLS. S. Dakota a state, 1889.
1876	Custer's forces massacred on the Little Big Horn, Montana.
1854-1871	Copper, silver and gold deposits discovered in ARIZONA. Ajo, La Paz, Wickenburg, Clifton-Morenci. 12 bloody years of COCHISE'S vendetta.
1877	Discovery of TOMBSTONE'S silver. Notorious sagas of the West.
1877	The copper wealth of BISBEE, Arizona discovered.
1885	W. A. Clark opens UNITED VERDE mine, Jerome, Arizona.
1898	Gold Rush to the KLONDIKE, THE YUKON, NOME.
1900	Discovery of silver-rich TONOPAH, NEVADA
1902	Fabulously rich GOLDFIELD, NEVADA starts production.
1945	Atom bomb test, Alamogordo, New Mexico opens ATOMIC AGE. (1942, First chain reaction pile, University of Chicago.)
(1945)	The ATOMIC BOMB ENDED WORLD WAR II
1949	Carnotite (uranium ore) discovered at Haystack Butte, New Mexico. Marked the beginning of the URANIUM RUSH.
1951	Great Jackpile uranium mine discovered by Anaconda Company on Laguna Indian Reservation.
1952	Charles Steen discovers Big Indian uranium district, Moab Utah. Glamorization starts URANIUM STAMPEDE.
1952	Vernon Pick finds uranium on Dirty Devil River, Utah
1969	FIRST MEN ON THE MOON, followed by other Apollo Missions.
1970	Conference of scientists, Houston, Texas, re: moon findings.
1971	Apollo 15 lands at base of Apennine Mountains on the moon.
1972	Apollo 17 lands in Taurus-Littrow highlands, the moon.
1973	Skylab—Space Laboratory

SELECTED PUBLICATIONS

The books and publications concerning anthropology, archeology, history, geology, economics, technology and world mineral resources are innumerable. The following list is offered merely as a general guide to those specialized works which contain more detailed information on the subjects covered in this book. They can be found listed in the files of most major libraries.

ADY, C.M. Lorenzo de Medici and The Renaissance in Italy, London, 1955

AGRICOLA, GEORGIUS. De Re Metallica. Translated by Herbert C. Hoover and Lou Henry Hoover, New York, 1950

A.I.M.E. Transactions, Vol. 42, History of the Geology of the Ancient Gold Fields of Turkey, by L. Dominian, 1911

ANATI, EMMANUEL. Palestine Before The Hebrews, New York, 1963

ANDREWS, C. M. The Colonial Period of American History, 1934

ARDAILLON, EDOUARD. Les Mines du Laurion dans l'Antiquite, 1897

BANCROFT, HUBERT H. The Works of—Histories. San Francisco, 1882

BAIKE, J. The Sea Kings of Crete, 1910

BARRACLOUGH, G. The Origins of Modern Germany, Oxford, 1946

BINING, A. C. Pennsylvania Iron Mfg. in the 18th Century, 1938

BLANCE, B. M. Early Bronze Colonists in Iberia, Antiguity, 1961

BLEGEN, C. W. Troy, 1950-58

BLOCH, RAYMOND. The Etruscans, 1958

BOLTON, HERBERT E. The Spanish Borderlands, 1921. Coronado, 1949

BRAILSFORD, J. W. Late Prehistoric Antiquities of The British Isles, 1953

BRAIDWOOD, R. J. Prehistoric Men, 1957. Prehistoric Investigations in Iraqui Kurdistan, Chicago, 1960

BREASTED, JAMES H. A History of Egypt, N.Y., 1909. Ancient Times, N.Y., 1916, 1944. Conquest of Civilization, 1926

BROOKE, C. N. Europe in The Middle Ages, London, 1964

BROWNE, J. ROSS. Adventures in Apache Country, N.Y., 1878

BURN, A. R. Minoans, Philistines and Greeks, 1930

BURNS, WALTER. Tombstone, New York, 1929

CAMBRIDGE. Economic History of Europe. Vol. II, Trade & Industry in the Middle Ages. Vol. III, Economic Organization and Policies of The Middle Ages.

CARMEN, H. J. & Syrett, H. C. A History of The American People, N.Y. 1952

CARPENTER, RHYS. The Greeks in Spain, London, 1925

CARTER, HOWARD. The Tomb of Tutankhamen, London, 1927

CHALFANT, W. A. The Story of Inyo. Gold, Guns & Ghost Towns, 1947

CHAMPDOR, A. Babylon, New York, 1958

CHANDLER, L. V. The Economics of Money and Banking, N.Y., 1948

CHARLESWORTH, M. P. Trade Routes & Commerce—Rome, 1926

CHILDE, V. GORDON. The Dawn of European History, N.Y. 1957
——————. Prehistoric Migrations in Europe, 1950.
—————— Prehistoric Commerce in the British Isles, 1940

CHITTENDEN, H. A. History of The American Fur Trade, Stanford, 1954

CLARKE, J. G. D. Prehistoric Europe, London, 1950.

CLARKE, GRAHAME. World Prehistory, Cambridge, 1950.

CLELAND, R. G. From Wilderness To Empire, N.Y. 1944. This Reckless Breed of Men, 1950. A History of Phelps-Dodge, 1952

COMAN, KATHERINE. Economic Beginnings of The Far West, 1912

CERAM, C. W. Gods, Graves & Scholars, N.Y. 1961. The Secret of The Hittites, N.Y. 1956

COOPER, HENRY S. Moon Rocks, New York, 1970

DAVIES, O. Roman Mines in Europe, Oxford, 1936

DANA, E. S. A Textbook of Mineralogy, N.Y. 1898-1926

Del MAR, ALEXANDER. A History of The Precious Metals, London, 1902

DE QUILLE, DAN. The Big Bonanza, New York, 1947 (Reprint)

DE VOTO, B. The Course of Empire, N.Y. 1952

DIAZ, BERNAL. Discovery and Conquest of Mexico, N.Y. 1956 (Reprint)

DIXON, PIERSON. The Iberians in Spain, Oxford, 1940

DOBIE, J. F. Apache Gold & Yaqui Silver, Boston, 1947

DOMINIAN, L. Geology of The Ancient Gold Fields of Turkey. A.I.M.E. Transactions, Vol. 42, 1911

DUNBAR, CARL O. Historical Geology, N.Y. 1954

DURANT, WILL. The Story of Civilization. Ten Volumes.
——————. The Lessons of History, N.Y. 1968

EHRENBERG, R. Finance of The Fuggers, 1912

ELLIOTT, J. H. Imperial Spain, 1469-1716. London, 1963

EMERY, W. H. Nubian Treasure, 1948. Royal Tombs of Ballana, 1938

EMMONS, W. H. Gold Deposits of The World, N.Y. 1937

EVANS, A. E. The Palace of Minos at Knossos, 4 Vols. 1921-35

FICHTENAU, H. The Carolingian Empire, Oxford, 1957

FORBES, R. J. Metallurgy in Antiquity, Leiden, 1950. Studies in Ancient Technology, Vols. VIII & IX, Leiden, 1964

FRANKFORT, H. The Birth of Civilization in The Near East, N.Y. 1959

FRENCH, L. H. Seward's Land of Gold, N.Y. 1900

GARROD, D. E. & BATE, D. A. The Stone Age of Mount Carmel, 1937

GARSTANG, J. The Hittite Empire, 1929

GHIRSHMAN, R. Iran From Earliest Times, 1954

GIBBONS, E. The Decline and Fall of The Roman Empire, N.Y. 1960

GLASSCOCK, C. B. War of The Copper Kings. The Golden Highway, 1935.

GOWLAND, WM. Early Metallurgy of Silver & Lead, Archaeologia, 1903

GRANT, MICHAEL. The World of Rome, N.Y. 1960

GRAY, JOHN. The Canaanites, 1964

GRISWOLD, D. L. Leadville, Denver, 1951

GURNEY, O. R. The Hittites, 1961.

HAFEN, L.R. Settlement of Western America, 1941

HAGEN, VICTOR. Realm of The Incas. N.Y. 1957

HALL, H. R. The Civilization of Greece in The Bronze Age, 1928

HALL, R. N. Great Zimbabwe, 1905. Prehistoric Rhodesia, 1909

HAMILTON, W. R. The Yukon Story, Vancouver, 1964

HARDEN, DONALD D. The Phoenicians (Ed. Dr. D. Glyn), London, 1962

HARGRAVES, E. H. Australia and Its Gold Fields, London, 1855

HERRMANN, PAUL. Conquest By Man, N.Y., 1954

HILL, JAMES M. Mining Districts of The Western United States, 1912

HOUGH, EMERSON. The Passing of The Frontier, 1918.

HULBERT, A. B. The Forty Niners. The California Trail, 1931

HUSSEY, R. C. Historical Geology, N.Y. 1947

JACKSON, J. H. Anybody's Gold, N.Y. 1941

JENKIN, A. K. H. The Cornish Miner, 1927-48

JORALEMAN, IRA B. Romantic Copper, Its Lure & Lore, N.Y. 1934

KEES, HERMAN. Ancient Egypt, Chicago, 1961

KENYON, K. M. Archeology in The Holy Land, 1959

KNIGHT, M. Economic History of Europe to the End of The Middle Ages, Harvard, 1926

KRAMER, SAMUEL NOAH. The Sumerians, Chicago, 1936. History begins at Sumer, 1958. Enmerker and The Lord of Arrata, Philadelphia, 1952

LATOUCHE, R. The Birth of Western Economy, London, 1961

LAVENDER, DAVID. The Story of the Cyprus Mines Corporation, Huntington Library, San Marino, California, 1962

LEAKEY, L. S. B. Adam's Ancestors, 1953

LEEPER, A. W. A History of Medieval Austria, Oxford, 1941

LEWIS, GEORGE R. The Stannaries, 1908

LINDGREN, WALDEMAR. Mineral Deposits, N.Y. 1933

LLOYD, S. Early Anatolia, 1956

LORAIN, S. H. Iran Mineral Report, U.S. Bureau of Mines, 1964

LUCAS, A. Copper in Ancient Egypt, London, 1927. Ancient Egyptian Materials & Industries, London, 1962

LUDWIG, EMIL. The Germans, 1941

LYMAN, G. D. Saga of The Comstock Lode, N.Y. 1944. ————. Ralston's Ring, N.Y. 1947

LEWIS, OSCAR. The Silver Kings, 1947

McDIVILL, J. F. Minerals and Men, 1965

McGUIGAN, DOROTHY. The Habsburgs, N.Y. 1966

MARYON, H. Metalworking in The Ancient World, American Journal of Archeology. 1949

MASON, BRIAN & MELSON, W. G. The Lunar Rocks, N.Y. 1970

MASON, J. A. The Ancient Civilizations of Peru, 1960

MACIVER, D. R. The Villanovans and Early Etruscans, 1924

MARCOSSON, I. F. Anaconda, N.Y. 1957

MARTIN, D. D. Tombstone Epitaph, New Mexico, 1951

MOORE, RUTH. Man, Time & Fossils, N.Y. 1953

MORISON, S. E. Admiral of The Ocean Sea, Boston, 1942

MULDER, WM. & MORTENSEN, A. R. Among The Mormons, N.Y. 1958

MUMFORD, LEWIS. Technics and Civilization, N.Y. 1934

MURDOCH, ANGUS. Boom Copper, N.Y. 1945

MYLONAS, G. E. Ancient Mycenae, 1957

NADEAU, REMI. Ghost Towns of The West. The City Makers, N.Y. 1948

NETTELS, C. P. The Roots of American Civilization, 1938

NEUGEBAUER, O. & SACHS, A. The Exact Sciences in Antiquity, 1957.

NEVINS, ALLAN. Chronicles of America. The Gateway to History, 1938

NINIGER, R. D. Minerals For Atomic Energy, N.Y. 1954

NUCLEAR GEOLOGY. A symposium, Wiley & Sons, N.Y. 1954

OAKLEY, K. P. Man The Tool Maker, 1958

OLMSTEAD, A. A History of The Persian Empire, 1948

OSBORN, HENRY F. Men of The Old Stone Age, N.Y. 1915

OSGOOD, H. L. The American Colonies in The 18th Century, 1904-07

PARKMAN, FRANCIS. The Oregon Trail, N.Y. Pioneers of France in The New World, 1907

PARROT, A. Sumer, N.Y. 1961

PARRY, J. H. The Age of Reconnaissance, N.Y. 1962

PAUL, RODMAN. Mining Frontiers of The Far West, N.Y. 1963

PAYNE, ROBERT. The Gold of Troy, N.Y. 1959

PEAKE, HAROLD. The Bronze Age and Celtic World, 1922

PEATTIE, RODERICK. The Black Hills, N.Y. 1952

PETRIE, SIR W. F. Researches in Sinai, 1906. Prehistoric Egypt, Royal Tombs of 1st Dynasty, 1901-20

PICARD, G. Everyday Life in Carthage, 1961

PIRENNE, HENRI. Economic & Social History of Medieval Europe, N.Y. 1937

POLANYI, C. & PEARSON, H. W. (Arensberg & Oppenheim). Trade & Markets in The Early Empires, N.Y., 1957.

POWELL, T. G. E. The Celts, Revised 1960

PRESCOTT, W. H. History of The Conquest of Mexico and Peru, London, 1843—Reprinted in N.Y., Random House

PUBLICATIONS: U.S. Geological Survey Bulletins, Professional Papers and Folios on various mining districts.
————. U.S. Bureau of Mines: Yearbooks, Area Reports, Mineral Facts & Problems. Available at U.S. Government Printing Office, Washington, D.C.
———— Also: Mining Bureaus and Geological Surveys of the various states publish area reports.

QUIETT, GLENN C. Pay Dirt, N.Y. 1936

QUIGGEN, A. H. A Survey of Primitive Money, London, 1949

RICKARD, T. A. Man and Metals, N.Y. 1932. The Romance of Mining, Toronto, 1945. A History of

American Mining, A.I.M.E. Series, N.Y. 1932. The Copper Mines of Lake Superior, 1905. Journeys of Observation (Mexico), San Francisco, 1907.

ROSTOVTZEFF, J. J. Social and Economic History of The Hellenistic World . . . and of The Roman Empire, London, 1947

SCHLIEMANN, HEINRICH. Troy and Its Remains, London 1880. Mycenae, 1878. Tiryns, 1886.

SCRAMUZZA, V. M. & MACKENDRICK, P. L. The Ancient World, N.Y. 1958

SHOEBOTHAM, H. M. Anaconda, 1956

SINGER, C. A History of Technology, London, 1954

SINGLEWALD, J. T. & MILLER, B. L. Mineral Deposits of South America.

SMITH, GRANT. The History of The Comstock Lode, Univ. Nevada, 1943.

SMITH, G. ELLIOT. The Invention of Copper Making, Man, 1916-26.
————. The Ancient Egyptians, 1923

SOUTHWORTH, J. R. The Mines of Mexico. Heritage Europe.

SPENCE, C. C. Mining Engineers & The American West, 1970

SPIESER, E. A. Excavations of Tepe Gawra, 1935

SPRAGUE, M. Money Mountain, Boston, 1953

SPURR, JOSIAH E. Through The Yukon Gold Diggings, 1900.
————. Mines and Mineral Resources of Spain.

STONE, IRVING. Men To Match My Mountains, N.Y. 1958

TATON, RENÉ (Ed.) History of Ancient & Medieval Science, N.Y. 1965

TAYLOR, BAYARD. Eldorado, London, 1850

TRIMBLE, W. J. The Mining Advance Into The Inland Empire, 1914

TURNER, F. J. The Frontier in American History, N.Y. 1928

TWAIN, MARK. Roughing It, Hartford, 1872

UNITED STATES PUBLICATIONS. See PUBLICATIONS

VACANO, O. W. The Etruscans in The Ancient World, 1960

VAILLANT, G. C. The Aztecs of Mexico, N.Y. 1941

VANDERWILT, J. W. Mineral Resources of Colorado, Denver, 1947

WATERS, FRANK. Midas of The Rockies, Denver, 1949

WEED, W. H. The Copper Mines of The World, N.Y., 1907

WEINBERG, A. K. Manifest Destiny, 1935

WELLMAN, PAUL. Glory, God and Gold, N.Y. 1954

WELLS, H. G. The Outline of History, N.Y. Revised, 1949

WHITE, STEWART E. The Forty Niners, 1921

WIRTH, F. P. The Discovery and Exploitation of The Minnesota Iron Lands, 1927

WOOLLEY, SIR C. L. Excavations at Ur, London, 1926. The Sumerians, London, 1929. The Royal Cemetery of Ur, 1934

WORMINGTON, H. M. Ancient Man in North America, 1957

INDEX

ILLUSTRATIONS

MAPS